MOZART'S
WOMEN

JANE GLOVER

MOZART'S
WOMEN

His Family, His Friends, His Music

HarperCollins*Publishers*

HarperCollins books may be purchased for educational, business, or sales promotional use. For information, please write: Special Markets Department, HarperCollins Publishers, 10 East 53rd Street, New York, NY 10022.

First published in Great Britain in 2005 by Macmillan, an imprint of Pan Macmillan Ltd.

FIRST EDITION

Printed on acid-free paper

Library of Congress Cataloging-in-Publication Data

Glover, Jane
    Mozart's women : his family, his friends, his music / Jane Glover.—1st ed.
      p. cm.
    Includes bibliographical references and index.
    ISBN-10: 0-06-056350-8
    ISBN-13: 978-0-06-056350-9
    1. Mozart, Wolfgang Amadeus, 1756-1791—Relations with women. 2. Mozart, Wolfgang Amadeus, 1756-1791—Family. I. Title.
    ML410.M9G645   2004
    780'.92—dc22
    [B]

                                                   2005052699

06 07 08 09 10 SSL/RRD 10 9 8 7 6 5 4 3 2 1

CONTENTS

In memory of Stephen

Prelude

~

AT THE end of the 1820s, three elderly widows lived in two separate households in Salzburg. One of them, bedridden and blind, led an almost reclusive existence in a third-floor apartment in Sigmund-Haffnergasse (whose back windows overlooked, had she been able to see them, those of the house in Getreidegasse where she had been born). The other two, sisters whose lives had converged again after the deaths of their husbands, enjoyed marvellous mountain views from their house and garden in the Nonnberggasse, a narrow street running along the cliff under the shadow of Salzburg's fortress. Between them, these women had shared, witnessed and contributed to the life of the greatest musical genius the world has ever known, Wolfgang Amadeus Mozart.

Although much of the story of Mozart, and of the women in his life, took place elsewhere, it is in the town of Salzburg that it begins, episodically continues, and ultimately (posthumously) ends. He himself was born there on 27 January 1756. He was the last of seven children, of whom only he and his sister Maria Anna (known as Nannerl) survived, born to Leopold and Maria Anna Mozart. At a very early age Wolfgang's phenomenal musical gifts were recognized by his parents, and much of his childhood was spent travelling through the major cities and capitals of Europe, where the small child played, composed and grew. His sister too was musically gifted, so at first the whole family travelled together, parading the two children on more or less equal terms. Later, when Nannerl approached adulthood, the women were left behind in Salzburg.

Yet despite the dazzling distribution of young Wolfgang's talents, and for all that his brilliance was universally recognized and praised, he could secure no permanent employment in any of the places he visited. He returned to Salzburg in his late teens, and joined his father in the musical service of its Prince-Archbishop. At the age of twenty-one he undertook another long journey in search of more stimulating employment, this time accompanied by his mother. But this trip resulted only in disaster, and yet again Wolfgang found himself back in Salzburg, where he felt trapped and unappreciated. During a temporary residence in Vienna, still in the service of his Salzburg Archbishop, he allowed himself to be ignominiously dismissed from his employment, and so entered the wholly precarious world of life as a freelance musician. But by now he had made many excellent contacts with musical patrons and friends, and for the next decade he poured his music into the opera houses, concert halls and musical salons of the Austrian capital. He married Constanze Weber, from another gifted musical family, and she bore him several children, of whom, again, only two survived. But the monumental achievements of the 1780s actually occurred against a backdrop of endless struggle, hardship and loss: the young couple were regularly short of money. By the time Wolfgang's fortunes were recovering, in 1791, his never-robust health had collapsed. He died in Vienna in December 1791, at the age of thirty-five.

In the years after Mozart's death, his widow Constanze, supported continually by her mother and sisters, gradually began to organize his musical legacy, arranging performances and publications. In 1809 she remarried. Her second husband, Georg Nissen, was a Danish diplomat, and in 1810 she returned with him to Copenhagen where they lived for ten years. On his retirement in 1820 they moved to Salzburg, for Nissen was undertaking the first major biography of Mozart. He died in 1826 before finishing it, but Constanze saw it into publication. She lived out the rest of her life in Salzburg, where she was treated with the greatest respect: at last, in the mid-nineteenth century, the town was beginning to appreciate the extraordinary genius it had raised, and lost. Constanze's gentle dignity and her quietly civilized lifestyle were noted by her visitors. She shared her last years with her younger sister Sophie, by then also widowed, and later still, in the 1830s, with her one remaining older sister Aloysia, whom, as it happened, Mozart had loved before he married Constanze.

Mozart's sister Nannerl, meanwhile, had been largely concerned with domestic responsibilities since her retreat from her brother's limelight. In 1784, at the relatively late age of thirty-three, she had married a much older widower, Johann Baptist Franz von Berchtold zu Sonnenburg, moved to St Gilgen where he was Prefect, and acquired five stepchildren. Only after the death of her brother in 1791 did she filter back into the Mozart narrative, supplying early memories and anecdotes to biographers. When her husband died in 1801, she returned to live in Salzburg, supporting herself and her own children by giving piano lessons, until her failing eyesight and physical frailty prevented this. She outlived her brother by nearly forty years.

And so, at the end of their lives, the women who had been closest to Mozart were all back in the town of his birth, observing caring, courtesies in their communications with one another. In fact they head a whole roster of women who inspired, fascinated, supported, amused, aroused and sometimes hurt Mozart throughout his life. And since he was the creator of some of the most vividly drawn and brilliantly understood women on the operatic stage, his entire rich female acquaintance bears close examination.

～

THIS CONCENTRATION ON women by no means ignores the importance to Mozart of male company and friendship. He was naturally gregarious, and from his childhood quite at ease in any company,

whether in an Imperial palace or his local inn. His closest friends
were often fine musicians too – the clarinettist Anton Stadler, the
violinist Franz Hofer (who married Mozart's sister-in-law Josefa
Weber), and of course Joseph Haydn. With all these and many
others, Mozart enjoyed a warm camaraderie, which embraced both
profundity and buffoonery. He liked male clubs, societies and
fraternities, and became a Freemason in his late twenties. And the
most important single influence in his life was his father Leopold, in
whose company he spent practically every day of his first twenty-
one years. The relationship between father and son was highly
complex, and deteriorated distressingly after Wolfgang escaped his
father's daily scrutiny. Ultimately the remarkable Leopold Mozart
emerges as a tyrannical and paranoid man, who did and said unfor-
givable things to his son. But the bond between them was based on
deep love and shared experience of travel and music. Leopold's
death in 1787 was a major loss to Wolfgang, from which he never
really recovered.

Mozart's large and diverse circle of female acquaintance similarly included many extremely talented musicians – singers and
instrumentalists – with whom he enjoyed that most fulfilling
experience, artistic collaboration. But beyond that, he turned
unfailingly to women for support: for the whispering of confidences and the baring of his soul, for playful release from
the mental and emotional pressures of constant creativity, for the
boisterous normality of a domestic hurly-burly, and for the physical joy and comfort of sexual relations. Much of his attitude to
women, his respect, his sympathy, his perspicacious understanding,
can be gleaned from his music. And then there are the letters – from
him, to him, and about him. The surviving material inevitably has
many gaps in it, some of extremely eloquent significance.
Nevertheless it is a rich source of information, which in the case of
Mozart's own letters offers insights too into his compositions. He
was as fluent and inventive with words as he was with music. His
letters have pace, narrative, dramatic contrast and great passion. At
times they seem to be verbal equivalents of his famed improvisa-

tions at the keyboard: he could take an idea (be it descriptive, or practical, or even scatological), and develop it with fantastical imagination. He loved jokes and puns and ciphers, and often wrote in a veritable counterpoint of languages.

And from this brilliant store of self-expression, the personality of Mozart emerges. The sunny, sweet, willing child, entirely nonchalant about his genius which he nonetheless recognized, displayed a spirit of optimism which proved invaluable to him as he grew up. This essential cheerfulness was frequently battered, and therefore became somewhat embittered, in the course of an adult life which can only really be described as a monumental struggle, for all its dazzling achievement. So we perceive immense courage and fortitude too, and a heartrending vulnerability. Mozart clearly needed emotional support from those closest to him. And from the many women who loved him – his mother and sister, his wife and her sisters, his colleagues in the theatrical communities where he was so much in his element – he received it.

Mozart's Family

~

MOZART NEVER knew either of his grandmothers. His mother's mother, Eva Rosina Pertl, died in the care of her pregnant daughter a few months before he was born. His father's mother, Anna Maria Mozart, could have heard her seven-year-old grandson perform in Augsburg in 1763, but had long since fallen out irreparably with her own son Leopold, and kept her obstinate distance. But both these women, the one a victim and the other a culprit of historical absenteeism, had a strong influence on the lives and natures of their own children, Mozart's parents; and thus they left their mark on the early awareness of their grandchildren.

There was music on both sides of Mozart's family, but more perhaps in the maternal genes. His grandmother Eva Rosina's father and her first husband were both Salzburg church musicians. Her second husband, Nikolaus Pertl, was also musical, with a career path initially not dissimilar to that of his future son-in-law. Pertl attended the Benedictine University in Salzburg, sang bass in the choir of St Peter's Abbey and taught at the monastery school. But his main study was law, which after graduation brought him jobs in Salzburg, Vienna and Graz. He was forty-five when he married Mozart's grandmother in 1712. He then held the fairly senior post of District Superintendent (or Pflege) in St Andrae, but in 1715 suffered a near-fatal illness, which left him greatly debilitated. The

Pertls moved to the quieter waters of the Abersee, and the small village of St Gilgen, where Nikolaus he held a similar but lesser-paid position. As his health continued to decline, he increasingly found himself having to borrow money, especially after the birth of his two daughters, Maria Rosina Gertrud in 1719, and Maria Anna in 1720. When he died in March 1724, his debts amounted to more than four times his annual salary. His effects were confiscated, and Eva Rosina, with her two little girls, returned to Salzburg to live on a meagre charity pension. Four years later, in 1728, her elder daughter died. Eva Rosina and Maria Anna, survivors of this all-too-common cycle of family tragedy, were thrown ever closer together.

The future mother of Mozart thus had a somewhat difficult start in life. Torn from the peaceful lakeside beauty of St Gilgen at the age of four, bereft of her father and soon also to lose her sister, she was bewilderingly transplanted into the city-state of Salzburg – prosperous, independent of its neighbours Bavaria and Austria, and gleamingly modern. Ruled since the thirteenth century by a series of Prince-Archbishops, Salzburg reaped great revenue from its far-flung territories with their salt mines, livestock farming and forestry. Over the centuries it had also grown as a cultural and intellectual centre. The Benedictine University was founded in 1623, and, also in the seventeenth century, under a series of rulers whose imaginations were fired by the Italian Baroque, the city's architecture was transformed. The first major works of Fischer von Erlach, who later brought similar innovation to Imperial Vienna, were four of Salzburg's finest churches. By the beginning of the eighteenth century, the city had nearly 16,000 inhabitants. Its ecclesiastical royal Court was the centre of important social and cultural events. Its merchants had distant trading connections, which gave them immense wealth individually. There was a wide range of public institutions and social services: schools, museums, libraries, hospitals and almshouses. Salzburg looked after its poor as well as its wealthy. In the 1720s it was just this supportive security that the widow Eva Rosina and her small child needed.

Little is known of Maria Anna's upbringing, except that she was not especially healthy. She probably had no formal education. Perhaps she and her mother supplemented their charity pension by making lace — an industry which thrived along the shores of the Abersee. In the one adult portrait of Maria Anna, she is depicted holding a piece of lace in a rather proprietorial manner, which suggests that she had made it herself. But she was clearly a bright, observant and intelligent child. Through caring for her mother, which she continued to do until Eva Rosina's death in 1755, she developed a strong sense of resourcefulness, compassion and duty. These qualities were to sustain her through her eventual marriage to a charismatic but difficult man.

Sometime in her early twenties, Maria Anna met a young Court violinist. Leopold Mozart had been born and raised in Augsburg. His father, Johann Georg Mozart, was a well-to-do bookbinder; his mother, Anna Maria Sulzer (Johann Georg's second wife, married within a few weeks of the death of his first), the daughter of a weaver. Leopold was the eldest of nine children. He had received an excellent education in Augsburg's Jesuit schools, and after the death of his father in 1736, when Leopold was seventeen, it was the Jesuits who had effectively taken care of him. His mother had seemed almost to relinquish responsibility for her eldest son, concentrating instead on her younger children, and this was probably the origin of an ever-widening rift between them. As the years progressed, mutual mistrust festered and grew. Anna Maria may have disapproved of Leopold's erratic choices of career. First he forsook the family firm (her younger sons would continue the bookbinding business); next he abandoned the Jesuit path, for he left Augsburg in 1737 and entered the Benedictine University in Salzburg, where he studied law; and then, after only a year there, he was dismissed, with the chilling indictment of having been 'unworthy of the name of student',[1] and began to pursue his abiding passion, music (he was a talented violinist, organist and composer). This was too much for his mother. Finally dismissing him as some sort of family black sheep, she effectively cut him off, never allowing him to receive his family inheritance. Both Leopold and his mother were cunning, blinkered, stubborn, and ultimately unforgiving – maybe this was what lay at the heart of their antagonism: they were simply too alike.

How and when Leopold and Maria Anna met is not known, but, much as they came to love each other, times were difficult and they had to wait for several years before they actually married. The hot-headed student of Leopold's youth was growing up into a man whose caution with money was extreme. After a brief period as a violinist in the service of Count Johann Baptist Thurm-Valassina und Taxis, he became fourth violinist at Court in 1743. But his salary was minimal, and, without his share of the family money, he had to supplement it by taking on extra pupils. Maria Anna, virtu- ally penniless, could bring nothing to their union, apart from her beloved mother: wherever she went, Eva Rosina would come too. And in addition to the family's own insecurities, there was the War of Austrian Succession (1740–48), between Bavaria and the young Maria Theresa's Habsburg Empire, which unsettled the whole region. But Leopold's financial state did gradually take on a firmer footing, and at last he reckoned it was safe to enter 'the order of the patched trousers'.[2] Leopold Mozart and Maria Anna Pertl were married in Salzburg's Cathedral on 21 November 1747. He was twenty-eight, she just over a year younger.

A month after their wedding, Leopold applied to retain his Augsburg citizenship, wanting perhaps to keep his options open as to where he and his new wife (and indeed his mother-in-law) might live. In a petition full of staggeringly brazen untruths, he claimed that his father was still alive, and had sponsored him through University; that his wife was the daughter of a prosperous family; and that he himself, having been a distinguished scholar, was now a valet at Court. Whether this was self-deluding fantasy or wilful lying, Leopold failed to appreciate the stupidity of such reckless hyperbole (surely all these facts could have been checked?). But his petition was in fact successful; and it was by no means the last occa- sion on which he would bend the truth to embroider his own status.

After their marriage, Leopold and Maria Anna rented a small third-floor apartment on Getreidegasse from one of Salzburg's prosperous merchants, Johann Lorenz Hagenauer, and moved in, together of course with Eva Rosina. The Hagenauers were to become lifelong friends of the Mozarts. Johann Lorenz assisted Leopold with financial matters, providing a network of contacts through many different cities and countries whereby Leopold on his travels could send and receive monies; and he was also the recipient of dozens of letters from Leopold describing these experiences. The Mozarts were to live in the Getreidegasse apartment for the next twenty-six years, and it was there that Maria Anna went through her series of virtually annual pregnancies, beginning immediately after her marriage.

Between July 1748 and January 1756 Maria Anna bore Leopold seven children, five of whom died in extreme infancy. The first three were born within two years, from August 1748 to July 1750, and they all died in the same period (at respectively five and a half months, six days, and eleven weeks). So in the summer of 1750 Maria Anna went to take the cure for four days at Bad Gastein. The Mozarts could ill afford it, but she needed it, and it did her good. Her next child was born within a year. Maria Anna Walburga Ignatia, always known as Nannerl, was born on 31 July 1751, and would live into her seventy-ninth year. But there was more loss to come. Two more children were born, and died, in 1752 and 1754. And in 1755 Eva Rosina died, at the age of seventy-four. She was buried in the cemetery of St Sebastian, the first occupant of what would become a chaotically constituted family grave. At the beginning of the following year, on 27 January 1756, Maria Anna gave birth, with dangerous difficulty, to her seventh and last child: Johann Chrysostomus Wolfgang Theophilus. (This last name would appear in other synonymous forms in the course of Mozart's life, as Gottlieb and, most especially, as Amadeus.)

Leopold was becoming impatient with the domestic turbulence of Maria Anna's childbearing. In the mid-1750s he had decided to publish a treatise on the fundamental principles of violin-playing,

based on his by now considerable, and evidently extremely successful, teaching experiences. His *Versuch einer Grundlichen Violinschule*,
a meticulous if somewhat uncompromising book, with its scholarly
preface and authoritarian tone, was eventually printed in Augsburg
by Johann Jacob Lotter. Writing to Lotter on 12 February 1756, just
two weeks after Wolfgang was born, Leopold confided: 'I can
assure you I have so much to do that I sometimes do not know
where my head is . . . And you know as well as I do, when the wife
is in childbed, there is always someone turning up to rob you of
time. Things like that cost you time and money.'[3] But for all
Leopold's apparent irritability at the arrival of his latest child, his
priorities were to change very quickly. He and Maria Anna soon
realized that their children were extremely gifted.

Years later, it was Nannerl herself who became the chief source
of information on their early childhood. She was approached after
Wolfgang's death by the German scholar Friedrich Schlichtegroll,
who regularly published volumes of obituaries. For his *Nekrolog auf
der Jahr 1791* he sent a questionnaire to Nannerl, asking her for
information on her brother's early life, and she replied eagerly and
in great detail. (She had over 400 family letters in her possession, as
well as her own diaries, for she had been a great chronicler of daily
events.) Encouraged by her compliance, Schlichtegroll then sent
her a list of supplementary questions, at which point Nannerl
enlisted the help of an old family friend, the Court trumpeter and
poet Johann Andreas Schachtner. From the reminiscences and anecdotes of both Nannerl and Schachtner, the story of a remarkable
family life unfolds.

Like their mother, neither Nannerl nor Wolfgang received any
formal education at all. They were schooled entirely at home, at the
brilliant hands of their painstaking father. With imagination and
resourcefulness, he taught them to read and write, to do arithmetic,
and learn some basic history and geography. Both children had
good handwriting, read widely, drew well and were extremely
articulate. And then, of course, there was music. The children
would have absorbed it from the cradle, for Leopold's fellow Court

musicians were constantly in and out of the Getreidegasse apartment, rehearsing, playing, teaching. And when Nannerl was seven she too began piano lessons with her father. Soon the creative Leopold compiled a music book ('Pour le clavecin') for her, touchingly inscribed, '*Ce livre appartient à Marie Anna Mozart, 1759*'. It contained several short pieces, by himself and other contemporary composers, arranged in order of difficulty. Apparently little Wolfgang, aged only four, also began to play these pieces, and, as Nannerl recalled, 'the boy at once showed his God-given and extraordinary talent'.[4] Her music book is studded with annotations by their astonished father: 'This piece was learned by Wolfgangerl on 24 January 1761, three days before his fifth birthday, between nine and nine-thirty in the evening.' And, as Nannerl continued in her memoir, Wolfgang 'made such progress that at the age of five he was already composing little pieces, which he played to his father who wrote them down'.

Schachtner similarly recalled Wolfgang's early genius. He recounted an occasion for instance when he and Leopold returned from church duties to discover the four-year-old boy writing some music which he claimed to be a piano concerto. When the amused father took the ink-smudged, childishly written manuscript from his son, 'he stared long at the sheet, and then tears, tears of joy and wonder, fell from his eyes'.[5] He also recalled the child's phenomenal sense of pitch ('Herr Schachtner, your violin is tuned half a quarter-tone lower than mine, if you left it tuned as it was when I last played it') and, most fascinatingly, his fear of Schachtner's own instrument, the trumpet. 'Merely to hold a trumpet in front of him was like aiming a loaded pistol at his heart. Papa wanted to cure him of this childish fear and once told me to blow [my trumpet] at him despite his reluctance, but, my God! I should not have been persuaded to do it. Wolfgangerl scarcely heard the blaring sound, than he grew pale and began to collapse, and if I had continued, he would surely have had a fit.' In due course the child clearly overcame this phobia; but his own adult writing for the instrument often reflects this early terror.

As the captivating skills of both children developed, Leopold and Maria Anna began to contemplate showing them off to a more discerning audience than that in Salzburg. In 1762, when Nannerl was ten and Wolfgang six, they took their first tentative steps into a wider world. They travelled to Munich for three weeks in the depth of winter, and played before the Elector Maximilian III. Encouraged by the success of this trip, Leopold then took his family to Vienna the following September. The children were displayed everywhere, including the palace of Schönbrunn, no less, where they played before the Empress Maria Theresa herself, together with 'the grown-up Archdukes and Archduchesses',[6] as Nannerl later recalled. But they met the younger generation of Archdukes and Archduchesses too, who were their own age, and even inherited some of their clothes, in which they later had their por-traits painted. The Vienna visit was temporarily marred by Wolfgang's falling ill (this was unquestionably a taste of things to come), but in general it was a triumph. Leopold relayed breathless accounts of their hectic schedule to Hagenauer (who was no doubt expected to broadcast these throughout Salzburg). He listed every member of the Viennese nobility who had attended their perform-ances. He described the universal admiration that his children ('the boy especially'[7]) had aroused. And he pocketed a considerable sum of money. By the end of the first week in Vienna he could send home more than he had earned in the last two years.

Count Zinzendorf, then a councillor at the Treasury and an energetic chronicler, was one of those who heard the children per-form. On 17 October he wrote in his diary: '. . . the little child from Salzburg and his sister played the harpsichord. The poor little fellow plays marvellously, he is a Child of spirit, lively, charming; his sister's playing is masterly, and he applauded her.'[8] Wolfgang was clearly therefore the chief focus of attention, but, as Zinzendorf noticed, he was touchingly generous to his sister. And this Vienna trip did indeed cement for the children the foundations of what would become a pattern as they travelled in the years ahead. On their long journeys they were thrown exclusively into each other's company, and into a shared sibling world of games and make-believe. Their appearances together before the great and the good could almost have seemed an extension of this world, their extraordinary abilities, their nonchalant perfectionism and their very delight in music-making (which neither of them ever lost) all simply being part of what they did together. They probably saw themselves as a little team.

~

INTOXICATED WITH THESE social and financial jackpots, Leopold began to think further afield.

In one visionary sweep, backed up by formidable preparation of almost military precision, he planned to advance on three major capitals of northern Europe: Paris, London and The Hague. Lorenz Hagenauer's trading connections would supply what were effectively banking facilities in all the major cities en route, and Leopold could call upon various members of his own network among the aristocracy to write letters of recommendation to friends and colleagues, who in turn would do the same. Thus Leopold's trail was blazed, and his remarkable family could enter each new town and city with fanfares of publicity and attention. Although he had a general idea of the itinerary, various events would dictate changes, either of direction or of length of stay, and there would therefore be a certain amount of improvisation. But the main purpose of this large journey was to show off Nannerl and Wolfgang in the highest society in Europe, and here Leopold succeeded brilliantly.

The Mozart family set off from Salzburg on 9 June 1763. Wolfgang was seven, Nannerl nearly twelve. Spirits were high: it was early summer, and the rural highways and byways looked marvellous. 'My wife takes the greatest pleasure in the country-side,' reported Leopold. They travelled in their own privately hired coach, together with their servant Sebastian Winter. They stayed mainly in inns (Leopold was always on the lookout for a good price), where they would take a large room with two beds, one for Leopold and Wolfgang, the other for Maria Anna and Nannerl.

On long journeys of several hours in a single day, the children entered the imaginary realm they had created for themselves, which they called 'Das Königreich Rücken' (The Kingdom of Back): Wolfgang was its King, and Nannerl the Queen, and sometimes their servant Sebastian would join in, doing little drawings of their alternative world. Everywhere they stopped they would perform, and were well rewarded. Thirty years later, Nannerl could remember every city and town on that immense tour.

Their first stop was in Munich, where again they played to the Elector Maximilian III. Attention was focused on the seven-year-old Wolfgang, and it was only when the Elector himself asked to hear Nannerl as well that, two days after Wolfgang had first appeared, she played too, and was warmly applauded. This early experience in Munich did rather set a pattern for Nannerl, and almost certainly she began to feel somewhat sidelined. Her parents probably noticed this too. Leopold later reported to Hagenauer, 'Nannerl no longer suffers by comparison with the boy, for she plays so beautifully that everyone is talking about her and admiring her execution.'[10] But it cannot have been easy for Nannerl. Her adored brother, to whose age level she constantly descended when they created their secret worlds and games, was accelerating past her own already remarkable musical achievements, and drawing all the attention. Highly talented and hardworking though she was, she simply could not keep up.

After Munich, the family went to Leopold's home town, Augsburg, where they stayed for two weeks. His estranged mother still considered his whole lifestyle reprehensible, and steadfastly ignored the visit. Although the children gave three concerts, their grandmother did not attend them, her dogged intolerance tragically denying her an experience of which most grandmothers can only dream. Nor did these concerts make much money: Leopold complained to Hagenauer that they had barely covered the cost of their expensive inn. Nevertheless they did buy a portable clavier from the instrument-maker J. A. Stein, with whom Wolfgang would do more business in adulthood. And they managed to renew contact with at least one member of Leopold's family. His brother Franz Alois, who had inherited the bookbinding business, did welcome them. And so did his excitable four-year-old daughter, Maria Anna Thekla, whom they nicknamed the 'Bäsle' (little cousin). She too would reappear, rather spectacularly, in Wolfgang's later life.

The first main focus of the tour was Paris. Travelling via Frankfurt (where Goethe's father heard the children play) and Brussels, the Mozarts arrived in the French capital in mid-November, and stayed for five months. With extreme tenacity, a certain amount of self-aggrandization (Leopold did not hesitate to have himself described as 'Kapellmeister' to the Prince-Archbishop of Salzburg, when in fact he was only the Vice-Kapellmeister), and the considerable assistance of good friends, Leopold eventually secured the children appearances at the court of Louis XV, and in public. Wolfgang's first publications appeared. Baron Grimm, critic and author of *Correspondance Littéraire* between 1753 and 1773, became a great source of support. He and his mistress, the glamorous Madame d'Epinay, befriended the Mozarts, introducing them to all the right people, advising them on propriety, diplomacy and publicity (Grimm wrote the flowery dedications to Wolfgang's publications), and bestowing all manner of gifts on them. Maria Anna received a red satin dress (was this the dress in which she had her portrait painted in 1775?), a fan and an amethyst ring from Madame d'Epinay. And Grimm commissioned a painting of Leopold and the children from Carmontelle, engraved copies of which would effectively serve as their visiting card, or publicity photograph, in the months ahead.

There was some sightseeing too. Over the Christmas period the children were taken to Versailles, and Leopold, ever the inspiring teacher, fired his daughter's imagination with his explanations of the mythological sculptures that she saw in the gardens. The twelve-year-old Nannerl's diary for this outing includes her interpretations of the statues on the Latona fountain: 'How latona changed the farmers into frogs, how neptune stopped the horse, diana in the bath, the rape of brosperina, very beautiful vase of white marble and alabaster.'[11] (How she would have enjoyed Florence and Rome.) In a very individual way, these children were receiving the most wonderful education. They were speaking new languages. They were hearing and absorbing more new music (ballets, operas). They were learning to appreciate beauty in art and architecture, and often the historical and mythological basis for them. And they were developing discerning tastes for elegant clothes, fine fabrics, jewels and hairstyles. In future years, most of the direct communications between Nannerl and her mother, when they were apart, were about fashion and ornament; and Wolfgang too would confess to a female friend, 'I should like all my things to be of good quality, genuine and beautiful.'[12] And all the time their own skills continued to blossom. By the summer of 1764, Leopold wrote to Hagenauer, 'What it all amounts to is this, that my little girl, although she is only twelve years old, is one of the most skilful players in Europe, and that, in a word, my boy knows in his eighth year what one would expect only from a man of forty.'[13]

Eventually, in April 1764, the family left Paris and set out for the central pivot of this great tour, London. For the first time in their lives they saw the sea, and the captivated Nannerl described its waves in her diary: 'In Calais I saw how the sea runs away and comes back again.'[14] The fascination probably palled quite quickly, for they were all horribly seasick on the crossing to Dover. But they evidently recovered well, for within days of their arrival in London they were already playing at the Court of George III and his young German queen, Charlotte. They stayed in London for fifteen months, a period in which, again, the skills and awareness of the children, especially Wolfgang, continued to develop astonishingly. They learned yet another language, met a new circle of people (including Johann Christian Bach, son of the great Johann Sebastian) and heard completely different music (symphonies, oratorios). Leopold continued his unorthodox but ingenious education of his children, and, initially at least, accrued goodly sums of money and many more gifts.

The London schedule was frenzied. In the first six weeks the children played twice at Court (each time coming away with the handsome sum of 24 guineas) and at various public venues, whose press announcements billed Nannerl and Wolfgang as 'Prodigies of Nature'. There were private events too, in the drawing rooms of London's nobility, where the children were put through their now familiar paces. In addition to performing (pieces by himself as well as others), Wolfgang was subjected to various tests. He might be given a melody but no bass, which he had to supply, or the reverse, a bass line without a melody, which he had to supply. He might be asked to identify pitches of various instruments, or even of non-instruments (bells or clocks); to read at sight, often from a full score of five or more staves; to play with a cloth over his hands so he could not see them, and no doubt other spontaneous challenges. Wolfgang sailed through all this (though none of it, in fact, would be much of a problem for a technically gifted child with perfect pitch and a pushy parent). London was initially entranced by the boy, and murmured appreciatively too about the pianistic skills of Nannerl, and more sums of money were sent by Leopold back to Hagenauer in Salzburg.

Then setbacks began. First, as summer arrived, London emptied, and opportunities for more of these private events vanished. Second, Leopold became ill. He caught a chill which, probably through a bad reaction to a prescribed medicine, developed into infections throughout his body and nervous system. It was necessary for the family to move out of the centre of London to the country (to what is now Ebury Street, in Chelsea), where they remained for two months; and, because of the dangerous state of Leopold's condition, the children were required to maintain absolute silence within the house, not even being allowed to play a keyboard. And so, fired by having met J. C. Bach and heard his symphonies, the eight-year-old Wolfgang decided to compose some symphonies of his own. With his sister beside him to write them out, Wolfgang took his first steps into full orchestral scoring. 'While he composed and I copied,' she remembered, 'he said to me, "Remind me to give something good to the horn!"'[15]

This monumental advance, so delightfully made, was for them another exciting game shared by brother and sister.

Maria Anna must have had great anxiety throughout this difficult summer, but she clearly took responsibility for the family, organizing their move to Chelsea, nursing her sick husband, and eventually also taking over the cooking. She lost weight, but gained rare praise from her convalescent husband, who reported back to Salzburg, 'My wife has had a great deal to do lately on account of my illness . . . In Chelsea we had our food sent to us at first from an eating-house; but as it was so poor, my wife began to do our cooking, and we are now in such good trim that when we return to town next week we shall continue to do our own housekeeping. Perhaps too my wife, who has become very thin, will get a little fatter.'[16] But after a summer of medical expense and no takings, it was necessary to recover some losses, and Leopold thought hard about their winter activities. He considered presenting the children in a subscription series run by a Mrs Cornelys at Carlisle House in Soho Square. One of the great society hostesses, the Italian-born Teresa Cornelys had been a mistress of Casanova (who had fathered her daughter). Now she organized masked balls for anything up to 600 people, and Leopold cannily reckoned that her contacts were as good as any. But if the Mozart children did play for Mrs Cornelys, there is no record of it. As spring approached, and Leopold contemplated the family's departure from London, he resorted to increasingly desperate measures.

He took out newspaper advertisements offering the public 'an Opportunity for all the curious to hear these two young Prodigies perform every day from 12 to 3'. This gruelling daily exposure began in March 1765, when the price of a ticket was half a guinea. By May he had reduced the children's hours from three to two, but also halved the cost of admission to five shillings. And in July, as a final thrust, he rented a room in a pub, the Swan and Harp Tavern in Cornhill, and made Nannerl and Wolfgang play there, again on a daily basis. Humiliatingly, the price was halved again.

Eventually the Mozarts left London at the end of July, heading now for Holland. They spent a day at the races in Canterbury on their way to Dover, and this time survived the crossing to Calais with no ill effects. In Lille they learned of the death of Francis, husband of the Empress Maria Theresa. He was succeeded as co-Regent by their twenty-four-year-old son, Joseph II, who would later play his part in Wolfgang's adult life. As the family reached Holland, Nannerl became extremely ill with intestinal typhoid. For two months Leopold and Maria Anna nursed their daughter night and day (Maria Anna always on the night shift), barely leaving their rooms, but by 21 October Nannerl was so ill that she actually received the last rites. Leopold reported gruesomely to Salzburg: 'Whoever could have listened to the conversations which we three, my wife, myself and my daughter, had on several evenings, during which we convinced her of the vanity of this world and the happy death of children, would not have heard it without tears.'[17] And then, just as Nannerl was recovering, Wolfgang succumbed as well, causing real financial anxiety on top of everything else, for he was already the family's chief bread-winner. But he too recovered, having on this occasion got off rather more lightly than his sister. Nannerl's own 1792 memory of this horrendous time for their parents was quite clear about which of the children had been more dangerously ill: 'When the daughter had recovered from her *very* grave illness, the son fell sick of a *quite* grave illness.'[18]

Eventually the convalescent children could be put on show again, and they performed in Utrecht, Amsterdam, Antwerp and Brussels. Then at last the family began the return journey to Salzburg. They spent two more months in Paris, where Baron Grimm noticed changes in both children in the two years since he had last seen them: 'Mademoiselle Mozart, now thirteen years of age, and moreover grown much prettier, has the most beautiful and most brilliant execution on the harpsichord . . . Her brother alone is capable of robbing her of supremacy.'[19] He also noticed that Wolfgang had 'hardly grown at all', and was altogether concerned about the general health of the child. As the family headed off to Switzerland, Madame d'Epinay wrote to her friend, the author and philosopher Voltaire, instructing him to attend any concert the children gave in Geneva – though in the event Voltaire was ill and missed them. Finally, after an extremely laborious journey, generally of one- or two-night stops en route, and one more appearance before the Elector Maximilian III in Munich, they arrived back in Salzburg on 29 November 1766. They had been away for three and a half years.

Despite their near-disasters and recurring anxieties, the Mozart family had reaped enormous benefit from this Grand Tour. Both children had developed musically, Wolfgang out of all possible recognition or even expectation, and their names were now circulating throughout the Courts of northern Europe. Although there had been alarming lapses in their takings during the periods of illness, they had made a great deal of money, more than Leopold would ever divulge even to his closest friends in Salzburg, and acquired a dazzling quantity of snuffboxes, watches and jewellery. The children's imaginary 'Kingdom of Back' had been fed by their encounters with real palaces, real kings and queens, real ostentatious splendour. They could regale their wide-eyed young friends with tales of their experiences; and they chattered away to each other in several languages. But there had of course been a physical price to pay for all this: both Nannerl and Wolfgang were fundamentally quite frail, and continued to fall prey easily to infection and disease for the rest of their lives, as if somehow their resistance had never been given the chance to develop fully. This was certainly observed at the time. Grimm even feared that 'so premature a fruit might fall before maturing',[20] while the British minister to The Hague, Baron Dover, believed both children to be 'not long-lived'.[21] Leopold too had had his own serious indisposition in London. If Maria Anna had suffered, nobody particularly remembered or mentioned it, beyond remarking that she had grown thin. But for all of them, this tour had been a momentous experience; and for Maria Anna and Nannerl, literally the experience of a lifetime.

～

FATHER BEDA HÜBNER, librarian to St Peter's Abbey in Salzburg, was a great chronicler, and recorded the triumphal return of the Mozarts.

> Today the world-famous Herr Leopold Mozart, Vice-Kapellmeister here, with his wife and two children, a boy aged ten and his little daughter of thirteen, have arrived to the solace and joy of the whole town . . . These past two years nothing has been more frequently discussed in the newspapers than the wonderful art of the Mozart children: the two children, the boy as well as the girl, both play the harpsichord, or the clavier, the girl, it is true, with more art and fluency than her little brother, but the boy with far more refinement and with more original ideas, and with the most beautiful inspirations, so that even the most excellent organists wondered how it was humanly possible for such a boy, who was already so good an artist at the age of six, to possess such art as to astonish the whole musical world.[22]

The whole town was agog with how the children had changed and how Wolfgang now had the skills of a Kappellmeister; with how much money they had made, and indeed where the family might go next. Hübner himself got completely carried away, speculating that the Mozarts would 'soon visit the whole of Scandinavia and the whole of Russia, and perhaps even travel to China'. Leopold adored this limelight, and could not stifle his instincts of vulgar exhibitionism, for he put all the trophies of their tour on display in their house, and invited the admirers in. Hübner was one of them:

> I afterwards saw all the tributes and presents which the aforesaid Herr Mozart and his children had received from the great monarchs and princes during their costly journey: of gold pocket watches he has brought home 9; of gold snuff-boxes he has received 12; of gold rings set with the most handsome precious stones he has so many that he does not know himself how many; ear-rings for the girl, necklaces, knives with golden blades, bottle-holders, writing-tackle, toothpick boxes, gold *objets* for the girl, writing-tablets and suchlike gewgaws without number and without end; so much, that merely to see all this *raptim* and *obiter*, you

would have to spend several hours doing nothing but look, and it
is just like inspecting a church treasury.

When the excitement died down, some changes were made in
the small Getreidegasse apartment. Maria Anna and Leopold could
at last share a bed again. But Nannerl, now fifteen, was growing up
in all senses (she was even considered 'marriageable', according to
her father). It was wholly inappropriate for her to share a room
with her ten year-old brother, but since there was no alternative, a
special bed was built for her, with curtains around it for privacy.
Leopold resumed his humble duties at Court. But he longed for
more of his two intoxicating drugs, travel and universal admiration.
Within nine months of their return to Salzburg an opportunity
arose, and he seized it.

Vienna was preparing for the marriage of Maria Theresa's
daughter, the Archduchess Maria Josefa, to the young Ferdinand
IV, King of Naples. In her fierce determination to protect her territories and forge strong links with her neighbours, Maria Theresa
was ruthless in the distribution of her children. She had produced
sixteen of them between 1737 and 1756, and those who survived
beyond puberty, and were in good health, were soon earmarked for
strategic marriage. Joseph, her eldest son and now co-Regent, had
married first Isabella of Parma, and then, after Isabella's early
death, Maria Josefa of Bavaria (whom Joseph loathed and therefore cruelly ignored). Maria Theresa's younger sons were to be
similarly deployed: Leopold would marry Marie Louise of Spain,
and Ferdinand would secure the House of Modena in the person of
Maria Beatrice d'Este. The young Archduchesses were also part of
this board game. Maria Christina married Albert of Saxe-Teschen,
and snared Upper Silesia; Maria Amalia would bring back the
House of Parma, temporarily distanced after Isabella's death. Most
spectacularly of all, the Empress's youngest daughter, Maria
Antonia, would change her name to Marie Antoinette and
marry Louis XVI of France. But in these early days of political
manoeuvres, it was the Bourbon King of Naples that Maria Theresa

had in her sights. Originally she had planned that Maria Josefa's
older sister Johanna Gabriella would head for the Kingdom of Two
Sicilies, but she had died in 1762, aged only twelve. So now it was
Maria Josefa who was to be shackled to the unattractive Ferdinand.
They were both sixteen years old.

In Salzburg, Leopold heard of the elaborate celebrations that
would attend this royal wedding. Probably hoping that his old
acquaintance with the Empress would persuade her to invite his
children to take part, he got leave from his ever-indulgent and
supportive employer, Archbishop Schrattenbach, and the Mozart
family once more packed their bags and set off for Vienna. Leopold
should perhaps have realized that Maria Theresa, still in mourning
for her late husband and all but inaccessible, would not receive them
as readily as she had in 1762. But even he could not have foreseen
the other great problem awaiting them, an outbreak of smallpox in
Vienna. At first the Mozarts were unaware of it, and while they
waited in vain for a summons to the Empress, they busied themselves going to operas and plays. But then, on the very eve of her
wedding, the Archduchess Maria Josefa died of smallpox, contracted, it was ghoulishly rumoured, through visiting the family
vaults in the Kapuzinerkirche with her mother. (Eventually, at her
third attempt, Maria Theresa would succeed in marrying her
thirteenth child, Maria Carolina, to the illiterate young Ferdinand.)
Far from mounting glorious wedding festivities, Vienna went into
mourning all over again.

Leopold panicked when he realized the severity of what had now
become an epidemic of smallpox; indeed there had been three cases
of it in the very house on Weihburggasse where the family were
staying. He looked for new lodgings, and, failing to find anything
big enough for the four of them, just took Wolfgang away, leaving
the evidently more expendable Maria Anna and Nannerl in the
infected house. But he did then decide to remove the whole family
from Vienna, and a week later they travelled first to Brno, where
they called on Archbishop Schrattenbach's brother, and then on to
Olmütz. It was however too late: Wolfgang had already contracted

smallpox. Although he and Nannerl, who also then caught it, both recovered, the family yet again found itself grounded in a strange city for two months, dealing with potentially fatal illness. They returned to Brno and the Schrattenbachs for Christmas, and were back in Vienna in early January.

And then, at last, their Imperial Highnesses agreed to see them. Nannerl recalled the occasion: 'On 19 January the children performed before the Emperor Joseph; there was no one present but the Empress Maria Theresa, Prince Albert of Saxony and the Archduchesses.'[23] Leopold's account to Hagenauer of this highly privileged, two-hour private audience is more telling. It was only when the Empress learned that the Mozarts too, with their talented children, had been infected with the disease that was wreaking such havoc in her own family (both she and her daughter Elisabeth had caught it, and recovered) that she summoned them: 'For hardly had the Empress been told of what had happened to us in Olmütz and that we had returned, when we were informed of the day and the hour when we should appear.' But for Leopold, who had been building such hopes on the success of this encounter, the visit was bitterly disappointing. There was no reward beyond a medal ('beautiful, but so worthless that I do not even care to mention its value'); and Joseph II, to whom Maria Theresa handed over the formal hosting of the occasion, merely showed 'amazing graciousness'. Leopold concluded acidly, 'The Emperor . . . enters it in his book of oblivion and believes, no doubt, that he has paid us by his most gracious conversations.'[24]

But for Maria Anna, the visit must have been one of the highlights of her life. It was she who was taken into the company of Maria Theresa while Joseph listened to her children. The two women, approximately the same age, compared notes and shared their recent experiences. As Leopold described it, 'you cannot possibly conceive with what familiarity Her Majesty the Empress conversed with my wife, talking to her partly of my children's smallpox and partly of the events of our grand tour; nor can you imagine how she stroked my wife's cheeks and pressed her hands.'[25]

Leopold may have left their Imperial presences in a state of frustrated discontent, but Maria Anna had had a quite wonderful afternoon.

There was, though, one straw to be grasped from the content of those 'gracious conversations'. The Emperor 'asked the boy twice whether he would like to compose an opera and conduct it himself. Wolfgang said, Yes.' Leopold seized on this fragment of Imperial smalltalk, and chose to interpret it as an invitation. He made contact with Giuseppe Affligio, the manager of the Burgtheater, and initiated a series of meetings, as a result of which the twelve-year-old Wolfgang was given a libretto, *La finta semplice*, by the theatre's poet, Marco Coltellini. Leopold now rebuilt his hopes on this. Wolfgang's exposure at the heart of Vienna's operatic activity would surely bring him a permanent position, and the whole family could move from Salzburg. But although Wolfgang composed his *La finta semplice*, K51 (46a), it was not performed. There were intrigues and conspiracies at many levels – rumours that Leopold was trying to pass off his own composition as his son's, and resistance among the theatre's musicians who did not want to play music written by a child. All this took virtually a whole year, during which the Mozarts stayed in Vienna. Leopold generally made a nuisance of himself, writing a long and petulant petition to Joseph II which in fact served only to alienate the Court, and in so doing actually gambled with his own security too. He was ordered by Salzburg to return, for his salary was being paid in his absence and it was time he started earning it. But he ignored the summons, and his salary was indeed suspended. There were, at least, two musical compensations in this chaotic year. In the autumn Wolfgang's *Bastien und Bastienne*, K50 (46b), was performed at the private house of the controversial Dr Franz Anton Mesmer (whose magnets would reappear some years later in *Così fan tutte*); and in December he conducted his *Waisenhausmesse*, K139 (47a), at the Orphanage Church in the presence of five members of the Imperial family. But this was a meagre tally for over a year spent away from home; and the return to Salzburg at the end of 1768 was a far cry from the triumphal re-entry the family had made two years earlier.

Nannerl's 1792 memoir, despite its telegraphic style of reportage, is eloquent of the way in which she remembered that troubled year. 'The Emperor told the son he should write an opera buffa.[26] The Emperor informed the Impresario who leased the theatre. The Impresario arranged everything with the father. The son composed the opera. But it was not performed . . . although Kapellmeister Hasse and the poet Metastasio praised it uncommonly. The opera was called; *La finta semplice*.'[27] Her childhood loyalty to her brother was easily retrieved, and she recalled the praise of distinguished men. If she remembered the tensions and difficulties caused by Leopold's bungled negotiations, she remained loyal to him too, and did not betray them.

Leopold's salary in Salzburg was eventually reinstated, but only after he had had to petition for it, and he meekly took up his duties again. Wolfgang had several of his compositions performed (church music and chamber music), and in the autumn of 1769 he was appointed, unpaid, to the post of Konzertmeister at Court. But, for all his compliance, Leopold was not idly treading water in those summer months in Salzburg. He was planning their next escape, and this time to the country he had had in his sights for years, Italy. He called on many of his recently acquired influential contacts, for instance Hasse in Vienna, and got them to write letters of introduction. He arranged for Wolfgang, like other Salzburg musicians before him, to be given a bursary of 120 ducats towards the cost of the journey. The departure date was set for 13 December. But this trip would be different from all the others: only Leopold and Wolfgang would travel. Maria Anna and Nannerl would have to remain in Salzburg.

~

THE DECISION TO leave the women behind, and so to split the family for the first time, was clearly not taken lightly, but, quite simply, Leopold was determined to keep the costs down. Maria Anna and

Nannerl were miserable, not merely at being excluded from experiences which up to this point the whole family had shared equally, but, in Nannerl's case, at now having her own gifts utterly ignored. In the mid-1760s, while the Mozarts had been on their Grand Tour, three teenage girls from Salzburg had been sent to Venice to further their musical studies. On their return, at the end of 1765, they had been appointed as Court singers. As they all shared their travelling experiences, Nannerl would have looked upon these three young women, only a few years her senior, with considerable interest. And she might naturally have assumed that a spell of study in Venice would be the next possible option for her too: she had after all been depicted as a singer in the 1763 Carmontelle portrait of Leopold, Wolfgang and herself. But it was not to be. Perhaps it was never appropriate, as her skills were decidedly pianistic rather than vocal (her cheeky brother, in a typical sibling tease, once referred to her 'unbearable voice'.[28]) But it is most likely that Leopold never even countenanced the idea that Nannerl should travel abroad to pursue her own training: he had a very much greater talent to nurture.

Wolfgang and his father made three trips to Italy in the next four years and never once took the women with them. Like the rest of Salzburg, they could share in the Italian experience only second-hand. Maria Anna would now become the chief recipient of Leopold's letters describing their activities, while Wolfgang's added postscripts were addressed to Nannerl. Just before Wolfgang left for Italy, he and Nannerl performed together at a private party at the Hagenauers' country house in Nonnthal, an event which effectively concluded their shared stellar childhood. For Wolfgang and his father, the Italian journeys ahead would signify some of the best of their experiences, of travel, of music, of growth, of approbation and of great achievement. For Maria Anna and Nannerl, they marked the end of their direct involvement in Wolfgang's development, an end which though temporary for Maria Anna, was for Nannerl permanent.

'ON 12 DECEMBER 1769, father and son went alone to Italy,'[29] recalled Nannerl twenty-three years later. That first Italian journey lasted fifteen months, until March 1771; yet again Wolfgang met new composers, heard new music (an abundance of Italian opera, but church music too in Italy's most magnificent cathedrals), and, as he absorbed all these influences, continued his own astonishing development. Nannerl's 1792 account of that trip again demonstrated her touching sibling pride in her brother, as, two decades later, she remembered with all the wide-eyed enthusiasm of the teenage sister specific details which had impressed her at the time.

In Verona, an early stop, Wolfgang 'played the organ at St Thomas's Church, where they could not reach the organ through the church because of the crowd, and had to go through the monastery cloisters'. In Milan there were 'many concerts at the house of Count Firmian', who was Viceroy there and therefore the real power. (Firmian's uncle had been Archbishop of Salzburg before the current incumbent, Schrattenbach, and therefore Leopold's first employer at Court. Firmian was extremely supportive therefore to young Wolfgang, and commissioned an opera from him for the 1771 Carnival.) In Florence they were 'summoned at once to the Grand Duke, with whom they spent five hours'; and it was here too that 'the son made friends with an Englishman, Tommaso Linley, a boy of fourteen years and the same age as Mozart. A pupil of the famous Nardini, this boy played the violin quite enchantingly. This Englishman and the young Mozart performed in turn, not like boys but like men.'

In Rome, Wolfgang famously heard Allegri's *Miserere* in the Sistine Chapel, and wrote it down from memory later that day. But it is Nannerl's account of this which provides the most telling human detail: 'The next day he went back again, holding his copy in his hat, to see whether he had got it right or not.' In Naples, 'when the son was playing in the Conservatorio alla Pietà, everyone thought that the magic was due to his ring, [so] he took the ring off and only then was everyone filled with astonishment'. In Bologna the great teacher and contrapuntist Padre Martini tested Wolfgang for entry into the elite Accademia Filarmonica. 'He was locked up quite alone, and had to set an antiphon for four voices, with which he was ready in a good half hour.' Nannerl also lengthily recalled a bad injury to Leopold's foot, which necessitated suspending their travelling while he recovered (in extreme luxury) at the home of Count Pallavicino outside Bologna. For Maria Anna and Nannerl back in Salzburg, anxieties about Leopold's health still took precedence over all other considerations. Even after twenty-two years, that injured foot was given greater space than the one-line description of what was the greatest honour of the whole trip: 'The Pope wanted to see the son, and gave him the cross and the brief of a militiae auratae equus.' But Nannerl did remember the great success of Wolfgang's first Italian opera, *Mitridate, re di Ponto*, K87 (74a), given in Milan: 'This opera was performed more than twenty times consecutively. That the opera was applauded can be deduced from the fact that the management at once gave him a written commission for the year 1773.' And she added proudly, 'When he wrote the opera he was fourteen years old.'

Nannerl's recollections were drawn no doubt partly from conversations she had had with the travellers on their return, but also from the letters that she and her mother had regularly received from them. The first of these, written only one day after departure, carries the slight implication that Nannerl had been ill when they left ('How is your sore throat?'[30]), which was often and with greater seriousness to be the case at future partings. Leopold was insistent that none of their letters should be lost or discarded. Like his earlier letters to Hagenauer, they were to be distributed around Salzburg, and were effectively newsletters for the whole community. Even on the day after their departure he wrote, 'You must keep all our letters';[31] and again a month later, 'I hope you are carefully collecting all our letters.'[32] His style in the reporting of events therefore has a somewhat impersonal quality, conscious perhaps of the inquisitive glance of posterity. But Leopold was quite shameless about yet another instance of telling lies about himself, in order to further their cause. In Naples, as he reported proudly,

I announced everywhere that I was the steward of the Imperial
Ambassador, because in these parts the stewards of such person-
ages are very highly respected. Thus not only did I ensure a safe
journey, but I was given good horses and quick service; and at
Rome it was not necessary for me to go to the Customs Office for
the usual examination, for at the gate I was received with a deep
bow.[33]

There were private sections too ('For you alone'), in which in a
fierce stream of consciousness he shows a continual need to control
everything, as much in Salzburg as on the road. Two days after their
departure, for instance, he returned the key to a clavichord, which
he had accidentally taken away with him, out-rageously adding,
'See that it is not lost.'[34] A few weeks later, in a postscript, he
demanded to know (in a most telling order of preference), 'Have
our two guns been cleaned? Is Nannerl practising the harpsichord
regularly?'[35]

Just as Leopold wrote home regularly, so he instructed his wife
to write back to him, frequently charging her with failing to do so
('You are very lazy'[36]) when in fact she had, and never offered an
apology for such hasty accusations. On 17 November 1770 he tore
into his wife and daughter for not having sent him congratulations
on his name-day. But they had written, on the 9th; and he only
acknowledged this weeks later on 1 December. Even Wolfgang had
been upset by the ferocity of his chiding ('Wolfgang . . . became
rather sad and said: "I am truly sorry for Mamma and Nannerl,
because in his last letter Papa wrote such cutting remarks"'[37]). But
there was never any regret if Leopold or Wolfgang neglected their
side of things: 'We forgot to congratulate Nannerl on her name-
day,'[38] he wrote casually; and again, later, 'Wolfgang read Nannerl's
long story with great pleasure, but as he has gone out driving with
the Countess, he cannot write back.'[39] And on top of all this there
were endless instructions and recriminations concerning the sales of
the *Violinschule*, for which Maria Anna was evidently now respon-

sible, and about which Leopold regularly felt it necessary to crack the whip.

All this must have been extremely hurtful to Maria Anna, as on the one hand she read of all sorts of experiences, excitements and honours from which she had been excluded, and on the other was somehow seeming to be chastised for everything she had or had not done. When, desperate for more personal information about her family, she had asked some specific questions, Leopold replied as impatiently as if he were filling out a dull questionnaire: 'You want to know whether Wolfgang still sings and plays the fiddle? He plays the fiddle but not in public. He sings, but only when some text is put in front of him. He has grown a little. I am neither fatter nor thinner; and we have got accustomed to Italian food.'[40] And meanwhile he heartlessly continued to tantalize Maria Anna and Nannerl with descriptions of their experiences, while at the same time congratulating himself on his decision to leave them behind: 'Though I am glad that neither of you undertook this journey with us, yet I am sorry that you are not seeing all these Italian towns, and especially Rome. It is useless and quite impossible to describe it in a few words. Once more I advise you to read Keyssler's *Reisebeschriebung*.'[41] He exaggerated the dangers of travel, giving lurid accounts of bandits on the road between Rome and Naples, and, even when they were staying in grand houses, played down the true extent of their luxurious surroundings. Only rarely did he show genuine affection towards his wife, beyond the conventional formulae with which he closed his letters ('We kiss you and Nannerl a thousand times and I am your old MZT'). One of the very few confidences he wrote to her revealed his extreme nervousness as the premiere of *Mitridate* approached: 'On St Stephen's day . . . picture to yourself Maestro Don Amadeo seated at the clavier in the orchestra and myself a spectator and a listener in a box up above; and do wish him a successful performance and say a few paternosters for him.'[42]

In contrast to his father's essential meanness of spirit, Wolfgang was generally extremely cheerful throughout this Italian trip. 'I simply love travelling,'[43] he wrote from Naples. His letters to Nannerl were exuberant, generous and positive. He loved to show off his multilingualism, on one occasion writing in no fewer than three languages (German, Italian and French) and two dialects (Salzburg and Swabian). And with his sister he continued their shared pastime of word-games and riddles, and was completely unselfconscious in expressing his fascination with basic bodily functions. None of the family, in fact, was especially reticent about these (a common affectionate exchange between them, for instance, was 'Shit in your bed and break it'[44]); but Wolfgang's improvisations on this particular theme were, like all his others, more involved and more brilliant than those of anyone else. One whole sentence took as its recurring verb *tun* (to do), which can also mean to relieve oneself or even to have sexual intercourse. Since Wolfgang was apparently sending greetings to one of Nannerl's current admirers, Herr von Schiedenhofen, there is little doubt that his sniggering pun was here intentional.

> . . . und *thue* gesund leben, und *thue* nit sterben, damit du mir noch hanst einen brief *thuen*, und ich hernach dir doch einen *thun*, und dan *thuen* wir immer so vort, bis wir was hinaus *thuen*, aber doch bin ich der, der will *thuen* bis es sich endlich nimmer *thuen* last, inzwischen will ich *thuen* bleiben.

> . . . and *do* keep well and *do* not die, so that you may *do* another letter for me and I may *do* another for you and that we may keep on *doing* until we are *done*, for I am the man to go on *doing* until there is nothing more to *do*.[45]

Ten days after sending Nannerl this, Wolfgang was still proud of it. ('I hope that you received my letter,'[46] he chuckled.)

But beyond the smuttiness, the loving relationship between brother and sister was still touchingly evident throughout his correspondence with her. He wanted to share everything with Nannerl, as he always had, whether notated descriptions of a particular singer's astonishingly wide range; or bad trumpet-playing in Bologna; or a new game ('after lunch we play boccia. That is a game I have learnt in Rome. When I come home I shall teach it to you'[47]); or Rome itself ('I only wish that my sister were in Rome, for this town would certainly please her'[48]). He did at times seem to be genuinely homesick ('Every post day, when letters arrive from Germany, I enjoy eating and drinking far more than usual'[49]). But he continued to encourage and support Nannerl's own music-making, including composition ('You have set the bass exceedingly well and without the slightest mistake. You must try your hand at such things more often'[50]), and showed great interest in the attentions of her male admirers ('Does Diebl often visit you? Does he still honour you with his entertaining conversation? And the Honourable Karl von Vogt? Does he still listen to your unbearable voice?'[51]).

Meanwhile Wolfgang himself, now in his early teens, was experiencing physical changes too. He was constantly sleepy and hungry, partly through continual excitement and, later, exhausting pressure, but partly also because, quite simply, he was growing. And he recognized these changes himself, and confided to Nannerl his playfulness with the Wider family in Venice, to whom the Mozarts had been introduced through Johann Baptist Hagenauer. There were four daughters, whom Wolfgang nicknamed the 'pearls', and with them Wolfgang had joined in all sorts of arcane Carnival activities:

> Tell Johannes that Wider's pearls, especially Mademoiselle Catarina, are always talking about him, and that he must soon come back to Venice and submit to the *attacco*, that is, have his bottom spanked when he is lying on the ground, so that he may become a true Venetian. They tried to do it to me – the seven women all together – and yet they could not pull me down.[52]

Although Leopold liked and admired the Wider family, he subsequently referred to Venice as 'the most dangerous place in all Italy',[53] where young people needed careful supervision. It is unlikely that he approved at all of such adolescent high spirits.

Wolfgang's references to Nannerl's own admirers do prove that she was enjoying some social life. She was now nineteen years old, and had grown into a strikingly handsome young woman, with a keen eye for fashion, an extremely elaborate hairstyle, and a steady, intelligent gaze. Two young men who paid attention to her during 1770 were Herr von Mölk (son of the Court Chancellor) and Herr von Schiedenhofen. Both were from respectable Salzburg families, and their interest would have pleased Nannerl and her mother too. In the autumn of 1770 Schiedenhofen invited them to stay at his country estate at Triebenbach, greatly to Leopold's approval, for even this small journey was a real treat for the women, and distracted them from their constant sadness of exclusion.

In March 1771 Leopold and Wolfgang returned to Salzburg and were reunited with Maria Anna and Nannerl. But already there were plans to go back to Italy, for they had a commission for another opera for Milan. Maria Theresa's son, the Archduke Ferdinand (a mere two years older than Wolfgang) was to marry Beatrice d'Este in one of the most spectacular weddings in the whole of eighteenth-century Europe. It was a canny commission from the Habsburg family, who, as Nannerl's memoir recalled, had taken care in their choice of composers: 'As H: Majesty had appointed Hr Hasse, the oldest Kapellmeister, to write the opera, he had chosen the youngest to write the serenata.'[54] Johann Adolph Hasse, then aged seventeen-two, was a German composer from Hamburg who had acquired his confidence, his métier and indeed his wife (the celebrated soprano Faustina Bordoni) in Italy. He divided his time between Vienna, where he had taught Maria Theresa herself, and Venice, where he would die in 1783. He was enormously gifted and respected, and represented everything in a composer's career and lifestyle that Leopold envied. He had met Leopold and Wolfgang in Vienna in 1767, befriended them over the debacle of *La finta semplice*, and then written enthusiastic letters of recommendation for them to his colleagues in Italy. And now Hasse and the Mozarts were to be working side by side in Milan.

Nannerl recalled again the exact date of the departure of her father and brother for their second Italian journey, 13 August 1771; and she no doubt also remembered the intense coded requests she received from her brother (now sixteen) with regard to his own developing infatuations. Buried among descriptions of great heat, and the seasonal fruits he and his father were consuming on the journey, he wrote, 'What you promised me (you know what, you dear one!) you will surely do and I shall certainly be grateful to you';[55] and again, a week later, 'I beg you to remember the other matter, if there is nothing else to be done. You know what I mean.'[56] But once he had received the libretto for his serenata (*Ascanio in Alba*, K111) and begun setting it to music, he wrote less to his family. As ever it was Leopold who conveyed to the women the thrilling details of their crammed schedule, and of Milanese excitement as European royalty and nobility gathered for the festivities. In the event, *Ascanio in Alba* clearly outshone Hasse's *Ruggiero*, and, try as he might, Leopold could not conceal his Schadenfreude ('It really distresses me, but Wolfgang's serenata has killed Hasse's opera more than I can say in detail'[57]). Wolfgang was quietly generous about his elderly colleague, going repeatedly to performances of *Ruggiero*, which of course he knew by heart.

Again, Maria Anna and Nannerl were wretched at being excluded from all this. Although for the second year running they spent part of October at Triebenbach with Herr von Schiedenhofen, they would far rather have been in Milan. The more they heard about this second trip, its glamour and pace even more dynamic than the last, the more they knew that they were missing out. And again Leopold was tetchily defensive, especially after a Salzburg visitor brought him some pills from home (ordered through Maria Anna) and reported on the women's longing to be in Milan too. This infuriated him. He flung it all back in their faces: 'Chaplain Troger . . . told me that you and Nannerl would have liked to come with us. If this was your real feeling it was very wrong of you not to tell me so quite frankly, though the expense of the outward and return journeys alone would have meant a difference of at least 60 ducats',[58] and referred repeatedly to what he clearly considered to be their treachery in confiding in a third party. His staggering insensitivity to the women's feelings can only have exacerbated their bitterness when, in the midst of reports of his own glittering experiences, he grudgingly gave them permission (in a postscript) to get some new clothes: 'If you need some clothes, get what is necessary made for you, for neither you or Nannerl must do without necessities. What must be, must be. And do not buy inferior materials, since to buy shoddy stuff is no economy.'[59]

Wolfgang meanwhile continued to be utterly charming to his mother and sister. Occasionally they would have noticed his old homesickness ('I often let off my whistle, but not a soul answers me,'[60] he wrote to Nannerl – was there perhaps some calling-signal between the siblings?), and his exhaustion ('I am quite well, but always sleepy'[61]). But in general he was in great spirits and, for all the pressure, absolutely on top of his duties. He wrote exuberantly about the community of musicians where they were staying, and how the resulting cacophony actually inspired him: 'Upstairs we have a violinist, downstairs another one, in the next room a singing-master who gives lessons, and in the other room opposite ours an oboist. This is good fun when you are composing! It gives you plenty of ideas!'[62] Although Nannerl was now a young woman of twenty, their enclosed sibling world of games and secrets persisted. Just after leaving Salzburg, he spun her an energetic series of synonyms: 'You may trust, believe, opine, hold the opinion, cherish the constant hope, consider, imagine, think, and be confident that we are well.'[63] And his own physical growth continued, as even Leopold acknowledged in a curious little sentence, 'Thank God we are both like two deer, but, I should add, we are not on heat!'[64]

After the great success of *Ascanio in Alba*, Leopold delayed their departure from Milan. He was still desperately trying to find permanent employment in Italy: this after all had been the ultimate aim of all the Italian trips. In his letters to Maria Anna he concocted a series of stories about bad rheumatism and other ailments, which prevented him from travelling (for this was the narrative to be circulated throughout Salzburg), and all the while he was hanging on in the hope of receiving good news. Evidently unaware of the reputation he had acquired, he believed his Habsburg connections in Milan and Florence might bring some prestigious offer for Wolfgang and himself. And at least one Archduke did actually consider it. No doubt pleased with his wedding serenata, Archduke Ferdinand suggested to his mother Maria Theresa that he should give Wolfgang a job in Milan. On 12 December 1771, the Empress's reply was blistering:

> You ask me to take the young Salzburger into your service. I do not know why, not believing that you have need of a composer or of useless people. If however it would give you pleasure, I have no wish to hinder you. What I say is intended only to prevent you burdening yourself with useless people and giving titles to people of that sort. If they are in your service it degrades that service when these people go about the world like beggars. Besides, he has a large family.[65]

Not surprisingly, Ferdinand dropped the whole idea.

So although Leopold and Wolfgang began their return journey with some remnants of optimism ('the affair is not quite hopeless,'[66] Leopold wrote), in fact they had no prospects at all. They arrived back in Salzburg on 15 December 1771 and on the following day Archbishop Schrattenbach died. The era of the supportive employer was over.

~

THERE WERE THEN ten months of family life at home. Wolfgang and Nannerl resumed their music-making, and he wrote the first of his piano duets, the sonata in D, K381 (123a), for them to play together. This most basic form of chamber music, for two players at one keyboard, their bodies touching, their hands intertwined, became for later composers a vehicle not just for shared expression and virtuosity, but also for flirtation and seduction. (Schubert was particularly enthusiastic about this aspect of the activity.) But for Nannerl and Wolfgang, physical proximity was entirely uninhibited and familiar. They had played and performed together throughout their childhood, and this D major piano duet can be seen as a touching portrait of their sibling relationship at this later stage of their lives. Quite apart from Wolfgang's enjoyment of the whole range of the keyboard being shared through the dimensions of four hands rather than two, and his continuing invention with regard to colour, texture and the exploration of keys, the duet has a lively conversational style, punctuated with wit and cheeky humour (the return to the recapitulation in the last movement positively chuckles), and a slow movement of tender poignancy. It is significant that there is absolute parity between the Primo and Secondo parts: as a player, Nannerl was entirely Wolfgang's equal. They derived great pleasure from playing their new sonata, and no doubt gave the same to their listening parents.

At Court, Schrattenbach's successor was appointed. The new Archbishop was Count Hieronymus Franz de Paula Colloredo, son of the Imperial Vice-Chancellor. Like Joseph II himself, he was a man of the Enlightenment, who encouraged scholarship and freedom of enquiry, but at the same time resisted excessive decoration in ecclesiastical buildings and similarly preferred his church music to be simple and unadorned. One of his first tasks was to reform the musical household he had inherited, for in Schrattenbach's last years disciplines and standards had slackened considerably. Domenico Fischietti was appointed as a second Kapellmeister, equal in status to the current incumbent, Giuseppe Francesco Lolli – a move to which Leopold took the greatest exception. Despite his prolonged absence from Salzburg over the years, he had somehow assumed that the next promotion of this type was bound to be his own. Leopold never really recovered from being passed over, and held Colloredo, together with Fischietti, Lolli and indeed all Italian composers, in barely concealed contempt from then on. In his eyes his new employer had not got off to a good start. Leopold's seething resentment must have created an uncomfortable atmosphere in the tiny Getreidegasse apartment.

But despite this hostility towards usurping Italians, Leopold and

Wolfgang did have one more Italian journey to make. After the success of *Mitridate* for the 1771 Carnival, Wolfgang had been commissioned to write another opera for 1773. And so, for the third and last time, father and son made the long trip through the Dolomites to Milan in October 1772. The women, as usual, remained at home.

In comparison with the elated excitement of the last two visits, this final Italian sojourn was considerably more muted. Wolfgang was under great pressure with the composition of his opera *Lucio Silla*, K135, and Leopold's job-seeking energies had lost their edge of true conviction. Maria Anna must have noticed her husband's genuinely deteriorating spirits. In November he hinted at home-sickness and depression: '. . . now that I have been here for almost a fortnight, some trifling disorders have begun to plague me again; indeed I drop into thinking about Salzburg and, without noticing it, I go on brooding for some time.'[67] And a week later, in an isolated flash of true tenderness towards his wife, he acknowledged: 'Today is the anniversary of our wedding day. It was twenty-five years ago, I think, that we had the sensible idea of getting married, one we had cherished, it is true, for many years. All good things take time!'[68]

If Maria Anna noticed these changes in her husband, Nannerl may not yet have perceived any in her brother. Almost out of habit he continued the shared sibling secrets ('I thank you, you know for what'[69] on 21 November) and games ('I have learnt a new game here in Milan, called *Mercante in fiera*, and as soon as I come home, we shall play it'[70] on 5 December). There were puzzle-letters too. On 16 January he wrote to tell his sister about a new commission, for his motet 'Exsultate, jubilate', K165 (158a), ('I have to compose a motet for the primo uomo which will be performed tomorrow at the Theatine Church'), only he scrambled the order of his words: 'I for have the primo a uomo motet compose which to tomorrow at Church the Theatine performed be will.'[71] He still wanted to show off to Nannerl. In one letter, of 18 December, every other line was written upside down, there was a comic drawing, and much repetition of the phrases 'dear sister' and 'my child', almost like a musical leitmotif. But these flourishes of exuberance were now less frequent, and were perhaps conduits for the release of his own nervous tension (the 18 December letter was written immediately before the premiere of *Lucio Silla*), as was to be increasingly the case later in his life. His cheeky physicality was still there ('Please please, my dear sister, something is biting me. Do come and scratch me'[72] – whatever that meant); but so too were his touching homesickness and vulnerability. 'We kiss Mamma 100,000 times (I did not bring any more noughts with me) and I kiss Mamma's hands and prefer to embrace my sister in person than in imagination.'[73]

Perhaps Wolfgang too was now disenchanted with the huge labour, ultimately unrewarded, of operas for Milan, and fundamentally alarmed about his immediate lack of prospects. For indeed he had none. And by 13 March 1773, when the family was again reunited in Salzburg, they must surely have stared at one an other and wondered what to do next. Leopold's salary was meagre, especially in comparison with those of his superior colleagues, and he resented 'every kreuzer spent in Salzburg'. At the very least, Nannerl should start teaching too. Leopold had written to Maria Anna on 12 December, 'I send greetings to Nannerl and a message urging her to practise hard and to teach little Zezi conscientiously. I know well that she herself will benefit if she accustoms herself to teaching someone else very thoroughly and patiently. I am not writing this without a motive.'[74] But for Wolfgang, since he had failed to secure any employment in Italy, it was perhaps time to have another try in Vienna itself.

∽

'IN JULY 1773 the father made a short visit with the son to Vienna, in October they came back.'[75] Even taking into account Nannerl's customary telegraphic style, the baldness of this 1792 recollection speaks volumes. Nothing was achieved. The timing was not good: many people were away from the capital during the summer months. But Leopold was determined to go anyway, and equally determined that, once more, it would be far too expensive to bring the women along too. So Maria Anna could only read about their staying with old friends (the Mesmers) in lovely accommodation, meeting other friends who asked fondly after her and Nannerl and expressed surprise that they were not in Vienna too. Again Leopold was carelessly mean-spirited in justifying his actions: 'If I had known Frau von Mesmer's circumstances, which, as you know *were very doubtful*, I could have brought you both with us. But not only was it not possible for me to know them, there were other difficulties.'[76] His grumpiness continued when Maria Anna did not think to make use of a Salzburg visitor to Vienna to bring something he might need ('did no shimmer of an idea occur to you, prompting you to make use of this convenient opportunity and send a cloth travelling coat of mine?'[77]). He was bad-tempered again after the Empress granted another cool audience to the Mozarts: 'Her Majesty the Empress was very gracious to us, but that was all.'[78] (Little did Leopold realize her true feelings towards them.) Poor Maria Anna was as usual the ultimate repository for all Leopold's anxieties and frustrations.

But Wolfgang at least was in cheerful spirits now that he was away from Salzburg, and he shared these with his sister in his usual eccentric way. Just as his musical composition frequently teases the ear by delaying the perfect cadence, instead spinning ever more intriguing departures from the home key, so his epistolary composition effortlessly pursued all manner of diversion, to delay the full stop. His letter of 14 August, where in addressing her as his 'queen' he surely refers to their imagined childhood realm, the 'Kingdom of Back', is a case in point:

> I hope, my queen, that you are enjoying the highest degree of health and that now and then or rather, sometimes, or, better still, occasionally, or, even better still, qualche volta, as the Italians say, you will sacrifice for my benefit some of your important and intimate thoughts, which ever proceed from that very fine and clear reasoning power, which in addition to your beauty, and although from a woman, and particularly from one of such tender years, almost nothing of the kind is ever expected, you possess, O queen,

so abundantly as to put men and even graybeards to shame. There now, you have a well-turned sentence. Farewell.[79]

He might sign his name backwards ('Gnagflow Trazom'), or send his sister one line, but in four languages: 'Hodie nous avons begegnet per strada Dominum Edelbach, welcher uns di voi compliments ausgerichtet hat, et qui sich tibi et ta mère empfehlen lässt. Addio.'[80] ('Today we met in the street Herr Edelbach who has given us your compliments, and who asks to be remembered to you and your mother. Farewell.') He asked after the dog, and sent greetings from 'Her Majesty the Empress'. And all the while, according to his father, he was composing enthusiastically, and had some of his music performed, including his Dominicus Mass (K66), which Leopold conducted at the Jesuits' Church. Although there was no sign of a permanent job for him, he clearly felt energized and at home in Vienna.

Leopold and Wolfgang returned to Salzburg empty-handed, in September 1773. And then the family did make one enormous change in their lives, which somewhat belied Leopold's constant carping about money: they finally left the small apartment in Getreidegasse. They had wanted to move for some time. As early as 1765, when his young children were well into their boisterous years, Leopold had continually shown anxiety about the lack of space for the family and the hoards of acquisitions from their Grand Tour. But with Wolfgang and Leopold away from Salzburg so much between 1769 and 1773, Maria Anna and Nannerl had in fact been quite comfortable in the small Getreidegasse apartment. It was only after the three Italian journeys and the 1773 Vienna trip had all failed to secure the job that would take the family away from Salzburg altogether, that a move to a larger space was recognized as being not merely desirable but essential. So Leopold entered into negotiations with Anna Maria Raab, who owned the Tanzmeisterhaus in Hannibalplatz (now Makartplatz) on the other side of the river, and rented from her a spacious eight-room apartment on the first floor. With its large main room (the former dancing master's hall) serving as a magnificent music room, and its small garden at the back where they could play skittles or *Bölzlschiessen* (a form of darts shot with air-guns at specially designed targets), the Mozarts regularly entertained their friends and acquaintances here. If they had become resigned to being in Salzburg, at least they were now living in some considerable style.

Family life in the new home continued for just over a year. Wolfgang wrote another piano duet, K358 (186c) in B flat, for himself and Nannerl to play. And like his father he toed the Salzburg line at Court, writing the sort of music that would please his new employer – concertos, serenatas and well-behaved, old-fashioned Masses. But he did receive a most welcome commission, to write an opera (*La finta giardiniera*, K196) for Munich in the coming Carnival season. Colloredo gave him and his father permission to go, and even planned to attend a performance himself. And at last Leopold agreed that Nannerl, who had been so longing to travel again, should be allowed to join them for the opera's premiere. Only Maria Anna would remain in Salzburg while the rest of her family were away.

Wolfgang and Leopold arrived in Munich on 9 December. Wolfgang was invigorated by his new opportunity and resumed his high spirits, expressing them to Nannerl, together with his feelings about pretty girls (he was now almost nineteen), in his usual flamboyant way: 'Johannes Chrysostomus Wolfgangus Amadeus Sigismundus Mozartus Mariae Annae Mozartae matri et sorori, ac amicis omnibus, praesertimque pulchris virginibus, ac freillibus, gratiosisque freillibus.'[81] ('Johannes Chrysostomus Wolfgangus Amadeus Sigismundus Mozartus sends many greetings to the Maria Anna Mozarts, mother and sister, and to all his friends, and especially to the pretty girls, and Fräuleins, and gracious Fräuleins.') Nannerl herself was to join her father and brother three weeks later, by which time Leopold would have found suitable accommodation for her. This proved to be more problematic than he had anticipated – he was of course very fussy – and he even suggested at one point that Nannerl should not come to Munich at all. (How

tantalizing it must have been for poor Nannerl to read that.) But
Leopold did eventually find something appropriate, and then con-
centrated on issuing her with the most detailed instructions about
absolutely everything else. 'Nannerl must certainly have a fur rug
for the journey, or she will not be able to stand the cold in the half-
open coach. She must wrap up her head well and she must protect
her feet with something more than felt shoes only, which after a
time do not keep out the cold. She ought therefore to slip on the fur
boots which she will find in the trunk under the roof',[82] and so on.
(Did he really think that Maria Anna and Nannerl could not have
thought of these things for themselves? Nannerl was twenty-three
years old.) He told her what to do about her hair, her make-up,
which music to bring and which pieces she should especially practise – he was clearly expecting her to perform too in Munich. And
at the last minute he also told her to bring 'five or six copies of the
copper engraving of our Paris portrait'.[83] This Carmontelle painting had of course been done eleven years previously, when the children were twelve and seven, and surely had no relevance now to
either Wolfgang's or Nannerl's abilities. But for poor Leopold, perhaps it still defined his own position in his son's life, and so he
required several copies of it to give to his Munich acquaintances.

Nannerl arrived, with her bulging trunks and two girlfriends, on
4 January 1775, and Wolfgang was delighted to see her: 'She is
drinking coffee with Wolfgang at this very moment,'[84] reported
Leopold to Maria Anna. She was still her brother's best friend, and
he had much to share with her. She sent the briefest of notes to her
mother to confirm her arrival, but kept a daily diary (now lost) of
her activities, which she would read out to Maria Anna on her
return. Her only other letter home was written at the very end of
her stay, when she asked after her pet birds and her pupils (in that
order). For all her elaborate preparation and practising, there is no
evidence that she ever did take part in any music-making, public
or private. But she had a thrilling time, attending Wolfgang's
premiere, going on visits to castles and palaces, to many balls and
dances (dressed as an Amazon for one of them), and generally

getting caught up in the whole whirl of Munich Carnival. 'We are never at home the whole day long,'[85] Leopold recounted.

It was Wolfgang himself who sent his mother an account of his opera's success. He alone seemed to realize that she must have felt left out of a glorious family occasion, and therefore included her by his detailed description of it.

> Thank God! My opera was performed yesterday, the 13th, for the first time and was such a success that it is impossible for me to describe the applause to Mamma. In the first place, the whole theatre was so packed that a great many people were turned away. Then after each aria there was a terrific noise, clapping of hands and cries of 'Viva Maestro'. Her Highness the Electress and the Dowager Electress (who were sitting opposite me) also called out 'Bravo' to me. After the opera was over and during the pause when there is usually silence until the ballet begins, people kept on clapping all the time and shouting 'Bravo'; now stopping, now beginning again and so on. Afterwards I went off with Papa to a certain room through which the Elector and the whole Court had to pass and I kissed the hands of the Elector and Electress and Their Highnesses, who were all very gracious. Early this morning His Grace the Bishop of Chiemsee sent me a message, congratulating me on the extraordinary success of my opera. I fear that we cannot return to Salzburg very soon and Mamma must not wish it, for she knows how much good it is doing me to be able to breathe freely.'[86]

The sweetness of this account must have touched Maria Anna considerably, for she only received increasingly acerbic letters from her husband. (Colloredo had indeed decided to come to Munich, greatly to Leopold's displeasure.) By February he claimed that he was 'really tired out' from all the restless activity that Nannerl was enjoying so much, and he was longing for Carnival to be over. For all its success, *La finta giardiniera* had not brought Wolfgang any appointment in Munich, and Leopold was beginning to feel familiarly resigned. As their return journey approached, he sent his usual cool catalogue of commands to his wife, so that she might prepare the house to his instruction.

~

FOR TWO AND a half years after the return from Munich, all the members of the Mozart family stayed in Salzburg. It was their longest period of uninterrupted time together since their Grand Tour; and indeed it was to be their last. Nannerl as usual kept her diary,[87] and its surviving pages for these years are the greatest source of information on family life in the Tanzmeisterhaus. As in her few surviving letters, she was reluctant ever to express her feelings (unlike her father and brother, and to a lesser extent her mother). Nannerl was a chronicler of facts, a reporter of events, a keeper of lists and statistics. But for all their tantalizing inarticulacy of emotion, her diaries do shed fascinating light on middle-class life in mid-1770s Salzburg.

Nannerl recorded her daily attendance at early Mass, her teaching, visits the family made and received, walks they took around the neighbourhood (with or without their fox terrier Bimperl), the games they played of cards or *Bölzlschiessen*, and the weather. She reported major public events, including the comings and goings of the Archbishop and some of his visitors (among them, arrestingly, the 'equerry of the King of England, Herr v. Eyerer [Ayre?] . . . with his wife and a travelling companion' – was this someone with whom she might have recalled her own meetings with George III just over a decade earlier?). There were parades and processions, various community deaths, Mass compositions in a number of different churches. And there were more exotic events, such as the arrival of an elephant (which Nannerl had trouble spelling: '[*Elopfant*] *Elephant*') and its subsequent departure twelve days later. She mentioned over 170 individuals. Among the Mozarts' close family friends were the Gilowskys (Johann Wenzel Andreas was the Court surgeon, and his children Katherl and Franz Xaver Wenzel were the same ages as Nannerl and Wolfgang), the Barisanis (another family of physicians), the Robinigs, two of whom had accompanied Nannerl to Munich for *La finta giardiniera*, and the Abbé Bullinger, a Jesuit teacher to aristocratic families in Salzburg. Nannerl named some of the musicians at Court, including the oboist/cellist Fiala, and the trumpeter Schachtner, whose instrument had so frightened Wolfgang as a child, but who would in due course collaborate with him on a theatrical project, *Zaïde*, K344 (336b). There were many passing references to 'Papa' and her 'bruder', and indeed to Bimperl. She never mentioned her mother at all.

Wolfgang frequently hijacked Nannerl's diary and made entries of his own. His contributions are always fascinating, with occasional comments on performers ('frightful ass!' [*ershröcklicher esel!*] for a violinist), and little fantasias on Nannerl's themes. He wrote with the same shared conspiratorial humour, often lavatorial, of his Italian letters to her, sending her up, inventing new and often ambiguous words, continuing, in fact, their entirely normal sibling relationship. But there was virtually no reference from either of them to his own composition in those years, which in fact was plentiful and increasingly miraculous, nor to their music-making together.

One name that Nannerl did not enter into her diary was that of Josefa Duschek; but she would unquestionably have made her mark on the entire Mozart family. The young Czech soprano had recently married her teacher, Franz Xavier Duschek, and was in Salzburg with her new husband to visit her grandfather. The Mozarts probably met the Duscheks through their old landlord and friend, Johann Lorenz Hagenauer, whose wife was Josefa's grandfather's half-sister. Wolfgang was excited to meet a singer with a broader view of theatrical life than those employed at Court in Salzburg. He wrote an extensive concert scena for her, 'Ah, lo previdi', K272, to a text from Cigna-Santi's *Andromeda*. The versatility of Josefa's artistry is reflected in Wolfgang's flamboyant treatment of accompanied recitative, followed by a brisk aria and a concluding cavatina with a beguiling solo oboe — almost as if he were flexing his operatic muscles in a town where there was barely any theatre. He and Josefa Duschek were to meet again in Prague, ten years later, and the two families would remain emotionally, if not geographically, close.

But apart from the Duschek scena, most of Wolfgang's composition in the Salzburg years was instrumental rather than vocal. These were the years of symphonies, divertimentos and serenades, of his major violin concertos, possibly even to be performed by his father; and it was also the time when he laid the formidable foundations for a genre of composition that was to become highly significant for him, the piano concerto. Later these concertos would be performed by himself, but in the Salzburg years they seemed often to be composed for women, including of course his sister. Early in 1776 he wrote two of them, those in B flat, K238, and in C, K246, the latter for Archbishop Colloredo's niece, the Countess Lutzow, who had recently arrived in Salzburg and was a gifted pianist. He also wrote his concerto for three pianos, K242, for Countess Lodron and her two teenage daughters, who would shortly become Leopold's pupils (as indeed their younger sisters would in due course become Nannerl's pupils). And then he received a commission for another concerto from an old friend. Victoire Jenamy was the daughter of the celebrated French-Swiss dancer and choreographer Jean-Georges Noverre, whom Wolfgang and Leopold had met in Milan at the wedding of the Archduke Ferdinand in 1771, and again later in Vienna in 1773. For the gifted 'Mademoiselle Jenomy' (or 'Genomai', or 'Jeunehomme', as she has successively been labelled) Wolfgang wrote his first truly extraordinary piano concerto, that in E flat, K271. With its dazzling dialogue between piano and orchestra initiated in the very opening bars of the first movement, its utterly sublime slow movement, and its finale interrupted by an extra minuet – a tribute perhaps to the profession of Mademoiselle Jenamy's father – Wolfgang made another leap within his unique world of originality and invention. Staying in the key of E flat, he also wrote his concerto for two pianos, K365 (316a), probably for himself and Nannerl, their natural duetting partnership now happily extended to embrace an orchestra too.

Enjoyable and productive though this time was, Wolfgang clearly felt completely stifled by the restrictions of his Salzburg employment. The memory of his glittering childhood triumphs was always there to frustrate and tantalize him, and he longed for greater challenges in wider circles. In desperation he wrote to Padre Martini in Bologna. He told him of his recent success in Munich with *La finta giardiniera*, and also of the motet he had written for the Elector; and he sent Martini a copy of it, asking for his comments ('I beg you most earnestly to tell me, frankly and without reserve, what you think of it'[88]). But the main purpose of the letter was really to alert Martini to the fact that he was still on the lookout for a job. He went on, 'Oh how often have I longed to be near you, most Reverend Father, so that I might be able to talk to you and have discussions with you. For I live in a country where music leads a struggling existence,' and so on, complaining about the state of music in Salzburg, where there was no theatre, where his father had 'served this Court for thirty-six years and knows that the present archbishop cannot and will not have anything to do with people who are getting on in years', and finally sending his 'devoted remembrances to all the members of the Accademia Filarmonica' and especially to Martini himself, 'that one person in the world whom I love, revere and esteem most of all'.

This letter was written in Italian, and in Leopold's hand, and surely was the work of Leopold himself. The glowing reference to Leopold's own selfless service of Salzburg (ignoring of course the many years that he was absent from it), and the general uncomfortable blend of discontent and obsequious flattery, seem to represent the style and sentiments of father rather than son. Wolfgang of course would have had no disagreement with the object of this exercise. But in fact it led nowhere, for although Martini wrote Wolfgang a marvellous reply, admiring his motet and encouraging him to continue composing, nothing more ever came of it. Martini had probably seen through the whole ruse.

The Mozarts continued to live en famille in the Tanzmeisterhaus for another year. And then they tried again. In another letter written in Leopold's hand, Wolfgang applied to Colloredo for permission to travel. Unlike the careful flattery of the Martini letter, this petition adopted a somewhat petulant tone. It referred to previous occasions when either Leopold or Wolfgang had sought similar permission but had been turned down, and to newer obstacles which now seemed to be in their path ('Your Grace has been pleased to raise certain objections'). So for this latest attempt, Leopold called upon not only his entire family and their security and stability as ballast to his argument, but also the Holy Gospel:

> Parents endeavour to place their children in a position to earn their own bread; and in this they follow alike their own interest and that of the State. The greater the talents which children have received from God, the more they are bound to use them for the improvement of their own and their parents' circumstances, so that they may at the same time assist them and take thought for their own future progress. The Gospel teaches us to use our talents in this way. My conscience tells me that I owe it to God to be grateful to my father, who has spent his time unwearyingly upon my education, so that I may lighten his burden, look after myself and later on be able to support my sister. For I should be sorry to think that she should have spent so many hours at the harpsichord and not be able to make good use of her training.[89]

The Prince Archbishop could not endure sermons from his own employees. Like the Habsburgs perhaps, he was by now heartily sick of the whole Mozart family. He kept them waiting nearly a month for his reply, but then hurled back at Leopold the very Gospel which he had so unwisely cited: '. . . in the name of the Gospel, father and son have my permission to seek their fortune elsewhere.'[90] He had sacked them.

The Mozarts must have been thrown into total turmoil by these events. They simply could not survive without at least one salary, so Leopold swallowed an enormous amount of pride and managed to get himself reinstated. But the wording of the Archbishop's decree leaves no doubt as to the reputation of his exceptionally troublesome employee:

> To signify to the petitioner that His Grace desires that there should be real harmony amongst his musicians. In gracious confidence therefore that the petitioner will conduct himself calmly and peaceably with the Kapellmeister and other persons appointed to the court orchestra, His Grace retains him in his employment and graciously commands him to endeavour to render good service both to the Church and to His Grace's person.[91]

Meanwhile, Leopold had decided that Wolfgang should indeed travel, but not alone. (He was twenty-one years old.) The family would therefore be split again, but the other way round: Maria Anna would go with her son, and Nannerl would remain in Salzburg with her father. This decision was taken and acted upon very quickly, for barely a month after Colloredo's release, Maria Anna and Wolfgang left. They planned to return to three great cities of music, Munich, Mannheim and Paris. In one of these, surely, the young composer would find an appointment. But the trip was conceived against a background of chaos, disharmony and dismay, and was probably doomed before it began. As the day of departure loomed, Leopold fell ill; and when, early on the morning of 23 September 1777, the travellers' carriage trundled away from the Tanzmeisterhaus, Nannerl too collapsed completely. Leopold described the bleakness and misery of that 'dreadful day' in his first letter to his wife and son.

> After you both had left, I walked up our steps very wearily and threw myself down on a chair. When we said goodbye, I made great efforts to control myself in order not to make our parting too painful; and in the rush and flurry I forgot to give my son a father's blessing. I ran to the window and sent my blessing after you; but I did not see you driving out through the gate and so came to the conclusion that you were gone already, as I had sat for a long time without thinking of anything. Nannerl wept bitterly and I had to

use every effort to console her. She complained of a headache and a sick stomach and in the end she retched and vomited; and putting a cloth round her head she went off to bed and had the shutters closed. Poor Bimbes [the dog] lay down beside her. For my own part, I went to my room and said my morning prayers. I then lay down on my bed at half past eight and read a book and thus becoming calmer fell asleep. The dog came to my bedside and I awoke. As she made signs to me to take her for a run, I gathered it must be nearly noon and that she wanted to be let out. I got up, took my fur cloak and saw that Nannerl was fast asleep. The clock then showed half past twelve. When I came in with the dog, I woke Nannerl and ordered lunch. But she had no appetite, she would eat nothing and went to bed immediately afterwards, so that . . . I passed the time lying on my bed, praying and reading. In the evening she felt better and was hungry. We played piquet and then had supper in my room. After that we played a few more games and, with God's blessing, went off to bed. That is how we spent that sad day which I thought I would never have to face.'[92]

One almost feels sorry for him.

~

IN CONTRAST TO the desolation in the Tanzmeisterhaus, the travellers were in very good humour. For years Maria Anna had been longing to journey again with Wolfgang, and now her turn really had come. For all that she hated leaving her husband and daughter, she probably felt perfectly equal to any task ahead. Her childhood had been shot through with hardship and deprivation, but in adulthood she had taken care of her elderly mother, raised a young family, and cared for them over three and a half years of peregrination. She had kept house, done the cooking, and dealt with near-fatal illnesses in strange cities. So she was practical, level-headed and experienced; and she adored her brilliant son, in whom she had total confidence. She probably imagined that he would be offered some glorious post within a very short period, and that her family would soon be reunited. On 26 September she wrote cheerfully to her husband from Munich, 'Thank God, we are in good trim and only wish that you were with us, which, with God's help, will happen some day. Meanwhile, do not worry, and shake off all your troubles. Everything will come right in the end, when the hooks and eyes have been put on. We lead a most charming life – up early – late to bed, and visitors all day long. Addio ben mio.'[93]

And, without question, Wolfgang himself was thrilled to have got away from Salzburg. 'I am always in my best spirits,' he wrote, 'for my heart has been as light as a feather ever since I got away from all that humbug.'[94] He too was confident about dealing with all the practicalities of travel, reassuring his father, 'I am quite a second Papa, for I see to everything. I have begged Mamma to let me pay the postilions, for I can deal with these fellows better than she can.'[95] And the high spirits of both mother and son were reflected in the affectionate language with which they signed off their early letters. Wolfgang referred repeatedly to his 'brute of a sister'. And Maria Anna reached into the family's customary lexicon of lavatorial catchphrase, to cheer her gloomy husband: 'Keep well, my love. Shove your arse into your mouth. I wish you good-night, my dear, but first shit in your bed and break it.'[96]

Eventually Nannerl began to pull herself together, and by 29 September, less than a week after the travellers' departure, she bravely tried to reply to their chirpy letters in the same vein. (She was actually twenty-six years old, but her letter reads like one from a kid sister.)

> I am delighted to hear that Mamma and Jack Pudding are cheerful and in good spirits. Alas, we poor orphans have to mope for boredom and fiddle away the time somehow or other. That reminds me, Bimperl, please be so good as to send me soon a short pre-ambulum. But write one this time from C into B flat, so that I may gradually learn it by heart.
>
> I have no news to send you from home. So I kiss Mamma's hands and to you, you rascal! you villain! I give a juicy kiss and I remain Mamma's obedient daughter and your sister who is living in hopes – MARIE ANNE MOZART

Miss Pimpes too is living in hopes, for she stands or sits at the door whole half-hours on end and thinks every minute you are going to come. All the same she is quite well, eats, drinks, sleeps, shits and pisses.'[97]

When she heard that they were well received in Munich but could see little prospect of permanent employment, Nannerl seconded her father's advice to them to move on to Mannheim (perhaps at his instruction?) with a postscript of touching certainty in her brother: 'It would do us far more honour if you could succeed in obtaining a post under some other great lord. You will surely find one.'[98] In her mother's absence she was now responsible for the running of the household, not without some tense little domestic scenes, apparently, as Leopold rather glowingly reported:

Our maid Thresel finds it extraordinarily funny that Nannerl should be for ever poking her nose into the kitchen and scolding her daily about its dirty condition. For Nannerl does not overlook the least thing; and when Thresel tells a lie, Nannerl at once points out to her that it is an untruth. In short, Thresel's eyes are getting wider and wider, for Nannerl says everything to her without mincing matters, though indeed she becomes quite calm again after it is all over.'[99]

But she was still reticent about supplying her own news, and when she did, literally copied out her drily recorded schedule from her diary.

The chief pleasure for Nannerl and her father remained music-making, which they continued to do every evening, for hours at a time. And they took especial pleasure when something new arrived from Wolfgang. On 15 October they received the pieces Nannerl had asked for, and Leopold wrote to his son: 'The preludes you sent Nannerl are superlatively beautiful and she kisses you a million times for them. She plays them very well already.'[100] And three days later, after another delivery, this time of duets, he reported, 'We lit our candles at once, and to my delight Nannerl played them off . . . without the slightest hesitation and . . . with taste and expression.'[101]

At the end of the month, Leopold was still singing Nannerl's praises: 'she plays as much as she can and is an excellent accompanist. Every evening we practise for two or two and a half hours at least.'[102] Perhaps Nannerl, like many musicians, was only really happy when she was immersed in her music.

In Munich, meanwhile, the travellers were enjoying themselves with friends and music, but living was costly and there was no actual financial gain. Wolfgang discovered that it was no longer easy to arrive somewhere and simply put on a concert, as they had done when he and Nannerl were children: a child prodigy (or, even better, two) was of interest, but a grown-up one was not. There were some old friends in Munich to whom they could turn for advice, and among these was the Bohemian composer Joseph Mysliveček, whom Leopold and Wolfgang had repeatedly met on their Italian travels. Mysliveček had then agreed to try to get Wolfgang an opera commission for Naples. Sadly, he was now suffering from syphilis, and was in Munich to receive medical treatment, with hideously disfiguring facial results. On hearing all this, Leopold's claim that 'everyone must be shunning and loathing him'[103] – on both physical and moral grounds, presumably – no doubt reflected his own thoughts, and he ludicrously tried to dissuade his son from seeing him: 'If . . . Mysliveček hears or has heard that you are in Munich, your excuse . . . will have to be that your Mamma forbids you to do so.'[104] But Wolfgang would have none of it: 'Was I to know that Mysliveček, so good a friend of mine, was in a town, even in a corner of the world where I was and was I not to see him, to speak to him? Impossible! So I resolved to go and see him.'[105] He was indeed dreadfully shocked by Mysliveček's appearance, which lingered in his mind's eye for days and kept him awake at night. But on the day before he left Munich, he went back to see him again, and this time, perhaps even in defiance of Leopold's suggestion, he asked his mother to come with him. And Maria Anna, ever practical and compassionate, took it completely in her stride. She wrote to Leopold, 'He is indeed to be pitied. I talked to him as if I had known him all my life. He is a true friend to Wolfgang, and has said the kindest things about him everywhere.'[106]

There is perhaps the slightest hint, in these early days in Munich, that Maria Anna, left to her own devices as Wolfgang scurried about the city, countered the beginnings of deep loneliness by resorting to drink. On 6 October Wolfgang referred to his mother being unable to write because she had a headache; five days later (after the Mysliveček visit) he reported that they had been to a coffee party, where however she 'drank no coffee, but two bottles of Tyrolese wine instead'.[107] And indeed, as she struggled to pack up all their belongings for their journey on to Augsburg (Wolfgang meanwhile being at the theatre) her little insertion into Wolfgang's unfinished letter home did not exactly suggest total sobriety:

> I am sweating so that the water is pouring down my face, simply from the fag of packing. The devil take all travelling. I feel that I could shove my feet into my mug, I am so exhausted. I hope that you and Nannerl are well. I send most cordial greetings to my dear Sallerl and Monsieur Bullinger. Please tell Nannerl not to give Bimperl too much to eat, lest she should get too fat. I send greetings to Thresel. I kiss you both millions of times. MARIA ANNA MOZART
> Munich, 11, at eight o'clock in the evening,1777.[108]

She was of course accustomed to alcohol in Salzburg, where everyone drank copiously, largely because Court employees were generously supplied with wine as part of their earnings. Inebriation was even known to be the cause of embarrassment among the musicians as they carried out their duties (Michael Haydn was a regular offender, as was his wife, the Court singer Maria Magdalena Lipp), and had perhaps been partly responsible for the fall in standards that Colloredo was so keen to arrest.

From Munich, Maria Anna and Wolfgang travelled on to Augsburg, where they stayed for two weeks. Wolfgang gave two concerts, though they brought little reward. But the Augsburg visit was extremely significant for the change wrought in the chemistry of the Mozart family. Wolfgang was reunited with his bookbinder uncle, Franz Alois, and therefore with his young cousin Maria Anna Thekla (the 'Bäsle'). Up until this point, Wolfgang's interest in girls had been cheerful, adolescent and spasmodic. The Wider 'pearls' in Venice had excited him, and later he had sent greetings and possibly little gifts through Nannerl to a number of their Salzburg friends. But no single girl had made serious inroads into his emotional attention. His best friend, and his closest confidante, was still his sister.

All that changed when Wolfgang caught up with the 'Bäsle'. They had met twice as children, in June 1763 at the very beginning of the family's Grand Tour, when Wolfgang was seven and the 'Bäsle' four, and then again at the end of the same tour three years later. Now, at twenty-one, Wolfgang was bowled over by his nineteen-year-old cousin. He wrote to his father: 'I declare that our little cousin is beautiful, intelligent, charming, clever and gay; and that is because she has mixed with people a great deal, and has also spent some time in Munich. Indeed we two get on extremely well, for, like myself, she is a bit of a scamp. We both laugh at everyone and have great fun.'[109]

Despite Wolfgang's customary hyperactivity in Augsburg, meeting family friends and fellow musicians, and especially trying out new Stein pianos, which he was to admire so much for the rest of his life, he and his cousin delighted in each other's company. They spent enormous amounts of time together, becoming mutually infatuated on many levels, not least physically. The family habit of expressing affection through analogy with basic bodily functions was naturally extended to include the 'Bäsle', and they seem to have become almost inseparable. She accompanied him to lunches and visits and concerts – and, significantly perhaps, to a wine shop with Maria Anna.

Wolfgang's infatuation with his cousin was observed and received cautiously by the rest of the family. The ebullient optimism that Maria Anna had shown at the start of her trip seems already to have become muted in Augsburg, just a few weeks after departure. She entered much less into the exchange of lengthy letters between Leopold and Wolfgang, adding just one cover-all line, for instance, on 14 October, 'All sorts of messages from me to all my good friends.'[110] She made no reference at all to the 'Bäsle', nor therefore to any changes in Wolfgang's behaviour, but began to take less and less part in daily activities, refusing invitations because 'the cold has given me pains in the belly'.[111] Nannerl, however, did seem to notice the change in her brother. Her letters to him became a little more agitated, even exasperated ('Not a single letter!'[112] on 27 October) as she perhaps began to feel that she was losing him. As for Leopold, the 'Bäsle' herself had written to him, probably at Wolfgang's suggestion (he was later also to encourage his future wife, Constanze Weber, to write to his father in the early stages of their relationship); and despite its idiosyncratic spelling and style, her letter expressed all the right sentiments.

> MY PARTICULARLY LOVABLE UNCLE,
> It is impossible for me to express the great pleasure which we have felt at the safe arrival of my aunt and of such a dear cousin and indeed we regret that we are losing so soon such excellent friends, who show us so much kindness. We are only sorry that we have not had the good fortune to see you here with my aunt. My parents send their humble greetings to you both, my uncle and my cousin Nannerl, and they hope that you are well. Please give my greetings to my cousin Nannerl and ask her to keep me in her friendship, since I flatter myself that I shall one day win her affection. I have the honour to send you my greetings and I remain with much respect
>   Your devoted servant and niece
>   M.A. MOZART
> Augsburg, 16 October 1777
>   My father cannot remember whether he informed you that on 31 May 1777, he gave Herr Lotter four copies of your 'Violin-schule', and two more on 13 August 1777.[113]

Leopold responded with reserve, bizarrely warning his son that his cousin had 'too many friends among the priests'.[114] (This actually proved to be prophetic, for a few years later his niece gave birth to an illegitimate child, fathered by a local canon.) Wolfgang hotly denied this. In his eyes, the 'Bäsle' could do no wrong.

But in fact Leopold was more worried about the bigger picture, his son's total failure to achieve either good money or, better still, permanent employment. His immense letters – unedited streams of consciousness, with little care any longer for that eye of posterity – became increasingly domineering. He issued instructions, worried about minutiae, reprimanded his son for not writing and therefore not answering his questions; and he began a line of guilt-inducing challenge. Often he stooped to exploiting his wife and daughter in his arguments. 'Honour and care for your mother, who in her old age is having much anxiety,'[115] he wrote on 23 October. (Maria Anna was fifty-seven.) Nor did he have qualms about emotional black-mail: 'Nannerl and I, alive and dead, are the old faithful, abandoned orphan and grass widower and everything that is sad.'[116] And yet, even as he urged Wolfgang to move on to Mannheim, he foresaw the down side:

> Now you must be well on your guard, for Mannheim is a danger-ous spot as far as money is concerned. Everything is very dear. You will have to move heaven and earth to obtain a hearing, then wait interminably for a present and in the end receive at most ten carolins – or 100 gulden, a sum which by that time you will have probably spent. The Court is packed with people who look on strangers with suspicion and who put spokes in the wheels of the very ablest. Economy is most necessary.'[117]

And so on. Such negative prediction cannot have been helpful to the travellers.

On 26 October 1777 Wolfgang and Maria Anna did leave for Mannheim, where they were to spend the next four months. The Electoral seat of the Palatinate had a long reputation as one of the most brilliant Courts in all Europe. The Elector since 1742 was Carl Theodor, a keen music-lover who had continually expanded his orchestra: by 1778 it numbered ninety. The players were excellent, and the orchestra was universally admired for its sound and its virtuosity. The Mozart children had played at the Elector's summer residence, Schwetzingen, in 1763, and Wolfgang and Maria Anna must have been eager to return, hoping now for permanent employment in this haven of musical excellence and opportunity.

As soon as he possibly could, Wolfgang engineered a meeting with the Elector. Carl Theodor was gracious, but distant and ultimately dismissive. (He did have other things on his mind: he was awaiting news from Bavaria, where indeed the Elector was about to die, passing his inheritance to Carl Theodor. In the following summer, Carl Theodor would move his entire Court from Mannheim to Munich.) Quite simply, there was no need for another musician, however brilliant, in his Court: he already had a clutch of Europe's finest in his possession. And Wolfgang greatly enjoyed the company of those very composers and instrumentalists, especially the Konzertmeister, Christian Cannabich, and the flautist Johann Baptist Wendling, whose families were extremely welcoming to Wolfgang and his mother, and whose friendship endured beyond the Mannheim stay. But Wolfgang's frustration at not landing the job he sought occasionally manifested itself in arrogance and defiance, and, except within his immediate circle of friends, he began, like his father, to get a reputation as a nuisance. As early as the day after his arrival, he was taken by Cannabich to a rehearsal. Some musicians were 'very polite and fearfully respectful'[118] to him, while those who had not the least idea who he was 'stared wild-eyed, and certainly in rather a sneering manner'. In this, Wolfgang's first Mannheim letter home (on 31 October), he added crossly, 'They probably think that because I am small and young, nothing great or mature can come out of me; but they will soon see.' And most significantly, for it became a pattern, he assuaged his feelings of tension and discouragement by writing the first of his now-famous letters to the 'Bäsle'. Though not yet of the profoundly scatological nature of his later letters to her, this first has a nonsensical date, and is full of light-hearted tomfoolery – the sort of letter, in fact, that he used to write to Nannerl. His sister, it seems, had been deposed.

Wolfgang's situation soon became precarious, as hope for any permanent employment evaporated. Leopold was increasingly exasperated by his son's lack of success, and again his letters multiplied in length, recrimination, instruction and emotional blackmail. He continued to make references to Maria Anna and Nannerl, deploying them as ballast for his arguments. On 13 November, for instance, when lengthily expounding on the advisability of staying in Mannheim to try to secure the elusive post, and the tactics Wolfgang might adopt, he suggested, 'you could give as a good excuse to the Electress your mother's age and the strain of a winter journey, which would be very uncomfortable indeed for an elderly woman,'[119] adding later, 'Women sympathize with one another, and Her Highness knows what old age means.' The general tone of this massive letter is overbearingly dictatorial. And for all that Wolfgang was still breezily pretending that all was well, his father's letters were beginning to upset him. They must have caused misery too both to Nannerl, who endured Leopold's moods even as he wrote them, and to Maria Anna, who received and read them as well. The contest of wills between father and son was growing in intensity, and the unhappy spectators were powerless to stop it.

Between themselves, Maria Anna and Nannerl communicated little, and when they did, their concerns were mainly practical and domestic. (Wolfgang wrote on 4 November, 'Mamma asks me to tell Nannerl that the lining for the coat is at the very bottom of the large box on the right hand side. She will find all sorts of bits for patching, black, white, yellow, brown, red, green, blue and so forth.'[120]) Only when Nannerl began to feel shoved aside in Wolfgang's affections did she turn more to her mother, discussing their shared interest in fashion and hairstyles – 'women's chat',[121] as she put it rather pointedly.

But Maria Anna was increasingly homesick. She longed for news of all her Salzburg friends, and of Bimperl, her beloved dog. On 23

November she issued what amounted to another of her questionnaires:

> You do not tell us very much about Salzburg. Are there no players
> [Maria Anna meant actors] there? Are no operas being performed?
> Is Dr Barisani still out of favour? Does our Chief Purveyor still
> pay attention to Fräulein Tonerl? I should like to know all these
> things in detail . . . This very moment Nannerl will lay aside what-
> ever she is doing and give Bimperl a kiss on her little paws and
> make it smack so loudly I can hear it in Mannheim. Remember me
> to the Hagenauers, Robinigs, Frau von Gerlichs, the Barisanis,
> Jungfer Mitzerl, Katherl Gilowsky, to whom we send congratula-
> tions on her coming name-day. Remember us too to Theresa [the
> maid]. Now I think I have sent greetings to all and our compli-
> ments and thanks.[122]

But as Leopold's salvos became ever more furious, Maria Anna
too began to resent his accusations, and to retaliate. When Leopold
suggested it was all a waste of time and money to stay on in
Mannheim, she coolly and factually defended their remaining, and
in fact showed herself to be extremely lucid on financial matters.
By December she had found out everyone's salary in Mannheim
('Rather different from Salzburg: it makes your mouth water'[123]).
And after she had received frenzied complaints from Leopold that
nobody had told him how much anything had cost, she did so,
firmly and in great detail. Countering his accusations of their
inefficiency and lack of trust in his considerable experience in these
matters, she retorted, 'Travelling expenses have gone up a lot since
everything became so dear. It is not like it used to be, you would
be surprised.'[124] And, as they all considered the next move, that
Wolfgang should travel on to Paris with two Mannheim musicians
and she should return alone to Salzburg, she agreed to go along
with the plan, however much she dreaded the journey in the middle
of winter ('I can't bear to think of it'[125]). Although she was cold and
miserable, she was always loyal and selfless and brave. (And perhaps she continued to seek consolation in alcohol. Congratulating

Leopold on his name-day, she wrote, 'We shall now drink your health in a good Rhine wine.'[126]) But she was not just longing to get home; she was desperately lonely. After another of her questionnaires about all her Salzburg friends, she added, 'Wolfgang has not come home yet . . . He has to go to one place for his meals, to another to compose and give lessons, and to yet another when he wants to sleep.'[127] In other words, she had been virtually abandoned.

Wolfgang was indeed doing all those things. But the constant haranguing from his father was distressing him, and after composing lengthy and determinedly optimistic replies, he let off steam by writing to his cousin. His three 'Bäsle' letters from the end of 1777 (5 and 13 November, 3 December) were all written immediately after he had dealt with his father. And for him the release into his cousin's earthy, childlike world, into their shared obsession with all matters lavatorial and physical, became a theme upon which he extemporized with huge energy, glee and boundless imagination. He was clearly still infatuated with his cousin, from whom he had only recently been parted. And his heading to the second of these three letters even suggested that for him she was the embodiment of all women: 'Ma très chère Nièce! Cousine! Fille! mère, soeur et épouse!'[128] These explosions of fantastical verbal gymnastics and word-games include sexual innuendo ('one has the purse and the other has the gold' – the implication being that you put one into the other; and then, 'And what do you hold it with? With your hand, don't you?!'[129]) Their exploration of each other's bodies in Augsburg seems to have been entirely thorough. And Maria Anna probably knew all about this. Wolfgang's letter to the 'Bäsle' on 13 November apparently quotes what his mother had just said to him: 'Now do send her a sensible letter for once.'[130] So she was quite aware of the sort of language he normally used with his cousin, and everything that it entailed, and she remained unshocked.

The coarseness of these 'Bäsle' letters can seem profoundly puzzling, and hard to equate with a composer whose music is of the utmost sublimity. And yet, as the letters of all the Mozart family regularly demonstrate, the discussion of basic bodily functions was a matter of complete normality. That the excitable and sexually aroused Wolfgang developed this practice to such startling proportions should, in truth, be no surprise, for it was no more than what he did when improvising with infinite brilliance and originality at a keyboard. And amidst all the 'muck' and nonsense, he did produce some real poetic fantasy:

> Do go on loving me, as I love you, then we shall never cease loving one another, though the lion hovers round the walls, though doubt's hard victory has not been weighed and the tyrant's frenzy has crept to decay; yet Codrus, the wise philosopher, often eats soot instead of porridge, and the Romans, the props of my arse, have always been and ever will be – half-castes.[131]

Like all the women he loved, the 'Bäsle' certainly inspired Wolfgang's brilliant creativity.

~

As 1777 TURNED into 1778, dramatic events took place in Bavaria. The Elector Maximilian III died on 30 December, and Carl Theodor ('our' Elector, as Maria Anna approvingly called him) was declared his successor, leaving for Munich immediately. Both Munich and Mannheim went into mourning, and everything closed down. 'There are no operas, for which I am truly sorry,' wrote Maria Anna, 'all plays, balls, concerts, sleigh-rides, everything has been stopped . . . it is deadly quiet and thoroughly boring . . . Salzburg will be a much jollier place this winter.'[132]

The Mozart family exchanged New Year greetings, and both Maria Anna and Nannerl revealed deep dissatisfaction with their current unresolved situations. Maria Anna hoped that the new year would be 'better than the last',[133] and Nannerl expressed her longing to see her mother and brother again, 'provided it is not in Salzburg'.[134] She kept in her sights the original goal, that Wolfgang would land a plum job in a plum Court, and they would all move to join him. ('We are both longing for you to make your fortune'[135]). But her life in 'this dull Salzburg' was still enlivened by music-making, especially when more new compositions arrived from Wolfgang. She greatly admired his latest piano sonata, K309 (284b), observing astutely, 'One can see from its style that you composed it in Mannheim'[136] (by which she presumably meant its sudden changes of mood and dynamic, and its sense throughout of orchestral colour and texture). And while Leopold had peevish reser-vations about its 'Mannheim mannerisms' (perhaps he was now determined to be negative about every aspect of Mannheim), he proudly reported how both the new sonata and Nannerl's fault-less performance of it had thrilled some fellow musicians at the Tanzmeisterhaus. And indeed, these evenings of music at home, when Nannerl joined her father and other Salzburg colleagues to play through piece after piece by her brother, were ever the happiest of times for her. In a curious way, it was Wolfgang's music that was providing her with the release that she needed, just as corresponding with their cousin was a release for him. The tyranny of life at home with Leopold can only have been stifling. ('Nannerl has had a cold,' Leopold wrote on 12 January 1778, 'and I am not letting her go out.'[137] Nannerl was twenty-six years old.)

Leopold continued to fuss about the forthcoming travel arrange-ments, weighing up every possible permutation of Maria Anna's proposed return journey to Salzburg. She herself seemed to be steadier at this prospect, encouraging her husband: 'Do not worry, for we shall think of the best way to arrange it.'[138] On Wolfgang's behalf Leopold wrote letters to old contacts in Paris who might be useful to him, and made more elaborate arrangements for his journey there. Two Mannheim wind-players, the oboist Friedrich Ramm and the flautist Johann Baptist Wendling, would accompany him. Not having met either of these men, Leopold fretted too about the temptations that might beset Wolfgang in Paris, where he would be without any parental supervision whatsoever. Mindful perhaps of his son's previous antics with the Wider girls in Venice, which had so dismayed him, Leopold was forthright on the subject of French women. 'You should refrain from all familiarity with young Frenchmen,' he wrote on 29 January, 'and even more so with the women, who run after people of talent in an astonishing way in order to get at their money, draw them into their net, or even land them as husbands.'[139] A week later he returned obsessively to his theme: 'I shall say nothing about the women, for where they are concerned the greatest reserve and prudence are necessary, Nature herself being our enemy. Whoever does not use his judgement to the utmost to keep the necessary reserve with them, will exert it in vain later on when he endeavours to extricate himself from the labyrinth, *a misfortune which often ends in death.*'[140] (For all that Leopold had a loyal and devoted wife, he was fundamentally riddled with misogyny.) But, regardless of all these anxieties, plans for both Wolfgang and Maria Anna at last seemed to be taking shape, and the Mozarts were discussing which bits of their luggage should go in which direction. And then Wolfgang suddenly changed his mind. He had become infatuated with another young woman.

Aloysia Weber was the daughter of Fridolin Weber, a Court singer in Mannheim who supplemented his lowly salary by prompting at the opera theatre, and by hiring himself out as a music copyist. His four daughters, then aged between fifteen and nineteen, were all gifted musicians, especially the seventeen-year-old Aloysia. Wolfgang first mentioned her in a letter to Salzburg on 17 January 1778, as he prepared to go for a long weekend to Kirchheim-Bolanden with her and her father, to play for the Princess of Orange. 'She sings most admirably, and has a lovely pure voice,'[141] he wrote. So they packed up arias for her, and sonatas and symphonies for him, and set off to earn, they hoped, good money. Maria Anna was left alone in Mannheim.

With everything still closed for official mourning, the city was eerily silent. 'One hears nothing at all here,' she wrote on the 24th, 'it is as quiet as if one were no longer in the world.'[142] She seized on kindnesses of young people who occasionally visited her 'to see how I was getting along without Wolfgang', and tried to enliven the evenings she was obliged to spend with her host family by getting them to play games: 'We do needlework until it gets dark, and after supper we play "fire and murder" (which I have taught them).' She was no doubt happy to receive an immensely lively poem from Wolfgang, clearly in the best of spirits with his new friends. But its central message must have caused her to raise her eyebrows. In between his customary family references to shitting and farting, she would have detected the beginnings of a new plan in her son's mind:

Die Wahrheit zu gestehen, so möcht ich mit den Leuten
Viel lieber in die Welt hinaus und in die große Weiten,
Als mit der Tac-gesellschaft, die ich vor meiner seh,
So oft ich drauf gedenke, so thut mir der Bauch weh;
Doch muß es noch geschehen, wir müssen noch zusamm —
Der Arsch vom Weber ist mehr werth als der Kopf von Ramm
Und auch von diesem Arsch ein Pfifferling
Ist mir lieber als der Mons: Wendling.

(Indeed I swear 'twould be far better fun
With the Webers around the world to run
Than go with those bores, you know who I mean,
When I think of their faces, I get the spleen.
But I suppose it must be and off we shall toddle,
Though Weber's arse I prefer to Ramm's noddle.
A slice of Weber's arse is a thing
I'd rather have than Monsieur Wendling.)[143]

Their carefully considered strategy, laboriously agreed through lengthy correspondence between Mannheim and Salzburg, was about to be ditched.

Wolfgang announced his change of heart as soon as he returned from his jolly week away. (They were having such a good time that they spent a few extra days extending their return journey.) He wrote to his father on 4 February 1778, at first describing his experience in Kirchheim-Bolanden in detail, and in the process continuing his praise of Aloysia's singing and playing. He enumerated everything they had all performed for the Princess, and complained about the fees they had been paid. Then came the bombshell – and here Wolfgang pulled his mother into the argument ('Mamma and I have talked the matter over'[144]). Wendling and Ramm were now considered disreputable types ('libertines', with 'no religion whatever'), and were therefore not trustworthy. As his little poem had implied, it would be far better not to go to Paris at all, but to travel with the Webers to Italy. Wolfgang warmed to his theme: 'I have become so fond of this unfortunate family that my dearest wish is to make them happy'; and added the supremely tactless miscalculation, '[Fridolin Weber] is just like you and has exactly your way of thinking'. He therefore asked his father to write to all their contacts in Verona, Venice and so on, and help him launch Aloysia on the Italian stage. On their way to Italy they would of course stop in Salzburg, when (dragging Nannerl now into the argument) 'my sister will find a friend and companion in Mlle Weber, for, like my sister in Salzburg, she has a reputation for good behaviour'.

Later that night while Wolfgang was out, Maria Anna added a postscript to his letter, beginning with the wry observation, 'You will see from this letter that when Wolfgang makes new acquaintances, he immediately wants to give his life and property for them.' But she was much shaken by her son's complete abandonment of all they had agreed. She continued:

> True, she [Aloysia] sings exceedingly well; still, we must not lose sight of our own interests. I never liked his being in the company of Wendling and Ramm, but I never ventured to raise any objection, nor would he have listened to me.
>
> But as soon as he got to know the Webers, he immediately changed his mind. In short, he prefers other people to me, for I remonstrate with him about this and that, and about things which I do not like; and he objects to this. So you yourself will have to think over what ought to be done. I do not consider his journey to Paris with Wendling at all advisable. I would rather accompany him myself later on. It would not cost so very much in the mail coach. Perhaps you will still get a reply from Herr Grimm. Meanwhile we are not losing anything here. I am writing this quite

secretly, while he is at dinner, and I shall close, for I do not want to be caught.

While Wolfgang was writing his bombshell letter, and his mother was adding her anxious postscript, Leopold in Salzburg was composing a letter of his own. Confidently expecting this to be his last before Wolfgang left for Paris, he was nevertheless extremely perturbed about him going without any parental guidance at all, and therefore tried to instil some adult responsibility in his son. Hauling out all their family history to strengthen his arguments, including the children who had died in infancy, and – as in his earlier petition to Archbishop Colloredo – invoking the Almighty, he applied the most appalling pressure:

> It must be clear as noonday to you that the future of your old parents and of your good sister who loves you with all her heart, is entirely in your hands. Since you were born, or rather since my marriage it has been very difficult for me to support a wife, seven children, two maids and Mamma's own mother on my monthly pay . . . and to meet the expenses of childbirths, deaths and illnesses . . . When you were children, I gave up all my time to you in the hope that not only would you be able to provide later on for yourselves, but that also I might enjoy a comfortable old age, be able to give an account to God of the education of my children, be free from all anxiety, devote myself to the welfare of my soul and thus be able to meet my death in peace . . . My dear Wolfgang, . . . I place all my trust and confidence in your filial love. Our future depends on your abundant good sense.[145]

And in a postscript to Maria Anna, he confessed that he had written his appeal with tears in his eyes, and would not even let Nannerl read it.

These two desperately unfortunate letters crossed on the road between Mannheim and Salzburg. Upon their respective arrival, there was inevitable dismay on both sides. Leopold worked himself into such a state that he could not sleep, and only after two days could he begin to reply. But when he did sit down to write, on

11 February, his floodgates opened. 'I have read your letter of the
4th with amazement and horror,'[146] he began, and continued for over
3,000 words – quite his most monumental letter yet. With the
fiercest possible intensity he reminded Wolfgang of the whole purpose of his journey: to get a good appointment so that he might
support his mother and sister, and of course his father. He pointed
out the alternative endings that Wolfgang might face, as a result of
a good or bad choice made at that moment, either earning himself
an honest place in history as a famous Kapellmeister, or (with melodramatic flourish), 'utterly forgotten by the world, captured by
some woman, you die bedded on straw in an attic full of starving
children'. He listed the girls with whom Wolfgang had become
infatuated, including 'your little romance . . . with my brother's
daughter'. He redoubled his criticisms of his son's administrative
and behavioural hopelessness on the tour so far. He ridiculed the
notion that an inexperienced German girl of eighteen could have a
chance on the Italian opera stage: 'Tell me, do you know of any
prima donna who, without having first appeared many times in
Germany, has walked on to the stage in Italy as a prima donna?'
(In fact, some foreign singers of less than eighteen were doing
just that.) If Wolfgang was to hitch his fortunes to those of the
impoverished Weber family, the Mozarts would be the object of
derision in Salzburg. The only possible course therefore was that
Wolfgang should continue on his way to Paris, as planned. ('Off
with you to Paris! And that soon! *Aut Caesar, aut nihil!*') He had a
few dismissive words for Aloysia Weber (she should take advice
from an experienced singer, like the elderly Mannheim tenor Anton
Raaff). And finally he returned to the effect that all this had had on
him: 'Think of me as you saw me when you left us, standing beside
the carriage in a state of utter wretchedness. Ill as I was, I had been
packing for you until two o'clock in the morning, and there I was at
the carriage again at six o'clock, seeing to everything for you. Hurt
me now, if you can be so cruel!' Only in his postscript did he
remember his wife and daughter, but still managed to find them
useful. Nannerl was an emotional tool, Maria Anna a physical

one: 'Nannerl has wept her full share during these last two days';
and, on the cover of the letter, the bluntest of instructions, 'Mamma
is to go to Paris with Wolfgang, so you had better make the arrangements.'

Wolfgang and his mother were naturally devastated by
Leopold's letter. Wolfgang replied very carefully, retracting most
of his plans, but maintaining a certain scorched dignity. He
answered Leopold's postscript with one of his own: 'Tell [Nannerl]
she must not cry over every trifle, or I will never go home again.'[147]
And then, having written his difficult reply (and as so often with the
Mozart family in times of stress), he became ill and took to his bed
for two days. Maria Anna unquestionably took her son's side. 'We
are both awfully sorry that our letter horrified you so. On the other
hand, your last letter of the 12th distressed us greatly.' But she continued calmly, 'Why, everything can be made right again.'[148] She
agreed to go to Paris with Wolfgang, never once mentioning that in
so doing she obviously had to abandon her own great desire to
return home. And indeed, in the many exchanges of letters during
the four weeks before they did leave, it was Maria Anna who was
the steadiest of them all. Throughout this family crisis, Leopold
was hysterical, self-pitying, often irrational, melodramatic, verbose
and manipulative. Wolfgang was defensive, wounded, a little petulant, but fundamentally guarded now (although he did defiantly
continue to praise Aloysia Weber's musicianship to the skies).
Nannerl was virtually silent. She did, however, and with the utmost
generosity, send her brother 50 gulden from her own savings, for
which Wolfgang thanked her seriously and sweetly – almost
operatically in fact ('Happy is that brother who has such a good
sister'[149]). Maria Anna was calm and practical, never directly
expressing her homesickness. She now pinned her hopes on reunit-
ing her family in Paris: 'I do hope that Wolfgang will make his
fortune in Paris quickly, so that you and Nannerl may follow us
soon. How delighted I should be to have you both with us, for nothing could be better.' But her sad little postscript about her beloved

dog revealed her real longings: 'A kiss for Bimperl, who will by this time have forgotten me and will no longer recognize me.'[150]

And so Wolfgang and his mother prepared to depart. Leopold rallied and instructed, worrying as ever about every single detail. Maria Anna could not wait for the transition period to be over ('I shall be delighted to be out of this'[151]). And Wolfgang found time to write once more to the 'Bäsle', releasing the tensions and pressures of the past dreadful weeks in his old familiar mixture of nonsense, fantasy and lavatorial humour. 'Perhaps you think or are even convinced that I am dead? That I have pegged out? Or hopped a twig? Not at all,'[152] he began, and continued: 'Don't believe it, I implore you. For believing and shitting are two very different things! How could I be writing such a beautiful hand if I were dead? How could that be possible? I shan't apologize for my very long silence, for you would never believe me. Yet what is true is true. I have had so many things to do that I had time indeed to think of my little cousin, but not to write, you see.'

Very soon his letter deteriorated into a childish refrain ('Muck! – Muck! – Ah, muck! – Sweet word! Muck! Chuck!' and so on); but then recovered as he spun the 'Bäsle' a long, hilarious, veritably surreal tale about a shepherd and 11,000 sheep. His head and heart may have been turned by Aloysia Weber, but his passionate friendship with his cousin – a member of the family, but (unlike Nannerl) at a safe remove from Leopold – was still essential to his spiritual equilibrium.

~

WOLFGANG AND MARIA Anna left Mannheim on 14 March 1778. Wolfgang was distraught at having to tear himself away from his Aloysia and her family. In his first letter home after their arrival in Paris, he described in great detail the 'farewell' concert of his music at Cannabich's house in Mannheim, at which Aloysia had both sung and played the piano, and then the tearful two hours he had spent with the Weber family on the very eve of his departure. Maria Anna's letter, as usual briefer than her son's, described more directly the conditions of their journey: 'We had the most beautiful weather for eight days, bitterly cold in the morning and warm in the afternoon. But during the last two days we were nearly choked by the wind and drowned by the rain, so that we both got soaking wet in the carriage and could scarcely breathe.'[153] By the time they arrived in Paris on 23 March they were exhausted, and Maria Anna was probably not in the best of health.

But they were determined to be optimistic about Wolfgang's prospects. He had been a sensational success in Paris as a child, and the Mozarts still had extremely good and influential contacts there, notably Baron Grimm and his mistress, Madame d'Epinay. There were two concert series to which Wolfgang might contribute; and since Paris had seen his first-ever publications (at the age of seven), he was hopeful that he might also publish some of his latest works. He hurried about the city in his first days, renewing all his old acquaintances and making new ones, and within weeks had established quite a network of support. Family tension eased. Leopold's letters became altogether more relaxed, approving his family's presence now in a capital offering so much more opportunity than Mannheim had: 'Thank God, Nannerl and I are both well, and I am now free from all worry and thoroughly happy, knowing that our excellent friend Baron de Grimm is taking an interest in you and that you are in a place which, if you are industrious, as you are by nature, can give you a reputation throughout the world.'[154] Remembering the gifts that Madame d'Epinay had bestowed on Maria Anna when they had last left Paris in 1766, he gaily observed, 'So my dear wife has seen Paris again, and so have Madame d'Epinay's red satin gown and fan.'[155] He continued to advise his wife and son on every aspect of diet, health and expenditure. But he also reported at length on Salzburg activities, on much music-making for both himself and his daughter ('Nannerl accompanies . . . like a first-rate Kapellmeister'[156]), on their respective pupils, and on their various friends in town – exactly the sort of gossip, in fact, that Maria Anna always adored.

But while relationships between father and son were improving,

Maria Anna was still very unsettled. By the beginning of April she could report proudly and positively on Wolfgang's activity ('Words fail me to tell you how famous and popular our Wolfgang is'[157]), but she could not conceal her continuing anxieties about the small amount of money they had, and how she was trying to economize ever more. Nor could she hold back her gathering misery at her own circumstances: 'As for my own life, it is not at all a pleasant one. I sit alone in our room the whole day long as if I were in gaol, and as the room is very dark . . . I cannot see the sun all day long and I don't even know what the weather is like. With great difficulty I manage to knit a little by the daylight that struggles in.'[158] Her depression was no doubt exacerbated by not feeling well – that cold, wet journey had taken its toll – and, on 1 May, in her first letter for three weeks, she confessed that she had been 'plagued with toothache, sore throat and earache'.[159] Her composure had recovered a little, but she was still basically miserable: 'I don't get out much, it is true, and the rooms are cold, even when a fire is burning. You just have to get used to it.' And, worryingly, she asked if somebody from Salzburg could bring her some more black powders (*pulvis epilecticus niger* – a fever-reducing preparation taken by the Mozart family at the first sign of any malady), as she had 'almost come to an end of our supply'. Clearly she had been dosing herself for weeks.

Leopold replied a week later. Most of his letter was as usual full of instruction and exhortation to his son, and it was only in the postscript that he finally turned his attention to his wife. He urged her to be bled, and suggested that she try to find their black powders 'at some chemist's shop'. And indeed Maria Anna's next letter, on 14 May, was altogether more cheerful. She was a little calmer about money, because Wolfgang had better prospects, particularly once the slack summer season was over. She had extremely practical plans to halve their outgoings by renting rooms, buying furniture, and doing the cooking herself. Like the rest of Paris she was fascinated by the pregnancy of Marie Antoinette, whom of course she had known as a child in Schönbrunn ('The Queen is pregnant; this is not yet public property, but there is no doubt about it, and the French are absolutely delighted'[160]). Her constant thirst for Salzburg news prompted another of her eager questionnaires: 'How is Frau Adlgasser? Is little Victoria still with her? And how are Barbara Eberlin and Berantzky? Do they still come to our house sometimes? Does Nannerl go to Andretter's every week as usual? Is young Andretter still in Neu-Otting? I mean since all these changes have taken place in Bavaria? Do Fräulein von Schiedenhofen and Nannerl Kranach still come to shoot?' Maria Anna was intrigued by how much Paris had changed in the twelve years since their last visit ('I have a new map of the town, which is quite different from our old one'). For her daughter ('Here is something for Nannerl') she was full of news of Paris fashions, describing minutely the jewellery, hairstyles, hats and necklines, and telling her to get herself 'a pretty walking stick', as all the women in Paris carried them. By the end of May she was extremely interested in the current political situation (there was the War of Bavarian Succession between Austria and Prussia, and a possible war also between France and England), and she summarized succinctly and intelligently the various relationships between Russia, Turkey, Sweden, Denmark and Prussia. And she was equally lucid about prices, enumerating them for her husband and concluding, 'Everything is twice as dear as it used to be.'[161] But amidst all this excellent detail, she revealed that she was still not well, and furthermore desperately homesick: 'Wolfgang and I . . . often and often . . . talk about our friends in Salzburg when we sit at supper together in the evenings.' And Wolfgang's postscript confirmed their shared depression: 'I often wonder if life is worth living.' Mother and son were both truly miserable, but bravely trying to be cheerful.

In Salzburg, however, Leopold and Nannerl were in excellent spirits. Leopold was indulging in distinct Schadenfreude since Colloredo, seeking a new Kapellmeister, had sent messages all over Europe with no result. After he himself had been passed over, he was resigned to observing these manoeuvres from the sidelines, and it amused him that nobody seemed to want the job. His relationship with his new Archbishop had never recovered from that poor start, but he was on good terms with the Archbishop's sister, who seemed in a position of influence with her brother, and Leopold was fairly confident that she would be useful in getting Wolfgang a better position at Court should he ever want one. And meanwhile, as always, he and Nannerl were continually in the thick of music-making. (Between them, though, they had completely neglected to pay their maid Theresa in the nine months since Maria Anna had left. On 11 June Leopold had to ask 'what wages Theresa should get'.[162] He clearly had no idea.)

In Paris, spring turned to summer, and there were signs of hope. Although Maria Anna and Wolfgang were now borrowing money, Wolfgang had two significant performances in June. His music for his old friend Noverre's ballet *Les Petits Riens*, KAnh.1 (299b), was performed at the Opéra on the 11th, and then his 'Paris' symphony in D, K297 (300a), was played at the Concert Spirituel on the 15th. The weather was glorious, and Maria Anna claimed to be feeling better. She had been enjoying the company of Anton Raaff, the Mannheim tenor who was also now in Paris. He came to see her every day, called her 'Mamma' (he was actually six years older than she), and often sang to her ('for I am quite in love with his singing'[163]). Another friend was the horn-player Franz Joseph Heina, whom Leopold had first met in 1763. He and his wife also visited Maria Anna regularly, and on 10 June invited her for lunch and then to visit a picture gallery in the Jardin du Luxembourg. But this day out exhausted her. Although her next letter was animated, intelligent and wide-ranging (it included a carefully considered explanation of lightning conductors), she confessed that on the day after her outing with the Heinas she had been bled, and she ended her letter rather abruptly ('I must stop, for my arm and eyes are aching'). It was the last letter she ever wrote. A few days after that, according to Wolfgang, she 'complained of shivering and feverish-ness, accompanied by diarrhoea and headache'.[164] They had of course long since run out of their black powders, and failed to find any more. Maria Anna's condition deteriorated rapidly; she lost her

voice and then her hearing. But she refused to let Wolfgang call a
doctor, probably because they could not afford one. Eventually
Baron Grimm and Madame d'Epinay, appalled to hear of her
plight, sent their own doctor; and Wolfgang was now so anxious
about his mother that he stopped composing ('I could not have
written a note'[165]). By 26 June he was told that she should make her
final confession, which she did on the 30th. At 10.21 on the evening
of 3 July, with a nurse and Heina and her beloved Wolfgang beside
her, Maria Anna died.

Maria Anna Mozart's lifespan of fifty-eight years has an almost
circular shape to it. She was born into a family facing great financial and medical crises, and her childhood was one of bereavement,
humiliation and dependence upon the support of others. Her last
years too were threaded with melancholy, illness and deprivation,
and her end, virtually alone in a strange city, has many hallmarks of
genuine tragedy. And yet her life, as she herself would surely have
agreed, was in its way glorious. From the most troubled of
beginnings she had made a good marriage and found domestic
security. She had borne and raised not one but two children of
prodigious talent, and through them gained an experience of the
world which very few women of her time, of whatever social background, could ever enjoy. She had travelled extensively, lived in
many different cities and absorbed their language and their culture.
She had moved in the highest circles, meeting a huge roster of
people, including the Empress Maria Theresa, France's King Louis
XVI and England's King George III. After the family's move to the
Tanzmeisterhaus in 1773 she found herself at the respectable hub of
Salzburg's social and musical life, and she enjoyed the company of
extremely good friends. And, most important of all, one of her
children was Wolfgang Amadeus Mozart. As she attended his performances across Europe and witnessed the astounded admiration
that he universally aroused, and probably too as she just listened to
him playing at home, the joy and loving pride that she must have
felt are unimaginable. Maria Anna was a woman of immense
fortitude, loyalty, patience and love, who struggled and suffered

probably more than most of her female acquaintance. But in the final analysis, her life was quite singularly blessed.

~

IMMEDIATELY AFTER MARIA Anna's death, Wolfgang sat down and wrote two letters. The first was to his father, warning him of 'sad and distressing news',[166] but by no means telling him the whole truth. He claimed merely that his mother was 'very ill', and that, while everything was being done to save her, her ultimate fate was in the hands of God. Astonishingly in the circumstances, he then went on to describe in the greatest detail the rehearsals and performance of his symphony on 18 June, and his prospects at the opera; to report the death of Voltaire; to advise on the wages of the maid Theresa; and to explain his reluctance to accept the post of organist at Versailles. To all intents and purposes this was almost a normal letter. But then, at what was now two o'clock in the morning, he wrote to his good friend in Salzburg, the Abbé Bullinger. In an unbearably moving letter, he told him the whole truth ('Her life flickered out like a candle'[167]), and begged Bullinger to prepare Leopold and Nannerl for the shock ('Watch over my dear father and my dear sister for me'). Later that day, 4 July, Maria Anna was buried in the churchyard of Saint-Eustache, in the presence of Wolfgang and Heina.

Wolfgang's strategy worked. On 13 July Leopold was writing to Paris, ironically to congratulate his wife on her forthcoming nameday (26 July), when he received Wolfgang's letter. Both he and Nannerl were knocked sideways. She wept and vomited, and eventually took to her bed, while he too was distraught for some time. Nevertheless he went back to his letter, a typical admixture of grief, desperation and accusation, before breaking off again to greet friends arriving for lunch and one of their shooting parties. Bullinger was among them; and after the rest of the group had left, he stayed behind and confirmed the awful truth. Leopold went back yet again to his letter, and begged Wolfgang to let him know everything about his Maria Anna's death. Yet in these first moments of unendurable bereavement, he offered no consolation to his son, no sympathy for the terrible ordeal he had witnessed. Rather, he initiated a little seam of blame, holding Wolfgang at least partly responsible for the death of his mother. To greater or lesser degrees, he would shamefully return to this for the rest of his life.

In the following weeks Wolfgang complied with his father's demands, supplying in the greatest detail repeated accounts of Maria Anna's final illness. He also then attempted to divert Leopold with other news and narrative. But he could not staunch the flow of recrimination. He himself was certainly in a wretched state of grief and shock and loss ('I have been dreadfully sad and depressed,'[168] he confessed on 20 July). His friends had helped: Heina had made the funeral arrangements, and Baron Grimm and Madame d'Epinay had immediately taken Wolfgang into their house, away from the deathbed apartment. But in truth he probably did feel guilty. He certainly became more overtly, and touchingly, concerned about his sister, and wrote to congratulate her on her name-day (the same, of course, as their mother's). Without a shred of the familiar, crude sibling banter that had characterized most of his messages to her, this letter was as sweet and tender as anything he ever wrote:

Dearest Sister!
Your name-day has arrived! I know that you, like myself, do not care a lot about words and that you realize that not only today but every day I wish you with all my heart all the happiness you desire – and that too as sincerely as is to be expected from a true brother, who loves his sister.

I am sorry not to be able to send you a present of a musical composition, such as I did a few years ago. But let us hope that the happy future is not far off when a brother and sister, so united and affectionate, will be able to talk to one another and tell one another all their most intimate thoughts and feelings. Meanwhile farewell – and love me, as I do you. I embrace you with all my heart, with all my soul, and ever remain your sincere – your true brother

W. Mozart[169]

And when, ten days later, he did send her a prelude (which she memorized on the day she received it), he repeated, 'Remember that you have a brother who loves you with all his heart and will always think of your welfare and happiness.'[170]

In many ways, the twenty-one-year-old Wolfgang had behaved admirably in these terrible circumstances. He had considered carefully how best to inform his family. With the help of the devoted Heina, he had dealt with the disposal of his mother's body, attended her funeral, and packed up her possessions, dispatching them to Salzburg. (The only omission, which of course was spotted by Leopold on the arrival of these effects, was the amethyst ring given to Maria Anna by Madame d'Epinay. Wolfgang explained much later that he had removed this from his mother's body and given it to the nurse who had attended her – presumably in lieu of payment.) But all the professional frustrations that he had been harbouring for some time were exacerbated in his state of scattered bereavement. He was clearly becoming irritated by the indifference of the Parisians, writing, with some astuteness, to Leopold on 31 July, 'What annoys me most of all is that these stupid Frenchmen seem to think I am still seven years old, because that was my age when they first saw me.'[171] He began to fall out with those closest to him, most seriously his greatest supporter, Baron Grimm. And in fact he was also preoccupied with another matter, which could indeed have been distracting him during his mother's last days. He was once more corresponding with the Webers.

After the death of Maximilian III and the accession of Carl Theodor as Elector of Bavaria, the structure and routine of the Mannheim Court were disrupted. Most of the Court employees were transplanted to Munich, and the musicians had to choose between making this move or staying behind in a centre of depleted activity. Fridolin Weber and Wolfgang were evidently in vigorous correspondence about this throughout the month of June. It would clearly be to everyone's advantage to go to Munich, but, as Fridolin confessed, he had debts in Mannheim which prevented him from leaving. He therefore appealed for advice. Wolfgang, still besotted with 'my beloved Mlle Weber' as he rather thoughtlessly referred to her in a letter to his father, made some earnest but thoroughly impractical suggestions, one of them being that the Webers should all come to Paris where he would take care of them. (At the time he was virtually penniless and living on the kindness of Madame d'Epinay.) In trying to enlist Leopold's help as well, Wolfgang only made matters worse. The letters from father to son throughout those high-summer months of 1778 are among the most domineering, self-pitying and ultimately distressing they wrote to each other.

And so eventually Wolfgang left Paris on 26 September. For the first time in his life he was truly alone, without any parental presence to consider. Although he inevitably received streams of advice and instruction from his father ('Take care of yourself! Do not strike up a friendship with anyone on the journey! Trust no one! Keep your medicines in your night-bag, in case you should need them. Look after your baggage when you get in and out of the coach',[172] and so on), he had to make all arrangements and take all decisions entirely for himself. So he dawdled on his long journey home. First he lingered for over a week in Nancy, causing Leopold, who had not heard from him for days, to dread the very sight of poor Bullinger ('I watch his features with the greatest attention'[173]) lest some new catastrophe had occurred. He spent three weeks in Strasbourg where he gave two concerts but lost money. He then continued on to Mannheim to stay with the Cannabichs, and had many joyful reunions. Frau Cannabich and he became 'best and truest friends',[174] and he spent hours in her company: perhaps at last he had found someone to whom he could really bare his soul. But the Webers were no longer there. With Cannabich's help, Fridolin had sorted out his debts, and both he and Aloysia were now earning good salaries in the newly constituted establishment in Munich. So Wolfgang headed off there, with Leopold continually issuing instructions and recriminations in the background. But if Wolfgang's main intent was to be reunited with Aloysia, he was planning another reunion too. He wrote to his cousin, the 'Bäsle', and asked her to join him in Munich.

The 'Bäsle' did not disappoint Wolfgang, but Aloysia did. She was utterly changed towards him, appearing cool and condescending, and he was devastated. While he managed to maintain an air of defiant nonchalance in her presence, his letters home do reveal his distress: 'I really cannot write, my heart is too full of tears.'[175] Aloysia's rejection of him was the last straw. He was already suffering from his bereavement (and all the concomitant trauma of dealing with it on his own); from his failure in Paris, and his ignominious departure from it, having finally also offended those who had most helped him; from the build-up of rage and emotional pressure from his father; and from the humiliation of his only visible future prospect, a lowly job in a place he had convinced himself he loathed. Repeatedly he expressed his contempt for the Salzburg musicians, whom he considered to be slovenly, dissolute and, as he wrote damningly to Bullinger, 'rich in what is useless and superfluous, but very poor in what is necessary, and absolutely destitute of what is indispensable'.[176] He had certainly worked himself into a fierce state of negative prejudice. After his glittering childhood in the grandest circles in Europe, was he reduced to this? Truly Wolfgang was at an emotional nadir.

His one saviour, as ever, was his cousin. The 'Bäsle' cheered him up, to the extent that by the beginning of 1779 they wrote jointly to Leopold suggesting that she came back to Salzburg with Wolfgang. (He certainly wanted an ally as he re-entered the city as some sort of disgraced renegade.) Leopold grudgingly offered a welcome to his niece – anything to bring Wolfgang home – and issued final instructions for the last leg of the journey. Wolfgang was back in Salzburg, a changed man, by the middle of January. Through the good offices of Leopold's friends at Court (he did actually have some), there was indeed a job waiting for him. And although the post of Court organist with some orchestral duties was far below the status he had been seeking, it really was necessary that he take it, and start collecting a salary. On top of everything else, the journey with Maria Anna to Germany and France had been a financial disaster. A period at home, where of course Leopold could keep an eye on his prodigal son, was essential. His appointment was confirmed on 17 January 1779, and Wolfgang was to remain in Salzburg for nearly two years.

~

LITTLE IS KNOWN about the reunion of the broken family, of their adjustment to life in the Tanzmeisterhaus without Maria Anna, of what recrimination and resentment hovered above or below the surface of reconciliation. The neutral presence of the 'Bäsle' must have eased the situation. For all that Leopold fundamentally disapproved of her influence on Wolfgang, she was a close member of the family, and could spend time with both her cousins. After she had returned to Augsburg, Wolfgang wrote her another of his nonsense letters of zany poetry and sexual innuendo ('one has the purse and the other the gold'[177] again), and, almost a year later, in a slightly calmer letter, he referred to her stay with them, and to the activities she had shared with him and Nannerl. She was probably good for both her cousins.

Certainly the relationship between brother and sister seems to have been restored. Nannerl's diaries, still fundamentally detached chronicles of daily events, survive from much of 1779, and again were considerably enlivened by additions from her brother. She was probably delighted with his annotations (she certainly did nothing to stop him making them), for she retrieved the jokey, sibling relationship of their childhood. At first Wolfgang imitated her style, listing their guests and reporting the weather. But, as so often in his letters to her and to others, he gradually distorted these accounts. On 20 April 1779, for instance, he improvised poetically on the weather conditions: 'The sun went to sleep in a sack – at 10 o'clock it rained, with a pleasant stench; – odour; – the clouds lost themselves, the moon allowed itself to be seen, and a fart allowed itself to be heard, a promise of good weather tomorrow.'[178]

One entry, however, is eloquent of Wolfgang's pervading mood

in these long Salzburg months. On 27 May 1780 he punctuated
every thought and itemization of their day with the expression 'or
something like that': 'At half past seven I went to Mass, or something like that, then was at the Lodronpalais, or something like
that . . . played cards at Countess Wicka's, or something like that.'[179]
Here the banality of his contributions reflects the banality of a
restrained and repetitive existence in Salzburg. Although he could
take some refuge in his composing (he produced symphonies, concertos and some church music in these years), the very fact that
even these activities were restricted was a source of the utmost
frustration to him. After over a year of it, Wolfgang was almost
screaming with claustrophobia.

One positively enjoyable development was the arrival of theatre
troupes. Colloredo had opened a public theatre in Salzburg in 1775,
and it was situated directly across the square from the Tanzmeisterhaus. Travelling companies visited regularly, performing plays,
operettas, ballets and melodramas. One such company, led by
Johann Böhm, had already often appeared at the Court theatres in
Vienna. They became well acquainted with the Mozart family, who
entertained them often at the Tanzmeisterhaus. In the winter of
1780–81 another troupe arrived, led by Emanuel Schikaneder. He
and Wolfgang struck up a deep friendship, which was to become the
basis for artistic collaboration in the future. But not only was this
daily proximity of intense theatrical activity some kind of training
ground for Wolfgang; the very presence of these companies
enlivened the winters for Nannerl too, who kept lists of the plays
she had seen and the artistes she had entertained. When the companies left in the springtime, Salzburg must have seemed a much
duller place again.

In the autumn of 1780 Nannerl was very ill with what seems to
have been a severe bronchial infection. Her father nursed her faith-
fully, as he had done when she was a child, supervising every meal
and every form of medication with even more determination and
intensity. By the time she had fully recovered, Wolfgang had left
Salzburg. He had obtained six weeks' leave from the Archbishop to

fulfil a commission for the opera *Idomeneo, re di Creta*, K366, in Munich. The librettist, Giambattista Varesco, was also Salzburg-based, and the two of them had worked on the structure of the opera during the summer months. Wolfgang left on 5 November 1780, waved off by his father and his new friend Schikaneder.

This major commission from the Elector of Bavaria, for an opera to be performed by musicians and singers whom Wolfgang had got to know so well in Mannheim before they were transplanted to Munich, was an enormous piece of good news. After nearly two years of frustration and boredom, he felt his spirits soar as he escaped his loathed employer and returned to operatic work among people he loved. *Idomeneo* was to be played by the best orchestra in Europe, which no doubt accounts for the brilliance of its orchestral writing. Wolfgang corresponded vigorously as usual with his father, who acted as an intermediary between him and Varesco in Salzburg, and was in fact extremely helpful and knowledgeable in the musical advice that he offered. Nannerl too was occasionally involved, as for instance when an intelligent and practical act on her part facilitated a necessary speedy decision, as Leopold proudly reported to Wolfgang: 'As your letter arrived while I was out, your sister read it, looked up the passage in Metastasio, and sent the letter and the book after me to Varesco's.'[180]

Leopold and Nannerl were both planning to travel to Munich for the premiere of *Idomeneo*. Leopold was particularly excited about hearing the orchestra. ('You can imagine that I am looking forward with childish delight to hearing that excellent orchestra.'[181]) But his old autocratic habits died hard. At first he seemed to want to slip back into his customary dictatorial role in his letters, issuing formidable instructions on every possible non-musical topic, and even applying his emotional thumb-screws again. He complained about his own health, and Nannerl's; he described his melancholy on the eve of his wedding anniversary; and, worst of all, he referred to Maria Anna's death again, implying that he could have saved her life if he had been there. And Wolfgang was still potentially vulnerable, with his heavy workload and the knowledge that he must make a success of the opera. (He did even seem to have a sort of composer's block, most rarely for him, though eventually he came triumphantly through it.) But he was stronger about dealing with pressure from his father. 'Pray do not write any more melancholy letters to me,' he wrote, 'for I really need at the moment a cheerful spirit, a clear head and an inclination to work, and one cannot have these when one is sad at heart.'[182] And, as the time of the premiere approached, and Leopold was still giving him trouble, he was increasingly firm in dealing with him: 'Join me in Munich soon – and hear my opera – and then tell me whether it is wrong of me to be sad when I think of Salzburg!'[183]

Wolfgang was in fact extremely well sustained by his old Mannheim circle in Munich. The elderly tenor Anton Raaff, who had been so good to Maria Anna in Paris, was struggling a little with the title role. The female leads were taken by two members of the Wendling family: Ilia by Dorotea, wife of Wolfgang's flute-playing friend Johann Baptist, and Elettra by Elisabeth Augusta, wife of Johann Baptist's brother Franz Anton. And the fine orchestra was led by Christian Cannabich, whose whole family were hugely supportive to their young friend. Wolfgang reported to Leopold on 1 December 1780: 'The Cannabichs and all who frequent their house are really true friends of mine. When I walked home with Cannabich to his house after the rehearsal . . . Madame Cannabich came out to meet us and embraced me, delighted that the rehearsal had gone off so well . . . The good lady – a true friend of mine – who had been alone in the house with her sick daughter Rosa, had been absorbed in a thousand anxieties on my account.'[184]

～

BACK IN SALZBURG, Nannerl was recovering from her debilitating illness and beginning to go out again. On 30 November 1780, at Wolfgang's request, she sent him a list of all the plays presented by Schikaneder's company since he had left, and described her own attendance – her first outing since taking to her sickbed – at a completely disastrous performance of Uezel's *Rache für Rache*. (It was

four hours long, and dismal in execution; the Archbishop left before
the end, and Schikaneder was roundly booed.) But Nannerl was
looking forward inordinately to her first journey out of Salzburg
since attending the premiere of *La finta giardiniera* nearly five years
earlier, so much so that she was rather cavalier about the final illness
of the Empress Maria Theresa, no less. 'You probably know already
that the Empress is so ill that at any moment she may play us a
pretty prank,' her letter continued. 'If she dies now, your opera may
still be performed; but if she dies later, my whole pleasure may be
spoiled.'[185] In fact Maria Theresa had obligingly died the previous
day, and Nannerl's next concerns were with her mourning clothes.
A very expensive black dress was made (which Leopold assumed
Wolfgang would pay for, since he was the one member of the
family earning well at the time). She was also, as always, greatly
concerned about her hair, for the Mozarts were once more having
their joint portrait painted. On 30 December she wrote to her
brother: 'I am writing to you with an erection on my head and I am
very much afraid of burning my hair. The reason why the Mölks'
maid has dressed my hair is that tomorrow for the first time I am
sitting for the painter.'[186] She must also have been brushing up her
keyboard skills again, for she too was going to perform while in
Munich. Wolfgang had sent her some teasing cajolement back in
November: 'My sister must not be lazy, but practise hard, for people
are already looking forward to hearing her play.'[187]

Leopold and Nannerl arrived in Munich on 26 January 1781.
On the following day, Wolfgang's birthday, there was the dress
rehearsal of *Idomeneo*, and the premiere took place on the 29th.
Other friends had come from Salzburg too – the Barisanis and the
Robinigs, though not in the end Nannerl's great friend Katherl
Gilowsky, much as she had wanted to come. There must have been
real family celebration at Wolfgang's triumph again at the Court of
Bavaria. They all stayed throughout the Carnival season which
Nannerl had so much enjoyed on her previous visit, and she joined
in some of the music-making, as planned. And after the Carnival
was over the three Mozarts went to Augsburg where Wolfgang and

Nannerl played together. For Nannerl this must have been an incredibly precious time. She had recovered some of the limelight of her childhood, performing again with her brilliant brother in the most illustrious of company, and there was a moment of real family harmony after the horrific tensions of the previous years. But it was only a moment. Both Leopold and Wolfgang had been granted leave from Salzburg, and both had outstayed it by considerable periods. Archbishop Colloredo had moved his household to Vienna, partly out of deference to the death of Maria Theresa and the full accession of her son Joseph II, and partly also because his own father Prince Rudolph Joseph was extremely ill. He had taken much of his Court with him, and was expecting some obedience now from the troublesome, truant Mozarts. When the family arrived back in Munich from Augsburg, there were stern orders awaiting them. Wolfgang went swiftly to join his employer in Vienna. Leopold, with Nannerl, equally swiftly returned to Salzburg to resume his own duties.

Upon his arrival in Vienna Wolfgang was immediately put to work as a lowly member of the Archbishop's household. *Idomeneo* still rang in his ears, as a little postscript in a letter home, on 4 April 1781, surely demonstrates. 'My compliments to all – all – all,'[188] he wrote, in a direct quotation of the repeated 'tutto, tutto, tutto' in the chorus 'Placido è il mar'. After his triumphant success he deeply resented his Cinderella status, so eloquently denoted in the dining arrangements where, as he reported with disgust, he had to sit 'above the cooks but below the valets'.[189] This was a humiliating anticlimax to Munich, and over the next three months his anger and frustration simmered, seethed and eventually exploded. He had a series of insolent meetings with the Archbishop or his representatives, in which first voices and then fists too were raised. On 8 June 1781, Wolfgang was literally thrown down the stairs of Colloredo's Viennese residence and dismissed for ever from his service, 'with a kick on the arse, by order of our worthy Prince Archbishop',[190] as Wolfgang reported to his father the following day.

Tensions in Salzburg must have been unbearable as these events unfolded in Vienna. It was Paris all over again, except that now the future of the whole Mozart family was threatened. Leopold could not bring himself to sympathize, let alone side with his son; far too much was at stake. He received Wolfgang's lengthy descriptions of conflict ('I hate the Archbishop to madness'[191]) and his verbatim reports of exchanged insults, with total horror, and responded with what must have been increasingly hysterical explosions of his own. None of Leopold's letters from these months survives. But their content can be easily surmised from the intensity of Wolfgang's detailed replies. ('I do not know how to begin this letter, dearest father, for I have not yet recovered from my astonishment and shall never be able to do so, if you continue to think and write as you do.'[192]) When Wolfgang, not at all unreasonably, suggested to his father that they all cut their losses and come to Vienna, which offered so much opportunity for all three of them to do well, Nannerl was absolutely considered part of the package too. But Leopold simply could not countenance such an upheaval. For all the shame that Wolfgang's dismissal had brought upon the family, he and Nannerl would not leave the security of their life at the Tanzmeisterhaus. Nannerl herself might have been tempted by the notion – especially when her brother sent her ribbons for her dresses, and offered to find anything else she might want – but she clearly had no say in the matter.

This was the real turning point in the lives of all the Mozarts. Wolfgang's amputation from the Salzburg Court effectively meant breaking away also from his tyrannical father. They continued to correspond regularly, but the umbilical cord was at last severed, and Wolfgang really did achieve independence in Vienna, building a new life and a new family all of his own. And to an extent Nannerl began to fade from the picture. Her life as a first-class performer had effectively ended with those evenings in Augsburg. She and her brother corresponded sparingly, though always with affection, and at first he was eager for her to send him some form of her diaries which he knew so well: 'You are the living chronicle of Salzburg, for you write down every single thing that occurs.'[193] He continued to admire and encourage her playing. When, in 1783 for instance, he heard that she was working on some sonatas by Clementi (whom he dismissed as a charlatan), he wrote, 'I implore my sister not to practise these passages too much, so that she may not spoil her quiet, even touch, and that her hand may not lose its natural lightness, flexibility and smooth rapidity.'[194] He really did appreciate her talent.

But Wolfgang was most interested in Nannerl's suitors. Especially during and after his own courtship and marriage, he wanted her to find happiness, as he had. Towards the end of 1780, one important admirer of Nannerl's appeared first in her diary, and then from time to time in correspondence. Franz Armand d'Ippold (or Diepold) was a former military captain who was now director of the Collegium Virgilianum in Salzburg. He was twenty-two years older than Nannerl, and therefore much closer in years to Leopold than to his daughter. He evidently became very involved with Nannerl during the dreadful summer of 1781, and Wolfgang, not wishing to lose his sister as well as his father, begged her to confide in him: 'I should very much like to know how things are progressing between you and a certain good friend, you know whom I mean. Do write to me about this! Or have I lost your confidence in this matter?'[195] And when in September of that year he heard that Nannerl had been ill yet again, he was extremely forthright as to a remedy for her: 'The best cure for you would be a husband.'[196] He went on to name d'Ippold, pointing out that they had no prospects in Salzburg, and therefore encouraging them to come to Vienna, where she too could 'earn a great deal of money . . . by playing at private concerts and by giving lessons'. (He still had complete confidence in her as a musician.) He continued, 'before I knew that your affair with d'Ippold was serious, I had something like this in mind for you. Our dear father was the only difficulty.' But he now suggested that they all came to Vienna, and 'we could all live happily together again'. He really did seem to want this, for all their sakes.

But it did not happen. For whatever reason, the Captain withdrew from Nannerl's sights (though not completely from the family, for he was involved in the practicalities of Leopold's estate after his death). For the moment, Nannerl seemed ever more tethered to her father's side in Salzburg. Like many as yet unmarried women of her time, she conformed to contemporary ideals of womanhood, sacrificing herself to the needs of others, living a life of piety and modest restraint. Just as Wolfgang had felt trapped in Salzburg after his glittering years of childhood, so too must Nannerl have developed a complex view of her own predicament. Her considerable talent, which had once likewise been paraded across the Courts of Europe, was now all but ignored. Her teaching, her domestic music-making and her occasional forays into slightly wider circles of Salzburg music were all still controlled and ordained by her father, executed at his behest, and ultimately for his delectation and gratification. Other women of musical ability in Salzburg had been encouraged to travel, to develop their gifts in Italy or Vienna; but not she. This highly-strung young woman 'cried over the merest trifle', shouted at servants, succumbed to illness when crises occurred, chronicled daily events in a style of deadpan reportage, and kept almost obsessional lists. She had inherited much from Leopold. If from her mother she had also inherited a certain stoic competence when facing hardship, she seems to have lacked Maria Anna's warmth and compassion. But with her mother dead, and her brother far away, Nannerl probably imagined that she was destined to be at Leopold's irascible side for the rest of his life. The prospect cannot have been altogether appealing.

And, perhaps most distressing of all, Nannerl realized that she was losing her own best friend, the companion of her childhood, her co-Regent of their 'Kingdom of Back', her partner in piano duets which he created for their own delight, her utterly captivating, hilariously mischievous, supremely talented younger brother. For in truth, in Vienna Wolfgang had found his other family.

Mozart's Other Family

MOZART CAN hardly have believed his luck when, late in 1777, he first met the Weber family in Mannheim. In many respects the four daughters must have resembled the Wider sisters (his 'pearls') who had so delighted him in Venice. They were young: Josefa was eighteen, Aloysia seventeen, Constanze fifteen and Sophie fourteen; they were lively, good-looking and warm-hearted. They were also extremely talented.

The girls came from a colourful family. Their parents had been in Mannheim since 1765: Fridolin Weber was employed there as a bass singer at Court, a prompter at the Opera, and as a copyist. His wife Cäcilia (née Stamm), some six years older than Fridolin, had been born in Mannheim, which probably therefore seemed a logical place for them to live, after they had had to leave Fridolin's home town of Zell rather abruptly. (Fridolin had been charged with embezzlement, as had his own father before him, curiously. Both men were apparently innocent, but such accusations must have made a new start in a different environment rather desirable.) Fridolin's brother, Franz Anton Weber, meanwhile, having been dismissed from his post as financial councillor and district judge to the Elector of Cologne, set himself up as an impresario of itinerant opera companies. His wife had had a considerable fortune, which he had squandered; and when she died he married a sixteen-year-old singer, Genoveva Brunner. The first child of this union was none other than Carl Maria von Weber, who was to become one of the most progressive composers of the early nineteenth century, and a great virtuoso pianist. And Genoveva herself, younger in years than her nieces by marriage, would in due course become somewhat elliptically entwined with the Mozart family.

Fridolin and Cäcilia Weber in fact had six children, of whom their two sons, born respectively in 1759 and 1769, both died in infancy. But their daughters were all extremely healthy, and would enjoy long and fulfilling lives. They probably received their education at the Congregation of Notre Dame, a Catholic school in Mannheim, where they learned to read and write and to speak French, and received religious instruction. They must also have been taught music and singing by their father, and at least three of them became high-coloratura sopranos with quite exceptional techniques. Like Leopold Mozart, Fridolin Weber was clearly a remarkable teacher, and Wolfgang did not fail to make the comparison. ('Her father resembles my father, and the whole family resemble the Mozarts,'[1] he wrote to Leopold on 4 February 1778). Another similarity was that one of the Weber children was destined at a relatively young age to become the main breadwinner for the family. The most talented, both as a keyboard player and especially as a singer, was Aloysia. From the age of nineteen, any career move of hers dictated the uprooting of the entire family. She and Wolfgang had a lot in common.

Wolfgang fell for Aloysia instantly. Early in 1778, as he prepared for his visit to Princess Caroline of Orange in Kirchheim-Bolanden, in which he would be accompanied by Aloysia and her father, he was captivated by Aloysia's singing, her musicianship and her prospects of an exciting future:

> She sings most excellently my aria written for De Amicis with those horribly difficult passages, and she is to sing it at Kirchheim-Bolanden. She is quite well able to teach herself. She accompanies herself very well and she also plays galanterie quite respectably.

What is most fortunate for her at Mannheim is that she has won the praise of all honest people of good will. Even the Elector and the Electress are only too glad to receive her.[2]

The 'aria written for De Amicis' was the extremely tricky 'Ah, se il crudel' from his opera *Lucio Silla* of 1772; and just as Wolfgang had been excited then about the range and virtuosity of Anna De Amicis's singing, and indeed drawn to the warmth of her friendship through his admiration of her expertise, so did Aloysia entrance him. That her talents extended to superb pianism was a true bonus; and, after extolling Aloysia so fully in his letter, Wolfgang then asked his father to send him '*as soon as possible* . . . the two sonatas for four hands'. Clearly he had found someone other than his sister with whom he could share those intimate musical experiences.

By the time Wolfgang, Aloysia and Fridolin returned from their extremely convivial week in Kirchheim-Bolanden, Wolfgang's plans had made their dramatic volte-face. Even as he recklessly tried to persuade his father of his scheme to abandon France and travel instead to Italy with the Webers, he was continuing to shower Aloysia with music. On 4 February he wrote, 'She sings superbly the aria which I wrote for De Amicis, both the bravura aria and "Parto, m'affretto" and "Dalla sponda tenebrosa".'[3] Three days later, there was more: 'I have given her . . . the scene I wrote for Madame Duschek . . . and four arias from *Il re pastore*. I have also promised her to have some arias sent from home.'[4] And then, at last, he wrote something especially for her. In his letter to Leopold of 28 February (which included his remarkable credo, 'I like an aria to fit a singer like a well-made suit of clothes'), he described his new composition.

I have also set to music the aria *Non sò d'onde viene* etc [K294], . . . for Mlle Weber . . . When it was finished, I said to Mlle Weber, 'Learn the aria yourself. Sing it as you think it ought to go; then let me hear it and afterwards I will tell you candidly what pleases and what displeases me.' After a couple of days I went to the Webers and she sang it for me, accompanying herself. I was obliged to confess that she had sung it exactly as I wished and as I should have taught it to her myself. This is now the best aria she has; and it will ensure her success wherever she goes.[5]

The text for this aria (from Metastasio's *L'Olimpiade*) and the manner in which Wolfgang set it to music are the most eloquent expression of his feelings for Aloysia. Wolfgang was already familiar with Johann Christian Bach's setting, which he admired greatly, but this did not stop him from doing his own: 'Just because I know Bach's setting so well and like it so much, and because it is always ringing in my ears, I wished to see whether in spite of all this I could not write an aria totally unlike his. And indeed mine does not resemble his in the very least.'[6] The choice of text cannot be insignificant ('Non sò d'onde viene / Quel tenero affetto' – I have never before felt such tender affection). And there is something incredibly intimate about Wolfgang's tender and sensuous setting of these beguiling words. The layout of the text suggests a two-part aria, with a slow section (in which Wolfgang would certainly show off Aloysia's cantabile singing, about which he had written so enthusiastically to his father) followed by a fast one. At that point it is almost as if a private interchange has become more public, as the singer and the accompaniment jump into more decorous display. But Wolfgang brought back the opening couplet and its slow music, in ever more tender and yet intense representations. And it was here, not in the central fast section, that Aloysia could and did show off her spectacular range, her virtuosity and her control. The aria ends with a quiet orchestral postlude of tranquil joy. 'Non sò d'onde viene' can indeed be seen as a veritable turning point in Wolfgang's composition for the voice. It was not just that he was writing for a classy singer of whom he was fond, for he had done that before. This time he was including his own personality and that too of the aria's interpreter. And from this point on, all his vocal writing, especially for singers whom he knew, liked and even loved, was of extreme distinction.

The tidal wave of derision, recrimination and command from

Leopold in Salzburg had its desired effect. Wolfgang capitulated, abandoned his plan to take Aloysia to Italy, and agreed after all to proceed to Paris. Two days before he and his mother left, the Cannabichs put on a concert in their house of some of Wolfgang's compositions. The multitalented Aloysia was the star of the show. Not only did she sing again her special aria, now in its newly orchestrated version, but she played one of the solo piano parts in a performance of Wolfgang's concerto for three pianos, K242. The other two pianists were also teenage girls who had been Wolfgang's pupils in Mannheim: Rosa Cannabich, the fourteen-year-old daughter of the house, and Therese Pierron, aged fifteen. (Therese was the stepdaughter of Herr Serrarius, the Court attorney in whose house Wolfgang and his mother had been staying rent-free in exchange for Therese's lessons. Wolfgang referred to her as 'our house nymph.'[7])

Wolfgang was absolutely delighted with this concert, which had been meticulously prepared by the Cannabichs and the by now wholly supportive musicians from the Court orchestra. But he was desolate at having to leave Aloysia and her family. Fridolin, who had done all the copying of music for the concert at no charge, presented Wolfgang with a large supply of music paper and a volume of Molière's comedies – a touchingly thoughtful present for someone about to go to Paris. He also took Maria Anna aside and told her that her son had been their 'benefactor', and that they could never repay his generosity. Aloysia herself, 'out of the goodness of her heart', knitted two pairs of mittens 'as a remembrance and small token of her gratitude'. And on the night before they left, Wolfgang spent two hours at the Webers' house. 'They thanked me repeatedly, saying that they only wished they were in a position to show their gratitude; and when I left, they all wept. Forgive me, but my eyes fill with tears when I recall the scene.'[8] The bond between Wolfgang and the Webers was thoroughly sealed.

～

THROUGHOUT WOLFGANG'S CALAMITOUS six-month stay in Paris in
1778, Aloysia was constantly on his mind. Even the relentless chain
of failure, tragedy and bereavement could not divert him completely from his longing for her. In maintaining regular correspondence (little of which has actually survived) with her father
Fridolin, he was in fact keeping in contact with Aloysia. He even
claimed to have written on 3 July, the very day of his mother's
death. Perhaps this was a third letter written immediately after the
awful event, along with those to Leopold and to Bullinger, and in
it he was confiding his terrible news to the people he loved most.
Owing to the customary eccentricities of postal delivery, the
Webers did not in fact hear of Maria Anna's death directly from
Wolfgang, but indirectly through the Mannheim social network,
some weeks later. By then the rumour was that Maria Anna had died
'of some contagious disease', and that perhaps Wolfgang too had
perished. As Wolfgang warmly reported to his father, the Webers
'had all been praying for my soul, and the poor girl [Aloysia] had
gone every day to the Capuchin Church to do so. Perhaps you will
laugh? But I don't. I am touched and I cannot help it.'[9]

Wolfgang wrote to Aloysia herself as well as to her father. He
sent yet more music to her, and even instructed her in how she
should go about learning it. His advice affords a rare but glorious
glimpse into his own commitment to text and its emotional content
– in fact to his total theatricality and dramatic integrity. He asked
her to work on his 'Ah, lo previdi', K272, which he had written the
previous year for Josephine Duschek: 'I advise you to watch the
expression marks – to think carefully of the meaning and force of
the words – to put yourself in all seriousness into Andromeda's
situation and position – and to imagine that you really are that very
person.'[10] He begged her to write to him too ('You have no idea how
much pleasure your letters afford me . . . Please do not keep me
waiting and do not make me suffer too long') and ended his letter
with unbridled passion: 'I kiss your hands, I embrace you with all
my heart, and am, and ever shall be, your true and sincere friend,
WA MOZART.'

Inevitably, the astute Leopold was immediately alert to his son's infatuation. His exasperation was eventually calmed when he managed to secure Wolfgang the post of Konzertmeister and Court Organist in Salzburg. With that confirmation (as he believed) of Wolfgang's return, he began to cool his fiery antipathy to Aloysia. 'As for Mlle Weber,' he purred on 3 September, 'you should not think that I would be opposed to this acquaintance . . . You can continue your exchange of letters as hitherto,'[11] and he even astonishingly added that he would not try to read these letters. But such magnanimity was short-lived. A week later, on 11 September, Wolfgang wrote his father a long, troubled and indecisive letter, complaining about Baron von Grimm with whom he had now quarrelled, pathetically needing instructions for his journey home ('I don't yet know how you want me to travel'), and then asking for his father's permission to take a detour: 'I have another request which I trust you will not refuse. If it should happen, though I hope and believe it is not so, that the Webers have not gone to Munich, but are still at Mannheim, I should like to have the pleasure of going there to visit them. I know that this would take me a little out of my way, but it would not be much.'[12] Leopold's reply was predictable: 'Your idea of going to Mannheim is absolutely impracticable.'[13] But when he subsequently heard of the Webers' change of fortune – they had after all transferred to Munich with a considerable salary increase: Aloysia was receiving 1,000 gulden, and Fridolin 600 – he was once more mollified, claiming again to be 'not at all opposed' to Wolfgang's love for Aloysia. But he remained deeply suspicious of the entire Weber family. 'My dear Wolfgang, I am inclined to think that Herr Weber is a man like most of his type, who make capital out of their poverty and, when they become prosperous, lose their heads completely. He flattered you when he needed you – perhaps he would not even admit now that you had shown her or taught her anything. Those who have been poor generally become very haughty when their circumstances improve.'[14] (Leopold could more accurately have been speaking of himself.) Such deep-rooted

antagonism towards the Webers was to reappear, dangerously intensified, in future years.

Wolfgang did make his (in fact extremely lengthy) detour to
Mannheim, only to discover that it had all been fruitless, for the
Webers were no longer there. He did at least spend some time being
comforted and cherished by the ever-warm Cannabichs before
he headed back towards Munich. And there at last, in the final week
of his annus horribilis, he caught up with Aloysia. He arrived in
Munich on Christmas Day 1778, and went to stay with the Webers.
But, for whatever reason, Aloysia had completely changed her mind
about him. The rest of the family witnessed the uncomfortable
reunion; and, years later, one of them, Aloysia's younger sister
Constanze, told the story to her second husband, Georg Nissen.
In his biography of Mozart, Nissen described the scene:

> [The Webers] had to move to Munich due to the change of admin-
> istration, and there Mozart appeared on his return trip from Paris
> wearing a red skirt with black buttons, a French custom to mourn
> the death of his mother. But he discovered that *Aloysia* had
> changed her feelings for him. She who had once cried about him
> pretended not to recognize him when he walked in. Mozart sat
> down at the keyboard and sang loudly: 'I'm glad to leave the girl
> who doesn't want me.'[15]

But, for all that Wolfgang had put on an extremely brave face while
he remained in Munich, he could not even attempt to disguise his
utter misery in his letters home.

> I arrived here safely on the 25th, but until now it has been impos-
> sible for me to write to you. I am saving up everything until our
> happy and joyous meeting, for today I can only weep . . . I have
> naturally a bad handwriting, as you know, for I never learnt to
> write; but all my life I have never written anything worse than this
> letter; for I really cannot write – my heart is too full of tears.[16]

In fact it was his cousin, the 'Bäsle', who comforted him. She
came to Munich from Augsburg, as he had asked her, and drew him
back into whatever playful world they still managed to create

together. When at last Wolfgang returned to Salzburg in early 1779, he needed her help, as well as that of Nannerl and his old Salzburg friends, to try to erase Aloysia from his mind. As he settled reluctantly into his unchallenging job at Court, he probably imagined he would never see her or her family again.

~

FOR THE WEBERS, 1779 was to be a momentous year. In the late summer, Aloysia, not yet twenty years old, was engaged by the Burgtheater in Vienna, and the whole family moved with her from Munich. The Burgtheater had been the official home of opera and drama in German since 1776, and Aloysia made her auspicious debut there in September 1779, as Hännchen in the singspiel *Das Rosenfest von Salency* (with music by a conglomerate of composers, including Philidor). It was the start of an extremely distinguished career in Vienna's theatres. But, within weeks, this exciting new chapter in the family's lives was tragically interrupted. On 23 October Fridolin Weber died, aged only forty-six. The four daughters were put under the guardianship of Johann von Thorwart, an Austrian Court official who controlled the finances at the Burgtheater. Aloysia continued to be the main provider for her widowed mother and sisters.

It was in her first season at the Burgtheater that Aloysia met the twenty-eight-year-old German actor Joseph Lange. Extremely good-looking and with a famously mellifluous speaking voice, he had been working in Vienna since his debut (like Aloysia, at the age of nineteen) in 1770. He would develop into one of the finest actors of his generation, playing Hamlet and Romeo among many other roles and becoming an enormous favourite with the public. He was also a highly gifted painter, and was often commissioned to do portraits, and representations of theatrical scenes. In 1775 he had married an eighteen-year-old singer, Anna Maria Elisabeth Schindler, but she died, aged only twenty-two, in March 1779. Six months later, Aloysia Weber joined the company at the Burgtheater, and within a year she and Joseph Lange were married, on 31 October 1780. (She was pregnant at the time: her first child, Maria Anna Sabina, was born just seven months later, on 31 May 1781.) The pre-marriage contract between them, probably drawn up by her guardian Thorwart, guaranteed an annual contribution of 700 gulden from Joseph to his mother-in-law. Aloysia was to bear him six children.

Marriage and childbirth did not in any way curtail Aloysia's career. She and her husband remained central to the competitive intensity of Vienna's theatrical scene. From 1781 she was drawn into fierce rivalry with Vienna's favourite soprano, Caterina Cavalieri, five years her senior. Cavalieri was the protégée, and the mistress, of the Court composer and future Kapellmeister, Antonio Salieri. And it is very likely that Aloysia's sisters, too, were somehow involved in musical and theatrical activities. Josefa, the eldest, was taking singing lessons from the most sought-after teacher in the city. Vincenzo Righini (born in the same week as Mozart) was brought from Italy by Joseph II in 1780, to be the singing master to Princess Elisabeth of Württemberg (fiancée of the Emperor's nephew Francis) and also director of the Italian opera company. If Josefa was studying with him, so perhaps were Constanze and even Sophie. Certainly the seventeen-year-old Sophie was employed as an actress in the 1780–81 season at the Burgtheater. So despite the shock of Fridolin's death, within a year the Weber family had pulled itself together and found its way to the heart of Viennese musical and theatrical life.

It was into this heady milieu that the troubled Wolfgang tumbled in the summer of 1781. As his employment with Archbishop Colloredo gradually collapsed, he found increasing solace in the company of the Webers. By 9 May he had moved in with them, as he reported rather carefully to his father: 'Old Mme Weber has been good enough to take me into her house, where I have a pretty room.'[17] He was still unsettled by the close proximity of Aloysia (now in the final stages of her pregnancy), and not exactly generous about her choice of husband; but he was nonetheless greatly

comforted to be among old friends at such a difficult time. He wrote
to Leopold on 16 May:

> What you say about the Webers I do assure you is not true. I was
> a fool, I admit, about Aloysia Lange, but what does not a man do
> when he is in love? Indeed I loved her truly, and even now I feel
> that she is not a matter of indifference to me. It is therefore a good
> thing for me that her husband is a jealous fool and lets her go
> nowhere, so that I seldom have the opportunity of seeing her.
> Believe me when I say that old Mme Weber is a very obliging
> woman and that I cannot do enough in return for her kindness.[18]

Leopold's reaction to Wolfgang's new domestic arrangements
can only be imagined, as all his letters from this period are lost. But
he must have been in the firm grasp of apoplexy. His son was not
merely in the process of throwing away his whole livelihood, and
thereby bringing disgrace upon Leopold himself, he was also living in a household consisting of a widow and her three young,
unmarried daughters – a family furthermore whose earlier association with Wolfgang had led only to devastating loss followed by
months of agonizing uncertainty. Although the naive Wolfgang
cannot really have hoped for a smooth ride, he was deeply distressed by the force of Leopold's thunderous opinions: 'I do not
know how to begin this letter, my dearest father, for I have not yet
recovered from my astonishment and shall never be able to do so, if
you continue to think and write as you do. I must confess that there
is not a single touch in your letter by which I recognize my father!'[19]

But scandalous whispers were travelling from Vienna to
Salzburg and of course reaching Leopold's ears. Wolfgang, it was
rumoured, far from pining for Aloysia, was now deeply involved
with another of the Weber girls. Was he even planning to marry
her? Wolfgang was furious, and attempted to stamp firmly on these
'entirely groundless reports', on 25 July: 'Because I am living with
them, therefore I am going to marry the daughter. There has been
no talk of our being in love. They have skipped that stage. No, I just
take rooms in the house and *marry*. If ever there was a time when I

thought less of getting married, it is most certainly now.'[20] He did admit that he was now thinking of moving to different lodgings, but he had mentioned the possibility in an earlier letter and done nothing about it. And, to be sure, there was some fire beneath this smoke. Although Wolfgang never actually specified which of the girls was now enchanting him, it is clear that something was going on: 'I will not say that, living in the same house with the Mademoiselle to whom people have already married me, I am ill bred and do not speak to her; but I am not in love with her. I fool about and have fun with her when time permits . . . and that is all.' He added, with a flurry of true defiance, 'If I had to marry all those with whom I have jested, I should have 200 wives at least.' And in fact he continued to lodge with the Webers ('such friendly and obliging people') until early August. They looked after him extremely well, waited meals for him, and allowed him to come to the table 'without dressing'. He felt completely at home.

But in due course, Wolfgang did yield to pressure and move out. First he took a highly unsuitable room in a dismal, rat-infested house, found for him by the Auernhammer family, whose talented daughter Josefa was taking lessons from him. This grim interlude did at least supply Wolfgang with a not unhelpful diversion for Leopold's obsessive antipathy towards the Webers. Josefa Auernhammer fell in love with him. Wolfgang was merciless in his account of it all in his letters home, beginning with a cruel description of his pupil:

> If a painter wanted to portray the devil to the life, he would have to choose her face. She is as fat as a farm-wench, perspires so that you feel inclined to vomit, and goes about so scantily clad that really you can read as plain as print: '*Pray, do look here*'. True, there is enough to see, in fact quite enough to strike one blind; but – one is thoroughly punished for the rest of the day if one is unlucky enough to let one's eyes wander in that direction – tartar is the only remedy![21]

And he continued: 'But, what is worse still, she is *sérieusement* in love with me! I thought at first it was a joke, but now I know it to be a fact . . . Throughout the town people are saying that we are to be married, and they are very much surprised at me, I mean, that I have chosen such a face.'

In fact Josefa and Wolfgang became and remained good friends, and this heartless account of her infatuation may well have been a gross elaboration of the truth, and a smokescreen to conceal Wolfgang's continuing relationship with the Webers. For by the beginning of September he had left his filthy room and found better accommodation in the Graben. It was literally round the corner from the Webers' house.

Throughout this difficult summer of exchanges with his father, Wolfgang was careful to maintain contact with Nannerl. Knowing that his letters home would also be read by her, he would include her in his plans and offer the most enticing possibilities. 'My sister too . . . would get on much better in Vienna than in Salzburg,' he wrote on 18 May. 'There are many distinguished families here who hesitate to engage a male teacher, but would give handsome terms to a woman.'[22] (This was probably an astute observation.) And when he wrote directly to her, his letters were sweetly and quite cleverly composed to appeal to everything she loved. On 4 July, with the greatest affection, he offered to get hold of as many different ribbons for her as she wanted. Knowing her enthusiasm for the theatre, he described his own pleasure at attending plays. He continued to enquire obliquely about her admirer (Franz d'Ippold), and he kept her informed of his compositions for the clavier, promising 'of course' to send her anything new. If this was a calculating letter, designed largely to keep his sister on side, it was certainly a good one.[23]

But even as Wolfgang dug his heels in and fought off Leopold's onslaught of diatribe about his new arrangements, his spirits rose dramatically in that summer of 1781. By no means flung into the wilderness as a result of his severance from the Salzburg Court, he was in fact attracting rather a lot of attention. He was often to be found in princely halls and patrician salons; Viennese society was intrigued by the brilliant renegade from Salzburg. Through the Webers' activities at the Burgtheater, he made contact with Johann Gottlieb Stephanie, a playwright and librettist who at the time was in charge of German opera there. Wolfgang had tried to interest him in his unfinished singspiel, *Zaïde*, and, although Stephanie rejected it, he did keep Wolfgang in mind for other projects. In late July it was announced that the Grand Duke Paul of Russia, son of Catherine the Great, would visit Vienna that September (sent by his mother, needing allies against the Turks, to further her links with the Habsburgs). There was a flurry of artistic activity in preparation for this great visit, and Stephanie thought of Mozart. Wolfgang wrote to Leopold on 1 August:

> Well, the day before yesterday Stephanie junior gave me a libretto to compose . . . The subject is Turkish, and the title is *Belmonte und Konstanze*, or *Die Verführung aus dem Serail*. I intend to write the overture, the chorus in Act I and the final chorus in the style of Turkish music . . . The time is short, it is true, for it is to be performed in the middle of September; but the circumstances connected with the date of the performance and, in general, all my other prospects stimulate me to such a degree that I rush to my desk with the greatest eagerness and remain seated there with the greatest delight.[24]

In the following weeks, Wolfgang was completely absorbed in this exciting task. It was exactly the break that he had hoped for, and for many reasons one of the most fulfilling and successful commissions he ever had. First, there was its subject-matter. Stephanie's libretto (based on a play by Bretzner) was the story of a rescue, whose climax was marked by a monumental gesture of forgiveness. (A young Spanish nobleman comes to the Turkish seraglio of the Pasha Selim to rescue his beloved, together with her English maid and his own servant. As they are all recaptured, the Pasha Selim magnanimously pardons and frees them.) This was not only relevant with regard to the Grand Duke Paul, for the Turks were basically seen as the enemy. It was also entirely appropriate for his host, Joseph II, who wanted something in German, that espoused his Enlightenment values of courage, reconciliation and forgiveness. The opera certainly became an enormous success with the public, and was revived in many cities, countries and languages for the rest of Wolfgang's lifetime and beyond. And it also marked a quite extraordinary confluence of two tributaries of his life, the personal and the creative.

It is always dangerous to try to draw parallels between a composer's output and his own story. Some artists do reflect their circumstances in their creations, but in general Wolfgang was not one of them. There are countless examples in his music (the 'Jupiter' symphony, for instance) of the greatest exuberance actually being the product of an exceptionally desolate time for him. But here the parallels between art and life are too striking to be irrelevant or coincidental. Wolfgang received his commission for *Die Entführung aus dem Serail* (as the title became) just as his heart was opening to the Weber girl who would in due course become his wife. Her name, and that of the opera's principal character, was Constanze. He wrote his opera and oversaw its preparation and rehearsal in the months in which he tried to persuade his family of the suitability of his choice of bride. *Die Entführung* had its premiere on 16 July 1782; and just over three weeks later, on 4 August, Wolfgang and Constanze were married. Both literally and figuratively, her hand is in this ground-breaking score; and his heart, his strength of feeling for her, is in every bar of it.

~

AS HE WAS writing *Die Entführung aus dem Serail*, K384, Wolfgang sent his father progress reports. By 22 August, just three weeks after Stephanie had brought him the libretto, he had finished the first act, and soon he was ready to send Leopold some of it. What he dispatched was a copy of the first aria sung by the character Constanze, 'Ach, ich liebte, war so glücklich' (I was in love, and so happy), and it had been written out by Constanze Weber. Leopold cannot yet have known whose handwriting it was. Can it even have crossed his mind that Constanze, the daughter of a professional copyist, was involved in such tasks? Was Wolfgang trying another little ploy, to show how musically literate, and practically supportive, this particular Weber girl was? In his next letter, Wolfgang went into great detail to explain his compositional procedure, which he knew would fascinate his father. His analysis of the young nobleman Belmonte's first aria, 'O wie ängstlich, o wie feurig/ Klopft mein liebefolles Herz' (How eagerly, how ardently my lovesick heart is beating), perhaps tactfully avoids describing its heart-stopping opening, where Belmonte breathes the name 'Constanze!' and then 'dich wiederzusehen, dich!' (to see you again!) over the gentlest of string chords. But his explanation of his musical decisions is thoroughly eloquent of his own state of mind as he wrote this music, with his future wife beside him.

> Let me now turn to Belmonte's aria in A major, 'O wie ängstlich, o wie feurig'. Would you like to know how I have expressed it – and even indicated his throbbing heart? By the two violins playing octaves . . . You see the trembling – the faltering – you see how his throbbing breast begins to swell; this I have expressed by a crescendo. You hear the whispering and the sighing – which I have indicated by the first violins with mutes and a flute playing in unison . . . This is the favourite aria of all those who have heard it, and it is mine also.[25]

The visit of the Grand Duke Paul of Russia was delayed: he did not actually arrive in Vienna until November 1781, by which time all plans for entertaining him had been through many different phases. *Die Entführung* was not produced until the following summer, and Wolfgang's musical energies were diverted into many other projects, including teaching and performing. In late December he took part in a famous piano contest with Clementi, in the presence of the Grand Duchess Maria Feodorovna. (He won.) He also entered into an agreement with the publishing firm of Artaria, and his first Viennese publication at the end of 1781 was a set of six violin and piano sonatas. He dedicated these to Josefa

Auernhammer, who was also his partner in the first performance of his sonata for two pianos, K448 (375a): she had indeed become a good friend. But throughout these latter months of 1781, Wolfgang's relationship with Constanze developed intensely, and by December he knew he had to take the first, perilous step of informing Leopold. On the 15th, he wrote his father a long and extremely careful letter, almost symphonic in its carefully argued construction, with its contrasts of pace and tone, its serious message enlivened by flecks of humour and ribaldry. At one of the most crucial points of Wolfgang's personal life, his stream of consciousness flowed from reservoirs of passion and tenderness. Like so much of his musical composition, this letter emerged with an effortless but immaculate sense of formal structure.[26]

It began normally enough, listing various pieces of music he was sending to Salzburg, and then complaining about Salieri, to whom he had recently lost out (Salieri had been preferred over him as teacher to the Princess of Württenberg). These two items of business – a slow introduction, really, to the allegro argument that was to follow – led to an admission: 'I am very anxious to secure here a small but *certain* income . . . – and then – to marry!' Imagining the paternal consternation at this point, Wolfgang's tone quickly became conversational: 'You are horrified at the idea? But I entreat you, dearest, most beloved father, to listen to me. I have been obliged to reveal my intentions to you. You must therefore allow me to disclose to you my reasons, which are, moreover, very well founded.' And then came his 'reasons', three of them, carefully ordered and explained. The first, quite simply, was physical. 'The voice of nature speaks as loud in me as in others, louder perhaps than in many a big strong lout of a fellow.' But he could not bring himself to 'fool about with whores', despite the fact that 'to err is natural enough in a man'. Second, he argued, his disposition was 'more inclined to a peaceful and domesticated existence than to revelry'. And this was almost certainly true: however much he loved a party and good company, he had had twenty-five years of ceaseless travel, upheaval and hyperactivity, and now needed a still point in his turning world. His third reason was that he really needed someone to look after him, his 'belongings, linen, clothes and so forth': this had always been done for him (by his mother or sister, he meant), and without that supervision he was spending too much money (an argument bound to hit home with Leopold). He concluded therefore that he would 'manage better with a wife', with a 'well-ordered existence'; and for good measure he added his touching observation, 'A bachelor . . . is only half alive.'

As Wolfgang now approached the punchline, his tone dropped from oration back to conversation. 'But who is the object of my love?' he asked. 'Do not be horrified again, I entreat you. Surely not one of the Webers? Yes, one of the Webers – but not Josefa, nor Sophie, but Constanze, the middle one.' And then, almost as if hearing the shrieks of protest, he launched into an encomium of Constanze, beginning with distinctly uncharitable (as with poor Josefa Auernhammer) dismissals of her sisters:

> In no other family have I ever come across such differences of character. The eldest is a lazy, gross perfidious woman, and as cunning as a fox. Mme Lange is a false, malicious person and a coquette. The youngest – is still too young to be anything in particular – she is just a good-natured, but feather-headed creature! But the middle one, my good, dear Constanze, is the martyr of the family, and probably for that very reason, is the kindest-hearted, the cleverest, in short the best of them all.

And when he went on to describe Constanze, he did so with an almost detached practicality, hoping again, perhaps, that this would appeal to Leopold:

> I must make you better acquainted with the character of my dear Constanze. She is not ugly, but at the same time far from beautiful. Her whole beauty consists in two little black eyes and a pretty figure. She has no wit, but she has enough common sense to enable her to fulfil her duties as a wife and mother. It is a downright lie that she is inclined to be extravagant. On the contrary, she is accustomed to be shabbily dressed, for the little that her mother

has been able to do for her children, she has done for the two others, but never for Constanze. True, she would like to be neatly and cleanly dressed, but not smartly, and most things that a woman needs she is able to make for herself; and she dresses her own hair every day.

(That last attribute of Constanze's may well have been an unkind little dig at his own sister, for Nannerl never could dress her hair.) And after all this detail, Wolfgang's eulogy concluded, like so much of his music, with the simplest of phrases: 'I love her and she loves me with all her heart. Tell me whether I could wish for a better wife?'

Before Wolfgang could learn Leopold's reaction to this veritable bombshell, it was necessary for him to write another long, and somewhat less calm, letter. The Vienna gossips were making their mischief, and Leopold had heard all sorts of unflattering stories about Wolfgang, about his standing in Viennese society, and about his love for Constanze Weber. On 22 December Wolfgang began a letter which took him at least four days to complete, and in it he attempted to demolish all that had been said against him.[27] The 'arch villain' who had been spreading these 'disgraceful lies' was one Peter von Winter, a violinist in the Mannheim–Munich orchestra, who was at the time in Vienna. Chief among the stories that got back to Leopold were that Constanze was a slut ('*luder*'); that her mother and her guardian Herr Thorwart had tricked Wolfgang into signing a pre-marriage contract whereby he would marry Constanze within three years or otherwise pay her 300 gulden a year; and that Wolfgang himself was out of favour, even 'detested', at Court. With the same simmering rage that had permeated his letters during the crisis of his Salzburg dismissal, Wolfgang denied all these fables. Although Frau Weber had spoken up for him, Herr Thorwart had indeed made him sign a preposterous pre-marital contract, because he too had been told stories by 'certain busybodies and independent gentlemen like Herr Winter'. Once more in his conversational mode, Wolfgang asked his father:

What other course was open to me? Nothing in the world could have been easier for me to write. For I knew that I should never have to pay these 300 gulden, because I should never forsake her, and that even should I be so unfortunate as to change my mind, I should be only too glad to get rid of her for 300 gulden, while Constanze, as I knew her, would be too proud to let herself be sold.

But then, with true operatic flourish, Wolfgang drew Constanze herself into the narrative: 'But what did the angelic girl do when the guardian had gone? She asked her mother for the document, and said to me, "Dear Mozart, I need no written assurance from you. I believe what you say," and tore up the paper.' (So Leopold could see that Constanze had a mind of her own, and was clearly more than the demure martyr that Wolfgang had previously described.)

Wolfgang went on to dismantle the stories about his unpopularity at Court: 'If you really believe that I am detested at Court and by the old and new aristocracy, just write to Herr von Strack, Countess Thun, Countess Rumbeck, Baroness Waldstätten, Herr von Sonnenfels, Frau von Trattner, *enfin*, to anyone you choose.'

And for his nonchalant coup de theâtre, he produced his star witness: 'Meanwhile let me tell you that at table the other day the Emperor gave me the very highest praise, accompanied by the words "*C'est un talent, decidé*!"'

Wolfgang then dealt with Winter's labelling of Constanze as a slut:

> Of all the mean things which Winter said, the only one which enrages me is that he called my dear Constanze a slut. I have described her to you exactly as she is. If you wish to have the opinion of others, write to Herr von Auernhammer, to whose house she has been a few times and where she has lunched once. Write to Baroness Waldstätten, who has had her at the house, though unfortunately for a month only because she, the Baroness, fell ill. Now Constanze's mother refuses to part with her and let her go back. God grant that I may soon be able to marry her.

And, almost as a coda, he added a fascinating insight into the character of Leopold's informer, Winter himself:

> There is one thing more I must tell you about Winter. Among other things he once said to me: 'You are a fool to get married. Keep a mistress. You are earning enough money, you can afford it. What prevents you from doing so? Some damned religious scruple?' Believe now what you will.

For all Wolfgang's passionate protestation and eloquent explanation, Leopold, entirely predictably, would have none of it. In the weeks and months that followed, many heated letters were exchanged between Vienna and Salzburg. Only those of Wolfgang have survived, but the content of Leopold's can again easily be surmised by the manner in which Wolfgang had to deal with them. Gradually he changed his tactics. He continued to write about other matters – people he was seeing, music he was playing, stories from Vienna's society; but he never failed to include news of 'my dear Constanze' and expressions of his longing for Leopold to meet her. He also brought Nannerl into the campaign, confiding in her, sending her significant little gifts from Constanze (two caps which Constanze herself had made), and, from himself, his fantasy and fugue in C major, K394 (383a), for clavier, which he claimed was written because Constanze had begged him to write a fugue:

> My dear Constanze is really the cause of this fugue's coming into the world. The Baron van Swieten, to whom I go every Sunday, gave me all the works of Handel and Sebastian Bach to take home with me (after I had played them to him). When Constanze heard the fugues, she absolutely fell in love with them. Now she will listen to nothing but fugues, and particularly (in this kind of composition) the works of Handel and Bach. Well, as she had often heard me play fugues out of my head, she asked me if I had ever written any down, and when I said I had not, she scolded me roundly for not recording some of my compositions in this most artistic and beautiful of all musical forms, and never ceased to entreat me until I wrote down a fugue for her. So that is its origin.[28]

This was indeed a clever move on Wolfgang's part, to show Nannerl (and therefore Leopold) that Constanze was not merely a good housekeeper and cap-maker, but had extremely sophisticated musical tastes. And meanwhile he persuaded Constanze herself to write to Nannerl too, a somewhat stilted and formal letter, with the aim of creating a bond between the two women in his life. Occasionally in his letters to Leopold he included messages (about fashions, for example) from Constanze to Nannerl. And once he even let Constanze finish his own letter, as he had to rush out. He had certainly inherited, or at least observed, some of his father's manipulative skills, as in that first half of 1782 he tried to defuse all the Salzburg resistance to his marital plans.

At some point in the midst of all this, tensions arose between Wolfgang and Constanze themselves and their betrothal was broken off. The high-spirited Constanze went again to stay with the Baroness Waldstätten. The Baroness, who was in her late thirties and lived apart from her husband in the Leopoldstadt district of Vienna, was an extremely good friend to the young couple. In April 1782 there had been a lively party at her house, at which several of the ladies present, including both Constanze and the Baroness herself, had allowed a young man to take a ribbon and measure the calves of their legs. When Constanze returned home, she regaled her sisters and Wolfgang with a gleeful account of the party. Wolfgang was appalled, and said so. There was a major row: she told him she was doing no more than everyone else was doing, and announced (not for the first time) that she would have nothing more to do with him. Wolfgang was heartbroken, and now wrote Constanze the most careful of letters. Still firmly, almost prudishly, sticking to his opinions about propriety, he begged her to change her mind about dismissing him: 'I (to whom it means more than it does to you to lose the object of my love) am not so hot-tempered, so rash and so senseless to accept my dismissal. I love you far too well to do so.'[29] He gave her a rather obsessive little lecture about her honour (again not dissimilar to something Leopold might have produced), and discarded the poor Baroness, aged thirty-eight, as 'already past her prime'. But he concluded with passion and tenderness:

> If you will but surrender to your feelings, then I know that this very day I shall be able to say with absolute confidence that Constanze is the virtuous, honourable, prudent, and loyal sweetheart of her honest and devoted MOZART.

As in any marriage, there must have been countless occasions such as this for Wolfgang and Constanze. She certainly held her own in argument, and gave him as good as she got. But their genuine devotion to each other invariably pulled them together again, and reconciliation was always sweet. This particular row can even be detected in the composition of *Die Entführung*, which was still on Wolfgang's desk. In the quartet at the end of Act II, the two pairs of lovers, Constanze and Belmonte and their servants Blonde and Pedrillo, fall upon each other as the men come to rescue their sweethearts. But almost immediately the men accuse the women of having been unfaithful to them, Constanze with the Pasha Selim, Blonde with his servant Osmin. Constanze and Blonde are appalled, and painful consternation descends on the four of them. Blonde hits out at Pedrillo in her rage, and Constanze sorrowfully asks Belmonte, 'Ob ich dir treu verblieb?' (Do you have to ask if I have been true to you?). Blonde complains to Constanze that Pedrillo does not trust her, and after two bars of orchestral tension, Constanze replies by telling her of Belmonte's doubts. After two more orchestral bars, Pedrillo declares that Blonde must love him if she hit him; but, without waiting for his two bars, Belmonte comes straight in with 'Constanze ist mir treu, Daran ist nicht zu zweifeln' (Constanze is true to me, there's no doubt about it). Forgiveness and reconciliation – two of the vast themes of this apparently light-hearted singspiel – transform the lovers' tensions into rapturous joy, and Wolfgang's musical portrayal of this whole scene has the authentic ring of real human experience.

Die Entführung aus dem Serail was at last performed on 16 July 1782, at the Burgtheater. It was a huge success, and subsequent performances were packed out, in spite of 'frightful heat',[30] as Wolfgang reported to Salzburg. By now he was enormously busy, not only with his opera but with other commissions (a symphony for the Haffner family, and an arrangement of *Die Entführung* for wind instruments), and often worked through the night ('I must just spend the night over it, that's the only way'[31]). He remembered rather late to send name-day greetings to Nannerl for 26 July, but, still longing for his family's endorsement of Constanze, persuaded her to add her own rather self-conscious message to his. By 27 July Wolfgang was desperate to be married, and once again asked Leopold directly for his blessing:

> Dearest, most beloved father, I implore you by all you hold dear in the world to give your consent to my marriage with my dear Constanze. Do not suppose that it is just for the sake of getting married. If that were the only reason, I would gladly wait. But I realize that it is absolutely necessary for my own honour and for that of my girl, and for the sake of my health and spirits. My heart is restless and my head confused; in such a condition how can one think and work to any good purpose?[32]

But by the next post all he received was a 'cold, indifferent' letter from Leopold, ignoring his reports of the sensation that *Die Entführung* now was, not even having bothered to look at the score of it that Wolfgang had sent him, chiding him for not having finished his symphony for the Haffners, and accusing him of making enemies of the musical profession, as 'the whole world declares'. Wolfgang was furious: '*What* world, pray? Presumably the world of Salzburg, for everyone in Vienna can see and hear enough to be convinced of the contrary. And that must be my reply.' And now his pleas to his father were more urgent, more impatient:

> You can have no objection whatever to raise – and indeed you do not raise any. Your letters show me that. For Constanze is a respectable honest girl of good parentage, and I am able *to support her*. We love each other – and want each other. All you have

written and may possibly write to me on the subject can only be *well-meaning advice* which, however fine and good it may be, is no longer applicable to a man who has gone so far with a girl. In such a case nothing can be postponed. It is better for him to put his affairs in order and act like an honest fellow! God will ever reward that. I mean to have nothing with which to reproach myself.[33]

If there were tensions between the generations in the Mozart family, they seem to have been present in the Weber family too. In those scorching days of a Vienna summer, Constanze had again flown from her mother's house to the safe haven of the Baroness Waldstätten's in Leopoldstadt, where she could presumably see Wolfgang in privacy. But Frau Weber was enraged by this arrangement, and even threatened to send the police to fetch her back. Poor Sophie, Constanze's younger sister, had to bear the brunt of all this, and when a servant was sent to deliver some music to Wolfgang, she included a tearful message to let Constanze come home. This, with or without Leopold's blessing, probably pushed Wolfgang into extreme action. He wrote to the Baroness to tell her of Frau Weber's threats ('Are the police in Vienna allowed to go into any house?'[34]) and to ask her advice. Should they not just go ahead and get married?

On 2 August Wolfgang and Constanze went to confession and Communion together; on the following day their marriage contract was signed and witnessed. And on 4 August, in the presence of Frau Weber and Sophie, Constanze's guardian Herr Thorwart, Wolfgang's boyhood friend and best man Franz Gilowsky (now a surgeon in Vienna) and a district councillor, they were married at St Stephen's Cathedral. It was an emotional occasion: 'When we had been joined together, both my wife and I began to weep. All present, even the priest, were deeply touched, and all wept to see how much our hearts were moved.'[35] And afterwards the Baroness Waldstätten put on a magnificent feast for them at her house, 'more princely than baronial'. Wolfgang's present to his wife on their wedding day was a small gold watch, the first one he had been given in Paris as a child. She wore it for the rest of her life, regardless of others presented to her in later years. (When, in her late seventies, Constanze was visited by an English couple, Vincent and Mary Novello, she showed them the watch. She wore it 'at that very time in her bosom', and it was still 'going remarkably well'.[36])

And so the deed was done. Just after the wedding Wolfgang heard again from Leopold, still refusing to give his blessing and complaining now that Constanze was only after the Mozart family money, about which Wolfgang had probably misled her. Wolfgang replied calmly and with strength: 'You are much mistaken in your son if you can suppose him capable of acting dishonestly. My dear Constanze – now, thank God, at last my wife – knew my circumstances and heard from me long ago all that I had to expect from you.'[37]

He described the wedding, and their happiness, and he continued to send his father Constanze's affectionate greetings, as he always had. And he ended as if this was a completely normal letter: he declared that the outer movements of his 'Haffner' symphony, K385, should be played 'as fast as possible' (this was a clear indication of his energy in those momentous days), and casually reported that Gluck had loved *Die Entführung* and had subsequently invited him and Constanze to lunch. But this was not a normal letter. Wolfgang had taken a major decision against the wishes of his father, and Leopold had finally lost the battle. At the end of *Die Entführung*, the Pasha Selim says to Belmonte, 'Nimm deine Freiheit. Nimm Constanze' (Take your freedom. Take Constanze). Wolfgang had taken his Constanze, and was at last free of his father.

~

THE EXCITEMENTS AND upheavals of their courtship continued throughout the first year of marriage for Wolfgang and Constanze. In the space of nine months they lived in no fewer than four different apartments – all of them admittedly within a few hundred yards of each other, but the constant uprooting cannot have allowed them to feel particularly settled as yet. There were still problems with

Frau Weber, who could reduce Constanze to tears quite easily. By the end of August, only a few weeks after their wedding, Wolfgang resolved not to let his wife visit her mother any more, unless they were compelled to celebrate a birthday or name-day of one of the family. (Constanze's two unmarried sisters, Josefa and Sophie, were still living at home.) And there was constant pressure from Leopold to bring his daughter-in-law to Salzburg. Despite protestations that they could hardly wait to see Leopold and Nannerl again, Wolfgang and Constanze procrastinated continually. At the end of August Wolfgang was citing the uncertain movements of the Imperial Russian visitors as his reason for not yet being able to settle on a date. In October, 'the most profitable season in Vienna'[38] was just beginning, when people wanted lessons and concerts – and indeed it was in this month that Wolfgang did finally get to perform *Die Entführung* for the Grand Duke Paul, for whom the whole project had originally been conceived. By mid-November, Wolfgang was blaming the weather and, for good measure, Constanze's 'severe headache'[39] for the delay. A week later he finally admitted that they could not come until the spring 'for my pupils positively refuse to let me go'.[40] And, the best reason of all, Constanze was now pregnant.

The newly-weds were in fact extremely happy. Despite all the upheavals, they took great strength from each other's love, from their good connections, and from Wolfgang's burgeoning popularity among music patrons. They had extremely good friends, especially the Baroness Waldstätten and her new lodger Josefa Auernhammer. And now that Wolfgang was happily committed to Constanze, he could forgive Aloysia for the heartache she had caused him: the Langes and the Mozarts were regular visitors in each other's houses. Joseph Lange would in due course paint his sister-in-law, and begin though not finish the most powerful of all the portraits of Wolfgang. A second daughter, Philippina, had been born to the Langes in September; indeed, Aloysia and Constanze must have continually supported each other through their many confinements. (There was barely a time when one or other of them was not pregnant: between them they had twelve babies in ten years – not counting any possible miscarriages.) In January 1783 Wolfgang and Constanze were temporarily lodged in the Klein-Herbersteinhaus in Wipplingerstrasse, a generous apartment loaned to them by Baron Raimund Wetzlar, another good friend. There were two large and empty rooms adjacent to this apartment, so one night the Mozarts gave a private ball in them, lasting from six in the evening until seven the following morning, to which they invited all their friends. In describing this event to his father and sister, Wolfgang declared it would be impossible to name all the guests, but he did pick out the Baroness Waldstätten, his generous landlords the Wetzlars, his Salzburg friend and best man Franz Gilowsky, a crowd of people from *Die Entführung* including the librettist Johann Stephanie and his wife, and the Belmonte, Johann Adamberger, and his; and of course the Langes. In the same letter, Wolfgang asked his father to send his Harlequin costume (was this something he had acquired in Venice, when they were there in 1772?): it was Carnival time, and Wolfgang felt liberated. Pregnancy or no, the Mozarts were enjoying themselves.

The richness of the Mozarts' new Viennese acquaintance, and especially Wolfgang's rapprochement with Aloysia, gave him new waves of compositional energy. He was discovering that the piano concerto, played and directed by himself, was a marvellous new medium for concerts. Over the winter of 1782–3 he wrote three of them, K413 (387a) in F, K414 (385p) in A and K415 (387b) in C, plus a new rondo in D, K382, as an alternative ending to his earlier D major concerto, K175. And he remembered to send these, or news of them, to his sister, ever sensitive to her passionate need for all his piano music.

Wolfgang also wrote some more spectacular arias for Aloysia. The first of them, the rondo 'Ah, non sai qual pena', K416, was for a big concert in the Mehlgrube in January 1783, and here Wolfgang thrillingly renewed his musical partnership with the artist who had so inspired him five years earlier. Again he wrote for every facet of Aloysia's remarkable voice, her controlled cantabile singing, her high tessitura (this time he took her up to F in alt), her brilliant coloratura and her dramatic interpretative powers, this time portraying a grieving lover who vacillates between tenderness and desolation. Wolfgang's stretching too of tonal relationships gave the Mehlgrube audience music of an intensely new and modern vocabulary. Both he and Aloysia undoubtedly made their mark that evening. Two months later, in the early stages of her third pregnancy, she sang the aria again at a concert of her own at the Burgtheater. She also included their first collaboration from Mannheim, 'Non sò d'onde viene', K294 (so there were no insuperably uncomfortable memories there), and he conducted his 'Paris' symphony and played his D major piano concerto with its new rondo. Gluck was in the audience, and was so delighted with the concert that he again issued lunch invitations, this time to both the young couples, the Mozarts and the Langes. Leopold must have been impressed with that report, and even more so by that in Wolfgang's next letter, when he described his own concert, attended by the Emperor, no less: 'But what pleased me most of all was that His Majesty the Emperor was present and, goodness! – how delighted he was and how he applauded me!'[41] Again Aloysia was one of the soloists, and the whole concert was an enormous success. With Wolfgang's burgeoning concert activity, and an expanding circle of brilliant musical and theatrical acquaintance (he mentioned in passing to Leopold the new poet in town, 'a certain Abbate Da Ponte'[42]), he was energized and inspired.

But above all Wolfgang was loving his new private happiness. If he left the house before Constanze had arisen, he wrote little notes for her:

> Good morning, dear little wife! I hope that you have slept well, that nothing disturbed you, that you haven't got up too hastily, that you are not catching cold, that you are not bending or stretching, that you are not angry with your servants, that you don't fall over the threshold in the next room. Spare yourself household worries until I return. Only may nothing happen to you! I am coming at – o'clock etc.[43]

He reported regularly and proudly to Leopold and Nannerl on the progress of Constanze's pregnancy. In January he described his 'little wife who is quite plump (but only about the belly)'.[44] In April, Constanze was 'in such excellent health and has become so robust that all women should thank God if they are so fortunate in their pregnancy'.[45] And in May he wrote contentedly from the Prater, where they were enjoying marvellous spring weather, after eating lunch out of doors: 'My whole company consists of my little wife who is pregnant, and hers consists of her little husband, who is not pregnant, but fat and flourishing . . . For the sake of my dear little wife, I cannot miss this fine weather. Exercise is good for her.'[46] They had just moved house again, for the third time in five months, and now had a first-floor apartment in the Judenplatz. And it was here that their first child was born, on 17 June 1783. He was named Raimund Leopold, after their generous landlord and of course the child's grandfather.

The anxiety and excitement of childbirth brought about another important reconciliation with the Weber family, for Constanze's mother was involved. As she nursed her daughter and new grand-son, Frau Weber was forgiven for her preposterous past. Wolfgang's letter of 18 June has all the elation and exhaustion of every new father:

> Congratulations, you are a grandpapa! Yesterday, the 17th, at half past six in the morning, my dear wife was safely delivered of a fine sturdy boy, round as a ball. Her pains began at half past one in the morning, so that night we both lost our rest and sleep. At four o'clock I sent for my mother-in-law – and then for the midwife. At six o'clock the child began to appear and at half past six the trouble was all over. My mother-in-law by her great kindness to her daughter has made full amends for all the harm she did before her marriage. She spends the whole day with her.[47]

Never one to avoid describing the most basic bodily functions, Wolfgang went on to confide his anxieties about breast-feeding:

> From the condition of her breasts I am rather afraid of milk-fever.

And now the child has been given to a foster-nurse against my will, or rather, at my wish! For I was quite determined that whether she should be able to do so or not, my wife was never to feed her child. Yet I was equally determined that my child was never to take the milk of a stranger! I wanted the child to be brought up on water, like my sister and myself. However, the midwife, my mother-in-law and most people here have begged me and implored me not to allow it, if only for the reason that most children here who are brought up on water do not survive, as the people here don't know how to do it properly.

And three days later his report on his newly extended family (sandwiched between accounts of writing some more arias for Aloysia, and of possible plans for a new opera) was equally, joyfully, explicit:

Thank God, my wife has now survived the two critical days, yesterday and the day before, and in the circumstances is very well. We now hope that all will go well. The child too is quite strong and healthy and has a tremendous number of things to do, I mean, drinking, sleeping, yelling, pissing, shitting, dribbling and so forth. He kisses the hands of his grandpapa and his aunt.[48]

Truly, Wolfgang and Constanze were extremely happy: 'Little Raimund is so like me that everyone immediately remarks it. It is as if my face had been copied. My dear little wife is absolutely delighted, as this is what she has always desired.'[49]

Little Raimund's other aunt, Aloysia, was also around the Mozart household a great deal in these days. She was about to appear in Anfossi's opera Il curioso indiscreto at the Burgtheater, and Wolfgang was to write two arias especially for her, to be inserted into Anfossi's score. (This was quite normal practice, when a singer for whom a role had not been written went into a production.) In different ways, both these arias, 'Vorrei spiegarvi, oh Dio!', K418, and 'No, che non sei capace', K419, again confirmed the astonishing musical partnership of Wolfgang and Aloysia. Now writing for her without the pain of deep personal involvement, Wolfgang could reach to the extremities of her superb facility and of their shared emotional experience, and produce music of utterly breathtaking distinction.

The text of 'Vorrei spiegarvi' (by an unknown librettist) complies with a common enough formula:

> *Vorrei spiegarvi, oh Dio!*
> *Qual è l'affanno mio;*
> *Ma mi condanna il fato*
> *A pianger e tacer.*

> (I would like to tell you, oh God
> what is my desire,
> but fate has condemned me
> to weep in silence.)

But Wolfgang's setting sent it to Olympian realms. His choice of key, A major, is interesting, for that is so often associated with seduction in his music; and indeed the partner that he gave to the voice, an obbligato oboe, is also often the instrument of seduction. So it is almost as if this sad little text has become a love duet. And again Wolfgang exploited Aloysia's famously controlled slow singing, her emotional involvement with text, and her phenomenal high register; and he produced what is arguably his finest ever aria. Together with the flashier brilliance of 'No, che non sei capace', these two arias inevitably eclipsed the rest of *Il curioso indiscreto*. According to Wolfgang, Anfossi's opera 'failed completely with the exception of my two arias . . . which did inexpressible honour both to my sister-in-law and to myself'.[50] The combined family triumph caused some jealousies on the Viennese musical scene, and both Wolfgang and Aloysia were wary of their 'enemies', especially, in Aloysia's case, of a new young singer in town, the eighteen-year-old 'Mlle Storace'. Little did Wolfgang realize, when he first mentioned her in a letter to Leopold in July 1783, that Nancy Storace too would become an important and much-loved member of his circle.

But all these excitements continued to delay the promised family visit to Salzburg. Leopold and Nannerl had still not met Constanze, and once again Leopold began to accuse Wolfgang of having no intention of coming at all. Undoubtedly, both Wolfgang and Constanze were extremely nervous of this obligation, Wolfgang for political as well as family reasons – it was now over two years since he had got himself kicked out of Salzburg service, and he had no idea how he would be received there – and Constanze for the sheer ordeal of meeting her troublesome in-laws for the first time. She did at least have two young allies in Salzburg. Heinrich and Gretl Marchand were the children of Theodor Hilarius Marchand, director of the German Court Theatre at Mannheim and then Munich, and the Marchands had known the Webers in Mannheim. When Leopold had come with Nannerl to Munich to hear *Idomeneo* in 1781, he too had met the Marchands, and had offered to take the two children back to Salzburg and teach them. (Almost certainly, Leopold had been looking for the next generation of educable prodigy.) Now aged fourteen and fifteen, Heinrich and Gretl were living in the Tanzmeisterhaus with Leopold and Nannerl; and when Wolfgang and Constanze wrote a series of letters assuring his father and sister that they really would come to Salzburg, Constanze wrote a little note too to Gretl. As Vienna emptied for the hot summer, the young Mozarts could delay their visit no longer. Tearing themselves away from their six-week-old baby, whom they left with a foster-mother, and bidding farewell too to Aloysia, who was heading off to Frankfurt to sing the role of Constanze in *Die Entführung*, they left for Salzburg at the end of July. Wolfgang had not been there since November 1780, nearly three years earlier.

~

AGAIN BECAUSE OF the absence of letters in the three months that Wolfgang and Constanze spent in Salzburg, there is little information as to how this much-anticipated visit went. The chief chronicler, as always, was Nannerl, who continued laconically to record in her *Tagebuch* the basic facts of her daily activities – teaching commitments, visits, visitors, church attendance, weather reports and so on. These do however reveal that she and Wolfgang to an extent resumed their sibling relationship. Once more Wolfgang purloined the diary and made his own entries, gently (and not so gently) ridiculing her unemotional shorthand by improvising on it: 'Went walking in the Mirabellgarten at seven o'clock as one goes walking in the Mirabellgarten, as one goes walking, went walking as one goes. Looming threat of rain, but never rainfall, and gradually – the heavens smiled!'[51] Some of Wolfgang's contributions seem to follow Nannerl's voice so exactly that she might almost have been dictating to him at his side. Others are emphatically in his own voice and style, as ever full of puns, anagrams, puzzles and jokes. Whether intentionally or unintentionally, Wolfgang was reverting to childhood innocences and exuberances with his sister.

It is likely, given the months of build-up, that poor Constanze received a cool welcome from Leopold and Nannerl. But it does seem nonetheless that every proper effort was made to entertain her. Nannerl's diaries record sightseeing outings in carriages, many visits to other people's houses in Salzburg, and, most especially, enormous amounts of music-making in the Tanzmeisterhaus. There were, after all, six musicians actually living there, including the gifted Marchand children; and many of the Salzburg Court musicians also came regularly to take part – as they always had.

As in most family gatherings, especially when members are possessed of a distinct emotional volatility, there were inevitable strains and personality clashes. Years later, Constanze described to some English visitors one of those musical evenings. They were singing the quartet from *Idomeneo*, and Wolfgang became very upset: 'he burst into tears and quitted the chamber and it was some time before she could console him.'[52] Since the quartet focuses on Idomeneo's son Idamante having to take his leave of his father who has been behaving quite irrationally towards him, and involves too the princess Ilia whom he loves but who politically is his father's enemy, there must have been layers of potential for poignant distress on all sides. But these musical occasions afforded great pleasure too, and for Nannerl especially this must have been another precious time. Wolfgang probably wrote his piano sonatas in C, K330 (300h), in A, K331 (300i), and in F, K332 (300k), in those Salzburg months, and she would have been among their first interpreters. But the main musical event of the visit came right at the end of it: a performance of Wolfgang's new and enormous Mass in C minor, K427 (417a). The chief soloist was Constanze.

The genesis of this unfinished but major church composition is a little unclear, as two slightly different stories were told, one by Wolfgang and the other by Constanze. Wolfgang's version had appeared in a letter to Leopold in January 1783, when parental pressure was again being applied as to the precise date of their visit to Salzburg. Refuting the accusation of not intending to come at all, Wolfgang cited a half-finished Mass as evidence that they would indeed come, with the implication that he had always planned to bring his wife, and a Mass written for her and in honour of her, to Salzburg: 'The score of half a Mass, which is still lying here waiting to be finished, is the best proof that I really made the promise.'[53]

Constanze's version of the story is somewhat different, and she told it twice. First she informed Georg Nissen, as he planned his Mozart biography in the 1820s, that the Mass had been 'solemnly promised for his wife when her confinement was happily over'.[54] She repeated this in 1829 to her English visitors, the Novellos: the Mass was written 'in consequence of a vow that he had made to do so, on the safe recovery after the birth of their first child – relative to whom he had been particularly anxious.'[55] And in fact both these stories can go together. Wolfgang had probably always planned to write something for Constanze, which, like the music he wrote for her sister Aloysia, would show both of them off in an excellent light. During Contanze's pregnancy, when like any first-time expectant father he was nervous about the outcome, he vowed to finish the Mass when mother and baby were both doing well. And although in fact Wolfgang never did complete it (he must have drawn on his earlier church music for that first performance in Salzburg), its vast conception and 'tailor-made' solo writing for Constanze are spectacular indicators of his great love for his new wife, of his awareness of the music that she both liked and could sing, and incidentally of his great desire to show the whole of Salzburg just how versatile his writing now was.

Certainly, the C minor Mass is quite unlike any other church music of its time. It has double choruses (in the 'Qui tollis' and *Sanctus*) and mighty choral fugues ('Cum sancto spiritu'); its solo writing is often florid and ornate; the orchestral forces required are large (strings, oboes, bassoons, horns, trumpets, trombones, timpani and organ) and in addition there is some very prominent solo instrumental writing. All this flew in the face of current practice, for in Vienna Joseph II had restricted church music with instrumental accompaniment to the Court chapel or St Stephen's Cathedral: everywhere else the music had to be plain and congregational. And in Salzburg, Archbishop Colloredo had applied his own constraints, demanding the elimination of complexity (there were to be no fugues) and virtuosity (no solo sections), and decreeing that no Mass should last longer than forty-five minutes. In the C minor Mass, Wolfgang broke all these 'rules', almost as if he were deliberately defying his former employer. What he seems to have conceived here is an enormous work balancing old-fashioned polyphony in the style of Bach or Handel, whom he and Constanze both so admired, with more modern solo writing, and an overall orchestral sonority which would thrillingly fill St Peter's Abbey in Salzburg, where he knew the Mass would be performed.

Wolfgang never wrote beyond the capabilities of his performers (unlike Beethoven), but always challengingly stretched them to their limits. Judging by the solo writing in the C minor Mass, Constanze must have been a gifted singer with many of the same attributes as her sister Aloysia. This is not particularly surprising, since all four Weber girls had been excellently taught by their father, and their technique was exceptionally secure. And in preparing his wife for this very special, and exposed, performance, Wolfgang wrote some exercises for her, training her technique for the sort of music she would now be required to sing. The first glimpse of Constanze comes in the opening *Kyrie* movement, when 'Christe eleison' is given to the soprano solo. Like Aloysia, Constanze must have possessed a voice with a wide range and easy coloratura: despite the general solemnity of this music, its execution is always impressive and commanding of attention. In the next solo movement, 'Laudamus te' in the *Gloria*, he developed this: again both extremities of Constanze's register were exploited, and the coloratura writing was confidently and radiantly expanded. But the heart of Constanze's performance, for indeed it is the heart of any Mass setting, was the 'Et incarnatus est' in the *Credo*. Although Wolfgang's surviving music is incomplete, the vocal line together with solo instrumental parts for flute, oboe and bassoon are all extant, and the resulting aria has the same slow, controlled virtuosity as has the music that he had written for Aloysia, and, at the same time, a phenomenal sense of tranquillity and reverence. Constanze's vocal range evidently lay a little lower than her sisters' (where Aloysia, and indeed later Josefa, would go to F in alt, Constanze never went beyond a C), but she shared many of her family's traits, and Wolfgang had written to her strengths.

Wolfgang's new Mass was rehearsed in the last week of his Salzburg visit, and performed in St Peter's Abbey (significantly not the Archbishop's Cathedral) on 26 October, the night before he and Constanze were to leave. All his friends and ex-colleagues from the Salzburg orchestra were involved, and the Archbishop tactfully stayed away. Nannerl's typically succinct diary entry merely recorded that the performance had taken place, and that her sister-in-law had sung. But she and her father must have been overwhelmed by the sheer depth and versatility of Wolfgang's compositional range. Although the C minor Mass is unfinished, inviting speculation that the lasting impression of this first performance was one of disappointment, no musician could fail to respond to it with anything other than joyous wonder. The Salzburg visit had had its tensions, but it is tempting to suggest that it ended, literally, on a high note.

And so Wolfgang and Constanze came to the end of their stay. As they left the Tanzmeisterhaus, Constanze rather boldly asked Leopold if she could have one of the many gifts that Wolfgang had received on his earliest travels, but this was refused. Acceptance of Wolfgang's wife evidently did not extend to over-generosity with mementos. Wolfgang would never return to his birthplace, nor see Nannerl again. On the journey home they stayed for a few days in Linz, where Wolfgang wrote rather stiffly to his father and sister: 'My wife and I kiss your hands, ask you to forgive us for inconveniencing you for so long, and thank you once more for all the kindnesses we have received.'[56] They were however made to feel extremely welcome in Linz, where the Thun family (relations of a good Viennese patron) showered them with generous hospitality. Wolfgang returned this by giving them a concert; and, as he had no symphony with him, he simply wrote them a new one (the 'Linz', in C, K425), 'at breakneck speed'.

When Wolfgang and Constanze eventually arrived back in Vienna, there was terrible news. Their baby son Raimund had died on 19 August. For weeks they were both absolutely devastated. In an otherwise normal letter of news and business on 10 December, Wolfgang could not refrain from including the heartrending line: 'We are both very sad about our poor, bonny, fat, darling little boy.'[57] For Constanze especially, this must have been a bitter and utterly desolate homecoming, after a not particularly happy trip. She would have needed the support of her family at such a time, and it does seem that there were happy and productive reunions with the Webers. Aloysia's career was going from strength to strength. She was about to set off on a tour of several months, but before leaving, she was to perform in an opera for her benefit, and she loyally chose *Die Entführung*. She and her brother-in-law continued to bring great credit to each other. And, almost as if to redress the sororial balance in the family, Wolfgang closed his letter of 10 December with a postscript to Nannerl:

> We both send Nannerl
> (1) a couple of boxes on the ear
> (2) a couple of slaps on the face
> (3) a couple of raps on the cheek
> (4) a couple of whacks on the jaw
> (5) a couple of smacks on the jowl
> (6) a couple of cuffs on the mug.

With his wife's sister, his discourse was now one of sublime music. With his own, it was one of childish banter.

But 1784 was to be a much better year for the Mozarts. They began it by moving to a spacious apartment in a brand-new building on Graben, built and owned by the proprietor of a prominent Viennese bookshop, Johannes Thomas von Trattner. Trattner's wife Maria Theresa was a pupil of Wolfgang's, and the two families had become good friends. Almost immediately Constanze became pregnant again, so she and Wolfgang renewed their hopes of expanding their family. And, without stepping out of their new residence, Wolfgang could expand his musical activities too. The Trattnerhof, as it was now known, housed a private hall in which concerts could be given, and Wolfgang seized on this opportunity to mount three subscription concerts there, in March 1784. He collected an impressive list of 178 subscribers, which he sent in its entirety to Leopold, and wrote a new piano concerto for each of these concerts (those in E flat, K449, B flat, K450, and D, K451). As he was also taking part in other people's concert series, he seemed to be performing almost daily. But he still remembered to send these new concertos to Salzburg, thoughtfully advising Leopold and Nannerl that 'the E flat concerto . . . can be performed *a quattro* without wind instruments'[58] – that is, Nannerl could play it at home in a chamber version with single strings. He continued to try to maintain good relations between Nannerl and Constanze: 'My wife sends her love to my sister and will dispatch a smart fichu by the next mail coach. But she is going to make it herself, as it will be somewhat cheaper and much prettier.'[59] Constanze was practical with her hands, and Wolfgang lost no opportunity to praise her sterling domestic attributes. He also shared with Nannerl touching details of Constanze's pregnancy ('she finds it difficult to remain seated for long, because our future son and heir gives her no peace'[60]), knowing perhaps that, like most women, Nannerl would want to know every stage of its development.

~

IN FACT NANNERL'S interest in matrimonial bliss and new babies, in that summer of 1784, was somewhat closer than vicarious. At last, she herself was about to get married. Her future husband was not her great admirer from recent years, Captain d'Ippold, who, despite having continued to appear in her diary's list of callers at the Tanzmeisterhaus throughout the visit of Wolfgang and Constanze, had suddenly faded somewhat from the picture. In April 1783 she had recorded in her diary the death of one Jeanette Maria Berchtold. Just sixteen months later, on 23 August 1784, she married this young woman's widower, Johann Baptist Franz von Berchtold zu Sonnenberg.

Like Captain d'Ippold, Berchtold was considerably older than Nannerl: he was now forty-eight, she just thirty-three. He had been married twice already, but had lost both his wives in childbirth. The first, Maria, died producing her ninth child in ten years, and the second, Jeanette, giving birth to her second in two years. Of these eleven babies, five survived, four from Maria and one from Jeanette; and in marrying their father Nannerl took on these stepchildren as well. It was a tall order; and so was the subsequent domestic upheaval. By a quite extraordinary family coincidence, her new husband was now Pflege (Prefect) of St Gilgen, as her own maternal grandfather had been. Nannerl probably retained early memories of her grandmother Eva Rosina, who had lived with them in Getreidegasse until her death in 1755, when Nannerl was four. She was now to move to the very house in St Gilgen in which Eva Rosina had given birth to her own mother Maria Anna, beside the peaceful waters of the Abersee. The symmetry of this arrangement probably appealed considerably to Nannerl's ordered mind.

But it was indeed a major change of lifestyle. From her routine in the Tanzmeisterhaus as companion to her ageing and not altogether easy father, as teacher, caretaker and chaperone to their young protégés Heinrich and Gretl Marchand, and as a highly skilled musician at the heart of regular musical and social events among her wide circle of long-standing friendships, Nannerl was uprooted and transported to a tiny village at the edge of a lake. In August, when she married her husband and settled into her grand-mother's old house, the countryside would have been dazzlingly beautiful, and the cool air from the lake a welcome relief from the often stifling humidity of a Salzburg summer. But as autumn and then the cruel months of winter set in, awareness of what she had exchanged for this rural idyll must have hit her very hard. In effect, she had escaped from the clutches of one bullying man into those of another, for, after their initial contentment, Berchtold seems to have drawn away from his younger wife and responded less than sympa-thetically to her needs. Her stepchildren were hostile and unruly; she had problems acquiring servants in the village, and even greater problems keeping them (good relations with her servants had never actually been her strong point). And, most painful of all, she was completely isolated from any musical activity. Her father had generously given her a fortepiano as a wedding present. But as the cold weather arrived, and the snows effectively cut off this small community, her instrument could not cope with the icy dampness, and became unplayable. Nannerl had inherited her mother's courageous resourcefulness, and applied herself doggedly to her new tasks. Her lifelines to the outer world were her regular weekly correspondence with her father; the supplies that he sent her via her husband's official messenger (a local man who delivered documents from St Gilgen to Salzburg) or with a woman who brought glass from Aich to Salzburg; and, most especially, news of her brother's musical life in Vienna.

Wolfgang seemed genuinely delighted about his sister's marriage. He may also have been astonished by it: in his letter to her of 21 July 1784 there is no mention of Berchtold, nor indeed of any romantic attachment at all. But a month later, on 18 August, his excitement about her new situation revived all his younger-brother cheekiness:

> It is high time I wrote to you if I want my letter to find you still a vestal virgin! A few days more and – it is gone! My wife and I wish you all joy and happiness in your change of state and are only heartily sorry that we cannot have the pleasure of being present at your wedding. But we hope to embrace you as Frau von Sonnenburg and your husband also next spring both at Salzburg and at St Gilgen.[61]

And, after a more serious paragraph, confiding his anxiety now about Leopold, he ended with a poem of characteristically creative brilliance:

> *Du wirst im Ehstand viel erfahren*
> *was dir ein halbes Räthsel war;*
> *bald wirst du aus Erfahrung wissen,*
> *wie Eva einst hat handeln müssen*
> *daß sie hernach den kain gebahr.*
> *doch schwester, diese Ehstands Pflichten*
> *wirst du vom Herzen gern verrichten,*
> *denn glaube mir, sie sind nicht schwer;*
> *doch Jede Sache hat zwei Seiten;*
> *der Ehstand bringt zwar viele freuden,*
> *allein auch kummer bringet er.*
> *drum wenn dein Mann dir finstre Mienen,*
> *die du nicht glaubest zu verdienen,*
>   *in seiner üblen Laune macht:*
> *So denke, das ist Männergrille,*
> *und sag: Herr, es gescheh dein wille*
> *beytag – und meiner bey der Nacht.*

(Wedlock will show you many things
Which still a mystery remain;
Experience soon will teach to you
What Eve herself once had to do
Before she could give birth to Cain.
But all these duties are so light
You will perform them with delight.
Yet no state is an unmixed joy
And marriage has its own alloy,
Lest us its bliss perchance should cloy.
So when your husband shows reserve
Or wrath which you do not deserve,
And perhaps a nasty temper too,
Think, sister, 'tis a man's queer way.
Say, 'Lord, thy will be done by day,
But mine at night you'll do.')

~

FOR WOLFGANG AND Constanze, 1784 progressed with ever more musical and social activity and success. Their son Carl Thomas was born on 21 September. He was a healthy boy, and would live into his seventies. A week later the Mozarts moved house yet again (their sixth residence in just over two years of marriage), this time to a splendid apartment practically under the shadow of St Stephen's Cathedral, in Domgasse. They rented it from a family called Camesina: a generation earlier, its owner Albert Camesina had been Court plasterer in Vienna and also worked in Salzburg. One small room in the Domgasse apartment has a Camesina ceiling of stuccoed marble decoration, and Wolfgang would have felt considerable satisfaction at being able to enjoy his own version of what appeared all over the Archbishop's Palace in Salzburg. Certainly the location, and the plentiful and spacious rooms, of this new home were symbols of Wolfgang's current standing in Viennese society. And the two and a half years that they spent in Domgasse were indeed the best of times for Wolfgang and Constanze: reputation, success, artistic satisfaction and domestic happiness all peaked here. But if Wolfgang's social status was high, so too was the rent. Whereas they had paid 150 florins per month at the Trattnerhof, they now had to find 460. (In Salzburg, Leopold was paying only 90 florins per month for the Tanzmeisterhaus.) For a young family with no regular or secure income, this move was potentially very precarious.

As soon as Wolfgang and Constanze were settled into the Domgasse apartment, they renewed their invitation to Leopold to come and visit them. Here at last was a grandson they wanted him to inspect, and a home they wanted him to see. (The significance of the Camesina ceiling would not be lost on him.) In the new year of 1785 Leopold prepared to make the journey, and he brought with him his ex-pupil, Heinrich Marchand, now aged sixteen. (After Nannerl's marriage and departure from Salzburg, the Marchands had moved back to Munich.) Leopold's visit lasted ten weeks and was an almost unqualified triumph. He was bowled over by the frantic pace of Wolfgang's musical activities, by the brilliance of his new compositions and the excellence of their execution, by his dazzling acquaintance (both fellow musicians and their patrician patrons), by the charm of baby Carl, and, even, by the Weber family. For, at this most critical of testing times, Constanze had conscripted the support of her mother and sisters.

Almost as soon as Leopold arrived in Vienna, he was taken to lunch at Frau Weber's. This was the woman who, according to Leopold in 1782, should have been 'put in chains and made to sweep streets'[62] for having tried to trick Wolfgang into marrying her daughter: there was certainly potential here for an icy social occasion. But Frau Weber, together with her youngest daughter Sophie, came through with flying colours. (Josefa was away, earning her living as a singer.) She took great trouble over the meal and judged it perfectly. Leopold could not disguise his genuine admiration when he wrote to tell Nannerl all about it:

> We lunched on Thursday the 17th with your brother's mother-in-law, Frau Weber. There were just the four of us [Leopold, Wolf-

gang, Constanze and Heinrich], Frau Weber and her daughter Sophie, since the eldest daughter is in Graz. I must tell you that the meal, which was neither too lavish nor too stingy, was cooked to perfection. The roast was a fine plump pheasant; and everything was excellently well prepared.[63]

Leopold had caught a cold on the journey from Salzburg (he was always nervous of these, especially after his terrible experiences in London twenty years earlier), and for at least a day he had to miss out on many musical and social events. But while he remained at home, he was not alone. The carer of the Weber family, Sophie, came to sit with him: she gave him lunch and stayed until the late evening when everyone else returned from two separate concerts (Wolfgang had been playing at one for Count Zichy; Constanze had taken young Heinrich to another). And Aloysia played her part as well. On at least two occasions the Langes invited Leopold to their house. Each time she sang several arias for him, and on one of the evenings her husband did a sketch of him. Although Leopold was hypercritical of Aloysia's singing (she perhaps was the one Weber girl he residually found it hardest to forgive) he cannot have failed to appreciate her gifts, which had indeed brought her to the top of her profession in Vienna.

Probably the greatest effort to ensure that this all-important visit was a success was made by Constanze. And, like her mother, she seems cleverly to have judged it all very well. Carl no doubt played his part too, for Leopold was captivated by his five-month-old grandson: 'Little Carl is the picture of [Wolfgang]. He seems very healthy, but now and then, of course, children have trouble with their teeth. On the whole the child is charming, for he is extremely friendly and laughs when spoken to. I have only seen him cry once and the next moment he started to laugh.'[64] Leopold even praised Constanze's running of the house. Elsewhere in Vienna he was enjoying lavish and gourmet entertaining, but at home in Domgasse he appreciated Constanze's economies. He went so far as to include her in the affectionate formalities with which he signed off his letters to Nannerl ('Your brother, your sister-in-law, Marchand and I kiss you millions of times'[65]). This was truly a big step forward.

There was every reason for Leopold to incline uncharacteristically towards generosity. He was positively euphoric about the music he was hearing. He wept tears of joy at the first performance of Wolfgang's new and intensely dramatic D minor piano concerto, K466, with its ink still wet on the page, and then again at many other concerts when Wolfgang played his concertos. He heard once more the thrilling music from Constanze's C minor Mass, which Wolfgang had reworked into a cantata, *Davidde penitente*, K469, for the Tonkünstler-Societät (to a text by his new colleague Lorenzo Da Ponte). In the Domgasse apartment he heard Wolfgang's mould-breaking string quartets K387, 421(417b), 428(421b), 458, 464, 465: six of these would shortly be published and dedicated to Wolfgang's new friend and fellow quartet-player, Joseph Haydn (whose brother Michael was a colleague of Leopold's in Salzburg). He was basking in compliments paid to him on Wolfgang's behalf by absolutely everybody, and especially those of Haydn, who told him, 'Before God and as an honest man, I tell you that your son is the greatest composer known to me.'[66] He wallowed too in the attentions of the Emperor (who 'waved his hat and called out "Bravo, Mozart!"') and the entire Viennese aristo-cracy. He was particularly besotted with the Baroness Waldstätten, who had continued to be a wonderful ally to Wolfgang and Constanze after their marriage. She had corresponded warmly and tactfully with Leopold, who now referred to her as 'this woman of my heart'[67] (what can Nannerl have made of that?). And during Leopold's visit to Vienna, the Baroness did indeed pull out all the stops, inviting him out to her house in Klosterneuberg, and sending her carriage and horses for him.

But most important of all, Leopold was once more on the best of terms with Wolfgang. This was like the old days, on their Grand Tour, or the Italian trips. Along with success and adulation, there was again great harmony between father and son, and Constanze had undoubtedly played her part in the rebuilding of it. While

Leopold was in Vienna he became a Freemason, at the same Lodge that Wolfgang himself had recently joined (*Zur Wohltätigkeit* [Beneficence]). In this ideal society, unsullied of course by the presence of women, they could together enjoy friendship, social contact (useful for advancement), good food, recreation and the sort of ritual procedures that they both respected and valued. Wolfgang composed his cantata *Die Maurerfreude*, K471, for their Lodge, and it was performed there on the night before Leopold left the city. In the end, Leopold was utterly exhausted by the sheer pace of his Viennese schedule, but, in his own way, he had loved every minute of it.

~

HOW POOR NANNERL reacted to Leopold's dizzy accounts of his activities can only be imagined, as she shivered through the winter in her snow-bound 'wilderness', as she called it. She and her brother, once regarded as equals, were now seemingly poles apart. He was at the hub of cultural and artistic activity in one of the most vibrant cities in the world, successful, fulfilled, apparently well rewarded, and a happy husband and father. She was living in a freezing backwater with a husband she barely knew and five boisterous stepchildren who did not like her (Leopold actually described them as being 'troublesome, evil-minded children'), and she could not even touch a decent keyboard. There was at least one glimmer of, literally, new life in her: she was pregnant. She and Johann Baptist went to Salzburg in mid-May to welcome her father back to the Tanzmeisterhaus, and informed him of their good news. Between them all, it was decided that she should return to Salzburg again in the summer, when her baby came to term.

Leopold Alois Pantaleon Berchtold was duly born in the Tanzmeisterhaus on 27 July 1785. Leopold senior had gone to St Gilgen to bring Nannerl back to Salzburg in June, some six weeks before the birth, as her husband had not been willing to leave then. After the baby was born, Nannerl remained with her father for another month. But when she returned to St Gilgen, to her husband

and her unruly stepchildren, in early September, she left her own baby with his grandfather.

How Nannerl, Johann Baptist and Leopold arrived at this astonishing arrangement is not known. Little Leopold, or Leopoldl as he became known, had not been well before Nannerl left, and continued to be periodically troubled by illness for the first few months of his life. Perhaps when Nannerl left him behind, she believed it to be only a temporary measure, and that she would come and collect her baby once he had recovered. But then in the autumn months she herself became quite unwell, and, as the winter closed in, it was impracticable for a sickly baby to make a six-hour journey on difficult roads. By Carnival season of the following year, Leopold wanted to go to Munich to see the Marchands, and he asked Nannerl and Johann Baptist to come and look after Leopoldl themselves. But Johann Baptist refused to travel to Salzburg, claiming he had too much work in St Gilgen. Leopold was outraged, and now unleashed his fury, hitherto generally reserved for his son, on to his son-in-law:

> That my son-in-law should make the excuse that he couldn't travel in *because of the sheer amount of work* is something I really couldn't tell anyone without going red myself, since everyone knows *the extent of the little Pfleg of St Gilgen*, and can therefore deduce from that the terrible pile of work. I salute my son-in-law and ask him what he believes all reasonable people must think of a man who is capable of holding out for a whole eight or nine months, and perhaps even longer, without seeing his child, or maybe, which God forbid, ever seeing him again, when he's only six hours away from him? because he hasn't seen him for *five months*, and I'll hardly be able to take him out in under *four months* because of the weather – what might and must reasonable people think?[68]

And what, more to the point, did Nannerl think? She was not in fact to see her child again until he was almost a year old, when, in the following June, her husband could at last be persuaded to make the journey to Salzburg. Meanwhile Leopold, who had indeed gone to Munich, unfeelingly sent her more lively reports of the Carnival activities, which Nannerl had twice adored there, and of the burgeoning singing career of young Gretl Marchand. So Nannerl, who had been denied the opportunity to develop a musical career of her own, and watched longingly from the sidelines as her brother had swept along his brilliant path, now had to suffer the pain of knowing that her own protégée was leading the lifestyle that should and could so easily have been hers. Even her own child, like her talent, had effectively been taken from her. If Nannerl became withdrawn and embittered in St Gilgen, it is not altogether surprising. By whatever combination of circumstances, and for whatever reasons, her own will had been completely suppressed.

~

FOR THE YOUNG Mozarts in Vienna, the frantic pace of life continued after Leopold's departure. The sheer amount of music that Wolfgang composed between arriving at the Domgasse apartment in late 1784 and his next trip out of Vienna (to Prague, with Constanze, in January 1787) suggests an almost inhuman pace of labour. Beneath his Camesina ceiling he wrote two operas (*Der Schauspieldirektor*, K486, and *Le nozze di Figaro*, K492), at least six concertos, two string quartets and an enormous quantity of other chamber music in various combinations, vocal arias, duets and trios, and music for his Masonic Lodge. And the quality of all this music is utterly insuperable. Wolfgang was creatively at his zenith, and in demand on all sides for new music (for everything was rehearsed and performed as soon as it was written). It is no wonder that he pleaded overwork in a letter to Anton Klein in Mannheim, in May 1785: 'My hands are so full that I can scarcely ever find a minute to call my own.'[69] Nor is it surprising to find Leopold complaining regularly in his letters to Nannerl that he had not heard from Wolfgang for weeks ('I haven't had a single line from your brother'[70]).

Much of this new music was now being published. Wolfgang was doing business with both Artaria, the reputable Viennese firm

of art, map and music publishers, and Franz Anton Hoffmeister, a
composer of Wolfgang's age who had just started his own publishing business. But a letter from Wolfgang to Hoffmeister of
November 1785, when he was in the middle of this successful and
prolific period, is quite startling in its content: 'I turn to you in my
distress and beg you to help me out with some money, which I need
very badly at the moment.'[71] Wolfgang had been receiving decent
sums for all his compositions and performances at this time; but he
was clearly unable to control his spending of them.

Certainly, the gregarious Mozarts' social life was as hyperactive
as Wolfgang's creative genius. The Domgasse apartment was
always welcoming friends and colleagues for meals and music-
making. In addition to Wolfgang's composer friends Haydn,
Dittersdorf and Vanhal, with whom he regularly played string
quartets written by all of them, there were many singers. After
the great success of *Die Entführung*, which continued to appear
periodically in Vienna, the fashion for German-language singspiel
had been overtaken once more by the triumphant return of Italian
opera to the Burgtheater. From the 1783–4 season, there was therefore a large influx of singers, including the English soprano Nancy
Storace (together with her composer brother Stephen), the Irish
tenor Michael Kelly, and many Italians. The German opera company, including Aloysia, had moved to the Kärntnerthor-Theater in
1785. But singers from both companies found themselves in the
Domgasse apartment, and Wolfgang delighted in their vitality and
their talents. And in due course, as ever fitting his music like a good
tailor, he wrote for all of them.

The most hilarious occasion for the Mozarts' singing circle was
undoubtedly a party at Schönbrunn, organized by the Emperor
Joseph II himself. His sister Maria Christina was married to the
Governor General of the Netherlands, Duke Albert Kasimir of
Saxe-Teschen, and they were visiting Vienna early in 1786. The
Emperor asked Mozart and the Court composer Salieri each to write
a short work, in which the whole business of creating and perform-
ing opera was effectively sent up: singers were presented as being

temperamental, jealous and competitive, theatre managers as devious and neurotic, and composers and librettists as manipulative opportunists. Wolfgang's one-act opera, *Der Schauspieldirektor*, was to a text by his old collaborator from *Die Entführung*, Johann Gottlieb Stephanie, and other colleagues from the German opera company were brought in too. The two women associated with the role of Constanze in *Die Entführung*, namely Caterina Cavalieri who had created it, and of course Aloysia, played the rival divas Madame Silberklang and Madame Herz. The original Belmonte, Johann Adamberger, sang the tenor role of Monsieur Vogelsang. And the speaking parts were taken by a number of actors including Stephanie himself, his wife, and Aloysia's husband Joseph Lange. It was practically a family affair. After this came Salieri's *Prima la musica e poi le parole*, presented by the newer Italian opera company, whose singers included Nancy Storace, Francesco Benucci and Stefano Mandini, soon to be, respectively, Susanna, Figaro and the Count in *Le nozze di Figaro*. The two operas were presented one after the other at either end of the Orangery at Schönbrunn, with the audience sitting between them, and there was a magnificent banquet. It is hard to imagine a more brilliant occasion of first-rate music, superb individual performances and high-spirited, affectionate camaraderie.

Aloysia's appearance at this event in early February 1786 was happy confirmation of her good health. In 1785 she had apparently been 'gravely ill' for some weeks, and her return to work, as Constanze in *Die Entführung* at the Kärntnerthor-Theater, was an event of such importance that it was reported in the press. Even Leopold in Salzburg had heard of Aloysia's indisposition, and almost seemed disappointed when he cattily reported on her recovery in a letter to Nannerl in St Gilgen: 'Regarding the singer Lange, it's ridiculous, and can now be confirmed that she is not dead, for this appeared in the Regenspurger Zeitung from Vienna: "We would have lost the greatest singer". Then it goes on to discuss her husband, and give public testimonials of her faultless perform-ance, and so on.'[72]

Aloysia was indeed now at the forefront of her profession, having overtaken Caterina Cavalieri in popularity and accomplishment. The Irish tenor Michael Kelly recalled in his *Reminiscences*, some thirty years later:

> The first female singer was Madame Langé, wife to the excellent comedian of that name, and sister to Madame Mozart. She was a wonderful favourite, and deservedly so; she had a greater extent of high notes than any other singer I ever heard. The songs which Mozart composed for her in *L'Enlèvement du Sérail* [Kelly had evidently forgotten that Cavalieri, not Aloysia, had actually done the first performances] show what a compass of voice she had; her execution was brilliant.[73]

During Aloysia's illness her sister Constanze was concerned too, as she took care of her baby Carl and tried to keep up with the pace of her husband's life. They frequently had guests staying with them. Two Salzburg oboists, looking for work in Vienna, were there in January 1786. And they also took in the seven-year-old Johann Nepomuk Hummel, from Pressburg, who became Wolfgang's pupil. Wolfgang must have been especially sympathetic to a child prodigy, recognizing that strangely isolating gift that could bring both visionary joy and deep loneliness to a bewildered boy. He and Constanze treated the young Hummel as if he were their own son, and in adulthood Hummel always declared that, once he was successful, he would not fail to recompense Constanze for all the trouble she had taken, for the care he received, the cost of his board and lodging, and the lessons. (In fact he never honoured these effusive statements, greatly to Constanze's annoyance.) By the time of the Schönbrunn opera party, Constanze was pregnant once more, and her third son, Johann Thomas Leopold, was born on 18 October 1786. Sadly, this child also died within weeks of his birth, and again the Weber family, Constanze's mother and sisters, would have been on comforting hand. (Wolfgang did not even tell Leopold or Nannerl of this latest tragedy: they only found out months later, from a third party.)

Nannerl and Wolfgang had their
first performing portrait painted
in Paris in 1763. Their father
Leopold was included too;
for years afterwards he used
copies of the portrait as an
elaborate calling-card.

Leopold Mozart
in c. 1765.

Maria Anna Mozart
in 1775.

Opposite
After they had
performed for the
Empress Maria Theresa
in 1762, Nannerl and
Wolfgang were given
some of her own
children's clothes;
wearing these,
they then had their
portraits painted.

'You are the living chronicle of Salzburg, for you write down every single thing that occurs', wrote Wolfgang to Nannerl.

Top
A page from Nannerl's diary for 1764.

Bottom
Wolfgang would frequently hijack the diary, and make comments of his own.

Wolfgang's cousin,
Maria Anna Thekla Mozart,
known as the 'Bäsle'.
To her he wrote his most
startling letters, whilst
in his early twenties.

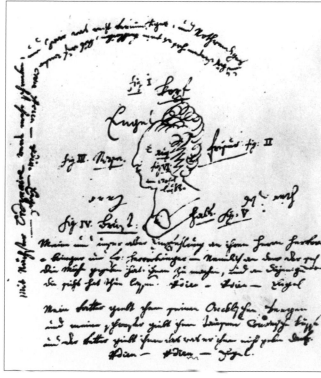

The young
Constanze Weber.

Wolfgang in 1777, wearing
the insignia of a Knight of
the Golden Spur.

Meiner lieben guten Mutter Caecilia Weber née Stamm.

Mozart's mother-in-law Cäcilia Weber, and her two most gifted daughters, Josefa (left), who created the Queen of the Night in *Die Zauberflöte* and Aloysia (right), Wolfgang's first love, and the inspiration for some of his greatest vocal music.

Leopold, Wolfgang and Nannerl were painted again in 1780.
By now Maria Anna was dead; but she was included,
as a loved portrait on the wall.

The Empress Maria Theresa, whose early enthusiasm for the Mozart family degenerated into impatient contempt as she described them as 'useless people'.

Joseph II, co-regent with his mother Maria Theresa, and then her successor. His own considerable musical appetite gave Mozart many opportunities for music-making at the highest level, but no permanent employment.

Dorotea Wendling, wife of Mozart's great friend, the flute player Johann Baptist Wendling. Dorotea created the role of Ilia in *Idomeneo*.

Elisabeth Augusta Wendling, wife of Johann Baptist's brother Franz Anton. She created the role of Elettra in *Idomeneo*.

Teresa Saporiti created
the role of Donna Anna in
Don Giovanni; apparently
she lived to be 106.

Josefa Duschek and her husband
Franz Xavier were good friends of the
Mozarts for many years. Wolfgang
wrote two concert arias for her, and
she and Constanze remained close
long after Mozart's death.

Actor, writer, composer and impresario,
Emanuel Schikaneder was one of
Mozart's closest collaborators. Together
they created *Die Zauberflöte*, and
Schikaneder played Papageno.

At the age of only twelve, Anna
Gottlieb created the role of Barbarina
in *Le nozze di Figaro*, and later,
still only seventeen, that of Pamina
in *Die Zauberflöte*.

Caterina Cavalieri (left) created the role of Constanze in *Die Entführung aus dem Serail*, and that of Madame Silberklang in *Der Schauspieldirektor*. The hugely charismatic Francesco Benucci (bottom) created the roles of Figaro, and of Guglielmo in *Così fan tutte*. Constanze's sister Aloysia married the actor Joseph Lange (top), who would later paint (though not completely finish) a portrait of Mozart. The two sisters and their husbands remained close until the end of Mozart's life. Stefano Mandini (right) created the role of the Count in *Figaro*.

The Residenztheater in Munich in Mozart's time.
Idomeneo was premiered here.

The Queen of the Night, in *Die Zauberflöte*, always had a spectacular entrance.

Mozart's men: three of his closest associates in Vienna.

Top left Joseph Haydn, passionate admirer, fellow composer and quartet-player, and dedicatee of six of Mozart's string quartets.

Top right Lorenzo Da Ponte, Mozart's collaborator on his three great 'modern' operas, *Le nozze di Figaro*, *Don Giovanni* and *Così fan tutte*.

Left Antonio Salieri, the charismatic operator at the heart of musical activity in Vienna throughout Mozart's time there. There was both mistrust and genuine affection between the two composers.

In womanhood,
Nannerl was described
as 'a regular beauty'.

The poignantly
unfinished portrait of
Mozart by Constanze's
brother-in-law, Joseph
Lange, Aloysia's
husband.

Constanze after Mozart.

Georg Nissen, Constanze's
second husband, and Mozart's
would-be biographer.

The 'family' grave in the cemetery of
St Sebastian in Salzburg.

When Constanze recovered, the Mozarts contemplated travel, inspired perhaps by their cosmopolitan acquaintance. Through their friendship with the Storaces and Kelly, they became keen on the idea of going to England. Wolfgang still retained happy memories of his childhood months in London, and once, after hearing with delight of an English victory over the French in 1782, even declared himself 'an out-and-out Englishman'.[74] He started brushing up his English, and wrote to ask Leopold if he would take care of Carl if he and Constanze travelled for a while. He had heard (not in fact directly from his father or sister) that Leopold was already looking after Leopoldl, and assumed therefore that he enjoyed having his grandchildren around him. He also trusted him to take good care of his child, as he had done of Nannerl and himself as children, in very extreme circumstances. But Leopold flatly refused. All the goodwill that had been so successfully nurtured and established during his visit to Vienna had totally evaporated in the ensuing months of poor communication. He wrote, somewhat hysterically, to Nannerl: 'So that is how the brilliant idea occurred to him or perhaps to his wife. Not at all a bad arrangement! They could go off and travel – they might even die – or remain in England – and I should have to run after them with the children.'[75]

In fact Wolfgang and Constanze abandoned their plan to go to England. But this was not because Leopold had refused to look after Carl. They had had another invitation.

~

WOLFGANG'S GROUNDBREAKING MASTERPIECE, *Le nozze di Figaro*, the first of his spectacular collaborations with Lorenzo Da Ponte, had been premiered in the Burgtheater in May 1786 to huge public acclaim. It was then taken up elsewhere, and in Prague it was a sensation. As Leopold reported to Nannerl, the Prague 'orchestra and a company of distinguished connoisseurs and lovers of music sent him letters inviting him to Prague and also a poem composed in his honour.'[76] So early in the new year of 1787, Wolfgang and Constanze set out, together with a small group of good friends including two musicians from the Vienna Court orchestra, a violinist, Franz Hofer, and a clarinettist, Anton Stadler. They left Carl in the care of some of Constanze's cousins, who were staying in the Domgasse apartment while they were away. On the morning of their departure, at five o'clock, Wolfgang wrote in the common-place book of twenty-one-year-old Edmund Weber (son of Constanze's uncle Franz Anton, and half-brother to the six-week-old baby Carl Maria von Weber): 'Be diligent – cultivate your work – and do not forget your cousin who loves you from his heart.'[77]

The five-week trip to Prague was a real tonic for Wolfgang and Constanze. As they travelled with their good friends, they were all in excellent spirits, and they whiled away the journeying hours by playing games, just as Wolfgang and Nannerl had done as children: 'We all invented names for ourselves on the journey. Here they are. I am Punkitititi. My wife is Schlaba Pumfa. Hofer is Rozka-Pumpa. Stadler is Natschibinitschibi.'[78]

When they arrived, Wolfgang was the toast of the town. 'For here they talk about nothing but "Figaro". Nothing is played, sung or whistled but "Figaro". No opera is drawing like "Figaro". Nothing, nothing but "Figaro". Certainly a great honour for me!'[79] Wolfgang conducted some performances of *Figaro* himself, and also gave a concert, which included a new symphony (the 'Prague' in D, K504), on 19 January. He and Constanze were royally entertained, slept a great deal, and had no time to write all the letters they had meant to write (though Constanze did manage to send one to her mother). When they left Prague, Wolfgang had a commission for a new opera, *Don Giovanni*, also in collaboration with Da Ponte. It was the beginning of a passionate relationship between him and the city of Prague.

But after this extremely agreeable start to 1787, things began to decline. When they returned to Vienna in mid-February, Wolfgang and Constanze did now seem financially stretched, and in April they reluctantly moved out of their splendid Domgasse apartment – those 460 florins per month were increasingly hard to find – to a much smaller one in the Landstrasse. And then Wolfgang received chilling news, probably from Nannerl. Leopold was seriously ill. In March, Nannerl herself had come in from St Gilgen to Salzburg, to take care of her father, and spent two months at his side. Wolfgang was profoundly shocked, but nevertheless wrote his father one of his very best letters, as, reacting also to the recent death of a close friend, he outlined his deeply positive views on the process, and indeed the purpose, of death:

> I have now made a habit of being prepared in all affairs of life for the worst. As death, when we come to consider it closely, is the true goal of our existence, I have formed during the last few years such close relations with this best and truest friend of mankind, that his image is not only no longer terrifying to me, but is indeed very soothing and consoling! And I thank God for graciously granting me the opportunity (you know what I mean) of learning that death is the key which unlocks the door to our true happiness. I never lie down at night without reflecting that, young as I am, I may not live to see another day. Yet no one of all my acquaintance could say that in company I am morose or disgruntled. For this blessing I daily thank my Creator and wish with all my heart that each one of my fellow-creatures could enjoy it.[80]

Leopold died on 28 May 1787, at six o'clock in the morning. He was sixty-seven-years old. Neither Wolfgang nor Nannerl was with their father at the end: Wolfgang was of course in Vienna; and even Nannerl in St Gilgen (to which she had only just returned) could not make it back to the Tanzmeisterhaus with any speed. For the same reasons, therefore, they did not attend Leopold's burial the following evening, beside his mother-in-law Eva Rosina, in the cemetery of the church of St Sebastian. When Wolfgang received the news, Constanze (pregnant again) was ill, and he was writing a note to his friend Gottfried von Jacquin: 'Please tell Herr Exner to come at nine o'clock tomorrow morning to bleed my wife . . . Today I received the sad news of my beloved father's death. You can imagine the state I am in.'[81]

But it had not been Nannerl who had written to Wolfgang. It

was Captain d'Ippold, her old friend and admirer, who had remained extremely close to Leopold after Nannerl's marriage and departure from Salzburg, and was also very attached to little Leopoldl. And although there was of course correspondence between brother and sister after Leopold's death, there was little real communication, or exchange of consolation. Wolfgang's letters to Nannerl in June 1787 are tight and formal, more concerned with the business side of Leopold's estate than with any sharing of grief. He certainly made no effort to visit Salzburg, either to comfort his sister or to be part of the process of sorting out Leopold's effects and the contents of the Tanzmeisterhaus. He could not afford the cost of the journey; he did not wish to leave his young family, especially in view of Constanze's pregnancy; and he had no time: *Don Giovanni* was due for performance in the autumn, and in addition he had as ever many smaller commissions. So he stayed where he was.

The death of Leopold was indeed a cataclysmic event for both Wolfgang and Nannerl. This stern, gifted, autocratic bully had been absolutely at the centre of their lives, not merely in childhood but way beyond it. 'After God comes Papa,' they would recite as children; and indeed it is almost as if Leopold saw himself as some sort of deus ex machina in their adulthood. When Wolfgang in particular went his own way, Leopold's frustration was intense. Nannerl had no doubt borne the brunt of this in her years at the Tanzmeisterhaus, but after her marriage, too, for he had continued to fuss over every detail of her life (her husband, her stepchildren, her servants, her health, her diet, even her bowels) in his weekly dispatches to St Gilgen; and of course he had also conveyed his judgements on the behaviour of her brother. But after the removal of this lifeline, St Gilgen must have felt even more remote. And, for all Wolfgang's stiff protestations of brotherly love and responsibility ('If you desire a kind brother to love and protect you, you will find one in me on every occasion'[82]), she knew she had effectively lost him too.

According to Leopold's will, Nannerl was to receive her father's money (no more than around 3,000 florins), and the property was to be divided between her and Wolfgang. She claimed certain items from the house, and put the rest up for auction. In the end, Wolfgang, in need of more immediate funds than the eventual proceeds of a long-drawn-out sale, relinquished his part in any of this, and requested instead a single payment of 1,000 florins. He only asked that his own music should be returned to him in Vienna. But he wanted no personal memento of his father, nor any of the memorabilia of the tours of his childhood, so many of which had literally furnished Leopold's house and lifestyle. He seemed to want the cleanest of breaks with his Salzburg past. It is probably significant that the first music that he wrote after Leopold's death was his outrageous *Musikalische Spaß* (Musical Joke), K522. This cruelly accurate and brilliant parody, of bad composition and bad performance, is completely hilarious. But, knowing Wolfgang's oft-stated contempt for all musicians in Salzburg, whether composers or performers ('rich in what is useless and superfluous, but very poor in what is necessary, and absolutely desititute of what is indispensable'), this *Spaß* can also be seen as his final, defiant, closing of the Salzburg gate.

~

In October 1787 Wolfgang and Constanze duly returned to Prague for *Don Giovanni*, K527. The new opera was originally planned to be part of the celebrations for the marriage of the Archduchess Maria Theresa, niece of the Emperor Joseph II, to Prince Anton Clemens of Saxony. In fact this had already taken place in Florence (Maria Theresa's father was the Archduke Leopold, Grand Duke of Tuscany) and then Dresden, but the Archduchess came to Prague in October. *Don Giovanni* was however immensely complex and difficult (its innovations included having three on-stage orchestras playing very different music at the same time, and some extremely challenging stage effects) and was not properly prepared in time for her visit, so *Figaro* was presented instead. Only after the Imperial departure was *Don Giovanni* finally

ready, and Wolfgang conducted the premiere on 29 October. Even
then he had had to stay up all night to write the overture, which,
according to a member of the orchestra at the time, 'had not even
been sketched'. Contanze's support in this last-minute crisis was
crucial:

> Mozart's wife, however, undertook that the overture should be
> finished in time. She accordingly sat up with her husband,
> although she found it difficult to keep awake. As he wrote, the
> sheets of the score were passed from his desk to those of a little
> army of copyists who were in attendance to transcribe the instru-
> mental parts. Again and again was the great maestro overpowered
> by sleep, and every time he was aroused by his vigilant help-
> mate . . . The ink . . . was hardly dry on some of the pages when
> they were placed on the desks of the orchestra.[83]

And yet the Prague musicians played this demandingly difficult
music at sight, and must therefore have been extremely able. No
wonder Wolfgang enjoyed working with them.

This was no doubt a somewhat fraught period for Wolfgang. Da
Ponte had only been with him in Prague for one week; and although
Wolfgang's good friends Josefa and Franz Xavier Duschek were
also in the city (he managed to write Josefa another concert aria,
'Bella mia fiamma', K528), he must have appreciated the supportive
and practical presence of Constanze. And she had her own support
too: her aunt Adelheid (her father's elder sister) had come to
Prague, and wrote affectionately in Wolfgang's album at the end of
their visit: 'He who knows not genuine, heartfelt, unselfish friendship does not know the best that men can give each other. This, dear
Mozart, is offered to you with a full heart by your true friend and
aunt Weber.'[84]

Wolfgang had always needed to write diary-like letters, giving
regular accounts of his dramatic activities, and now these had to be
directed to someone other than his father. But it was not to Nannerl
that he conveyed his reports, but to his young friend and pupil
Gottfried von Jacquin. Only after his return to Vienna did he

remember to write to Nannerl at all, and that was really because he wanted his own scores sent from Salzburg. And he did have another piece of news. The day before he and Constanze arrived back from Prague, Gluck had died. At the beginning of December, Wolfgang was appointed in his place as Imperial Court Composer (Kammermusikus) but at a considerably smaller salary (800 florins per annum) than that of Gluck (2,000 florins per annum). Although in reality he was only required to write dances for the Court's masked balls, he could at last sign himself 'I[mperial] & R[oyal] Chamber Musician'. This change of status encouraged Wolfgang and Constanze to move back into the heart of Vienna, to an apartment in Unter den Tuchlauben, very near Frau Weber. Constanze was about to be delivered of her baby, and they preferred to be near the rest of the family. Their daughter, Theresia Constanzia Adelheid Fredericke Maria Anna, was born on 27 December. There is no record of Wolfgang ever informing Nannerl of the arrival of her new niece.

There were changes for Aloysia too. Also in December 1787, the German opera company was finally disbanded, and Aloysia went over to the Italian company. Early in 1788 she was again involved in her brother-in-law's music: he wrote another concert aria for her, 'Ah, se in ciel, benigne stelle', K538 (very much to the successful formulae of those he had written for her earlier – when indeed this one may have been sketched – but lacking perhaps the deep emotional intensity of those first collaborations), and she also performed in Wolfgang's arrangement of C. P. E. Bach's Resurrection Cantata, when Wolfgang himself performed his new piano concerto in D, K537. Wolfgang would have been delighted by Aloysia's transference to the Italian opera company, for they were to present the first Viennese performances of *Don Giovanni*. And, sure enough, Aloysia was cast (most appropriately, for it was exactly her sort of music) as Donna Anna. Her long-time rival Caterina Cavalieri was given the role of Donna Elvira, and insisted on having some new music written especially for her ('Mi tradì quell'alma ingrata'), lest she be outshone by the new arrival in the Italian company. The rest of the cast included many old colleagues from the *Figaro* team. *Don Giovanni* had its Viennese premiere on 7 May 1788, and there were then fifteen more performances before the end of the year. But again, the inherent complexity of the work, quite apart from its startling subject-matter, meant that it was not the resounding success that Wolfgang had hoped it would be. According to Lorenzo Da Ponte, Joseph II had remarked coolly that it was 'not the food for the teeth of my Viennese'. When this Imperial judgement was reported to Wolfgang, he commented rather astutely, 'Let us give them time to chew it.'[85]

In that summer of 1788 there were both excitements and tragedies for the Weber sisters. Josefa, the eldest, married Wolfgang's great friend, the violinist Franz Hofer, on 21 August. (One of the witnesses, as he had been at Constanze's wedding, was Johann Thorwart, the Weber sisters' legal guardian.) It was Hofer who had accompanied Wolfgang and Constanze to Prague on their first visit in January 1787: he must have met Josefa through the Mozarts. And she too was about to become spectacularly involved in her brother-in-law's music. Her singing career had thus far been less prominent than Aloysia's, but she was soon to join the company at the Freihaus-Theater and assume a much larger profile in the Viennese musical scene. Conversely, Aloysia herself was withdrawing temporarily from the limelight. For one thing, she was pregnant again (which must have made her performances as Donna Anna especially interesting). But Austria was now at war with Turkey, and the country's finances were being drained, with inevitable repercussions on the cultural life of Vienna. Many companies, including the Italian opera company, were being disbanded, and Aloysia feared that her lack of employment might be more permanent after the birth of her baby. And for Constanze and Wolfgang there was another painful tragedy. Their own baby daughter Theresia died in June, aged only six months. Later that summer they moved yet again, away from the centre of Vienna to Wahringergasse in the suburbs, continuing therefore their almost gypsy-like regime of settling nowhere for longer than a few months at a time. This new lodging did have a garden, which Constanze loved very much, and was much healthier for their four-year-old son Carl as well as for themselves. And it was here, in those summer months, that Wolfgang composed his monumental last three symphonies (no. 39 in E flat, K543, no. 40 in G minor, K550, and no. 41 in C, K551). None of these was actually commissioned, so unusually there was no financial incentive, let alone reward, for writing them. And yet they represent the summit of Wolfgang's symphonic genius. For him the creation of these unquestionable masterpieces was an escape from his personal sorrows and professional anxieties: he entered an untroubled, alternative world – his adult 'Kingdom of Back' – where his gifts prospered and soared. The coda to symphony no. 41 in C, for instance, with its effortlessly brilliant five-part invertible counterpoint, is truly Olympian, hence, probably, its subsequently acquired sobriquet, the 'Jupiter' symphony.

Among the visitors to the Mozarts in the Wahringergasse that summer was a Danish actor, Johann Daniel Preisler, who was on a theatre-visiting tour of Europe. First he had met Joseph Lange, who took him home to meet Aloysia and persuaded her to sing for him, despite her pregnancy. Preisler was captivated, not just by Aloysia's commanding presence ('a melancholy ecstasy was to be read at once in her eyes'[86]), but by the fact that she accompanied herself 'like a Kapellmeister'. Lange then took Preisler to the Mozarts, and the scene he painted in his subsequent journal was of a blissful family idyll:

> There I had the happiest hour of music that has ever fallen to my lot. This small man and great master twice extemporized on a pedal pianoforte, so wonderfully! so wonderfully! that I quite lost myself. He intertwined the most difficult passages with the most lovely themes. His wife cut quill pens for the copyist, a pupil composed, a little boy of four walked around the garden and sang recitatives – in short, everything that surrounded this splendid man was *musical*![87]

But the reality of that summer was a long way from the lucky young Dane's euphoric interpretation. A clue might be found in his observation of Constanze cutting quill pens for the copyist (something she had probably done since childhood, for her copyist father): was this a sign of economy? It was in this summer that Wolfgang began a long and desperate series of letters to a fellow Freemason, Michael Puchberg. He was now having literally to beg for money.

The Mozarts had in fact been living beyond their means for some time. The ruinous rent of the Domgasse apartment had bled them dry, but they had stayed there for two and a half years because, quite apart from the joy and convenience of it, they needed to keep up appearances with their colleagues. Virtually everybody else they knew had regular salaries; and although Wolfgang frequently received commissions and subscriptions from his continual stream of compositions and performances in the mid-1780s, the very irregularity and unpredictability of this income only confirmed the truly precarious nature of existing outside the conventional system. All Leopold's fears for his son, after his perilous decision to live as an independent, freelance musician, were now being realized. It is indeed ironic that the first appearance of Michael Puchberg in the Mozart correspondence is in a letter from Wolfgang to Nannerl's husband Johann Baptist Berchtold about his share of Leopold's estate: he asked Berchtold to send his 1,000 florins straight to Puchberg. He was probably in deep trouble already.

Michael Puchberg was a Viennese merchant and fellow Freemason, who responded kindly over the years to Wolfgang's cries for help. From time to time he let him have small sums, varying from 10 florins to 300 florins. None of them was ever enough (on one truly desperate occasion in June 1788, Wolfgang had even wildly suggested that Puchberg lend him 'for a year, or two, one or two thousand florins'[88]), but every loan brought at least temporary relief, and the two men became good friends. On Wolfgang's next trip out of Vienna, when he and Constanze were to be apart for the first time since their marriage, she and their son Carl stayed with the Puchbergs. There was genuine affection between the two families.

Wolfgang was in fact rather in need of a change of musical scene. After his solid successes with the Viennese audiences in the mid-1780s, his star had waned somewhat. He had stopped putting on his own subscription concerts (no doubt the time taken to compose his two huge Da Ponte operas had precluded any great organizational activity), and other musicians were now capturing public attention. Not for the first time, he found he was no longer the sensation that he had been in his immediate past. But he did still have his staunch supporters, among them Baron van Swieten. This civilized, distinguished diplomat was the son of Maria Theresa's personal physician. In his early working years he had gained wide diplomatic experience in Brussels, Paris, Warsaw and Berlin, but since 1777 he had been back in Vienna as head of the Education and Censorship Commission. The Baron was a knowledgeable and passionate music-lover, and he befriended many of Vienna's foremost musicians, including Haydn, for whom in due course he would provide the texts of *The Creation* and *The Seasons*. It was he who had first introduced Wolfgang to the music of Bach and Handel, which he had learned to love in his days in Berlin.

Now in early 1789 the Baron asked Wolfgang to modernize some of Handel's choral masterpieces (for, in an era when all music was contemporary, anything even a few decades old was considered old-fashioned). Wolfgang duly made extremely deft and witty reorchestrations of Handel's *Acis and Galatea*, K566, and then *Messiah*, K572; and the equally loyal Aloysia was on hand to sing the solos in the performance of *Messiah* on 6 March. Wolfgang rather tactfully gave some of Handel's very florid choral writing (the really tricky sections of 'And he shall purify' and 'His yoke is easy', for instance) to his soloists, who also included Adamberger, his first Belmonte, knowing that their coloratura would cope easily with what many choristers find a challenge. He also wrote for Aloysia the one completely new movement, setting 'If God be for us' as an accompanied recitative. (Later that year, after the Italian opera company had been disbanded, Aloysia continued her Mozartian allegiance and identity by singing the role of Constanze, to great acclaim, in Hamburg and Berlin.)

Wolfgang himself planned a trip to Berlin, via Prague, Dresden and Leipzig. Like so many of his trips in the past, the object was to drum up support and employment, and in that regard, like the others, it failed. But it was undertaken in the company of Count Karl Lichnowsky (later a patron to Beethoven), another Freemason and possibly also a pupil of Wolfgang's. He probably subsidized Wolfgang's expenses, and Wolfgang borrowed too from yet a third fellow Freemason, Franz Hofdemel. He was away from Vienna for two and a half months.

Within hours of leaving, Wolfgang was desperately homesick, and he wrote the first in a series of touching letters to Constanze:

> Dearest little Wife! While the Prince is busy bargaining about horses, I am delighted to seize this opportunity to write a few lines to you, dearest little wife of my heart. How are you? I wonder whether you think of me as often as I think of you. Every other moment I look at your portrait – and weep partly for joy, partly for sorrow. Look after your health which is so precious to me and fare well, my darling! Do not worry about me, for I am not suffering any discomforts or annoyances on this journey – apart from your *absence* – which, as it can't be helped, can't be remedied. I write this note with eyes full of tears. Adieu.[89]

And although, throughout this long and fruitless trip, Wolfgang received a great deal of female attention, some from old friends and some from new ones, he continued to ache for his 'beloved little wife' ('Today is the sixth day since I left you, and, by Heaven! it seems a year'[90]) to whose portrait he apparently talked 'for a good half hour' every night and morning. He wanted to check that her own family were playing their part, and visiting her at the Puchbergs':

> I should very much like to know whether our brother-in-law Hofer came to see us the day after my departure? Whether he

comes very often, as he promised me he would? Whether the Langes come sometimes? Whether progress is being made with the portrait? What sort of life you are leading? All these things are naturally of great interest to me.[91]

(This almost sounds like one of his mother's questionnaires.) Some letters that Wolfgang and Constanze wrote to each other seem to have gone astray, to their shared misery and dismay. Perhaps they each began to doubt the other's loyalty, for Constanze accused Wolfgang of having forgotten her, and he anxiously begged her to be careful of her honour. When these tensions were at their worst, he made a meticulous list of all the letters he had sent and received (so the family passion for list-making had not completely passed him by, either), as if to prove that he himself was blameless in the mysteries of postal non-delivery. But he also had to warn Constanze that the hoped-for riches, that were the very purpose of this whole trip, were not forthcoming ('my darling little wife, when I return you must be more delighted with having me back than with the money I shall bring'). He actually blamed Lichnowsky, and parted company with him. As he made his long and disconsolate way home, he asked that his best friends Michael Puchberg and Franz Hofer come with Constanze to meet him at the first staging-post. But it was his physical longing for Constanze, and the prospect of being with her once more, that kept him going:

> Arrange your dear sweet nest very daintily, for my little fellow deserves it indeed, he has really behaved himself very well and is only longing to possess your sweetest [*word deleted*]. Just picture to yourself that rascal; as I write he crawls on to the table and looks at me questioningly. I however box his ears properly – but the rogue is simply [*word deleted*] and now the knave burns only more fiercely and can hardly be restrained.[92]

The homecoming at the beginning of June was no doubt as passionate as Wolfgang had hoped, not least because he learned that Constanze was once again pregnant. But in one sense this news would have appalled him. To incur the necessary medical expenses for childbirth (about which Leopold had complained at Wolfgang's own birth), and indeed to expand his family at all at this financially disastrous time, must have filled him with dread. Worse was to come: Constanze became dangerously ill. She incurred some infection in her foot, which became ulcerated, and even the bone was threatened. She was bedridden for a long time, and did not fully recover for eighteen months. Her family rallied round her. Sophie came to take care of her in the apartment in the Judenplatz, where the Mozarts were now living; and their mother came too, to look after the running of the house, but, as Sophie told Nissen, years later, 'secretly, for we did not want [Constanze] to realize how ill she was.'[93] Wolfgang was desperate with worry, and, as Sophie again was later to recount, would endure all manner of personal discomfort in the interests of Constanze's recovery:

> How attentive Mozart was when something was wrong with his dear wife. Thus it was once when she was seriously ill and I nursed her for eight long months. I was just sitting by her bed, Mozart too. He was composing at her side; I was observing her sweet slumber, which had been so long in coming. We kept as quiet as the grave so as not to disturb her. Suddenly an unmannerly servant came into the room. Mozart was terrified that his dear wife might be disturbed from her gentle sleep, tried to beckon the man to keep quiet, pushed the chair back behind him, but happened to have the pen-knife open in his hand. This impaled itself between the chair and the thigh in such a way that it dug in up to the handle in his flesh. Mozart, who usually made such a fuss, did not stir, but, biting back the pain, signalled me to follow him. We left the room . . . and our mother bound him up . . . Although he had to limp somewhat from the pain, he managed to conceal it from his dear wife.[94]

When Constanze was well enough, she went to take the cure at the nearby spa of Baden. The Mozarts could not afford this at all, but for every possible reason, not least Constanze's pregnancy, they felt she needed to go. Once more, Wolfgang had to beg for a large sum of money from Michael Puchberg, and, to an extent at least, Puchberg complied. By this time Wolfgang was working furiously on his third opera in collaboration with Lorenzo Da Ponte, *Così fan tutte*, K588 (a libretto which had first been given to Salieri, who had turned it down), and, what with that and writing new music for a revival of *Figaro*, he could not be with his wife all the time, though he did make quick visits to Baden to see her ('to stay here until the 19th without you would be quite impossible'[95]). And again, as was so often the case when they were apart, his anxiety about her led him to entertain jealous suspicion of her naturally high spirits, and therefore to write (almost like his father) stern moralistic homilies:

> Dear little wife! I want to talk to you quite frankly. You have no reason whatever to be unhappy. You have a husband who loves you and does all he possibly can for you. As for your foot, you must just be patient and it will surely get well again. I am indeed glad when you have some fun – of course I am – but I do wish that you would not sometimes make yourself so cheap. In my opinion you are too free and easy . . . A woman must always make herself respected, or else people will begin to talk about her.[96]

Constanze did benefit from her time in Baden, and returned to Vienna in the autumn. But when her baby, another girl whom they named Anna Maria, was born on 16 November, she was sickly and lived only one hour. And again, Wolfgang's only real escape from all this tragedy and alarming anxiety, was into his own creative world. At the end of 1789 he was writing not only *Così fan tutte*, but his exquisite clarinet quintet in A, K581, which his friend Anton Stadler performed at a 'Grand Musical Concert' presented by the Tonkünstler-Societät on 22 December. (Wolfgang's sister-in-law Josefa also took part in this concert, singing the soprano solos in a cantata by her former teacher Vincenzo Righini – whom Wolfgang rather despised.)

As the decade changed in 1790, apart from the immediate excitement of *Così fan tutte*, the future looked bleak. In her still feeble state, Constanze was probably shielded from the whole truth, but Wolfgang was again having to plead for cash with Michael Puchberg. Swayed perhaps by the seductive invitation to attend, with Haydn, some closed rehearsals of *Così fan tutte*, Puchberg duly handed over 300 florins. But throughout the first half of the new year Wolfgang continued to write to him regularly and pathetically, asking for more ('even though it be only the small sum you sent last time'[97]), and the loyal Puchberg generally complied. *Così fan tutte* was a success. Its apparently frivolous subject-matter appealed more than the shocking violence of *Don Giovanni* to Viennese audiences, who probably failed to recognize its damning indictment of human behaviour (their own). Count Zinzendorf described the music as 'charming, and the subject rather amusing'.[98] But there were only five performances, because in February Vienna and the whole of the Habsburg Empire were thrown into turmoil by the death of Joseph II.

For Wolfgang this was indeed the end of an era. Joseph had known him since boyhood, and, although he had never found the opportunity to give him a really prestigious post (perhaps he was still influenced by his mother Maria Theresa's dismissal of the Mozarts as 'useless people'), he had encouraged and applauded and to some extent even appreciated Wolfgang's gifts. Wolfgang had to begin all over again to create a relationship with Joseph's successor, his younger brother Leopold, Grand Duke of Tuscany. He began a letter to Leopold's son, the Archduke Franz, asking if he might perhaps be considered for the post of second Kapellmeister, but he never finished it. He seemed, at this time of crisis, to be completely lacking in confidence.

In the summer of 1790, Constanze was ill again. She went back to Baden to recuperate in its rural airiness, which she loved, and for a time Wolfgang stayed there too. He returned to Vienna without her, to conduct *Così fan tutte* again, and also to do some more Handel arrangements (*Alexander's Feast*, K591, and *Ode to St Cecilia*, K592) for the ever-enthusiastic Baron van Swieten. But when they were apart, Wolfgang's thoughts vacillated between deep longing for Constanze and irritability that she had apparently not replied to his letters. There were clearly tensions in the marriage at this point. And then he too became ill. His letter to Puchberg of 14 August shows just how low his spirits had sunk:

> Whereas I felt tolerably well yesterday, I am absolutely wretched today. I could not sleep all night for pain. I must have got over-heated from walking so much, and then without knowing it have caught a chill. Picture to yourself my condition – ill and consumed by worries and anxieties. Such a state quite definitely prevents me from recovering. In a week or a fortnight I shall be better off – certainly – but at present I am in want! Can you not help me out with a trifle? The *smallest* sum would be very welcome just now. You would, for the moment at least, bring peace of mind to your true friend, servant and brother.[99]

Yet more disappointment followed after the summer. In September there were big celebrations in Vienna for the double wedding of Maria Theresa and Louisa, daughters of King Ferdinand and Queen Karoline of Naples, to their Habsburg cousins, Archdukes Franz and Ferdinand. Among the festivities were operas by Salieri and Weigl, and concerts of music by a great number of composers, including Haydn. But Wolfgang was completely ignored. Similarly, when the new Emperor Leopold II was crowned in Frankfurt, several Viennese musicians were invited to go there to take part in the festivities. Again, Wolfgang was not one of them. In desperation he decided to go to Frankfurt anyway, under his own steam. He would put on his own concerts and attract the attention of all the gathered nobility of Europe. Once again, he asked his good friend and brother-in-law Franz Hofer to travel with him. (Since the death of his mother in Paris, and his chaotic return on his own, Wolfgang had hated to travel without company. His journey back from Berlin in the previous summer, after his falling-out with Count Lichnowsky, had likewise made him miserable; and he knew he would be better off with a companion.)

Hofer agreed to go, despite the fact that his own wife Josefa had just had a baby – a little girl also called Josefa, who in due course would continue the Weber family tradition and become a celebrated singer herself. Wolfgang somehow bought a carriage, which he adored ('I should like to give it a kiss!'[100] he wrote to Constanze) and set out. He and Hofer were away from their Weber wives for six weeks. As could really have been predicted, the trip was not successful at all, for although Wolfgang gave his concerts in Frankfurt and met many of the right people, he never even got close to the new Emperor, let alone performed for him. But there were some joys, for he and Hofer went on to Mainz, Mannheim and Munich; and he had happy reunions with many of their old friends including the Cannabichs and Marchands, who made a big fuss of him as always. He felt in considerably better spirits as he began his return journey, and even contemplated returning with Constanze the following year.

Meanwhile, Constanze had at last realized how desperate their situation was, and had begun to take control of it. If Wolfgang had tried to shield her up to this point, he had only got them deeper into trouble. So while he was away, Constanze directed her acute practicality towards solving the problems. First, with the help of Stadler, she negotiated a loan against all their furniture, not from Michael Puchberg but from another merchant, Heinrich Lackenbacher. The sum, 1,000 florins, was large enough to cover Wolfgang's debts and leave them something to live on, and was to be repaid over the next two years, at 5 per cent interest, through the profits of some new publications set up with Hoffmeister. Wolfgang knew she was now handling all this, and his letters from Frankfurt had a new and grateful respect for her, almost as a business partner. But he was determined to play his part too, and expressed this resolve with Chekhovian intensity: 'I am longing for news of you, of your health, our affairs and so forth. I am firmly resolved to make as much money as I can here and then return to you with great joy. What a glorious life we shall have then! I will work – work so hard – that no unforeseen accidents shall ever reduce us to such desperate straits again.'[101]

As well as trying to sort out their money problems, Constanze also organized another house move. She found a first-floor apartment on Rauhensteingasse, with enough room for Wolfgang's teaching and chamber music, and a courtyard below that could take his beloved carriage and horse. Wolfgang himself was anxious to see their new home, and could not wait to return to his family. Soon after their reunion, Constanze was pregnant again.

If Constanze was now to take greater control of their finances, Wolfgang kept to his side of the bargain and worked extremely hard. He produced sets of German dances, K599–607, for winter balls at Court, as was required by his appointment as Kammer-musikus; and he wrote chamber music for publication by Hoff-meister, as part of the loan agreement set up by Constanze. Some of this was first performed in their new home: Haydn joined them at the end of December, for instance, to play through a new string quintet in D, K593. Invitations started arriving, including not one but two to travel to England. The first was from a Mr Robert May O'Reilly, who tried to persuade Wolfgang to go for six months from December 1791, for a large fee (2,400 florins); and the famous London impresario, Johann Peter Salomon, came in person to Vienna to invite both Wolfgang and Haydn. Haydn was excited, as he had never before travelled very far afield, and he accepted his invitation. But Wolfgang declined his: he was no longer prepared to go anywhere without Constanze, and there was no question of travelling at all now before the arrival of the baby. Furthermore, there did at last seem to be other promising opportunities develop-ing in Vienna.

Possibly with the help of Aloysia, Wolfgang started appearing again on Vienna's performance scene. In March, he took part in a concert put on by the newest young sensation, a twenty-one-year-old clarinet virtuoso, Joseph Bähr. Wolfgang played his latest piano concerto, in B flat, K595, and Aloysia sang. In April, two huge con-certs, involving 180 musicians conducted by Salieri, were mounted by the Tonkünstler-Societät. Again, Aloysia was one of the singers: as an insertion into extracts from Paisiello's *Phedra*, she performed 'No, che non sei capace', which Wolfgang had written for her in 1783. And the programme began with one of Wolfgang's symphonies. There were other positive developments too. Also in April, Wolfgang successfully petitioned the Magistracy of Vienna for the post of assistant to the Kapellmeister: the job was unpaid, but carried with it a guarantee to succeed the present incumbent, Leopold Hofmann, upon his death or retirement. But the most exciting prospect of all came from a commercial venture, the Freihaus-Theater an der Wieden. Since July 1789 it had been run by Wolfgang's old theatrical friend, the multitalented writer, manager, singer, actor, dancer and composer, Emanuel Schikaneder.

The Freihaus-Theater was located in a large self-contained complex of buildings, including apartments, gardens, shops and a chapel. The theatre itself, which Schikaneder restored most elegantly, was well equipped and seated a thousand people. Schikaneder settled his company in this ideal living and working environment, inheriting some actors and singers from his predecessor, including Constanze's sister Josefa, and adding new ones, among them the latest teenage singing sensation, Anna Gottlieb (who had sung Barbarina in *Figaro* in 1786, at the age of twelve), the tenor and composer Benedikt Schack, the bass and composer Franz Xavier Gerl, and a young tenor, Jakob Haibl (who in due course would marry the youngest of the Weber sisters, Sophie). The company had had great success performing plays and singspiels to the Viennese public. And now, in the summer of 1791, Schikaneder and Wolfgang agreed to collaborate on a vast and fantastical spectacle, at once comic and serious, light-hearted and profound. This would be *Die Zauberflöte*, K620. Schikaneder himself would play the central role of Papageno, Schack would be Tamino and Gerl Sarastro. The Queen of the Night was to be sung by Wolfgang's sister-in-law, Josefa Hofer.

As if this exciting new assignment was not enough, Wolfgang received two more enormous commissions in the summer of 1791. The new Emperor Leopold II was now to be crowned King of Bohemia, and for those ceremonies in Prague, the Bavarian Estates asked Wolfgang to write an opera. (Salieri had been approached first, but, because of pressure of other work, had turned down the offer.) If Wolfgang had hoped to work again with Lorenzo Da Ponte, for their collaborations had always been so well received in Prague, he was thwarted: Da Ponte was no longer in Vienna. So an old libretto was chosen, one appropriate to the notion of a forgiving and benevolent emperor, Metastasio's *La clemenza di Tito*. Wolfgang would have to go to Prague in late August. Meanwhile he received his third commission, and this was the strangest of them all, for it was to remain a secret.

Count Franz Walsegg-Stuppach was a wealthy landowner with a sizeable estate on the edge of Simmering Forest, some 30 kilometres from Vienna. An unassuming eccentric, he was popular with his own tenants, and his acquaintance included members of the Imperial family, who would come annually to hunt and be entertained at Stuppach Castle. The Count was also a keen music-lover, and it was his custom to have string quartets and other chamber music played in his castle twice a week. His enthusiasms led him into deceitful action, however. He himself dabbled in composition, and loved the idea of having his own music performed. But when he found himself unequal to the task of actually producing it, he would purchase other composers' works, have them recopied with no indication of authorship, and pass them off as his own. After a piece had been played through, the instrumentalists would be asked to guess its composer. Years later, this procedure was affectionately described by one of the participants, a local schoolteacher and violinist, Anton Herzog: 'Usually our guess would be the Count himself, for he had composed some trifles now and then. He then would smile, pleased that he had tricked us, or so he thought. But we laughed that he would think us so naive. We were young then and thought that we were merely providing some harmless fun for the Count.'[102]

In February of 1791 the Count's young wife Anna had died at the tragically early age of twenty, and he wished to have a Requiem Mass composed for her. And, as was by now his accustomed practice, he almost certainly wanted to have it believed that he had written it himself. He would have known of Mozart, for he had some of his chamber music in his possession at the castle. And he knew how to get hold of him: one of his tenants at his Vienna residence, in Hoher Markt, was none other than Michael Puchberg. So the Count sent a note to him, via the administrator of one of his other estates, Franz Anton Leitgeb. Wolfgang was asked if he would undertake to write a Mass for the Dead, and if so to state his fee. Wolfgang accepted the undertaking and named his fee, though when Leitgeb returned again he brought 50 ducats (225 florins) as a down payment and the 'promise of a considerable additional sum, since Mozart's quoted fee had been too low'.[103] Leitgeb, who did not identify himself any more than he did his master, reiterated the specific instruction that Wolfgang should not attempt to identify his patron.

Wolfgang probably saw through all this weird subterfuge and went happily along with it, like the local musicians at Stuppach. He was never averse to hoaxes and practical jokes, and had been known in the past to compose for other people if necessary (he had once helped out an ailing Michael Haydn in Salzburg). He would have seen this new commission as another lucrative channel for putting the family finances on a more even keel, his only anxiety at this early stage being one of actually finding time to write his Requiem, given all his other heavy commitments.

With a little more money now in the coffers, Constanze went again to Baden at the beginning of June, there to prepare for her forthcoming confinement. She took their six-year-old son Carl with her, and a maid, and was also later joined by Wolfgang's twenty-five-year-old pupil Franz Xaver Süssmayr. Working as some kind of amanuensis to Wolfgang (his handwriting was almost identical to that of his teacher), Süssmayr organized such sections of *Die Zauberflöte* as Wolfgang sent to him or left with him after his own visits, and also looked after the needs of Constanze and Carl. The local schoolteacher and choirmaster, Anton Stoll, was closely involved in the Mozart party that summer, too. He helped arrange suitable accommodation for Constanze (on the ground floor, as her injured foot was still troublesome), and was close also to

Süssmayr, who later sent messages to a Baden girl through him. Wolfgang repaid his gratitude to Stoll that summer, on one of his visits, by writing him a motet for his church choir; and, on 23 June, the lucky Stoll directed the first performance of *Ave verum corpus*, K618.

Wolfgang's regular letters to Constanze when he was not with her reveal renewed energy and spirit. Sometimes he wrote to her in French (which she spoke well). He was getting up at 4.30 in the morning to compose, he told her. He still missed her desperately, and as always longed for their reunions ('I expect to find in your arms all the joy which only a man can feel who loves his wife as I do'[104]). But he was basically cheerful and lively, gently bossy about her regime ('Take an electuary if you are constipated – not other-wise. Take care of yourself in the morning and in the evening, if it is chilly'[105]), and full of light-hearted gossip about their friends. He sent her money regularly, so that she could pay for her baths. (On 3 July he apologized for only being able to send 3 florins, though on the next day he sent her 25, and promised that when he arrived in Baden he would pay all her bills. He had probably just received his large down-payment for the Requiem Mass, from Count Walsegg.) He also reported occasionally and self-deprecatingly on his work composing *Die Zauberflöte* ('From sheer boredom today I com-posed an aria for my opera'[106]), and, very rarely, even quoted from it ('I kiss you 1,000 times and say with you in thought: "Death and despair were his reward"!'[107]). Constanze evidently wrote long letters back, which cheered Wolfgang immensely when he was missing her so much. And she was also keenly involved still in their business and financial arrangements: 'Thank you,' he wrote, 'for your advice not to rely entirely on N.N.'[108] ('N.N.', shorthand for 'non nominato', or unnamed, was often used in Wolfgang's letters when he wished to be secretive about someone's identity, and con-ceal it from potentially prying eyes. In its numerous manifestations in the Mozart correspondence, 'N.N.' therefore referred to several different people; and in this instance was probably the Viennese iron merchant Joseph Goldhahn, who was tangentially involved in the Mozarts' financial affairs at the time.)

At last Constanze returned to Vienna, and their son Franz Xavier was born on 26 July. He was a healthy baby who would live into his fifties. But within a month she had to leave him in the care of Sophie and their mother, and also put Carl into a kindergarten in Perchtoldsdorf. She herself was to go with Wolfgang to Prague. As they were literally on the point of leaving, a stranger (to Constanze) appeared ('a ghostly messenger', as she described him to one of Wolfgang's early biographers). He touched her coat and asked, 'What about the Requiem?'[109] Wolfgang apologized, but explained that he had to go to Prague, and that he had been unable to inform his unknown commissioner about his Imperial duties there, as he did not know him; but that he would address himself to the Requiem as soon as he returned. This seemed to satisfy the messenger, and so the Mozarts went on their way. In his role still as Wolfgang's assistant, Süssmayr went too: he copied much of the material for *La clemenza di Tito*, K621, and even wrote the recitatives. And their close friend Anton Stadler also travelled to Prague, as he was engaged to play in the new opera (so Wolfgang made sure he wrote some spectacular clarinet solos). *Don Giovanni* was revived for the Emperor on 2 September, and the new opera was premiered on the 6th, with another old friend in the title role, Antonio Baglioni, who had created the role of Don Ottavio in *Don Giovanni*.

As soon as *La clemenza di Tito* was up and running, Wolfgang and Constanze rushed back to Vienna, for *Die Zauberflöte* was to open just three weeks later on 30 September. Wolfgang conducted the premiere himself, and the opera became an overnight success. The Mozarts were now much more secure financially, and for all possible reasons could once again hold their heads high. The crisis was over. But there had been a price to pay for this turnaround. After such a summer, with two huge operas presented one after the other in different cities, with the birth of a new child and many long journeys, both Wolfgang and Constanze were exhausted.

Constanze went back to Baden for another week in early October, taking little Franz Xavier with her, and also her sister Sophie, to continue to help with the baby. Süssmayr went to Baden too, and almost certainly stayed with Stoll. Wolfgang stayed in Vienna, to pay occasional visits to *Die Zauberflöte* at the Freihaus-Theater, to work on yet another new commission (Anton Stadler now wanted a concerto for his clarinet), and of course to continue writing his Requiem.

In that week in October when Constanze was in Baden – the last week in fact that she and Wolfgang were ever to be apart in his life-time – he missed her horribly as always ('I already feel lonely without you. I knew I would'[110]), but was otherwise in wonderful spirits. The huge success of *Die Zauberflöte* thrilled him ('What always gives me the most pleasure is the *silent approval*! You can see how this opera is becoming more and more esteemed'), as did reports from Stadler in Prague of *La clemenza di Tito*'s equally triumphant performances there. Wolfgang spent most of his time composing furiously, but broke off to take his meals, sometimes with his Weber family relations. His very last letter[111] to Constanze was radiant with contentment and confidence, and sweetly solici-tous for his family and friends. He described how he and Franz Hofer had taken not only Salieri and Caterina Cavalieri to *Die Zauberflöte*, but also his son Carl, and his mother-in-law. Frau Weber, according to Sophie, had become 'ever more fond' of Wolfgang, and he of her. He clearly visited her many times when Constanze was away, and he never arrived empty-handed. By now she was possibly quite deaf: Hofer had given her a copy of the libretto to *Die Zauberflöte* to read, on the day before they were to take her to the theatre, in order that she could do a little preparation ('she will *see* the opera but not *hear* it'). So perhaps she could not fully appreciate the extraordinary artistry of her eldest daughter Josefa, as, in her performance as the Queen of the Night, she threw off her coloratura roulades and her top Fs, in the best Weber tradition. Nor could she marvel at the wealth of invention of her son-in-law, whose genius had made of a popular singspiel one of the most profound creations in all opera. But she would have felt enormous pride and joy as she sat in Wolfgang's box with both her sons-in-law and her grandson, gazing at her daughter on stage. They all had dinner together after the performance, and she would have witnessed the delight of young Carl (aged seven) at having been included in such a grown-up evening. And in Baden the following day, Constanze and Sophie read Wolfgang's account of this happy family occasion, and of his concern for Carl's schooling, expressed in some astute paternal observations. What may have given Constanze cause for worry was Wolfgang's admission of his daily routine: he still seemed to start work at 4.30 in the morning, and never got to bed before midnight. He was burning every candle at both ends.

Sure enough, when Constanze returned from Baden at the end of the week, she found Wolfgang exhausted. He was increasingly enfeebled, and obsessively disturbed too by his current task, the writing of his Requiem Mass, K626. At one point, as they walked together in the Prater, he confessed to her that he believed he was writing his Requiem for himself. So she took it away from him, and called in a doctor. She persuaded him to work instead on a Masonic cantata, 'Laut verkünde unsrer Freude', K623, for the opening of a new temple at his Lodge on 18 November. But he returned again to his Requiem, even after his exhaustion turned to actual illness and gathering frailty made him take to his bed on 20 November. As she always had done when there was a crisis, Constanze called on Sophie to come and help her take care of him.

And perhaps Wolfgang did continue to fear that he was writing his own Requiem, for indeed, there is unquestionably something valedictory about it. Its very opening gesture, of throbbing syncopations in the strings accompanying mournful lines on basset horns and bassoons, is almost a quotation from the introduction to his own aria, 'Ah, non sai qual pena sia', K416, written for Aloysia in 1783. On that occasion the text was 'Anima mia, io più non ti vedrò . . . Addio per sempre' (My beloved, I will not see you again . . . Goodbye for ever). Was this some sort of subliminal message of farewell to his family? But, ill as he was, Wolfgang's creative genius was not destitute: the dramatic impact of the *Dies Irae* and the sublime intensity of the *Recordare* give every indication that yet another veritable masterpiece was flowing from him. But he could not physically manage the transcription of his ideas on to the page. His body swelled; his hands could not hold a pen; vomiting and fever ('hitziges Frieselfieber') began to drain his strength and spirit. So Constanze organized help for him too. The faithful Süssmayr came to try to write down what Wolfgang dictated. Constanze herself and three of his closest friends (his brother-in-law Franz Hofer, his Tamino and Sarastro, Benedikt Schack and Franz Xaver Gerl) sat with him and sang through some of what he had already written. And Sophie came every day, to support Constanze and the children, and help to nurse Wolfgang.

A quarter of a century later, it was Sophie herself who supplied the most poignant account of Mozart's last days. For Georg Nissen, his biographer (and Constanze's second husband), Sophie wrote a long and vivid memoir which, for all the simplicity of her expression, is devastatingly powerful. At this most critical of times for Mozart's 'other' family, Sophie encapsulates all the Weber spirit: their warmth, their practicality, their loving concern for the dying Wolfgang and also for one another. Her indignant memory of the behaviour of the professionals (the priests and the doctor, none of whom come out of this account at all well) is balanced by her own anxious capabilities (taking care of her mother as well as her sister), and by a heartrending portrayal of Constanze's ordeal. And, throughout, the central figure of Wolfgang himself is imbued with dignity, generosity, gratitude and grace.

Sophie's memoir[112] began on Sunday, 4 December, the day after a visit when Wolfgang had almost seemed to be on the mend.

> I was still young and, I admit it, vain – and I liked dressing up, but I never liked walking from our suburb into the town in my best clothes, and I had not the money for going by carriage; so I said to our good mother, 'Dear Mama, I shan't go in to Mozart today – he

was so well yesterday, so today he'll be better still, and one day more or less will make no difference.' She said, 'I tell you what, make me a cup of coffee, and then I'll tell you what to do.' She was rather concerned to keep me at home, for my sister [Constanze] knows how much she always wanted me to be with her. So I went into the kitchen. The fire had gone out; I had to light a taper and kindle the fire. But Mozart was still constantly on my mind. My coffee was ready, and my candle was still burning. I then saw how wasteful I had been to have burnt so much of my candle. The candle was still burning brightly, and I stared at it and thought, 'I wonder how Mozart is?', and as I was thinking this, and looking at my candle, it went out, it went out as if it had never been alight. Not even a spark remained on the wick. There was no draught, to that I would swear. I shuddered and ran to our mother, and told her. She said, 'All right, hurry up and take those clothes off and go in [to see him], but come back and tell me straight away how he is. Don't be long.' I hurried as fast as I could. My God! How frightened I was when my sister, half desperate yet trying to control herself, came to meet me and said, 'Thank God you've come, dear Sophie; he was so bad last night that I thought he would not make it to the day. Stay with me today, for if he gets bad again, he will die in the night. Go in to him for a little and see how he is.' I tried to control myself and went up to his bed, and he called to me at once, 'Ah dear Sophie, it is good of you to come. You must stay here tonight. You must be here as I die.' I tried to be strong and to dissuade him, but he answered to all my attempts, 'I have the taste of death on my tongue already' and 'Who will look after my dearest Constanze if you don't stay?' – 'Yes, dear Mozart, but I must first go and tell our mother that you would like me to be with you tonight, or she will think something dreadful has happened.' – 'Yes, do that, but come back soon.' God, how awful I felt. My poor sister came after me and begged me for heaven's sake to go to the priests at St Peter's and ask one of them to come, as if on a chance visit. So I did that, though the inhuman priests hesitated a long time and I had great difficulty in persuading them to do it. Then I hurried to our mother, who was anxiously awaiting me; it was already dark. How frightened the poor darling was. I persuaded her to go and spend the night with her eldest daughter, [Josefa] Hofer, who is now dead, and she did; and I ran back as fast as I could to my inconsolable sister. Süssmayr was there at Mozart's bedside, and the well-known Requiem lay on the coverlet, and Mozart was explaining to him how he thought he should finish it after his death . . . There was a long search for Clossett, the doctor, who was found at the theatre: but he would not come until the play was over. Then he came and prescribed *cold* compresses on his burning head, and these gave him such a shock that he did not regain consciousness before he passed away. The last thing he did was to try and mouth the sound of the timpani in his Requiem. I can still hear that now.

The timpani in his Requiem? We know that Mozart was working on the *Lacrimosa* in that final struggle, and that the last words that he set, therefore, were:

> *Lacrimosa dies illa*
> *Qua resurget ex favilla*
> *Judicandus homo reus*

> (Sorrowful that day
> when from the dust will arise
> the guilty man to be judged.)

What begins almost as a gentle, slow, lilting dance turns on the second line into an agonizing climb through an octave and a half, first with full-tone steps, and then, towards the peak, in more laborious semitones: the music has become a death march. The scale and its inevitable crescendo reach their summit at the devastating words 'Judicandus homo reus' (the guilty man to be judged). And it was here that Wolfgang instructed Süssmayr to add Sophie's timpani, together with their constant partners the trumpets, which had so frightened him as a child. And his life ended, on an unresolved dominant chord.

～

Or suonin le trombe:
Solenne ecatombe
Andiam preparar.

(Sound the trumpets:
Let us prepare
Solemn sacrifices.)

Idomeneo

Mozart's Women

~

ACCORDING TO Sophie, it was she who held Wolfgang in her arms as he died, shortly after midnight on 5 December 1791. And when it was all over, Constanze, completely distraught, crawled into the bed beside his body, as if to try to 'catch his illness and die with him'.[1] After the departure of the hopeless doctor, word travelled fast through the city, and by daybreak people had begun to gather in the street below. Close friends were admitted to the apartment, to view the body; and among them came the estimable Baron van Swieten, who, putting aside some shocking news of his own (he had been dismissed that very day from his Court post as president of the Education and Censorship Commission), took control of the practicalities. Van Swieten chose the most basic of funeral options, with no unnecessary adornments or extravagances. In Joseph II's time, the whole burial system had in any case been simplified in the interests of economy and hygiene. (The Emperor's own plain tomb, unobtrusively placed at the foot of the elaborate structure built for his parents in the Habsburg vaults of the Kapuzinerkirche, demonstrates the strength of his conviction.) Most Viennese people of the time, therefore, received an economy-class burial, and this was the obvious choice for Wolfgang. On the afternoon of 6 December, Constanze and her family, together with van Swieten and a few close friends, attended a simple ceremony in a side chapel of St

Stephen's Cathedral. Later, a rented private hearse, unaccompanied now by mourners, as was also the norm, took the coffin through the streets of the city to a cemetery in the suburban village of St Marx; and there it was deposited, in a 'normal simple grave'.[2]

Generations of music-lovers have mourned the loss of Mozart's human remains. Constanze's apparent indifference even to knowing the precise location of her husband's grave has brought her more charges of slovenly selfishness; and although there are now many appropriately placed monuments and shrines at which to worship, the very absence of those precious bones continues to unsettle an anxious world, and to feed it with the opportunity for recrimination, frustration and guilt.

Mozart himself would probably have been astonished at such dismay. Whether or not he shared the belief that all burials should be hygienic, economical and, above all, simple, he certainly never concerned himself with the graves of his own family. Of far greater importance to him was the notion that beyond death there was a 'true happiness',[3] and that this perpetual light surrounding departed souls was therefore a cause for celebration. The very setting of the words 'et lux perpetua luceat eis' in his own Requiem – in music that is positive, affirmative, truly radiant – is testimony to this profound optimism, and, even as he approached his own end through the agonies and anxieties of sickness and regret, to his essential solemn belief in the beauty of an afterlife.

Mozart would not therefore have given a second thought to the fate of his own bones. But he did care greatly for the preservation of his true legacy, his music. Like many composers, he rather dismissed his earliest works: 'my brother appreciated his older works less and less, the more he advanced in composition,'[4] wrote Nannerl in 1799 – poignantly, for these were the pieces with which she herself was most associated. But from 1784 until just three weeks before his death, Mozart meticulously kept a thematic catalogue of all his compositions.[5] This was not merely a manifestation of the family passion for lists, but a highly organized way of handing his creations down to future generations. For here, not in some dark tomb, is his immortality. In his unique and incomparable music, he lives on in the hands and hearts of his interpreters and their listeners. And so to an extent do the men and the women of his circle, for in creating his operatic roles for singers he knew, liked and sometimes even loved, he secured for them too their places in the firmament of posterity.

As in all Mozart's music, his operatic genius resides in the miraculous combination of a unique imagination and vertiginous risk-taking in his craft, all expressed with an apparently effortless fluency. But his imagination was informed too by experience. Mozart was a close observer of human nature, who, as Constanze reported, could seem to detach himself from his surroundings, but in fact missed nothing, and was never clinical. He loved the whole world of theatre and the people who inhabited it, and his happiest conviviality came through mingling with them, whether the Canna-bich company in Mannheim and Munich, or the devoted musicians in Prague, or Schikaneder's troupe in Vienna. With all his per-formers his standards were extremely high, and his condemnation of musicians who did not match up to them could be absolutely withering. From his earliest years, it was reported how he even became impatient with his father when he played wrong notes; and he held the Court musicians in Salzburg in collective, undiluted contempt. He demanded much more of a performer than a brilliant technique, famously dismissing the dazzling Clementi as a 'mere mechanicus'.[6] What he constantly sought was that extra ingredient of emotion and passion, not falsely or superficially applied, but fired from within the very soul of the interpreter. When he found anyone who could convey this, he was ecstatic. Aloysia could, and so could the young Beethoven, who once played to him and com-pletely captivated him. And for his beloved theatrical colleagues, in whose instruments (their voices) resided their passions and emo-tions at their most naked and vulnerable, he was especially inspired to make his most profound utterances. No character in a mature Mozart opera is therefore without interest. His creations are drawn with humanity, compassion and razor-sharp accuracy, and are some of the most multidimensional as any on the stage, Shakespearean in their variety, Chekhovian in their complexity.

As Mozart composed his operas, and created recognizable human beings for the stage, two ingredients were essential to his process. The first was the libretto. For his earliest operas he was, like all his contemporaries, given a ready-to-wear libretto (generally taken off the shelf by someone else), and made his own setting of it. The great Pietro Metastasio, Court poet in Vienna for over fifty years in the mid-eighteenth century, totally dominated opera composition in his time. He wrote over thirty texts for full-length operas, some of which were set as many as twenty-five times. There are therefore, staggeringly, over 800 different settings of Metastasio librettos. His great talent was to provide a cover-all style that was elegant, narrative and reflective, and that could accommodate all manner of compositional interpretation. The text of Mozart's 'Non sò d'onde viene' for Aloysia in 1778 was from a Metastasio libretto (*Alessandro nell'Indie*), and Mozart himself saw it as a challenge to produce something completely different from the setting by J. C. Bach that he knew so well and admired so much. But from 1780, he himself began to have direct input into the very structure of a libretto. First he collaborated with Schachtner in Salzburg on an aborted project, *Zaïde*, K344 (336b). Then for *Idomeneo* in Munich in 1781 he was deeply involved with Giovanni Battista Varesco in the shaping of the text and the pacing of the drama. And in Vienna his collaborations with Johann Gottlieb Stephanie, Emanuel Schikaneder and especially Lorenzo Da Ponte were completely symbiotic. As he himself put it, 'The best thing of all is when a good composer, who understands the stage and is talented enough to make sound suggestions, meets an able poet, that true phoenix.'[7] (The image of this rare bird was to reappear in the opening scene of the Mozart/Da Ponte *Così fan tutte*, when Ferrando and Guglielmo parry their praises for their sweethearts.) Mozart was absolutely clear in his mind about the importance of a properly shaped text:

An opera is sure of success when the plot is well worked out, the words written solely for the music and not shoved in here and there to suit some miserable rhyme (which, God knows, never enhances the value of any theatrical performance, be it what it may, but rather detracts from it) – I mean, words or even entire verses which ruin the composer's whole idea. Verses are indeed the most indispensable element for music – but rhymes – solely for the sake of rhyming – the most detrimental.

So Mozart's artistic creation began before a note of music existed even in his own head.

Second, and at the other end of the creative process, Mozart was deeply concerned with his performers' interpretation. He had very decided views on singing technique, and to an extent was able to train it himself, as demonstrated by the little exercises that he wrote for Constanze as he prepared her for their performance of his Mass in C minor. He loved good cantabile singing (at which Aloysia so excelled), but not if it became a calculated device for its own sake. In Paris in 1778 he criticized his good friend Anton Raaff for falling into mannerism ('he overdoes it, and to me it sounds ridiculous'), though he roundly praised his bravura singing and especially his 'excellent, clear diction, which is very beautiful'.[8] All these attributes were important to him, as was the use of vibrato in a singer, which again he loved when it was natural and beautiful, but could not abide if overused. One of the Salzburg singers, Joseph Meissner, was held up as an example of how not to deploy it: 'Meissner, as you know, has the bad habit of making his voice vibrate at times, turning a note that should be sustained into distinct crotchets, or even quavers – and this I could never endure in him. And really it is a detestable habit and one which is quite contrary to nature.' And he continued: 'The human voice vibrates naturally – but in its own way – and only to such a degree that the effect is beautiful. Such is the nature of the voice; and people imitate it not only on wind instruments, but on stringed instruments too and even on the clavier. But the moment the proper limit is overstepped, it is no longer beautiful – because it is contrary to nature.'[9]

Mozart's passion for naturalness in interpretation was particularly strong in the performance of recitatives; and when he heard two melodramas by Georg Benda, in which the dialogue was actually spoken over instrumental accompaniment, rather than sung, he was extremely excited: 'Do you know what I think? I think that most operatic recitatives should be treated in this way – and only sung occasionally, when the words *can be perfectly expressed by the music*.'[10] But again he required that his singers should always 'attend fully to the meaning and force of the words',[11] as he had instructed Aloysia, and was dismayed when, in the early rehearsals for *Idomeneo*, two of his singers – including, sadly, his good friend Raaff – failed to do this: 'Raaff and Dal Prato spoil the recitative by singing without any spirit or fire, and *so* monotonously.'[12] On the other hand, if anything was exaggerated or mannered, he was at his most forthright. Having met young Gretl Marchand on his visit with Constanze to Salzburg in 1783, he felt sufficiently strongly about her progress as a singer to offer her his own advice. And again the emphasis was entirely on naturalness and integrity:

> Please give a special message to little Greta, and tell her that when she sings she must not be so arch and coy; for cajolings and kissings are not always palatable – in fact only silly asses are taken in by such devices. I for one would rather have a country lout, who does not hesitate to shit and piss in my presence, than let myself be humbugged by such false toadyings, which after all are so exaggerated that one can easily see through them.[13]

So Mozart was a fierce taskmaster, who would never settle for anything less than total commitment to dramatic involvement and emotional truth. To sing beautifully was simply not enough.

~

THE TURNING POINT in Mozart's vocal writing was his initial and passionate encounter with Aloysia Weber in 1778; and in a not unrelated context, the opera that similarly took him to new heights of maturity, in all ways, was *Idomeneo* in 1781. He was then twenty-five years old. But throughout his teenage years he had been honing his craft: *La finta giardiniera*, for Munich in 1775 when he was nineteen, was in fact already his twelfth opera. Naturally the childhood and adolescent works do not begin to measure up to the miracles of what was to follow in his twenties and thirties. But they are all quite remarkable for their prodigious craftsmanship, their unfailing musico-dramatic instinct and their considerable beauty. They may have been written by a child, but they more than hold their own in the company of other contemporary operas. As with all Mozart's teenage composition, he was not merely copying styles and models; he was always personalizing, deepening, and in fact improving upon what he absorbed. And the better he knew his interpreters, the better the product. His early operas were all composed to ready-to-wear librettos, but the music that he wrote to these texts was, as he himself loved to put it, 'tailor-made'.

Mozart's creation of musical character began in 1767, when he was merely eleven years old. The family had just returned to Salzburg from their Grand Tour, and were drawing disappointing parallels between the musical resources available at Court and those they had encountered in Vienna, Paris and London. But there were in the service of the Prince-Archbishop three high-profile young sopranos, who, a little like the young Mozarts themselves, were cause for a certain amount of excitement and pride. In 1761, Maria Magdalena Lipp, aged sixteen, and Maria Anna Brauenhofer, aged thirteen, had been sent by Archbishop Schrattenbach himself to Venice, and there they had pursued their studies for two and a half years. In January 1764 they had been joined by eighteen-year-old Maria Anna Fesemayr, who, together with the Salzburg organist Anton Cajetan Adlgasser (in his mid-thirties) had similarly spent a year there. By the end of 1765 the three young women were back in Salzburg, and, now respectively aged twenty, seventeen and twenty-two, they were all appointed as Court singers. Their salaries were 8 florins per month, and also included – rather disastrously, as it turned out – a daily litre of wine.

The social lives of these Court musicians were somewhat

enclosed and claustrophobic: Brauenhofer's father was an organist in nearby Mondsee, and Lipp's a Court organist; and she was to marry a fellow Court musician, Michael Haydn, in 1768. Fesemayr eventually became the third wife of her Venetian companion and Court organist, Anton Adlgasser. Their world was therefore an intense little microcosm of the wider artistic community; and despite their earlier travels, the talents of many of these Salzburg musicians were to become dulled and stagnant, as they settled comfortably into their relatively undemanding routines, and enjoyed their free wine. (Both Michael Haydn and his wife Maria Magdalena would become excessive drinkers.) But in the mid-1760s, when they were all newly returned from their Italian sojourns, the skills of these 'Three Ladies' were considerable, and Mozart was to exploit them well.

The first glimpse of Wolfgang's musical tailoring is in his contribution to a sacred singspiel, *Die Schuldigkeit des ersten Gebots*, K35, in March 1767. This three-part work was to be performed in sections, on three successive Thursdays in the Knights' Hall of the Archbishop's Palace. Its text was by Josefa Duschek's grandfather, Ignaz Weiser, and two of the Archbishop's most accomplished composers were involved: Part Two was written by Michael Haydn, and Part Three by Adlgasser. Part One, given on that first Thursday, 12 March 1767, was by the eleven-year-old Mozart.

The singers for this serial singspiel were naturally drawn from the Archbishop's Court roster. In the three allegorical roles of Divine Mercy (Die göttliche Barmherzigkeit), Divine Justice (Die göttliche Gerechtigkeit) and Worldliness (Der Welt-Geist) were the 'Three Ladies', Lipp, Brauenhofer and Fesemayr. Two tenors, Joseph Meissner and Franz Anton Spitzeder, took the roles of a Christian and Christianity. In a score bubbling with ideas, both vocal and instrumental, and an astonishing command of orchestration, structural contrast and, that most challenging device, accompanied recitative, the music written for the two tenors is strong and straightforward. But the three women clearly had excellent technical agility as a result of their Venetian training, and for all of them Wolfgang wrote florid and acrobatic music. One of the three, Maria Magdalena Lipp, was especially challenged. She was widely acknowledged to be an excellent singer, but nobody much liked her, and in her later life she became difficult and obstructive. In her aria, 'Ein ergrimmter Löwe brüllet' (A furious lion roars), the animal-loving child in Wolfgang responded with glee both to the dramatic picture of the dangerous lion and perhaps too to the strong personality of the singer. He produced an aria of ferocious vocal leaps, balanced by threatening growling and prowling in low-lying chromatic scales. Among all his childhood output, this aria stands out as an early example of his being inspired not only by the text but also by the personality of the interpreter to produce something extraordinary.

The three Salzburg ladies were to appear again in Mozart's theatrical music. In 1769, after the family's rather unsuccessful fourteen-month stay in Vienna, and the disastrous episode of *La finta semplice*, Leopold did at least succeed in getting Wolfgang's unperformed Viennese opera put on back home, at the Archbishop's Palace. (He also succumbed to another of his little untruths, claiming on the title page of the printed libretto that Wolfgang was twelve, when in fact he was thirteen – a wholly unnecessary practice that he had regularly adopted in London.) Although Wolfgang had written *La finta semplice* for some excellent Viennese singers, he did not know them personally, and it is likely therefore that in his mind's ear he retained the talents of his three Salzburg ladies. And sure enough, the music for Rosina, Giacinta and Ninetta, whom they eventually came to perform, exactly follows the course of his earlier writing for Lipp, Brauenhofer and Fesemayr. Again it is that sung by the difficult but gifted Lipp which stands apart from the rest of the score. For her he produced his most original and successful experiments in orchestral accompaniment, writing for solo oboe and two cors d'anglais in the enchant-ing echo aria 'Senti l'eco' (Hear the echo), and for the fascinating dark colours of two bassoons and divided violas in 'Amoretti che ascosi qui siete' (You Cupids hiding here); and in both these arias the vocal writing is seductive and supremely assured. Wolfgang's 'Three Ladies' are detectable also in the church music that he wrote for Salzburg: there are glorious soprano solos in his three Litany settings, K125, K195 (186d) and K243.

Finally, in 1775, there is good music too in his little opera, or 'serenata', *Il re pastore*, K208, written for the occasion of the visit of Maria Theresa's youngest son, the Archduke Maximilian Franz (whom Wolfgang had known since 1762, when they had played together in the corridors of Schönbrunn Palace). The text by Metastasio is a gently symbolic tale of love, duty and magnanimity, set in an agreeable pastoral landscape, and it had already been chosen many times for similar occasions honouring Habsburg princes. But although Mozart (now nineteen) produced some extremely fine and very varied music, as ever challenging his performers and rewarding their skills with arias which would draw them enthusiastic archducal approbation, the virtuoso writing seems somewhat conventional, and not especially characterized. It is as if Wolfgang's heart was not fully engaged in this project. He had perhaps had his fill of Habsburg condescension, and the subject-matter bored him. And perhaps too he had grown out of his Three Ladies, and they no longer excited him. For by now he had been to Italy.

~

IN HIS MID-TEENS, Mozart wrote his three operas for Milan, *Mitridate, re di Ponto*, K87 (74a), in 1770, *Ascanio in Alba*, K111, in 1771, and *Lucio Silla*, K135, in 1772. The glittering surroundings of their performances, the highest Habsburg pedigree of their patrons and the enormous honour for Wolfgang, a fourteen-year-old boy, of being invited at all for these engagements, were still not the most significant challenge for him at this stage. He was now to write operas in the Italian language, for Italian singers and Italian audiences. This was a completely different experience from writing in Vienna for excellent Italian singers, but for audiences for whom Italian – if they understood it at all – was probably their third language, after German and French. It was certainly different from writing for German singers and audiences in Salzburg. But, as he always did when he was newly stimulated, Wolfgang more than rose to the occasion. The three librettos were all chosen for him, and in each case given to him only a few months before their scheduled performances. But they were all excellent examples of the opera seria concept (heroic tales of classical or historical figures, and with a strong focus on the pure and laudable virtues of love, loyalty and duty); and in the case especially of *Mitridate*, based on Racine's play, they were extremely well constructed. With all his teenage precocity, Wolfgang seized on their great merits, and, like Handel before him, succeeded in stretching the very format, adding emotional depth and stirring, inner drama to individual characters. And in this he was considerably helped by his singers. For, in the country that had invented the whole art-form of opera, he was now meeting its very best practitioners.

Three singers in particular were of momentous importance to Wolfgang in Italy. They were truly international performers, who busily traversed the whole of Europe in the mid-eighteenth century, and had enormous reputations and followings. Two of them were sopranos, Anna De Amicis and Antonia Bernasconi; the third was the castrato Venanzio Rauzzini. Wolfgang and his father knew of all three before they arrived in Italy. They had met Anna De Amicis in Mainz in 1763, when the thirty-year-old singer was at the height of her career. She had then been on her way back to her native Italy; they were just at the start of their Grand Tour. And they would have assuredly taken notice of each other, for in their own ways both she and the seven-year-old Wolfgang were extremely newsworthy. Four years later, when the Mozarts were in Vienna and Wolfgang was writing his ill-fated *La finta semplice*, they heard both Rauzzini, in Hasse's *Partenope*, and Bernasconi, creating the magnificent title role in Gluck's *Alceste*. And indeed, had *La finta semplice* been performed in Vienna, it is likely that Bernasconi would have taken the role of Ninetta (performed eventually in Salzburg by Fesemayr).

As Wolfgang waited with his father in Rome, in April 1770, for news of the first opera that he was to write, he was excited to learn that Anna De Amicis might be among the cast. He wrote to Nannerl, 'Some say that De Amicis will sing. We are to meet her in Naples. I should like her and Manzuoli to take the parts: then we should have two good acquaintances and friends.'[14] A month later, he and Leopold did indeed catch up with her in Naples, where she was now living with her husband and baby daughter. They heard her sing at the Teatro San Carlo and were greatly impressed. But it was not yet she whose great art would inspire Mozart in Milan. When the libretto of *Mitridate* was chosen, in July of that year, and sent to Wolfgang in Bologna, the cast list was sent too. The part of Aspasia was to be sung by Antonia Bernasconi; and the Mozarts were not disappointed.

In the mid-eighteenth century, the formal conventions of opera seria were potentially stifling to coherent narrative. Single-emotion arias in da capo form (whereby the first section is sung again after a middle section, but this time with much vocal decoration and ornament) temporarily arrested any dramatic thrust, for momentum was literally turned back on itself. Meanwhile the linking sections of simple, syllabic recitative, accompanied only by continuo instruments, propelled the action forward in ungainly bursts. In most cases the attraction of these operas was the opportunity that the arias gave for the singers to display their technical prowess: admiration of vocal pyrotechnics was a recognized practice, enjoyed equally by performers and worshippers. Frequently nobody paid any attention at all to the linking recitatives, nor, therefore, to any aspect of narrative. (In Metastasio's play *La cantante e l'impresario*, one character says to another: 'In the recitative you can sing in whatever language you like, for then, as you know, the audience generally has a good gossip.') But the greatest composers could make sense of this most uncomfortable of formats. For over thirty years in the first half of the century, Handel had burst through the straitjacket, sometimes simply breaking the rules, but most often finding ways to soften their edges. He developed the dramatically powerful accompanied recitative (recitativo accompagnato) as a musical bridge between simple recitative and aria, and as a vehicle for real development of dramatic thought. And in Vienna Gluck too had jettisoned the rigid structural conventions, and returned to a true balance between music and poetry, where the narrative purity was unsoiled by 'the mistaken vanity of singers' (as he rather cruelly wrote in his preface to *Alceste*). The young Mozart may well have heard operas in the style of Handel in London (for the great composer had been dead only five years), and had certainly heard operas by Gluck in Vienna; and like them he pursued paths of musico-dramatic truth. His orchestrally accompanied recitatives, and his richly varied arias, where the orchestra begins to reflect the emotional content of the moment, were devices which, even at this early stage, put his operas on a plane higher than those of his contemporaries.

Vittorio Amedeo Cigna-Santi's libretto of *Mitridate, re di Ponto* is a very competent reworking of Racine's great play. Although the story is ostensibly that of Mitridate's ultimate magnanimity in a huge gesture of forgiveness (that all-important Enlightenment passion), it is the role of Aspasia whose interaction with all the other characters propels the drama forward. Aspasia is betrothed to Mitridate, King of Pontus, but loves his younger son Sifare, and is also wooed by his treacherous older son Farnace. She is torn therefore between her love for Sifare and her duty to Mitridate, and dismayed by the advances of Farnace. When Mitridate discovers her true love for his son and condemns her to death, she resolves to take poison. But, in keeping with the Enlightenment desire for happy endings, Mitridate reprieves everyone when Farnace and Sifare unite to save his kingdom.

Antonia Bernasconi was evidently bowled over by the music that Mozart wrote for her as Aspasia. Leopold wrote to Maria Anna on 17 November 1770, 'The prima donna is infinitely pleased with her arias.'[15] And well she might have been. In her opening 'Al destin che la minaccia' (Save me from this cruel fate), where Aspasia longs to be free of Farnace, she could show off her energetic coloratura and acrobatic leaps, very much in the manner of Maria Magdalena Lipp's lion. But then the character of Aspasia gradually deepened and grew. Her second aria, 'Nel sen mi palpita' (My heart is pounding) calls for greater variety of singing, with sobbing interruptions to her text, and anxious chromatic lyricism. The central point of her role is the soliloquy in Act II, at the centre indeed of the whole opera. First in accompanied recitative and then in the aria 'Nel grave tormento' (In profound suffering) she expresses her deep torment as love and duty tear her apart. Two different tempos, adagio and allegro, alternate, as do her feelings; and the lyrical addition of flutes to the instrumental texture gives this section a sheen all its own. The second act ends with a duet for Aspasia and Sifare (the castrato Pietro Benedetti), 'Se viver non degg'io' (If I am not to survive), in which both singers, in equal vocal range, parry vocal virtuosity in a manner both alluring and thrilling. (Benedetti was absolutely delighted with this duet, and jokingly told Leopold that he would 'let himself be castrated again'[16] if it did not go well.)

But the most memorable music of all is Aspasia's third-act soliloquy, in which she contemplates suicide by poison. There is no place here for virtuosity. Mozart gave Bernasconi a slow and low-lying sustained line of unbearable emotional intensity, and then collapsed his aria's formal structure into an accompanied recitative as Aspasia raises the cup of poison to her lips. As her hand trembles, so too do the accompanying strings; as her fear breaks into panic, so too does the orchestra, in contrasts of pace, dynamic and gesture. An icy calm descends on her as she builds her final resolve, and the string chords surrounding her vocal line also assume a frozen stasis – before of course Sifare rushes in to knock the cup from her hand. For a fourteen-year-old boy to have grasped the concepts of love and duty with such success was already remarkable. For him to have begun to understand the unthinkable turmoil of a suicidal moment is almost frightening; and his interpreter, the creator of Gluck's Alceste, with performing attributes much greater than mere tech-

nical proficiency, had played her part in inspiring this step towards
maturity.

Mitridate, re di Ponto was an enormous success for Mozart and a
personal triumph too for Antonia Bernasconi: at the first performance her arias were all encored, and the running time of the opera
was stretched to more than six hours. Like his son, Leopold remembered for ever the dramatic impact of this impressive and
professional woman. And when, eight years later, Wolfgang fell for
Aloysia Weber in Mannheim and proposed to take her to Italy
where he was convinced she could have a great career, Leopold
drew Bernasconi into his fierce condemnation of his son's scheme:
'Tell me, do you know of any prima donna who, without having
first appeared many times in Germany, has walked on to the stage
in Italy as a prima donna? In how many operas did not Signora
Bernasconi sing in Vienna, and operas too of the most passionate
type, produced under the very severe criticism and direction of
Gluck and Calzabigi?'[17] Leopold knew that his argument would
hit home, for although Bernasconi may not have been their first
choice for Aspasia, she had created her role with the greatest
distinction.

Two years after *Mitridate, re di Ponto*, the woman Wolfgang and
Leopold had first wanted as Aspasia did at last come into their orbit.
At the time of *Lucio Silla*, Wolfgang's third opera for Milan, Anna
De Amicis was nearly forty, an age when most of her contemporaries had long since ceased to appear on stage. But this hugely
charismatic performer, of quite astonishing technique and with a
warm personality, was still very much in demand. She had sung all
over Europe, in Paris, Brussels, Dublin and London as well as
throughout Germany and her native Italy. Leopold and Wolfgang
heard her (singing 'marvellously well'[18]) in Naples before *Mitridate,
re di Ponto*, and again in Venice just after it. They got to know her
better during the period of Wolfgang's second Milan opera, *Ascanio
in Alba*, for Archduke Ferdinand's spectacular wedding festivities
in 1771. The principal soprano role in the other opera (Hasse's
Ruggiero) was initially taken by the English singer Cecilia Davies;

but on its opening night she was hissed and booed so cruelly by the Milanese audiences (whose practices have not changed much over the centuries) that she was 'banished for ever from the Italian stage',[19] and Anna De Amicis was rushed in to replace her. (This incident was to provide yet more ammunition for Leopold, as he argued against the likelihood of Aloysia succeeding in Italy.) So when the Mozarts returned to Milan for Wolfgang's third opera at the end of 1772, they would have been thrilled to learn that De Amicis was cast in the prima donna role of Giunia. Equally exciting was the news that Venanzio Rauzzini would play the part of Cecilio. The twenty-six-year-old castrato was also at the height of his performing career – which would stabilize just two years later when he moved to London and indeed became teacher to some of Mozart's later distinguished colleagues.

Wolfgang and his father arrived back in Milan in mid-November 1772. None of the principal singers was yet in residence, and, as ever, Wolfgang was reluctant to begin writing for them until he had met them, heard them and worked with them. But he could get started on writing the choruses and recitatives of *Lucio Silla*, and this he did in collaboration with the librettist, Giovanni de Gamerra, poet to the Teatro Regio Ducale in Milan. The story concerned the tyrannical Roman dictator, Lucius Cornelius Sulla, who had had a change of heart and bestowed prosperity on those who had suffered under him, and was therefore a perfect model for an Enlightenment spectacle. But, again, the opera's title role was not the most important. The fortunes of a banished senator, Cecilio (to be played by Rauzzini) and his wife Giunia (Anna De Amicis) propel the drama and provide all its emotional complexity. In Cecilio's absence Lucio Silla has taken Giunia into his household and plans to make her his wife. Giunia herself believes Cecilio to be dead, and is advised to marry Lucio Silla and then kill him. Lucio Silla publicly demands her hand as a way to end civil strife. Cecilio steals back to rescue his wife, but is seized and condemned to death. Giunia resolves to die with him, but Lucio Silla forgives everyone and abdicates.

There was in fact a major crisis about the casting of the title role of Lucio Silla. The tenor originally engaged, a Signor Cordoni, had to withdraw because of illness, and messengers were sent urgently to Turin and Bologna in search of someone who could 'not only sing well, but be a first-rate actor and have a handsome presence',[20] as Leopold nervously reported. In the end, one Bassano Morgnoni, a church singer from nearby Lodi, was hired, only eight days before the premiere. He was completely out of his depth, and Mozart had to adjust his ideas for Lucio Silla's music, which is therefore rather bland. But Rauzzini and De Amicis would have had no objection to all the dramatic and now musical emphasis too thus being trained upon them.

Rauzzini was the first to arrive in Milan. Wolfgang would have been greatly impressed again by his all-round musicianship and his striking dramatic presence: in that same year, the English music historian Dr Charles Burney had met him in Munich, and described him as 'not only a charming singer, a pleasing figure and a good actor; but a more excellent . . . performer on the harpsichord, than a singer is usually allowed to be.'[21] Wolfgang immediately wrote him his first aria, 'Il tenero momento' (The tender moment), full of exultant anticipation of the joy of seeing Giunia again; and he exploited his primo uomo's deft coloratura and wide range. As Leopold reported back to Salzburg, 'it is superlatively beautiful and he sings it like an angel.'[22] When Anna De Amicis arrived two weeks later (she had been performing in Venice, and was then delayed on her journey to Milan by appalling weather conditions and bad roads), Wolfgang could at last begin her music too. And, as with the role of Aspasia in *Mitridate*, that of Giunia was central to *Lucio Silla*. Torn between her love for her banished husband and the pressures to marry a tyrant in the interests of civil peace, she similarly has many opportunities for the noble contemplation of duty. And again, it is in the occasions where Mozart breaks away from the formal conventions of opera seria that he creates her most striking music.

Like Rauzzini's first aria, that for De Amicis, 'Dalla sponda

tenebrosa' (From the dark shore), defiantly resisting the advances
of Lucio Silla, is a highly impressive opener. There is the statutory
coloratura, though not yet at its most flashy, and interesting
chromatic writing. In the second act, 'Ah, se il crudel periglio' (Ah,
the cruel danger) describes Giunia's desperation as she fears for
Cecilio's safety. This phenomenally difficult aria – the real show-
stopper of the opera – really shows off Anna De Amicis's
technique, especially her flexible coloratura and extraordinary
breath control. Leopold wrote in amazement: 'Wolfgang has introduced into her principal aria passages which are unusual, quite
unique and extremely difficult, and which she sings amazingly
well.'[23] Her third aria, 'Parto, m'affretto' (I leave, I must hurry) is a
desperate soliloquy, in which Giunia resolves to die with Cecilio.
Her music is vivid, breathless and brave, and there is again real
emotional courage in the coloratura. And in her fourth and last aria,
after Cecilio has bid her a tender farewell, her accompanied recitative reflects her panic for them both, and takes her to the extremes
of emotion. (Wolfgang unusually uses a combination of both flutes
and trumpets to accentuate these extremes.) As she sees in her
mind's eye the bloodless corpse of her husband, her horror is
reflected in the orchestration too, which is both richer in its divided
violas and yet chillier in the manner in which Wolfgang deploys
them. In her arias alone, then, De Amicis's part of Giunia was
already a rounded character, with a true emotional journey to
travel, and with rich support from Mozart's ever-original orches-
trations. But there was yet another dimension to this role: De
Amicis's partnership with Rauzzini. And if there was the customary
competitive edge to the artistic collaboration between two high-
profile artists, Mozart brilliantly exploited this as well.

Two sections in *Lucio Silla* demonstrate both the quality of the
De Amicis–Rauzzini double-act and Mozart's breaking of opera
seria rules to bring out the best of it. In the first act, Cecilio is hiding in a burial ground, with its monuments to Roman heroes, and
contemplating these dour manifestations of death. Giunia comes in
with a group of 'young ladies and noblemen' (the chorus), and

Cecilio hides. Giunia sings to the tomb of her father. Cecilio cannot remain hidden: he embraces his astonished Giunia, and together they shed tears of joy. This whole scene is framed and supported by the orchestra: a brief introduction leads into Cecilio's accompanied recitative, and on into the chorus and Giunia's solemn invocation of her father, with its glorious cantabile line. The chorus immediately supports her, and Cecilio's emergence from hiding is again in the most dramatic accompanied recitative, before the joyful duet in which Rauzzini and De Amicis alternate their equal lines of coloratura. It is a quite brilliant scene. Both stars have great solo moments, and then come together to share a duet. There is no section of simple recitative, and no opportunity therefore for the audience to be anything other than swept along by Mozart's pacing.

The trio at the end of the first act is similarly tactful, deft and musico-dramatically alert. In effect it is a duet-plus-one, in that Lucio Silla, set apart from Cecilio and Giunia, observes their tenderness and passion, and is gradually moved by it. His own music, and therefore his tyrannical determination, is softened by the touching spectacle of fidelity. Poor Bassano Morgnoni, the startled church singer from Lodi, brought in at the eleventh hour to take the title role of Lucio Silla, must have been petrified at singing with two of the most celebrated performers in Europe. But Mozart took care of him too, without in any way compromising the dramatic moment. While De Amicis and Rauzzini sang in thirds, and exchanged gentle but not excessive coloratura, Morgnoni's music was straightforward and dramatically clear. The impact of this trio is by no means diminished, for all its musical inequality.

In the course of the writing of *Lucio Silla*, Anna De Amicis became extremely fond of her young composer. She regularly sent greetings to Maria Anna and Nannerl (whom she had never met) in Salzburg, and Leopold, as ever susceptible to the charms of exceptional women, was thrilled to be spending so much time in her company. 'De Amicis is our best friend,' he wrote excitedly on the day of the opening performance, adding, 'She sings and acts like an

angel and is extremely pleased. Wolfgang has served her extremely
well. Both you and the whole of Salzburg would be amazed if you
could hear her.'[24] In the event, that first performance was something
of a disaster. It started over three hours late, because the Archduke
did not arrive at the appointed time. When at last it did begin, therefore, the performers and waiting audience were already exhausted,
and it did not end until two o'clock in the morning. Then the
inexperienced Morgnoni, in a crude attempt at acting, made some
gesture that caused the audience to laugh. As Leopold reported,
'Signora De Amicis, carried along by her own enthusiasm, did not
realize why they were laughing, and being thus taken aback, did not
sing well for the rest of the evening.'[25] And the final straw for the
dismayed diva was that the Archduchess enthusiastically applauded
Rauzzini, because in fact she had been fed the information that he
was extremely nervous and really needed encouragement. This was
of course Rauzzini's own ploy to upstage his soprano colleague,
and it worked brilliantly. The Mozarts were highly amused by the
egotistical posturings of their Italian colleagues, but, as the performances settled down and De Amicis at last gave of her best, they
remained on the warmest of terms with her. And so they did with
Rauzzini too, for whom in the following month Wolfgang wrote his
spectacular motet 'Exsultate, jubilate', K165 (158a).

The writing and performance of *Lucio Silla* was in many ways a
traumatic and tense time for Wolfgang, as he had to contend with
late arrivals, a last-minute replacement, and high artistic temperament in his singers. But, as was often to be the case in his later life,
he thrived on this sort of energy. He wrote to Nannerl, 'I can think
of nothing but my opera, and I am in danger of writing down not
words but a whole aria.'[26] And the very language of his composition
developed immeasurably in the process. Faced with two incom-
parably distinguished singers, he raised his game accordingly: the
brilliance of their execution was the greatest spark to his creative
fire. After his Milan experiences he was not to meet such exceptional vocal talent again for several years. But when he did, in the
form of Aloysia Weber in Mannheim in 1778, it was De Amicis's

music from *Lucio Silla* that he immediately gave her. At last he had found someone else who could sing it.

~

AMONG THE REST of Mozart's operatic music before that great turning point, *Idomeneo*, two works were, in passing, significant. *La finta giardiniera*, composed for Carnival in Munich in 1775, marked another large leap for him, especially in terms of musico-dramatic structure. Following on from his developments in *Lucio Silla*, he continued to create long chains of drama-developing music whose sections were all accompanied by the orchestra, with no simple recitative at all. Over ten years before the miraculous finales to the second and fourth acts of *Le nozze di Figaro*, Act II of *La finta giardiniera* ends with a seamless progression through three arias, several accompanied recitatives, and a multisectional finale for all seven singers, amounting to over twenty-five minutes' music. And in general his harmonic language and instrumentation also became ever richer and more imaginative. If the individual characterizations are not as strong as in his Italian operas, it was due partly to the poor quality of the libretto (by Giuseppe Petrosellini), and partly to the poor quality of the cast. On 28 December 1774 Leopold reported drily to Maria Anna that 'The first performance has been postponed until January 5 in order that the singers may learn their parts more thoroughly and thus, knowing the music perfectly, may act with greater confidence and not spoil the opera.'[27] In fact the premiere was postponed again – the orchestra too needed more time to prepare it – and Rosa Manservisi, the soprano who sang Sandrina, the 'pretended gardener' of the title, was not especially well at the time. But she was possibly not of the greatest distinction anyway. Dr Charles Burney had heard her too, in Munich in 1772, and his approval was somewhat muted: 'Her figure is agreeable, her voice, though not strong, is well-toned, she has nothing vulgar in her manner, sings in tune, and never gives offence.'[28] Wolfgang and Leopold, and later Nannerl too, enjoyed their time in Munich, largely because they were not in Salzburg. But

Wolfgang would never consider *La finta giardiniera* to be among his most significant works.

In 1780 Wolfgang was back in Salzburg, after his disastrous tour of Mannheim, Munich and Paris. He had lost his mother, loved and lost Aloysia, and was now bleakly facing a dull future in the service of his loathed Archbishop. But he did embark on a new theatrical project, and one that might possibly take him in another direction. After the excitements of writing in Italian for Italian audiences, he was now intrigued by the idea of working in the vernacular for his German-speaking Salzburg audiences. In Mannheim he had attended performances of two melodramas by Georg Benda, *Medea* and *Ariadne auf Naxos*, with their German dialogue spoken over orchestral accompaniment, rather than being actually sung. It was at this point that he got together with his father's trumpet-playing friend, the poet Johann Schachtner, and began to work on a singspiel, *Zaïde*. The project was never finished (or, as Leopold was to say euphemistically, 'not quite completed'). But Wolfgang did write fifteen numbers, and again his advances are significant. He tried his hand at writing Benda-type accompanied dialogues, and they are strikingly effective, although, interestingly, he was never to repeat the experiment. He developed his abilities to write ensembles in which different emotions are expressed by different people at the same time. Where the trio in *Lucio Silla* was in effect a duet-plus-one, the quartet here in *Zaïde* is a duet-plus-one-plus-one, for two lovers are observed by two different commentators. And for Zaïde herself, Wolfgang did write some truly astonishing music, including the dramatic aria 'Tiger! Wetze nur die Klauen' (Tiger! Sharpen your claws!) – part of his Salzburg menagerie, perhaps, like Maria Magdalena Lipp's lion. But the most heart-stopping aria is the lullaby 'Ruhe sanft' (Sleep quietly) that Zaïde sings over the sleeping body of the man she loves. The accompaniment of muted strings and divided pizzicato violas supports not only the most gloriously alluring vocal line but also a solo oboe (Mozart's favourite instrument of seduction), and as such it anticipates the later wonders of his aria 'Vorrei spiegarvi, oh Dio', written for

Aloysia in 1783. When he and Schachtner worked on their experimental and ultimately aborted project, they had no performers or performance in mind – a totally rare occurrence for Mozart. But the very nature of this aria, its line, its accompaniment and its emotional content, surely indicate the truth of his vocal longings. For all her cruel rejection of him, his ears were still ringing with the voice of Aloysia Weber.

WHEN MOZART AND his mother spent the winter months of 1777–8 in Mannheim, it was not just the Webers who impressed him so profoundly. Other families too, solid like his own in musical talent, became immensely important to him, both in that trying period and beyond. Christian Cannabich, the composer and violinist who directed the stellar Mannheim orchestra, together with his wife Elisabeth and their gifted children Rosa and Carl, opened their home and their hearts to their young visitor and his mother. Two instrumentalists from the orchestra, the brothers Johann Baptist and Franz Anton Wendling, also became close friends. Johann Baptist was the flautist who, with the oboist Friedrich Ramm, was supposed to accompany Mozart to Paris on the next stage of his journey, but whose morals, religion and general behaviour were then so handily besmirched by Wolfgang, as he tried to concoct for Leopold his reasons for abandoning these arrangements and heading instead for Italy with Aloysia. If Johann Baptist Wendling ever knew of such disloyal and cavalier allegations, his friendship with Mozart survived them, for in Paris in 1778, where the young men did all meet up again, he was a supportive ally in an alien environment. Like Cannabich, he and his brother, both of whom had married superb singers and were also producing talented children, remained at the heart of Wolfgang's affections. And Wolfgang reciprocated the loving warmth that he received from all these Mannheim families by writing for them: arias for Johann Baptist Wendling's wife, sonatas for Cannabich's daughter, little songs for Franz Anton Wendling's daughter.

But beyond these important individuals, the entire Mannheim orchestra became for Mozart a beacon of musical excellence and achievement. The players who had initially eyed him with suspicion, but came together to play his farewell concert in February 1778, were acknowledged to be the best orchestra in existence, lauded throughout Europe. (In 1772 Burney had described them as 'an army of generals'.[29]) Wolfgang measured all other orchestras against the Mannheim yardstick, writing from Paris to his father in 1778:

> If only the [Salzburg] orchestra were as organized as they are at Mannheim. Indeed I would like you to see the discipline that prevails there and the authority which Cannabich yields. There everything is done seriously. Cannabich, who is the best conductor I have ever seen, is both beloved and feared by his subordinates. Moreover he is respected by the whole town and so are his soldiers. But they certainly behave quite differently from ours. They have good manners, are well dressed and do not go to the public houses and swill.[30]

He longed to write something really substantial for these beloved and admired musicians. And in 1780, by which time the Elector Carl Theodor had moved his entire musical establishment from Mannheim to Munich, Mozart at last had his opportunity.

For the Carnival season in Munich, in early 1781, Mozart was commissioned to write his opera *Idomeneo, re di Creta*. The libretto chosen by the Munich Court was an old text by Dauchet, originally set to music by Campra in Paris in 1712. Wolfgang turned to the Salzburg Court chaplain, Abbate Varesco, and invited him to make an Italian version of it. But he too was intrinsically involved in the project: throughout the summer of 1780 he and Varesco worked together on the structure, dramaturgy and poetry. This process continued long after Wolfgang had travelled to Munich in November 1780, for, as ever, it was only after he had met his cast and assessed their strengths that he began to write for them, and often the libretto was tweaked accordingly. Leopold, and to an extent Nannerl too, became intermediaries in the dialogue between Wolfgang and his librettist in Salzburg; and indeed the correspondence between father and son over the period of *Idomeneo*'s composition is enormously revealing of Wolfgang's methods, sensitivities and adaptability. His aim was not merely to produce a score of ravishing music, exceptional both in its complexity and its simplicity, but through this music to illuminate the dramatic narrative and the psychological conflicts abundant in it. And as he shared his experiences with his father, Leopold gave him his utmost support, offering advice that was practical, informed and scholarly. Between them they were tireless in preparing the libretto for publication, accommodating all alterations as they occurred in the process of composition and rehearsal. While not without tension and anxiety, the letters exchanged between Wolfgang and Leopold in this *Idomeneo* period are some of the most positive and most productive of their entire correspondence. And for Wolfgang, the whole process of *Idomeneo*'s creation and rehearsal in Munich was similarly happy. He was working with the best musicians in Europe, surrounded by close and loving friends whose support sustained him admirably through any problems. 'I went to that rehearsal', he wrote to Leopold, describing the orchestra's first reading, 'with as easy a mind as if I were going to a lunch party somewhere.'[31]

The plot of *Idomeneo* concerns the eponymous King of Crete, who is shipwrecked as he returns home from the Trojan wars. He begs the gods to spare his life, vowing to sacrifice the first person he meets if he is saved. That person turns out to be his own son, Idamante. Idomeneo tries to circumvent his vow by sending his son away, but Neptune produces another storm, together with a monster who ravages the island. Idamante kills the monster, and offers himself for sacrifice in proper fulfilment of his father's vow. But Neptune spares him, decreeing that Idomeneo should abdicate, and Idamante reign in his place.

This tough story of a classic conflict between paternal love and regal duty, laden with Enlightenment passion for loyalty, sacrifice and retribution, is enriched too by the important presence of two women. Ilia, daughter of King Priam of Troy, and therefore the enemy, has been sent as prisoner by Idomeneo to Crete, but has fallen in love with Idamante, and he with her. At the point of Idamante's sacrifice, she interrupts the ceremony, offering to die instead of him. The mollified Neptune decrees that she should marry Idamante and reign beside him as his queen. And then there is Elettra, the disturbed daughter of Agamemnon. She is also in love with Idamante. When Idomeneo tries to avoid killing his son by sending him away, it is to accompany Elettra back to Argos, and she is overjoyed. But Neptune's ultimate decree and resolution have no place for her, and she finally goes mad.

Idomeneo would therefore provide four singers with dramatically splendid roles, and Mozart was keen to discover who they would be. In the event, he was both delighted and dismayed, and, in the case of the protagonist of his title role, simultaneously. Idomeneo was to be sung by none other than his old friend Anton Raaff, who had enjoyed a successful international career throughout Germany, Italy, Spain and Portugal for several decades. In 1770, at the age of fifty-six, he had been engaged at Mannheim (where Wolfgang and his mother had first met him in 1777), and was thus high in seniority in the casting of operas for the Elector Carl Theodor's musical establishment in Munich. Now, at sixty-six, he was well past his prime; and his diminished capabilities were a cause of great anxiety to Wolfgang, who was torn between genuine affection for his friend and frustration at his level of performance. Not only were his vocal stamina and dexterity not up to the demands of the music that Wolfgang imagined for this tortured, central role; Raaff's acting abilities too were clichéd and shallow ('like a statue',[32] as Wolfgang protested in a letter to his father), and almost certainly failed to match up to the veritably Shakespearean demands of Idomeneo's conflicts and complexities. But Wolfgang was infinitely patient with him. He adjusted his own musical conception of the role, writing for Raaff a simpler version of the massive central aria 'Fuor del mar'; transferring the dramatic energy of the other arias from the voice to the orchestral accompaniment, thus making it an almost equal partner in the carrying of emotion; and presenting his final abdication speech as a monumental passage of accompanied recitative – in which Wolfgang himself spent hours coaching his friend. Throughout the rehearsal process Wolfgang dealt with Raaff with the sweetest tact and the kindest delicacy; their friendship endured, and *Idomeneo* was a triumph for both of them. But they were each no doubt sadly aware that by far the best role Raaff had ever been given had come several years too late.

There were major anxieties too about the casting of Idamante. The castrato Vincenzo Dal Prato, exactly the same age as Mozart, had just been hired by Munich, where he would remain in service for twenty years. But before they even met, Wolfgang had his doubts about him, telling Leopold that he had heard reports of Dal Prato being unable to sing long phrases. Once Dal Prato arrived, Wolfgang's misgivings were confirmed. He was ill-prepared, unimaginative both musically and dramatically, and seemed short of attention and concentration. Even Wolfgang's legendary patience with his colleagues was sorely tried, and eventually he reported in exasperation to Salzburg that Dal Prato was 'utterly useless'.[33] So, as ever, Wolfgang cut his musical coat according to the cloth of Dal Prato's vocal abilities, again transferring much of the musical energy to the orchestra. But his disappointment was exacerbated by the fact that Idamante was a role very close to his heart. The whole father–son relationship between Idomeneo and Idamante was something to which he was ever sensitive; and although for the rest of his life he continued to look back on the period of *Idomeneo* in Munich as one of his happiest, he was always affected by the paternal and filial tensions in the opera. As Constanze reported, in the course of a normal evening of domestic music-making at the Tanzmeisterhaus, during their visit to Salzburg in 1783, the assembled group launched into the quartet from *Idomeneo*, in which the passionate love between father and son is at its most disturbed by the vicissitudes of circumstance; and Wolfgang fled from the room in tears.

If Wolfgang was experiencing frustration, therefore, at the

casting of the two central male roles, the women who played Ilia and Elettra delighted him on every level, for these were the wives of his great friends, the Wendling brothers. Dorotea Wendling had married the flautist Johann Baptist when she was sixteen, in 1752, had produced their daughter Elisabeth Augusta in the same year, and, with her husband, had joined the musical establishment at Mannheim. In 1777, when Wolfgang and his mother had spent the winter in Mannheim, they had been regular guests of Johann Baptist and Dorotea, and, as Maria Anna had reported to Leopold, 'Wolfgang is a tremendous favourite with them.'[34] Dorotea was now, at forty-six, to take the role of the young Trojan princess Ilia. If Wolfgang had any misgivings at all about her ability to portray a woman half her own age, he never expressed them (any more than he had when the forty-year-old Anna De Amicis had sung Giunia in *Lucio Silla*). Rather, he would have been thrilled that an artist for whom he had already written a dramatic concert aria ('Basta, vincesti', K486a, in 1778, to a text which she herself had chosen) and whose voice he therefore knew completely, would now be in his opera.

Dorotea's sister-in-law, Elisabeth Augusta, was married to Johann Baptist Wendling's violinist brother Franz Anton. She was the younger by ten years, had joined the Mannheim Court at the age of fifteen in 1761, and married her husband in 1764. She too had produced a daughter, who would in due course also become a singer, and had named her Dorotea after her talented aunt. (That one Wendling brother had a wife Dorotea and a daughter Elisabeth Augusta, and the other a wife Elisabeth Augusta and a daughter Dorotea, has remained a challenge to admirers of Karl Theodor's musical establishment for centuries.) Elisabeth Augusta was cast in the dramatically thrilling role of Elettra. The educated Munich audiences, well versed like Leopold and Wolfgang in classical literature, would have been thoroughly familiar with this damaged product of the House of Atreus. So Elettra's presence in this story of Idomeneo, although potentially an ultimate irrelevance, was an added strand of violence, suffering, devotion and insanity. And, through Elisabeth Augusta Wendling, Wolfgang was to exploit all these emotions brilliantly.

Mozart's increasingly sophisticated methods of breaking the rules of opera seria, in order to give continual momentum to dramatic and emotional narrative, are immediately apparent at the end of *Idomeneo*'s energetic, tensely syncopated overture. Rather than coming to a resounding conclusion, inviting therefore the customary applause, the music subsides into soft and reflective string chords, out of which emerges the voice of Ilia: 'Quando avran fine mai l'aspre sventure mie?' (Will my harsh sufferings never end?). For the first time Mozart has let the orchestra take the audience directly into the body of the opera, and into the mind of this unhappy young woman; and the tumult of the overture has therefore been hers. As Ilia continues her soliloquy, she imparts essential narrative information: she has been shipwrecked in a storm, lost her father and brothers, been rescued by Idamante whom she believes loves Elettra, and has fallen for him. She expresses homelessness, grief, loss, bereavement, new amorous passion, and jealousy (of Elettra); and the orchestra follows her every mood-swing, supplying emotional commentary to Ilia's desolate story. Eventually she settles into a mournful, utterly beautiful aria, 'Padre, germani, addio' (Farewell my father and brothers), where again it is the orchestra which shadows Ilia's emotional fragility, in agitated syncopations, little stabbing forte-piano emphases, and, like a male dancer lifting his female partner, with supportive accompaniment as she soars through her long final melisma. After such an opening soliloquy, an audience might again have been expected to break into applause; and once more Mozart removes any possible opportunity to do so by not actually bringing her *scena* to a conclusion, but by cross-fading it directly into what follows. Idamante approaches, and the accompanying texture gradually unwinds into string-accompanied recitative, and then into simple recitative. It is a staggering opening to the opera. At a stroke, Mozart has put the audience firmly into the narrative picture, naming all the principal characters and establishing the relationships between them. He has issued firm instructions about not applauding, even for musicians of such quality. And with this initial scene of emotional intensity and music that is both beguiling and arresting, he has launched his friend Dorotea Wendling into her magnificent role of Ilia.

At the beginning of the second act Ilia has a most touching scene with the returned Idomeneo. (She is as yet unaware of his appalling conflict, nor of the decision therefore that he has made, to send Idamante back to Argos with Elettra.) She expresses her own sweet gratitude that he has been returned safely to his people, saying in her aria 'Se il padre perdei' that she now looks upon him as a father, since she has lost her own. And here, in the aria about a new family and peace of mind, Mozart wrote not only for Dorotea's glorious sustained singing, but for her husband Johann Baptist Wendling and his other friends in the orchestra too: 'Se il padre perdei' is enriched with solo instrumental lines for flute (Wendling), oboe (Friedrich Ramm), horn (Franz Lang) and bassoon (Georg Ritter) – the very same combination of instruments, and indeed players, for whom he had written a sinfonia concertante in Paris in 1778. The enhancement of the vocal line by these other solo strands gives the music a special sense of repose and transparency at this intimate expression of political reconciliation and personal gratitude. That it was, literally, a 'family' moment for the original protagonists is indicative of the intensity of Mozart's own gratitude to his dear friends, and a real gift to them as they all shared in it.

By the time Ilia reappears at the beginning of the final act, Neptune has thwarted Idomeneo's wild attempt to slide out of his vow, and sent his storm and monster to wreak havoc in Crete. But she is concerned only with her feelings for Idamante, wrestling with her deep desire to confess her love to him. In another aria for Dorotea Wendling's sustained cantabile singing, so admired by Mozart, Ilia invites gentle breezes ('Zeffiretti') to fly to her beloved and make her confession for her. Again this opening scene is enfolded by accompanied recitative, so there are no rigid divisions between the distillations of her thoughts; and the orchestra contributes emotional counterpoint to her longings, supporting and mirroring her own vocal lyricism. Ilia and Idamante at last confess their passionate love for each other, in a scene which Mozart builds from simple recitative to accompanied recitative, and eventually into the most tender of duets; and these two voices of equal range (if not ability) intertwine, blend and share. United now in thirds, they move into a rapturous allegretto, only to have their euphoria – and their duet – interrupted by the arrival of Idomeneo and Elettra. As Idomeneo insists that Idamante flees from Crete and seeks safe refuge elsewhere, four unhappy people then sing the most remarkable music in the whole opera, the quartet. Whereas in *Lucio Silla* Mozart's trio had been a duet-plus-one, and in *Zaïde* his quartet was a duet-plus-one-plus-one, here in *Idomeneo* the quartet consists of four separate voices expressing four separate miseries, united only by the fact that each of them is suffering: they come together to sing the lines 'Ah il cor mi si divide! / Soffrir più non si può' (My heart is breaking; there is no worse suffering). With brilliant control, Mozart focuses first on one character and then on another, bringing his or her musical line into sharp relief against the background of those of the others, and the audience thus has the impression of hearing and comprehending four strands of wretchedness at the same time; and the moments of shared suffering are heart-stopping. This utterly extraordinary quartet ends, as it began, with Idamante's framing line, 'Andrò ramingo e solo' (Alone I shall wander in the wilderness).

In spite of Idamante's triumphant slaughter of Neptune's monster, Idomeneo is persuaded by his High Priest and his own people that, for the sake of his country, he must go ahead with his avowed sacrifice; and in distress he at last discloses the identity of his victim. The ceremony begins, and Idomeneo prepares to kill his own son, in public view. But at the very moment of sacrifice, Ilia rushes in to interrupt it, arguing with admirable logic that Idamante is innocent, that the gods wish to rid Greece of its enemies not its sons, and that therefore she, as the daughter of Priam, is the one who should die. And, as in the tightly controlled exchanges of dignity and courage between Idomeneo and Idamante, this self-sacrificing speech is set entirely in accompanied recitative, with the orchestra as ever pointing and releasing every nuance of Ilia's dramatic utterance. Her offer to die for the man she loves, the finest and most noble gesture available to any human being, mollifies the gods, and Neptune now intervenes with his instructions for peace at last in Crete.

Dorotea Wendling's final appearance on stage in *Idomeneo* thus propelled the opera towards its dramatic denouement, and at the same time gave a superb conclusion to her role. Ilia is one of Mozart's first truly great creations, a thoroughly rounded character of sweetness, intelligence and courage, whose essential attributes would reappear, first, in Constanze in *Die Entführung aus dem Serail*, and then, a decade later, in Pamina in *Die Zauberflöte*. All the while that Wolfgang had been complaining in his letters to Leopold about the inadequacies of his male singers, he never breathed a word of criticism against his sopranos. Rather, he reported to Salzburg that Dorotea Wendling was 'arcicontentissima' with her music, implying therefore that he felt the same about her; and the double superlative speaks volumes. At the end of her career, she had received from her good friend a true gift of a role, and she had risen magnificently to the challenges, both musical and dramatic, within it.

But if Dorotea's character encapsulated all the nobility and goodness of human behaviour, her sister-in-law Elisabeth Augusta's was its complete opposite. The unstable Elettra, Wolfgang's only encounter with operatic insanity, is a startlingly original and utterly compelling role. From her very first appearance Mozart shows in the music that this woman is disturbed. She comes upon Idamante freeing the Trojan prisoners, and berates him for protecting the enemy; and then, after hearing of the supposed death of Idomeneo, she has her own first monumental soliloquy. Everything, she now believes, is conspiring against her: Idamante loves another, and will dispose of his heart and his realm as he pleases; a Trojan slave will share his throne and his bed, rather than herself, the daughter of a king; and in her jealous rage she hears the tormented cries of the Furies in Hades (the family problem), egging her on to seek her vengeance.

Elettra's soliloquy begins with a long accompanied recitative, where the opening six bars of agitated orchestral energy and her cry of 'Estinto è Idomeneo?' are immediately repeated, but, with spectacular musical verisimilitude, down a semitone, as if she herself is literally losing her grip. And Mozart continues in the same vein, using every advantage of accompanied recitative to convey the disjunct state of her mind: there are sudden changes of dynamic and tempo, of pace and rhythm, and a real collapse (musically represented in a chromatically sliding descent) at the words 'più non resisto' (I can bear it no longer). By the time therefore that Elettra launches into her aria, 'Tutte nel cor mi sento / Furie del crudo averno' (Within my heart I feel all the Furies of dismal Hades), the audience is in no doubt that she is completely unhinged. And the aria itself continues to characterize all her tensions and neuroses in the music. There are breathless arpeggios on a flute, like elusive fragments of thought. There are hysterical semiquavers in the violins, with sudden forte stabs appearing at irregular intervals, dispelling any confident assumption of the metrical security of the bar-line. There are wild leaps in Elettra's vocal line, and quasi-mindless repetitions ('vendetta e crudeltà'). And the most astonishing aspect of all comes as the aria seems to be approaching a da capo, with the return of the hysterical semiquavers and the displaced fortes. She arrives at a fermata on a diminished chord, and then does indeed repeat her opening music, but in a totally unexpected key. Even if a listener is unaware of what precisely has happened (the music is now in C minor, where it should be in D minor), the aural effect is as shocking as if one has suddenly stumbled off a pavement. Mozart then allows Elettra in the next fourteen bars to claw her way harmonically back to where she should have been. And as she rushes from the stage, the music of her mental storm hurtles straight into the real storm of Idomeneo's shipwreck. Elettra's first soliloquy is thus a scene of unprecedented musico-dramatic brilliance; and Elisabeth Augusta Wendling must have been an actress of fierce presence and intensity to enable Mozart to have created it for her.

But Elisabeth Augusta was not just a fiery performer. Like her sister-in-law, she could provide Mozart with what he so admired, a good cantabile singing line. In the second act, Elettra has a brief reprieve from her jealous insanities, for, when Idomeneo decides to send Idamante away, she becomes the beneficiary: she will be taken home to Argos by the man she adores. So her second soliloquy could not be in greater contrast to her first, as she now joyfully counts her blessings, and resolves to charm Idamante into forgetting her rival, Ilia, and loving her. Her string-accompanied recitative is gentle and confident, with delicate undulations from the orchestra: she seems completely healed by her rapture. And her aria ('Idol mio'), retaining its string-only accompaniment as if the orchestra too is stripped to its simplest, is a sweetly lyrical love-song, allowing Elettra her moment of serenity. Yet there is still something subliminally disturbing about it: the phrase lengths are made irregular by the seemingly arbitrary, even mindless, repetition of single bars (the fifth and tenth bars, for instance, of the introduction). If Mozart wanted subtly to undermine Elettra's temporary repose, he succeeded with a characteristic piece of musical prestidigitation. And again, as with so many arias in *Idomeneo*, her 'Idol mio' leads straight into the next music, here a march, which announces the imminent departure of her ship, and she hurries away to join it. At the port the assembled sailors and warriors of Argos and Crete sing a gentle departing chorus, 'Placido è il mar, andiamo' (The sea is quiet, let us leave), in the middle of which Elettra exhorts the gentle breezes ('Soavi zeffiretti') to calm the rage of the recent storm winds and spread love everywhere; and again Mozart deployed Elisabeth Augusta's immaculately controlled cantabile singing.

Elettra's radiant euphoria continues as Idomeneo and Idamante appear and bid each other taut farewells. At first she rides over their tensions in the ensuing trio, maintaining her calm line of contentment. But eventually she senses their mutual distress, and has a pre-monition of disaster ('Oh dio, che sarà?'), which moves the music from its gentle andante into an anxious allegro con brio; and here all three characters share a prayer to the fates to bring peace to every-one. But as they approach the ship, the storm flares up, the monster appears, and the act – together with Elettra's oasis of calm – ends in climactic disarray.

The third and final act of *Idomeneo* sees Elettra's inevitable return to insanity. Together with Idomeneo, she interrupts the ten-der love duet between Ilia and Idamante; and her contributions to the ensuing quartet call once more for vengeance. She joins with the others only for the communal line of suffering ('Soffrir più non si può'), but otherwise seems already to be consigned to the outer reaches of the central story. She witnesses the sacrifice scene, and therefore Ilia's heroic martyrdom; and, along with everyone else, she hears the voice of Neptune as he issues his decree. That she is utterly excluded from the happy resolutions pushes her firmly back over the edge, and she imagines herself in Hades along with the Furies and her brother Orestes. And here Mozart wrote a scene which, in that first Munich production, he was eventually obliged to cut: perhaps in the end Elisabeth Augusta Wendling could not maintain the stamina required for such a *scena*, for it is hugely demanding. Elettra shrieks at the Furies, at their serpents, at her brother, and at her own total grief, in repeated, fractured sentences and, finally, in manic laughter. This is another uncannily thorough musical treatment of insanity, and severely unsettles the composure of the audience at this stage of the opera. That Mozart simplified it for those first performances, leaving Elisabeth Augusta with a short accompanied recitative with which to rush distractedly from the stage, does suggest that, like Raaff in his central aria, she could not do the scene full justice. But there is still no doubt at all of Elettra's state of mind, and Mozart has created for another dear friend a role of spectacular and unforgettable dramatic intensity.

IF INDEED IT was a spirit of happy confidence in Mozart, supported as he was by the loving warmth of all his Munich friends, which propelled him into taking such monumental steps into operatic maturity with *Idomeneo*, it was an altogether different environment which was to challenge him in Vienna. A far cry from the almost cosy, family-oriented artistic milieu of Munich, that of the Austrian capital was a cut-throat world of competition, self-promoting intrigue and machination, and huge individual egos. Dominated by, but by no means limited to, activities at Court, Viennese music-making involved a large assembly of personalities, tightly contesting and jealously guarding their territories. Political manoeuvre, and the corruptions habitually associated with power, were rife and effective.

The central figure in all this was the Italian wunderkind, Antonio Salieri, who, only six years older than Mozart, had at the age of twenty-four (in 1774) been appointed as Composer at Court, and also as Director of Opera. Later, in 1788, he would succeed Giuseppe Bonno in the illustrious position of Kapellmeister. For the rest of Mozart's life these two composers would dance around each other in a complex relationship: Salieri did seem to block the path of his new rival, and possibly also to stir up cabals against him. But superficially at least they remained on the most courteous of terms; and beyond all the suspicion and mistrust there was unquestionably mutual respect, and, in the long run, affection too. And when in the spring of 1781 Mozart came to Vienna from Munich, he was unperturbed as he met head-on the challenges of this wholly different environment. For he was young, energetic, very noticeable, and above all extremely able; and there were abundant opportunities to be seized.

As the unfinished *Zaïde* had perhaps shown, Mozart had long had in his sights Joseph II's German National Theatre company at the Burgtheater. Since 1776, when this former real-tennis court and later home of French opéra-comique and Italian opera seria had come under the direct control of the Court, it had presented that thoroughly German theatrical art-form, singspiel, or comic opera in German with spoken dialogue. When Mozart arrived in Vienna, the director of the German National Theatre was Gottlieb Stephanie; and it was he who commissioned Mozart to write *Die Entführung aus dem Serail*, to his own adaptation of Bretzner's play. With both *Zaïde* and *Idomeneo*, Mozart had made significant contributions to the work of the librettist, exercising in collaboration first with Schachtner and then with Varesco his own supreme musico-theatrical instincts, and helping therefore to fashion a text that best served the musical and emotional development of the drama. Here in Vienna, he took this collaboration one step further, working literally beside Stephanie to set the musical structure and enable real development of character. And he found this process intensely satisfying. He wrote to Leopold, '[Stephanie] is arranging the libretto for me – just as I want it, in fact – to a hair.'[35] Mozart the musician and Mozart the dramatist were from now on inseparable.

The story of *Die Entführung aus dem Serail* concerns the unrequited love of an oriental potentate, the Pasha Selim, for his female prisoner Constanze; her attempted but foiled rescue by her lover Belmonte; and their eventual pardon by the magnanimous Selim. In addition to these three principal characters, there are their servants. Constanze's maid, Blonde, and Belmonte's manservant, Pedrillo, provide cheerful contrast to the nobility and seriousness of their masters. The overseer of the harem, Osmin, is ostensibly a cruel and unyielding figure, but he is smitten with love for Blonde and therefore, especially in the hands of Mozart, rendered truly multidimensional: human, tender, even vulnerable. And the cast that Stephanie assembled to perform this singspiel was of exceptional quality. After the uneven standards of the singers in Mozart's previous operas in Munich and even in Italy, the consistently high level of expertise in Vienna must have been for him an unprecedented delight.

At the time of *Die Entführung*'s commission and preparation, Mozart was lodging with Frau Weber, courting Constanze and rebuilding his bridges with Aloysia. It is tempting to speculate that he might have wanted Aloysia to assume the all-important role of

Constanze. But, had he even thought to suggest her, it is unlikely that she would have been able to take part, for she was rapidly producing children (her first daughter was born in May 1781, and by the beginning of 1782 she was pregnant again). And in fact a singer whose profile was even higher than Aloysia's was available. The twenty-six-year-old Caterina Cavalieri was the toast of Vienna. Trained by Salieri, and now his mistress too, she had made her debut in Vienna at the age of twenty in Anfossi's *La finta giardiniera* at the Kärntnerthor-Theater in 1775. In 1778 she had joined the singspiel company, and continued to sing in both Italian and German operas. She was a huge catch, and Mozart must have been thrilled to haul her in. Their relationship would continue long after *Die Entführung aus dem Serail*: she would go on to create Madame Silberklang in *Der Schauspieldirektor* in 1786, to sing Donna Elvira in the first Viennese production of *Don Giovanni* in 1788, the Countess in the 1789 revival of *Figaro*, and, in concert, in *Davidde Penitente* and Mozart's reworking of Handel's *Acis and Galatea*. Socially too she and the Mozarts remained close, visiting one another regularly. Wolfgang's final letter, to Constanze in October 1791, described with relaxed confidence how Cavalieri and Salieri sat in his box at a performance of *Die Zauberflöte*, along with his mother-in-law and young son, all in the greatest amity. They had become among his closest acquaintances.

The tenor cast as Belmonte was older: Johann Valentin Adamberger was over forty. He had studied in Munich under the renowned teacher Giovanni Valesi (who had just created for Mozart the small but magisterially important role of the High Priest in *Idomeneo*, and whose later pupils would include Constanze's cousin Carl Maria von Weber). In 1780 Adamberger had joined the German National Theatre; and by the spring of 1781 he was already central to Viennese musical activity, both theatrically and socially, gracing many an aristocratic salon in addition to the operatic stage. He too, together with his actress wife Maria Anna, would become close to Wolfgang and Constanze, exchanging visits and advising one another on their political manoeuvres at Court. For

Adamberger, Mozart wrote not just Belmonte, but also the tenor aria 'Per pietà, non ricercate', K420, to be inserted into Anfossi's opera *Il curioso indiscreto* in 1783 (when Aloysia sang her two arias, K418 and 419). In the event, Salieri, probably indeed trying to sabotage Mozart's brief exposure in Anfossi's opera, persuaded Adamberger that it would be inappropriate for him to sing this extra music (though Aloysia loyally and courageously went ahead and sang hers), and Adamberger's friendship with Wolfgang temporarily faltered. 'Now he is sorry, but it is too late,'[36] wrote Wolfgang to Leopold, relating the whole incident. But on numerous other occasions Adamberger did perform Mozart's music, and their mutual affection was restored.

Wolfgang would have been delighted that two old friends were also to be in his cast. He had known both Therese Teiber and Ludwig Fischer, respectively Blonde and Osmin, since the summer of 1773, when he and his father had made their rather fruitless visit to Vienna. Therese Teiber came from an extremely musical family: her father Matthias was a violinist at Court, her two brothers became celebrated as a violinist and an organist, and she and her elder sister Elisabeth would have successful careers as singers. Matthias Teiber had lent Wolfgang a violin in 1773, and, united perhaps by the fact that both he and Leopold were fathers of remarkable offspring, the families had spent time in each other's company. One day that summer, when both Wolfgang and Therese were in their teens, they had all gone together on a visit to Baden as guests of the promising young bass Ludwig Fischer. And now both these singers were to appear in Wolfgang's new opera. At twenty-two, Therese was the youngest of the cast, but had already been a member of the German National Theatre at the Burgtheater for three years, and would continue there, specializing in the soubrette repertory, for a further ten. She would also continue her association with Mozart, performing Giunia's 'Parto, m'affretto' from *Lucio Silla* in a concert of his at the Burgtheater in March 1783, and, later, taking over some performances of Zerlina in the first Viennese production of *Don Giovanni* in 1788.

At the time of *Die Entführung aus dem Serail*, Ludwig Fischer was in his mid-thirties, and extremely popular with audiences – 'he has the whole Viennese public on his side,'[37] Wolfgang wrote approvingly to his father in September 1781. His voice had developed most splendidly in its lower register, and Wolfgang was to exploit this fully ('I have allowed Fischer's beautiful deep notes to glow'[38]). He even seriously considered rewriting the role of Idomeneo for him, for Fischer was clearly a formidable actor as well as a distinguished and popular singer. Nothing ever came of that idea; but Mozart did revel in every aspect of Fischer's talent, and in his long-standing familiarity too with Therese Teiber, as he created the theatrically glorious relationship between Blonde and Osmin. Eventually Fischer would move to Paris, and Wolfgang helped him get established there by writing him letters of introduction. But he hated losing his charismatic friend, and wrote to Leopold in February 1783, 'The Viennese are making the foolish mistake of letting a man go who can never be replaced.'[39]

Contemporary with Fischer was the tenor and actor Johann Ernst Dauer, who was to take the role of Pedrillo. He too was enormously popular at the Burgtheater, where he specialized in lighter roles and remained a favourite with audiences for over thirty years. If his talents were more as an actor than as a singer (on the evening before the opening of *Die Entführung aus dem Serail*, he appeared in a German version of Sheridan's *A School for Scandal*), he was by no means a musical passenger; and in addition to his many contributions to ensembles, both comic and serious, Wolfgang rewarded him with a fine and heroic aria, 'Frisch zum Kampfe'. Finally, the non-singing but enormously important role of the Pasha Selim was taken by the fifty-year-old actor Dominik Joseph Jautz, who was a stalwart of the Burgtheater in both plays and singspiels. (He had performed the part of Horatio in the first Viennese production of *Hamlet* in 1773.)

There was thus not a single weak link in the cast: there was no Dal Prato, nor any last-minute replacement by a local church singer. And, for the first time in Mozart's operas, the ages of the performers were absolutely perfect. No longer did he have singers in their forties playing women in their twenties: rather, there was real dramatic verisimilitude in lustrous addition to vocal distinction. Mozart had largely shaped the libretto himself, with his natural instincts for characterization, pacing and structure, so recently refined in *Idomeneo*; and his own passions were energized by his freedom from Salzburg and his infatuation with Constanze Weber. All this would lead to another giant leap for him as he created his *Die Entführung aus dem Serail*.

Just as he had done when writing *Idomeneo* in Munich, Wolfgang kept his father informed of the whole process of composition. (His motive was perhaps now slightly ulterior: as Leopold disapproved so ferociously of all his current activities, he was determined at least to retain his obsessive interest in his music.) 'I thought it would afford you pleasure,' he wrote on 26 September 1781, 'if I gave you some idea of my opera.'[40] He described his work on the text with Stephanie, his preoccupation with key relationships, his specific use of 'Turkish' music (involving percussion and piccolos) in the overture, the choruses and some of Osmin's music, and, quite unselfconsciously, his effortless ability to write extremely good counterpoint in such a way as actually to enhance the dramatic moment. Of the trio 'Marsch, marsch, marsch' for the three men, for instance, he wrote:

> Now for the trio at the close of Act I. Pedrillo has passed off his master as an architect – to give him an opportunity of meeting his Constanze in the garden. Bassa Selim has taken him into his service. Osmin, the steward, knows nothing of this, and being a rude churl and a sworn foe to all strangers, is impertinent and refuses to let them into the garden. It opens quite abruptly – and because the words lend themselves to it, I have made it a fairly respectable piece of three-part writing.

But above all, Mozart's letter to his father demonstrates new depths of maturity and his ability to read a psychological state of mind and represent it in the music. He describes, for example, the acceleration in Osmin's final rage aria 'O wie will ich triumphiren' (claiming with modest confidence, 'this is bound to be effective'), and gives Leopold his wholly articulate reasons for deploying it:

> Just as a man in such a towering rage oversteps all the bounds of order, moderation and propriety and completely forgets himself, so must the music too forget itself. But since passions, whether violent or not, must never be expressed to the point of exciting disgust, and, as music, even in the most terrible situations, must never offend the ear but must please the listener, or in other words must never cease to be *music*, so I have not chosen a key foreign to F (in which the aria is written) but one related to it – not the nearest, D minor, but the more remote A minor.

Wolfgang has reached new levels of sophisticated human understanding, and found the means to achieve what he wants in his music.

All his characters are therefore well defined, and, for Fischer and Adamberger he wrote music that was challenging and greatly rewarding. For Therese Teiber he created the first in a series of roles that would develop later with Zerlina in *Don Giovanni*, Despina in *Così fan tutte*, and, most especially, Susanna in *Le nozze di Figaro*. Blonde's adorable perkiness and abundant common sense are perfectly expressed in her music. Her two arias are mainly syllabic, indicating both a matter-of-fact defiance in her dealings with Osmin and a beguiling and straightforward sweetness in her relationship with Pedrillo. But since Teiber evidently had a marvellous agility in her upper register, which Wolfgang exploited as happily as he did Fischer's low notes, Blonde has in her opening aria, 'Durch zärtlichkeit' (With tenderness) spectacular melismatic flourishes on the word 'entweicht' (banished), taking her far above the stave as she confidently brushes aside Osmin's boorish commands ('mürrisches Befehlen'). The duet between them, 'Ich gehe, doch rate ich dir' (I'll go, but take my advice and stay away), is a brilliant piece of subtle comedy for Wolfgang's two old friends. He delights in allowing Blonde to mimic Osmin's low notes, taking her way below her normal tessitura before springing her back up again over two octaves. In the central andante section, Blonde weaves a manipulative ornamental line above Osmin's bemused and syllabic bass line. And in the final allegro, 'Nun troll dich', which she constantly leads, she firmly threatens to scratch his eyes out ('Es ist um die Augen geschehen') in music which appropriately taunts and stabs. Not only is all this hilariously effective in clarifying Blonde's upper hand over Osmin, and hugely entertaining too as the two characters play off each other; it is also a perfect foil for what immediately follows, Constanze's most tragic aria, 'Traurigkeit'.

For indeed it is the music for this noble central character, as interpreted by the most distinguished singer of the day, which truly encapsulates Mozart's new depths of maturity. At Constanze's first appearance, in an exchange of dialogue with the Pasha Selim, they both behave impeccably while neither loses ground (he loves her passionately; she sweetly and apologetically desists); and when he begs her to explain what is holding her back, suddenly out of nowhere appears the plangent sound of a solo oboe, sustaining a single note. And tentatively, hesitatingly, Constanze begins to tell him her story: she loves another man, whom she has lost ('Ach ich liebte, war so glücklich' – I was in love, and so happy). Her sentences are broken, as if with the emotion of the narrative, and as ever Mozart reflects her tension in the orchestra too, whose repeated semiquavers at different dynamic levels suggest a world of deep unhappiness. As she rises to the full confession of her punch-line ('gab dahin mein ganzes Herz' – I gave him my whole heart), pausing for a sad little ornament on 'ganzes', she can restrain her passion no longer, and pours it all out in a highly strung allegro: 'Doch wie schnell schwand meine Freude' (But how quickly my joy vanished). Pairs of woodwind instruments float beside her; syncopated strings throb beneath her. And then Mozart unleashes Cavalieri's amazing vocal skills, with high, controlled and sustained passages of formidable coloratura. 'I have sacrificed Constanze's aria a little to the flexible throat of Mlle Cavalieri,' Wolfgang wrote admiringly to his father. The aria is unquestionably extremely demanding. But as it was Mozart's first presentation to, and of, Caterina Cavalieri, it was a real expression of her gifts, and of his respect for them as he deployed them so effectively.

By contrast, Constanze's soliloquy in the second act, 'Traurig-keit', is an almost slow-motion expression of her pain. Coming as it does after the fiery duet between Blonde and Osmin, the open-ing orchestral bars of its accompanied recitative immediately arrest the pace, and dissolve into the desolation of a simple vocal line ('Welcher Kummer herscht im meiner Seele' – What sorrow dwells in my heart). The strings of the orchestra sigh for her in frag-mented semiquavers, and lead into the aria itself, where four pairs of winds (flutes, oboes, basset horns and bassoons) now provide contrasting texture and colour. And here Constanze seems to be locked into her grief: in the course of this long aria, her music hardly ever settles on to a perfect cadence, but continues in relent-less and unresolved misery, punctuated instead by frozen silences, where her sorrow prevents her from uttering anything at all. Again, Cavalieri's technique allowed her to sustain this immensely challenging aria, in the course of which Mozart at a stroke turned the high comedy of the previous scene into lonely anguish.

Suddenly the Pasha Selim appears, and in a brief exchange of dialogue the temperature is changed again, for the Pasha, finally exasperated by her constantly refusing him, now threatens her with torture. And this releases the other side of Constanze, and of Cavalieri. Her defiant response is dazzling, as she throws the Pasha's threats back at him in determined, almost military explo-sions of eloquence: 'Martern aller Arten' (Torture of every kind). And, just as Mozart had done, in very different circumstances, for Ilia's aria 'Se il padre perdei' in *Idomeneo*, he adds four solo instru-ments to the swirls of virtuosity: Constanze is flanked by a flute, an oboe, a violin and a cello, which weave their own lines with both energy and poetry. At just twenty-seven, Caterina Cavalieri clearly had remarkable stamina, in addition to her phenomenal technique, as she delivered these two exacting arias one after the other. And, as before, as he honoured this stamina, Mozart included his respect for Vienna's instrumental soloists.

Constanze's next appearance is in the quartet which closes the second act. She and Belmonte finally meet again, share their joy, with Blonde and Pedrillo, and then both couples experience grave doubts about each other, before slowly overcoming these and returning to a state of shared happiness. It is an ensemble where a great deal happens, as the characters move from happy reunion, through dismay and reconciliation, back to a new joy, informed now by those moments of mistrust. And again, Mozart's musico-dramatic skills take him another step beyond his achievements in the *Idomeneo* quartet. There he portrayed four people expressing different emotions at the same time. Here four individuals are very clearly characterized, while they pair up in continually differing combinations. The opening joy is expressed first by Constanze and Belmonte, and then by Blonde and Pedrillo before all four sing together. But when Belmonte confesses his nagging doubt, the shared ecstasy dissolves suddenly, without warning, into the troubled hurt of a frowning andante. As both he and Pedrillo accuse their women of faithlessness, the joy collapses completely. The women's responses are entirely characteristic: Constanze weeps; Blonde hits Pedrillo across the face. Both men have had their reassurance, and there is a steady recovery towards reconciliation, which is sweet, resolving eventually, and literally, into pure harmony. And this is entirely an interpretation of Mozart's, for the women and men have different texts. The women sing of the injustice of the men's suspicious doubts, and the men of their realization that the women are beyond reproach; and Mozart unites these statements in an almost chorale-like moment of freeze-frame repose. As the men beg to be forgiven, the pace resumes, as does the shared joy, and the act ends in renewed hope. This quartet has somehow encapsulated so much of human relationships, of their understandings and misunderstandings, of their frailties and their strengths, of the calm of trust and the fervour of passion. With it,

Mozart again took a step further towards the perfection of his later operas.

In the final act, after the rescue attempt has been thwarted by Osmin, both Constanze and Belmonte are condemned to die, and as they wait for death they sing a ravishing duet. Most fascinatingly, it is Constanze who is the stronger character of the two. Belmonte apologizes constantly, but she sustains him with an expression of true fearlessness of death ('Was ist der Tod? Ein Ubergang zur Ruh!' – What is death? A passage to peace!) which Mozart surely shared. Like Ilia, Constanze is calmly prepared to die with the man she loves, and this confidence brings her true bliss ('Wonne ist mir dies Gebot'). And so she takes Belmonte into their allegro, and he too is strong. 'Ich will alles gerne leiden' (I will happily bear anything), he claims, and she replies that she will meet death in peace and joy. This most extraordinary duet, which had begun as a scene of condemned misery, ends as, together now in thirds and sixths, Constanze and Belmonte sing of their true rapture. It is little wonder that the Pasha Selim forgives them.

Where *Idomeneo* had been for Mozart a great step forward in the world of opera seria, here in *Die Entführung aus dem Serail* he took another, but now in the context of German singspiel, and again created a masterpiece of enormous emotional verisimilitude. However much there are moments of high comedy, the fundamental seriousness of the story's Enlightenment subject-matter imbues Mozart's whole score with a miraculous gravity. That Wolfgang was 'rescuing' his own Constanze at the precise moment of the creation of *Die Entführung* almost certainly contributed to the intensification of his own emotions, and therefore of the emotions expressed in his opera.

~

AFTER *DIE ENTFÜHRUNG*, Mozart produced no more opera for nearly four years. One reason for this was that he was preoccupied with other genres: piano concertos, string quartets, piano sonatas, arias, and of course his C minor Mass in Salzburg. But there was another reason too. The whole world of opera in Vienna was undergoing change, and again partly at the personal whim of the Emperor, who clearly saw himself as something of an impresario. He loved to have companies of singers staying at the palace of Schönbrunn, where he treated them royally in return for their entertaining him. He delighted in their acquaintance, and took trouble to get to know them personally. On his own frequent journeys to Italy he would often become a talent-spotter, selecting singers to be sent back to Vienna and employed by Salieri. He also had his spies in all the major Italian cities, performing the same function. And in Venice he was represented by the Austrian Ambassador and former director of theatre productions in Vienna, Count Durazzo. It was Durazzo who, in 1783, hired a handful of extremely talented singers for the Emperor. These singers would change the flavour not only of opera in Vienna, but, most significantly, of Mozart's operatic creations too.

Durazzo's haul included three Italian bass-baritones, Stefano Mandini, Francesco Benucci and Francesco Bussani, all in their mid-thirties; one eighteen-year-old half-Italian, half-English soprano, Nancy Storace; and a young Irish tenor, Michael Kelly. According to Kelly, whose hilariously engaging *Reminiscences* provide rich anecdotal information about their activities, Count Durazzo had been instructed to recruit some Italians because Joseph II had recently fired a group of French singers from Schönbrunn: apparently they had complained about his wine. Although this social faux pas may indeed have been some final contributory factor to the Emperor's changing his mind, it is more likely that he was influenced by Salieri, whose own operas were having great success in both Italy and Vienna. And sure enough, when the new influx of singers arrived in the summer of 1783, they all performed in Salieri's *La Scuola di gelosia*, to great public acclaim. Again according to Kelly, they were made to feel extremely welcome and given lavish accommodation: 'the apartments . . . consisted of an excellent first and second floor, elegantly furnished, in the most delightful part of Vienna. I was found, as usual, in fuel and wax candles, and a carriage to take me to rehearsals and to and from the theatre, whenever I performed.'[41] (It is not surprising that Wolfgang felt obliged to move into the expensive apartment in the Domgasse, if the Court's artistic personnel were living in such splendour.)

As Mozart, together with Aloysia and their German colleagues, witnessed this Italian invasion, there was a certain amount of consternation. Aloysia was particularly unsettled by young Nancy Storace, who, five years her junior, already had a glittering career behind her. Wolfgang, though, was excited, and longed to climb on to this bandwagon too: he had, after all, his own very impressive track record of Italian opera. He searched hard for a suitable libretto, but by now he was extremely choosy, and nothing that he saw appealed to him. He wrote to Leopold: 'I have looked through at least a hundred libretti and more, but I have hardly found a single one with which I am satisfied; that is to say, so many alterations would have to be made here and there, that even if a poet would undertake to make them, it would be easier for him to write a completely new text, which indeed it is always best to do.'[42] He was particularly intrigued by the arrival of 'a certain Abbate Da Ponte', whose rakish reputation and charismatic personality had caused quite a stir. Naturally Wolfgang was keen to collaborate with him, even if he still entertained residual (inherited) doubts about the trustworthiness of the Italian race as a whole. But for the moment Lorenzo Da Ponte was fully occupied with writing for Salieri and others, and Wolfgang knew he should wait his turn.

With these new Italian singers in mind, Mozart did however actually begin two separate projects, neither of which was ever completed. First he started work on *L'Oca del Cairo*, K422, a rather bizarre story of another rescue, this time from a castle and with the help of a large mechanical goose, into which the captives could be smuggled (a variation, perhaps, on the theme of the Trojan horse). If Wolfgang entertained hopes that Da Ponte would agree to write his libretto, he had to abandon them, and, since he was in any case about to go to Salzburg with Constanze, he turned instead to his old colleague from *Idomeneo*, Giovanni Battista Varesco, who did indeed produce a text. Wolfgang began work on it in the summer of 1783 in Salzburg, and continued to tinker with it after his return to Vienna. But he only sketched parts of seven numbers (three arias, two duets, a quartet, and a finale to Act I, involving all seven characters). Like all Mozart's unfinished fragments, these are full of glorious though unrealized promise. But their most striking aspect is the almost total lack of demanding coloratura singing. The new influx of Italian singers had many alluring attributes and no doubt fine technical abilities too. But the pyrotechnics that Aloysia Lange, Caterina Cavalieri and Therese Teiber all displayed so brilliantly were simply not part of their musical language, and so Wolfgang, realizing this, tactfully avoided them.

After abandoning *L'Oca del Cairo*, Mozart began another Italian comic opera, *Lo sposo deluso*, K424a, whose unattributed libretto might perhaps have been the work of Da Ponte. Mozart's own copy of the text indicates that he had very specific singers in mind for the six roles, for the names Storace, Cavalieri, Teiber, Benucci, Bussani and Mandini all appear in it: intriguingly, then, this was to be an amalgam of both the Italian and German factions. But this project too was abandoned.

In the course of the next two seasons, there was a certain amount of movement between the Italian and German opera companies. By 1785, Cavalieri, Adamberger and Teiber ('all Germans of whom Germany may be proud', Mozart reported patriotically to Professor Anton Klein in Mannheim) transferred to the thriving Italian company, leaving Aloysia as the stalwart of the German one. Wolfgang was clearly in two minds about these developments. On the one hand he was anxious to create opportunities to work with the Italians, but on the other, he was alarmed too at the potential loss of working in the vernacular. He continued his letter to Klein in a spirit of morose irony:

> The idea at present is to carry on the German opera with actors and actresses, who only sing when they must ... Were there but

one good patriot in charge, things would take a different turn. But then, perhaps, the German national theatre which is sprouting so vigorously would actually begin to flower; and of course that would be an everlasting blot on Germany, if we Germans were seriously to begin to think as Germans, to act as Germans, to speak German, and, Heaven help us, to sing in German![43]

And perhaps Joseph II himself was cannily aware of these conflicts and tensions in his musicians, and found a mischievous way to exploit them. He devised his evening of lavish entertainment for his sister and brother-in-law, the Governors-General of the Netherlands, in Schönbrunn on 7 February 1786, in such a way as actually to pit the opposing factions against each other, on separate stages at either end of the long Orangery. Perhaps deliberately aiming to provoke his employees into producing performances sharpened with a wholly competitive edge, the Emperor first asked Salieri to write an opera, with an Italian text, about the whole business of putting on an opera. Salieri and his librettist Casti produced the cumbersomely titled *Prima la musica e poi le parole* (First the Music, then the Words). He then asked Mozart to provide a vorspiel, but in German. (His guests, it seems, were to be greeted in their own tongue, and then entertained in the current language of high culture.) Mozart called on his old colleague from *Die Entführung*, Johann Gottlieb Stephanie, and their resulting curtain-raiser was *Der Schauspieldirektor* (The Impresario), K486.

The plot of *Der Schauspieldirektor* concerns the attempts of an impresario (Frank) and a comedian (Buff) to establish a theatre in Salzburg. After lengthy discussions between them on the repertoire they will present and the type of actors they are therefore seeking, they begin to view potential company members. Various artists are hired. But two sopranos quarrel over who is to be the 'prima' donna, and cannot be pacified. In the end, everyone agrees that all artists should do their very best, and that ultimately it is the audience who decides on the quality of the performance.

Caterina Cavalieri and Aloysia Lange, long-standing rivals at the German opera, but united now against the usurping incomers, sportingly agreed to play the two sopranos, portraying themselves and their very rivalry in high caricature. Adamberger was brought in as a potential (but fairly ineffectual) peacemaker, and the character actor Joseph Weidmann (whose long and successful career – of thirty-seven years – was entirely based at the Burgtheater) played the role of Buff, contributing as a singer too to a quartet. The other acting roles were taken by Stephanie himself and his wife, by Aloysia's husband Joseph Lange, by Adamberger's wife Maria Anna, and two others; and the spirit of family solidarity was dazzling.

Stephanie's almost slapstick text was perhaps a little overlong: Count Zinzendorf – whose diaries do admittedly reveal distinct philistine tendencies – pronounced it to be *'fort mediocre'*. But Mozart's musical numbers show how greatly he relished the truly glittering occasion, the passing patronage of the Emperor, the superb talents of his favourite singers, and his straightforward desire to outshine the team at the other end of the Orangery. The overture already is of a fiery brilliance, with high contrasts and arresting gestures. The next two numbers are effectively audition pieces for the rival sopranos, as first Madame Herz (Aloysia) and then Madame Silberklang (Cavalieri) show the impresario what they can do. And of course nobody knew what they could do better than Mozart, who wrote cheerfully to their great strengths. Madame Herz's 'Du schlägt die Abschiedsstunde' (The hour of parting is upon us) begins with a gentle larghetto in G minor, in which Aloysia's tender, sustained singing was shown to great advantage, followed by an allegro section in G major where her coloratura is at last allowed to fly. Madame Silberklang's rondo, 'Bester Jüngling' is similarly structured (though differently coloured – where Aloysia's accompanying wind group had bright oboes, Cavalieri's has warmer clarinets), and in her allegro section she too is given some brisk pyrotechnics. Neither Aloysia nor Caterina Cavalieri would have been overtaxed by these arias: compared to the music Wolfgang had already written for both of them, these were relatively undemanding. Perhaps by entering into the party atmosphere of the occasion, he was letting his divas relax and enjoy their showing off. But perhaps too he had taken to heart Joseph II's now legendary comment on *Die Entführung* ('too many notes' – a criticism surely of the prolonged passages of coloratura for both Cavalieri and Adamberger, which contrasted so strongly with the less florid technique of the new Italian singers), and modified his virtuosity accordingly.

The fun starts in the trio. Like the men's trio in *Die Entführung*, which Mozart had proudly claimed was good counterpoint as well as good theatre, this is extremely well crafted. But the text is hilarious, as the two divas now childishly exchange claims as to their status ('Ich bin die erste Sängerin!' – I am the foremost singer!). Wolfgang's music positively chuckles with the delight he must have felt as he wrote this, and the women themselves would have relished the opportunity perhaps to say what they really felt. They hiss vituperative asides to each other, and they each try again to show off their superior talents. Aloysia has a slow section, to the very word, 'Adagio', where Mozart takes her up to her top E flat and immediately down two octaves – the Weber trademark. Cavalieri's contrasting 'Allegro, allegrissimo' is a more flashy demonstration of her coloratura, after the manner of her triplets in 'Martern aller arten' in *Die Entführung*. And beneath all this, the equally game Adamberger, as the tenor Vogelsang, tries to calm them down, literally soothing the trio at its end with the words 'Calando! Mancando! Diminuendo! Decrescendo! Pianissimo!' It is tempting to imagine that this is just the sort of joke that Joseph II would have loved, and that Imperial shoulders were heaving at this point. The concluding quartet, in which Joseph Weidmann as Buff was allowed his little moment of glory, explaining that he only needed to add an 'o' to his name, and he'd become the first Buffo actor, drew its egalitarian theatrical moral; and Mozart's curtain-raiser was over. And the Schönbrunn audience turned its chairs to watch *Prima la musica e poi le parole* at the other end of the building.

Salieri's piece was longer, was the main feature of the double-bill, and presented the current stars of the Italian opera. Inevitably it got the greater part of attention. But it is unlikely that Mozart was unduly worried. He and his friends had put together their *Schauspieldirektor* in just two weeks, and they had had the most wonderful time at one of the society events of the year. He cannot any longer have felt threatened by the Italians, for by now he was writing music for all of them. On his desk, briefly put aside for the composition of *Der Schauspieldirektor*, was *Le nozze di Figaro*. Mozart had just embarked on the most thrilling, the most perfect, artistic partnership of his entire life.

~

WHEN TWO GREAT friends collaborate artistically and produce profoundly stirring results, there is no greater pleasure in life. But close friendship is by no means a prerequisite for such results, nor does it in any way guarantee them, for often the most unlikely alliances can produce extraordinary artistic issue. Two creators, or two performers, may have very little in common, and may not even particularly enjoy each other's company, yet the communication between them on a supermundane level can lead to a sharing of ideas, instincts and reflexes where the total exceeds the sum of the parts. On the face of it, the collaboration between Mozart and Da Ponte was not an obvious one at all: Da Ponte was a natural partner for Salieri (they were the same age, and of the same nationality), and did indeed produce librettos for him. But between Mozart and the 'new Italian poet' there were vast areas of agreement, likemindedness and vision, and it was perhaps only a matter of time before these two veritable geniuses would converge.

Lorenzo Da Ponte's upbringing had, in its own way, been almost as extraordinary as Mozart's. Originally called Emmanuele Conegliano, he was born in Ceneda (now Vittorio Veneto) in 1749, into a Jewish family, but had converted to Christianity, along with his father and brothers, at the age of fourteen, when his father had married his non-Jewish stepmother. At the same time he had assumed the name of the presiding Venetian bishop, Monsignor

Lorenzo Da Ponte. He seems to have had no formal schooling at all up to that point, yet by the age of twenty-one he was teaching literature at a seminary in Portogruaro, and writing poetry on all manner of subjects. He took holy orders, though he was wildly unsuited to the religious calling, and so acquired his title 'Abbate', affording him at least a veneer of respectability as he made his colourful progress through life. By 1773, when he was twenty-four, he was in Venice, where he made the acquaintance of Casanova, and himself had many adulterous affairs. One of these led to his eventual banishment from Venice in 1779, and his being forbidden to work anywhere at all in the Venetian Republic. After short spells in Görz (Gorizia) and Dresden, Da Ponte arrived in Vienna in late 1781. He made contact with his influential countryman, Salieri; and he met and received the approval of the legendary Court Poet, Metastasio, just before he died in 1782. When, a year later, Joseph II revived Italian opera at Court, Salieri encouraged Da Ponte to apply for the post of poet at the Burgtheater, and he was duly appointed. There, his tasks were to oversee the provision of all librettos for the theatre, whether translations or adaptations of plays or existing librettos, or original creations. As Mozart observed, Lorenzo Da Ponte had 'an enormous amount to do'.[44]

Da Ponte was never less than enthusiastic, admiring and courteous when discussing or making use of Metastasio's texts. But when he came to consider the librettos for the comedies that he was supposed to supervise, he was appalled. As he recalled in his *Memoirs*:

> . . . what trash! No plots, no characters, no movement, no scening, no grace of language or style! Written to produce laughter, anyone would have judged that most were written to produce tears. There was not a line in those miserable botches that contained a flourish, an oddity, a graceful term, calculated in any sense to produce a laugh. So many agglomerations of insipidities, idiocies, tomfooleries![45]

He therefore decided that 'it should not be a difficult matter to compose something better than that', and determined to write his own comedies:

> In mine, one would find, at least here and there, some clever turn, some smart quip, some joke; the language would be neither barbarous nor uncouth; the songs would be read without annoyance! Finding an attractive subject, capable of supplying interesting character and fertile in incident, I would not be able, even if I tried, to compose things as wretched as those I had read!

But despite this great confidence and optimism, the first original libretto that Da Ponte wrote for Salieri, *Il ricco d'un giorno* in 1783, was something of a disaster. And when it was followed by a work from the rival team of Paisiello and Casti, *Il re Teodoro in Venezia*, which became the most enormous popular success, Salieri was furious, and would not touch Da Ponte again for four years. For some time, therefore, Da Ponte retreated into the uncomfortable environs of disapproval from those in power, and it was not until 1786, which turned out to be a veritable annus mirabilis for him, that his fortunes turned. But his years in the frosty wilderness were by no means wasted, for he observed, absorbed and waited ('I eat and drink and write and think,' he wrote). Eventually he adapted Goldoni's *Il burbero di buon cuore* for the newest and most exciting arrival in Vienna, the Spanish composer Vicente Martin y Soler (protégé of the Spanish Ambassador's wife, who was herself said to be extremely close to the Emperor). The performances of this new opera, in early 1786, bejewelled as they were by the presence of Nancy Storace and Francesco Benucci, marked Da Ponte's return to the limelight. And by then he was working with Mozart on *Le nozze di Figaro*.

For all that Mozart and Da Ponte had been cautiously prowling around each other for three years, there was by now much common ground between them. In a crucially fundamental sense, they were both disenchanted with the Enlightenment. This intellectual movement, so beloved of Mozart's Emperor and therefore at the heart of all his reforms, had effectively turned society away from religion, and towards reason, as the chief tool for understanding human life. Education, and the idea of learning through experience, were part of this rationality, and most artistic works, including Mozart's operas, were passionate advocates for this new Age of Reason. Yet there was something essentially empty about it. At the end of his *Second Discourse*, Rousseau issued a warning to a society guided only by material values: 'We have only honour without virtue, reason without wisdom, and pleasure without happiness.' Mozart and Da Ponte both surely shared this view, as their collaborations indicate: all three works break through the barriers surrounding conventional society, with all its manners and proprieties, and release the emotional turmoil within.

Mozart and Da Ponte were both experienced in the theatre, and both had extremely definite ideas about the relationship between words and music. As it happened, these coincided perfectly, both of them realizing the very importance of text for music. Mozart had written to his father in 1781, 'Verses are indeed the most indispensable element for music,'[46] and Da Ponte clearly concurred: 'I think poetry is the door to music, which can be very handsome, and much admired for its exterior, but nobody can see its internal beauties if the door is wanting.'[47] Both Mozart and Da Ponte were highly and sensitively versatile. Just as Mozart 'tailor-made' his music expressly to suit specific singers, so Da Ponte realized that 'the actors . . . had to be studied individually that their parts might fit'[48]; he similarly chose different subject-matter for his different composers. (For the English Stephen Storace, for example, he adapted Shakespeare's *Comedy of Errors*, producing *Gli equivoci*; for the Spanish Martin y Soler he adapted a play by Luis Vélez de Guevara for *Una cosa rara*.) Both Mozart and Da Ponte were essentially outsiders, never fully accepted by the establishment; yet their peripatetic earlier lives, together with their current situation on the fringes of society, had furnished them with superb powers to observe, accumulate and interpret the infinite varieties of human behaviour. Each could therefore portray immense subtlety in theatrical characterization, whether for instance in the different modes of expression and colloquialism between the different classes, or in overt and covert manifestations of real human emotion – what is said not necessarily being what is felt, which nonetheless is acutely revealed. And, significantly, both Mozart and Da Ponte had experienced, first-hand, the splendid event of the Venetian Carnival. Mozart had been in Venice as a teenager, but never forgot his wild times there, with his Wider 'pearls'; and Da Ponte had resided in that most seductive, most liberal, most degenerate perhaps of cities, with its masks and its disguises, and its illicit assignations conducted under cover of watery darkness. All three of the Mozart–Da Ponte collaborations would draw on this richest of memories, using disguise as another device with which ultimately to discover the truth, in a manner at once entertaining and disturbing.

Above all, Mozart and Da Ponte were both prepared to take risks, and were therefore profound innovators. Before they agreed to collaborate, Mozart had trawled disconsolately through more than 100 librettos, and found nothing to fire his imagination. What Da Ponte put before him was utterly different. No longer were they to concern themselves with the remote classical plots of opera seria; no longer would they bother with rescue operas set in exotic Eastern harems, or rely on the conventional configurations of commedia dell'arte; and they would certainly no longer stoop to devices such as mechanical geese. The three librettos that Da Ponte prepared for and with Mozart, whether adaptations of existing stories (*Le nozze di Figaro, Don Giovanni*) or newly written (*Così fan tutte*), were all effectively portraits of the society in which they were both living, of the people who inhabited it, and of the ways in which these people treated one another and reacted to one another. In every possible way, this was truly contemporary opera.

At first glance, the selection of Beaumarchais' *La folle journée, ou Le mariage de Figaro* as the basis for the first collaboration between Mozart and Da Ponte was not such a provocative one. It was, after all, the sequel to *Le barbier de Seville*, which, in a setting by Paisiello originally written for Catherine the Great in 1782, had

been brought to Vienna in 1783 and performed by the Italian company (Storace, Mandini, Benucci) with great success. It was an
entirely logical move to continue Beaumarchais' narrative and
follow these characters into their next series of adventures. In *Il
barbiere di Siviglia*, Count Almaviva has, with the help of the
cunning barber Figaro, successfully won the hand and heart of
Rosina, the ward and intended bride of the elderly Dr Bartolo. But
now, in *Le nozze di Figaro*, some of these characters have undergone
a certain amount of transformation, and the whole energy of the
storyline has become considerably tougher. Where in *Il barbiere
di Siviglia* there was an essentially benevolent insolence lurking
beneath the comedy, in *Figaro* there is a positively dangerous spirit
of revolution. The marriage between Count Almaviva and his
(now) Countess has already disintegrated, and the Count is exercising his droit de seigneur with as many women and girls on his estate
as he pleases. Even on the day of Figaro's wedding to the
Countess's maid, Susanna, the Count tries to postpone the
ceremony for his own purposes. Figaro, Susanna and the Countess
devise a plot whereby the Count's infidelities are publicly, humiliatingly, exposed in front of his entire household. The French spirit of
the 1780s, of liberty, equality and fraternity, of the imperative need
for the bourgeoisie to rid itself of the ancien régime and all its outrageous practices, pervades every scene, whether overtly or subliminally. It is small wonder that Beaumarchais' play was banned in
Paris for three years, and banned again in Vienna, until it had been
much cut. That Da Ponte hoodwinked the authorities sufficiently to
obtain permission for its (presumably more acceptable) incarnation
as an opera buffa is testimony indeed to his formidable and eloquent
powers of persuasion.

Mozart and Da Ponte must have known the risks they were
taking in exposing some of the more vile foibles of their audiences
as well as their most engaging. And yet the concepts of fairness,
decency and propriety were, for all Mozart's passing preoccupations with the crude, utterly essential to him. Back in 1781, bristling
with rage after his treatment by the representatives of Archbishop

Colloredo, he had written to Leopold: 'It is the heart that ennobles a man; and though I am no count, yet I have probably more honour in me than many a count. Whether a man be a count or a valet, if he insults me, he is a scoundrel.'[49] In undertaking to collaborate with Da Ponte on this risky venture, Mozart was indeed settling some old scores.

But another great attraction of presenting the sequel to Paisiello's *Il barbiere di Siviglia*, and one which may indeed have swayed the authorities to grant permission for its performance, was that some of the same singers from 1783 were still enjoying enormous success and popularity in Vienna. The bass-baritone Stefano Mandini had played the role of Count Almaviva, and he could do so again, in this now considerably less sympathetic (and therefore more interesting) light, in the sequel. The two Francescos, Benucci and Bussani, had originally been Bartolo and Figaro. Now, three years later, they were to swap these roles: Benucci had become the absolutely favourite leading man with Viennese audiences, and was the more obvious choice for the title role. Bussani had assumed greater responsibility for stage direction, but could certainly play Bartolo, and also double as the drunken gardener, Antonio. His young wife Dorotea (at just twenty-three, nearly half his age) could play the page Cherubino, and Mandini's wife Maria could be the housekeeper Marcellina. Michael Kelly, the young Irish tenor engaged by Count Durazzo at the same time as all the Italians, and accustomed to playing comic roles of an age well beyond his own twenty-four years, could double the roles of Don Basilio (the music-master and general busybody) and the lawyer Don Curzio. Nancy Storace had originally played the part of Rosina in *Il barbiere di Siviglia* in 1783. But at the time of its 1785 revival, she had been undergoing a severe personal crisis, and Luisa Laschi, the newest arrival from Italy, had therefore taken the role. So she could continue to do so, now as the Countess Almaviva in *Figaro*; and Nancy Storace would be given instead the absolutely crucial and central role of Susanna. The small but dramatically riveting role of the gardener's daughter Barbarina was given to the twelve-year-old Anna Gottlieb, daughter of two actors at the Burgtheater.

It was however the relationship between Nancy Storace and Francesco Benucci that was fundamental to this opera. As representatives of an intelligent and sympathetic bourgeoisie, Susanna and Figaro would work together as a team (though not without their own little moments of mistrust) and succeed in humiliating their master. And so one of the most fascinating and satisfying characters ever written for the opera stage was to be created by an extraordinarily talented English girl of twenty-one. Nancy Storace's Italian father had been a double-bass player who had settled in London in the late 1750s, married an Englishwoman and, not unlike Leopold Mozart, produced two gifted children. Both Nancy and her brother Stephen were extremely musical. According to Michael Kelly's *Reminiscences*, Nancy could play and sing at sight at just eight years old, and 'evinced an extraordinary genius for music.'[50] While her brother was sent to Naples to study composition, she had singing lessons in London from none other than Venanzio Rauzzini (Mozart's old friend from *Lucio Silla*, and for whom he had also written his 'Exsultate, jubilate'), who would later teach Michael Kelly too. In 1778, aged only thirteen, Nancy travelled to Italy with her parents to visit her brother, and herself began a phenomenally prodigious career, performing on the stages of most of the major opera houses in Italy. At fifteen she sang at the Teatro alla Pergola in Florence, with such success that she caused jealous fury to the resident castrato Luigi Marchesi, who demanded – and succeeded in getting – her removal. (In 1786, in Salieri's *Prima la musica e poi le parole* in the Orangery at Schönbrunn, Nancy got her own back by hilariously mimicking her old adversary, and afforded great delight to the knowing audience.) Her eviction from the Teatro alla Pergola did not damage her career at all. She subsequently sang in Lucca, Parma, Livorno, Milan and Venice. And it was in the Teatro San Samuele in Venice that she was heard by Count Durazzo, and hired by him for Vienna's Burgtheater in 1783. She was still only eighteen years old.

Nancy Storace had met Michael Kelly in Livorno, and in his *Reminiscences* Kelly described the hilarious incident that brought them together and initiated a friendship that would endure for the rest of their lives.

> I had on a Sicilian *capote*, with my hair (of which I had a great quantity, and which, like my complexion, was very fair) floating over it: I was as thin as a walking stick. As I stepped from the boat, I perceived a young lady and gentleman standing on the Mole, making observations; as the former looked at me she laughed, and as I approached I heard her say to her companion in English, which of course she thought I did not understand, 'Look at that girl dressed in boy's clothes!' To her astonishment, I answered in the same language, 'You are mistaken, Miss; I am a very proper *he* animal, and quite at your service!'
>
> We all laughed until we were tired, and became immediately intimate; and these persons, my acquaintance with whom, commenced by this childish jest on the Mole at Leghorn, continued through life the warmest and most attached of my friends. All love and honour to your memories, Stephen and Nancy Storace![51]

The teenagers had a wonderful time together in Livorno, parted in tears, and joyfully met up again in Venice, where Nancy was 'quite the rage'. After they were hired by Durazzo, together with Benucci, Mandini and Bussani, they all remained a close-knit team in Vienna, appearing together constantly at the Burgtheater. Their workload was immense: in that first season (1783) alone, they performed in no fewer than six new operas, by Salieri, Cimarosa, Sarti, Anfossi and Paisiello. Nancy made a disastrous marriage to an Englishman named John Fisher, who apparently beat her ('it was said,' reported Kelly, 'that he had a very striking way of enforcing his opinion'[52]), and the paternalistic Joseph II, ever solicitous to his beloved singers, and extremely attached to Nancy, personally intervened to have Fisher removed from Vienna. But by this stage Nancy was pregnant with a daughter, who died soon after she was born. With all these personal crises and professional pressures, it is not surprising that, still only twenty, she had a major breakdown in 1785: but it was poignantly unfortunate that this should happen on stage, and at the opening night of an opera by her brother, *Gli sposi malcontenti* (a title of appallingly appropriate irony). Voiceless, she retired from the limelight for several months. When she returned, Da Ponte wrote her a celebratory poem, 'Per la ricuperata salute d'Ophelia', which was set to music by Salieri, Mozart and a mysterious (possibly pseudonymous) third composer, Cornetti. (Neither the poem nor its musical setting has survived.) Da Ponte and Mozart briefly considered Nancy for the role of the Countess in *Figaro*, for she had played Rosina so successfully in *Il barbiere di Siviglia*; but they transferred her to that of Susanna, to which in fact she was perfectly suited in every way, physically (she was short, and perhaps a little plump), musically and temperamentally.

As Michael Kelly had discovered on that quayside in Livorno, Nancy was lively, mischievous and extremely alert ('making observations'), missing nothing. She was comfortably confident in all company, including the most exalted. Kelly describes an incident at Joseph II's summer palace at Laxemburg, where he and Nancy were following a hunting expedition in one of the Emperor's carriages; when Joseph II himself rode up and asked if he could do anything for them, Nancy 'with her peculiar characteristic bluntness' asked for a glass of water (which was of course forthcoming).[53] But above all, she was a steadfast and loyal friend, full of compassion, common sense and extreme generosity. Kelly reports how his own single experiment at gambling ended in disaster, and at the end of the evening he owed 20 zecchinos to 'a gallant English colonel':

> In the morning, Nancy Storace called on me – 'So, Sir,' said she, 'I hear you were gambling last night, and not only lost all the money you had about you, but are still in debt – such debts ought not to be left unsatisfied a moment; you may one day or other go to England and, should the transaction of your playing for more money than you possessed become known among Englishmen, it might give you a character which I know you do not deserve; it must be settled directly.' She instantly produced the money, and

made me go and discharge the obligation. Such an act of well-timed disinterested friendship was noble, and never forgotten by me.[54]

All these characteristics and qualities were topped by a compelling stage presence, of, clearly, an alluring physicality. Count Zinzendorf may not have had a discerning ear, but his eye was always appreciative, and he more than admired Nancy's 'pretty figure, voluptuous, beautiful eyes, white neck, fresh mouth, beautiful skin, the naivety and the petulance of a child'. And, as she recovered at last from the physical and mental bruising of her marriage, Nancy became increasingly attached to her frequent on-stage partner, Francesco Benucci. By the end of 1786 their liaison was more than professional. In 1787 she finally returned to London, and she secured an invitation for Benucci to visit her there two years later.

Mozart too was delighted with Nancy Storace, whom he welcomed fondly into his closest circle. Before she left for London, she gave a farewell concert at the Burgtheater, and it was for this occasion that Mozart wrote a scena for her, 'Ch'io mi scordi di te', K505, with its tender, valedictory text ('I will never forget you'). For good measure he wrote a solo piano part in addition to the orchestral accompaniment, and so appeared with her at her final performance in Vienna. When he entered this work into his catalogue, he proudly added, 'for Mademoiselle Storace and me'. Nancy and her mother, together with Michael Kelly and the young Thomas Attwood (Mozart's pupil) returned together to England, passing through Salzburg on their way; and Wolfgang sent them to Leopold, asking his father to show them round the town. Leopold, with a not altogether good grace, duly obliged.

~

DA PONTE'S ELOQUENCE had persuaded the Court censors to pass the sequel to *Il barbiere di Siviglia* as an entertainment, and an extremely familiar and popular cast had been assembled to perform

it. But after that, nothing about *Le noɀɀe di Figaro* was predictable.
Da Ponte and Mozart relished the distinguished qualities of their
cast, both collectively and individually; they mined the rich seam of
social comment in Beaumarchais' play; they applied their own
particular geniuses to their collaboration; and they produced a work
whose premiere, on 1 May 1786, has to have been one of the most
important nights in the entire history of opera.

From the very first bars of the overture, it was clear that something was different. Rather than gather the audience's attention in
the normal way with a forthright and resounding opening, Mozart
instead began with a low, conspiratorial murmur in the strings and
bassoons, compelling the public to listen in an altogether new way.
Surprise after shocking surprise continued when the curtain went
up. First it revealed a barely furnished room ('Camera non affatto
ammobiliata'), in which Susanna and Figaro, the bride and groom,
were singing a duet, but, initially at least, paying not the slightest
attention to each other. At the revelation that Count Almaviva had
Susanna too in his sights, Figaro's revolutionary energy was immediately unleashed in an aria which began as a controlled minuet but
repeatedly collapsed into unruly bursts of rage. The audience
would have been struck by the contempt with which Figaro
deployed an insolent diminutive for his master ('Se vuol ballare,
signor Contino' – a subtlety entirely Da Ponte's, as he translated
Beaumarchais' 'Puis dansez, Monsignor'). The elderly Marcellina
and her lawyer Bartolo discussed a contract designed to entrap
Figaro into paying her money or marrying her. Susanna and
Marcellina exchanged ferocious insults (a development, certainly,
of those exchanged by Mesdames Herz and Silberklang in *Der
Schauspieldirektor*). A young page boy, Cherubino, confessed his
utterly bewildered adolescent obsession with women, and then had
to hide in a chair from the Count, in a scene bursting as much with
danger as it was with hilarity. When he was nevertheless discovered, having now overheard the Count's clumsy advances to
Susanna, Cherubino was summarily ordered to join the Count's
regiment; and this astonishing first act closed with a blazing aria for

Figaro ('Non più andrai') in which he teased the poor page about his imminent exchange of courtly elegance and frippery for the perilous realities of military life. Even at the first rehearsal of this aria, Benucci's mighty performance of it had elicited stupendous applause from his colleagues. At the fall of the curtain on 1 May 1786, the audience must have felt truly swept away by the sensational novelty of the journey they were now travelling.

And so it continued. The young Countess was discovered in tears, sorrowfully confronting her failed marriage. Susanna and Figaro outlined a plot publicly to expose her husband's infidelities, and in desperation she agreed to go along with it. Young Cherubino, besotted with the beautiful Countess as with all women, sang her a love song of his own composition, and was briefly dressed up as a girl by a now nervously playful Countess and her fun-loving maid. As Cherubino's infatuation with the Countess grew, the arrival of the Count again injected real danger into the scene: Cherubino was bundled into an ante-room, and the Count and Countess had an altogether ugly argument, indicating the cruel depths to which their marriage had sunk. Susanna's quick thinking temporarily rescued the situation, to the total mystification of the Count, and indeed the Countess. But the arrival of a drunken gardener (who had witnessed Cherubino's escape), followed by Marcellina and her supporters demanding that Figaro honour his contract, brought the act to a brilliant conclusion of total disarray, domestic, public and legal.

As the opera progressed, Count Almaviva was seen in all his ruthlessness, continuing his attempted seduction of Susanna, but expressing in the strongest possible language his hatred of his servant Figaro for enjoying pleasures he himself could not. Susanna somehow produced the money Figaro owed Marcellina, and brought it to relieve him of his legal obligation (true echoes here of Nancy Storace's bailing out Michael Kelly), but interrupted an incredibly touching scene in which it had been discovered that Marcellina and Bartolo were in fact Figaro's long-lost parents. The Countess and Susanna devised a letter intended to trap the Count, and during the wedding celebrations the Count duly took the bait. The gardener's young daughter, another passing conquest of the Count, was inveigled into carrying a message back to Susanna, but bungled it. Figaro, not yet knowing the full details of Susanna's plan, now in full swing, suffered almost violent jealousy, and became, along with everyone else, involved in a nocturnal tangle of mistaken identities, the Countess and Susanna having now exchanged clothes. As the Count discovered that the woman he had thought was Susanna was in fact his wife, he fell to his knees in front of his entire household, and begged her to forgive him. When she did, everybody else slowly accepted their uneasy truce, and life on the estate resumed; but the lives of them all had been utterly changed by the events of the mad day (the 'folle journée' of Beaumarchais' title).

And that original audience, too, should have felt utterly changed by their experience. They had been entertained by theatrical antics and beguiled by incomparable music; but they had also been shocked, in the same way perhaps as future audiences would be at the first performances of Stravinsky's *Sacre du Printemps*, or John Osborne's *Look Back in Anger*. They were left not just with the memory of strong music and stirring performances; they should have felt profoundly uncomfortable and in a way guilty. It had been a damning indictment of their own society, which Mozart and Da Ponte had exposed in the most glaring of arc-lights. And what was especially remarkable was that this essentially murky tale of domestic mayhem, for all that it touched on much wider, universal issues, was told by Mozart and Da Ponte with the greatest sympathy for the plight of women. Both men, utterly devoted to the opposite sex and as appreciative as anyone of their charms, firmly took the side of the Countess and Susanna, and even of Marcellina, whom they transformed from an almost stereotypical harridan at the beginning of the opera to a completely sympathetic mother at its end, strong, intelligent and supportive of her former adversary. 'Ogni donna è portata alla difesa del suo povero sesso,' she declares in the final act (Every woman comes to the defence of her own mistreated sex). All the male characters are unquestionably well drawn, especially of course Figaro himself, with all his attractiveness, warmth, vulnerability and dynamism; the ruthless Count; and even young Cherubino, whose enigmatic songs and desperate escapades reveal his struggle with the realities of adolescence. But it is Susanna and the Countess who effectively carry the opera. This sympathy for women was not a new departure for Mozart; but it was brought to a new level of relevance in *Figaro*, and was to shine too through both his next collaborations with the brilliant Da Ponte.

Susanna can be seen, in fact, as Mozart's perfect woman. Bright, quick, loyal and adorable, she is a superb friend to her beloved Figaro, to her Countess, and also to Cherubino. One of the longest and most rewarding roles in the soprano repertoire, Susanna leads (both musically and dramatically) every scene she is in. In the opening duets with Figaro, she is immediately established as being excited, a little vain (with her wedding hat), besotted with her Figaro, and extremely astute: she has worked out the full implications of the Count's choice of room for them (for his own easy access), and has gently but firmly to spell it out to Figaro. She is reluctant to engage in an exchange of insults with Marcellina; but the stream of bitchy and demeaning abuse from her menopausal adversary eventually provokes her, and she easily gets the upper hand. And, as in the *Schauspieldirektor* trio, Mozart's own glee at the spectacle of a scene so potentially embarrassing is nonetheless delivered with a perfect lightness of touch, diluting therefore the cruelties of Da Ponte's text. Susanna is playfully firm with young Cherubino, resolute in her rejection of the Count's advances ('Dritti non prendo' – I don't want your rights – she boldly declares); and she even manages to salvage the appalling situation of Cherubino's being discovered hiding in a chair, by pointing out that the page has overheard all his crude suggestions to her.

When Susanna is with the Countess, the two women talk almost as equals, paradoxically discussing the failure of one marriage just as another is about to begin. Having, with Figaro, informed the

Countess of the complicated plan designed to effect the Count's downfall, Susanna then, in playful mood, encourages the Countess to prepare for part of it (to send Cherubino, disguised as a girl, into the garden at night as a decoy) by dressing the page in women's clothes. And perhaps this stratagem held fond memories for Nancy Storace, as she recalled her first encounter with the long-haired teenager Michael Kelly in Livorno, when she mistook him for a girl: certainly her dressing-up aria, 'Venite inginocchiatevi', bubbles with youthful glee and laughter. It is Susanna's quick thinking that saves the Countess's own face, to the great bafflement of the Count, and in the finale to Act II Susanna and the Countess largely sing together in thirds (and even once in unison), utterly united against the hostile aggression of her Almaviva.

As Figaro's plan goes into operation, Susanna is essential to it. She makes her assignation with the Count, though not without some tough, ironic spirit as she endures his jibes. (He encourages her to use the Countess's headache remedy herself, to which she counters, 'Questi non son mali da donne triviale' – Girls of my class don't have these ailments – a reply worthy of Figaro himself.) As the Count begins his honeyed seduction of her ('Crudel, perche finora / Farmi languir così?' – Cruel one, why have you treated me so badly?) in A minor, she cannot bring herself to give in to it, and repeatedly gives the wrong answers to his little questions. But when she eventually gets it right, the music moves from the minor into A major (Mozart's key of seduction) for the Count's new confidence, over which Susanna mutters apologetically her miserable aside, 'Scusatemi se mento / Voi ch'intendete amor' (You who truly love, forgive my deception).

When, in true Storace fashion, Susanna brings in the money to absolve Figaro from his debt, she discovers him embracing Marcellina (for her supposed rival is, after all, his mother), and, after the manner of Blonde, she hits him. But as everything is explained to her, she too joins in the real joy of the new situation; the chemistry is now shifted, and Susanna and Figaro, Marcellina and Bartolo join together as a family and prepare for their double wedding. It is the Countess who now takes the lead as she and Susanna compose their letter to the Count, arranging the nocturnal assignation; and in the final act, Susanna's brief doubt of Figaro's own trust in her only makes their final understanding all the happier.

But the most miraculous moment for her comes almost at the end of the opera, in her aria 'Deh, vieni e non tardar'. She knows at this stage that Figaro has begun to entertain totally unjustified suspicions of her own fidelity; and as she continues to carry out the plan of deceiving the Count, she gently turns the tables on Figaro too. Sitting apparently alone in the garden at night, awaiting a supposed assignation with the Count but knowing she is observed by the hidden Figaro, she sings a tender, quiet aria anticipating the joys of love. But what begins as play-acting, with a slightly exaggerated vocal line ('godrò senza affanno' − I shall enjoy unreservedly) and giggling string punctuations, in fact becomes utterly sincere, as the profound truth and beauty of her emotions become real. The beguiling and sweet simplicity of her vocal line, gently supported in Mozart's inimitable fashion by a flute, an oboe and a bassoon which weave their own radiant lines through Susanna's, make this a moment of true theatrical perfection. (It is surely significant that these three solo instruments featured too in the sublime 'Et incarnatus est' that Mozart wrote for his Constanze, in their C minor Mass.) There is therefore a double dramatic irony: Susanna's world does indeed stop ('il mondo tace'), and her soul is refreshed ('il cor ristaura') as she sings these very words. At the end of the opera, the audience has the impression that, whatever else has happened, the marriage between Figaro and Susanna will be long, happy, and never dull. It is tempting to infer from *Figaro* some understanding of the relationship between Storace and Benucci; and perhaps too of the marriage of Wolfgang and Constanze.

And on the other side of the female coin there is the equally compelling portrait of the Countess, the lonely, restrained, courageous sufferer throughout most of the opera. Her opening soliloquy ('Porgi amor qualche ristoro') is an unbearable contemplation of her failing marriage. Changing the mood, pace and colour of the opera at the beginning of Act II, after the high activity of Act I, Mozart gives her an instrumental introduction to her aria, almost in the manner of a concerto. Clarinets, bassoons and horns supply sombre warmth, and set up the controlled vocal sorrow of what follows, rather like Constanze's 'Traurigkeit'. (Luisa Laschi too must have possessed a wonderful ability to spin a *cantabile* line, in the way Mozart so loved.) At the word 'sospir' (sighing), Mozart injects real pathos by giving the bassoon a G flat appoggiatura within an F minor chord, in the same way that he had, but in an exaggerated mood, on the words 'Aber, ach' for Madame Silberklang's 'Bester Jüngling' in *Der Schauspieldirektor*. Again as he had in 'Traurigkeit', Mozart delays the perfect cadence by using pauses and interrupted cadences; and then, having found the home key, gives the Countess the simplest and saddest of codas. After this demanding but brief aria (it is only 51 bars long), the audience is thoroughly supportive of a woman so tellingly introduced.

Throughout the dressing of Cherubino as a girl, the Countess is nervous, but she enjoys it too. This, and her touched reaction to his childlike distress, show her still to be desperate for both fun and affection; her brutal confrontations with her husband are cruel portrayals of broken communication. She publicly endures every revelation of the Count's philandering with icy dignity, and, in the final scene, quietly forgives him yet again, determined perhaps to give their marriage one last shot. But she has been fortified to do this by a quite extraordinary transformation in her, which took place in her third-act soliloquy. It is a scene which does not exist in Beaumarchais' play, and so was added by Da Ponte and Mozart; but even Da Ponte's text, brilliant and multilayered as it is, does not indicate the full variety and perspicacity of Mozart's interpretation of it. Unlike every other aria in the opera, this soliloquy begins with the Countess in one mood, and ends with her in quite another; Mozart has smashed yet another mould.

At the start of her scene, the Countess is nervously awaiting news from Susanna as to whether or not the Count has fallen for their ruse. She is impatient and anxious, and her tension turns to fear of her hotheaded and jealous husband. She tries to calm herself down: 'Ma che mal c'è?' (But what harm are we doing?). But as she runs through the whole plan again, that she must change clothes with Susanna, under cover of darkness, she suddenly breaks. 'O cielo! A qual umil stato fatale io son ridotta da un consorte crudel' (To what humiliation have I been reduced by a cruel husband); and in her despair she charts the dissolution of her marriage:

> . . . che dopo avermi
> Con un misto inaudito
> D'infedeltà, di gelosie, di sdegni,
> Prima amata, indi offesa, e alfin tradita.

> In a strange mixture of infidelity,
> jealousy and disdain,
> first he loved me, then neglected
> and finally deceived me.

And she arrives at her cruellest punchline:

> Fammi or cercar da una mia serva aita.

> Now he forces me to seek help from my own servant.

This 'servant' is Susanna: her friend, her devoted supporter. But at this moment of utter desolation, the Countess can see her only as an underling, to whom begging for help constitutes the worst social solecism. Truly, this Countess has only one foot in the burgeoning new world of egalitarianism; the other is still planted firmly in the ancien régime.

All these kaleidoscopic changes of emotion, swirling and conflicting in the Countess's mind, are of course expressed by Mozart in his matchless accompanied recitative, every nuance and subtlety mirrored and illuminated by the orchestra too. Having reached her nadir, the Countess moves into the most affecting aria of heartrending nostalgia: 'Dove sono i bei momenti di dolcezza e di piacer?' (What happened to the pleasures and delights of my marriage?). As she remembers the good times, a shadowy oboe (Mozart's instrument of seduction) completes her lines for her, recalling lost happiness. There is no virtuosity here, but simple, grieving beauty. Then as she returns to her opening, in what seems to be a regular *da capo* aria, a new thought strikes her:

> *Ah! Se almen la mia costanza*
> *Nel languire amando ognor*
> *Mi portasse una speranza*
> *Di cangiar l'ingrato cor!*

> Ah! If only my constancy
> in always yearning for him
> could bring me the hope
> of changing his ungrateful heart!

And this tiny glimpse of optimism, cautiously expressed at first, grows into an allegro section and a new, positive spirit of energy and excitement. She ends her aria, and her scene, in triumph, stronger, more determined and in some way healed. For the rest of the opera, up to and beyond her calm forgiveness of the Count, she is in control. And it was Mozart's fundamental generosity and philanthropy (for Da Ponte's text could have been interpreted in an altogether different way) that allowed his Countess her wonderful change of heart.

The mould was indeed broken. For all the stirring portrayals of character in the works of Mozart's predecessors and contemporaries, even indeed in his own operas, nothing before had ever discovered such astonishing depths of veracity. Between them, Mozart and Da Ponte had finally held the mirror up to the audience: 'This,' they were saying, 'is all about you.'

~

AFTER *FIGARO*'S SUCCESSFUL run of performances in Vienna, word travelled, and within six months of that May premiere, a new pro-

duction was mounted in Prague. Here, an Italian bass-turned-
impresario, Pasquale Bondini, was the director of Prague's
National Theatre. He was a great enthusiast for Mozart's music,
and had already presented *Die Entführung* twice, in Leipzig in 1783
and in Dresden in 1785. He moved swiftly to bring *Figaro* to
Prague, taking particular delight in the fact that this new Mozart
opera would provide his young wife Caterina, an extremely popular and accomplished member of his company, with the wonderful
role of Susanna.

Figaro was an immediate triumph in Prague and Bondini invited
Mozart and Constanze to come and see it, in January 1787. They
came; Wolfgang directed some performances of it, and he was well
pleased with what he found: the cast was more than equal to the
challenges of his score. Bondini, meanwhile, was planning ahead.
In the coming October, the Emperor's niece, Maria Theresa, would
visit Prague on the occasion of her marriage to Prince Anton
Clemens of Saxony. Joseph would need something special to
present to their Highnesses, and a new opera by Mozart would be
ideal. Bondini asked for a version of the Don Juan story – probably
because the greatest star of his company was the young Luigi Bassi,
a man with a magnificent voice, charismatic stage presence, and
extremely good looks. (Beethoven later described him as a 'fiery
Italian'.) Bassi had performed the Count in the Prague production
of *Figaro*, so Mozart too had appreciated his great talent. Wolfgang
was delighted to accept this new commission, to celebrate an august
occasion in a civilized city with impressive musical and theatrical
talent; and on his return to Vienna he naturally asked Da Ponte to
join him on the project.

As it happened, Da Ponte was already heavily committed, working on two librettos, *Tarare* (for Salieri) and *L'arbore di Diana* (for
Martin y Soler), both of which were required imminently.
Producing something for Mozart, for performance in nine months'
time, was a tall order. But he too was greatly attracted by the
occasion, and he was strongly drawn to the subject-matter
(that Venetian friendship with Casanova was now about to pay

dividends). With Wolfgang's enthusiastic advocacy for the Prague team, and Da Ponte's own knowledgeable sympathy with the hero, he found the project irresistible. And to help him through a pressurized period of meeting three deadlines at once, Da Ponte devised wholly appropriate ways of keeping himself alert and inspired:

> I sat down at my table and did not leave it for twelve hours continuous – a bottle of Tokay to my right, a box of Seville to my left, in the middle an inkwell. A beautiful girl of sixteen – I should have preferred to love her only as a daughter, but alas . . . ! – was living in the house with her mother, who took care of the family, and came to my room at the sound of the bell. To tell the truth the bell rang rather frequently, especially at moments when I felt my inspiration waning.[55]

For all that *Don Giovanni*, the new opera by Mozart and Da Ponte, was to be described on its title pages as a *dramma giocoso*, this was a very dark reading of the popular story. Da Ponte based his own version on one given in Venice, earlier in 1787, when Bertati had prepared a libretto for Gazzaniga. It would describe the final day in the life of the celebrated seducer of women. As Don Giovanni is trying to add young Donna Anna to his list of conquests, her father the Commendatore comes to her rescue: they fight, and the Commendatore is killed. Unabashed, Giovanni, accompanied by his servant Leporello, continues his pursuit of other women, next trying to seize a young peasant girl, Zerlina, on her wedding day (a development, certainly, of a theme begun by the Count and Susanna in *Figaro*). But Donna Anna, together with the man to whom she is betrothed, Don Ottavio, and Donna Elvira, a miserable reject from Don Giovanni's pile of past (and passing) conquests, doggedly pursue Giovanni, determined to put an end to his reckless and harmful philandering. When in a graveyard at night Giovanni and Leporello come upon the statue of the late Commendatore, the fearless Giovanni invites it to join him for supper. The statue does indeed appear at his table, demanding that

Giovanni repent his ways; and when Giovanni refuses, he is consumed by hellfire. The lives of all those involved in Giovanni's last
day (Leporello, Anna, Elvira, Ottavio, Zerlina and her husband
Masetto) continue. But they have all been irrevocably changed
by their encounter with Don Giovanni, and by the trauma of his
dramatic end.

Despite the greatly more melodramatic nature of *Don Giovanni*,
beginning and ending as it does with violent death, and portraying
during its course other unspeakable horrors, there are many
similarities of theme, and of device, to those of *Figaro*. First, young
Cherubino's infatuation with women, seen essentially in adolescent
fumblings but expressed in music of poignant appeal, has in Don
Giovanni himself become something brutal, though no less charming, in adulthood. 'Le donne!' says Giovanni to Leporello, 'Sai
ch'elle per me son necessarie più del pan che mango, più che l'aria
che spiro' (Women are more vital to me than the bread that I eat or
the air that I breathe). Da Ponte's portrayal of this grown-up
obsession seems to have been partly based on his observation of his
friend Casanova, who did in the course of seduction promise
marriage to many women, but then vanished after achieving his
conquest. Yet the irresistible allure of the music that Mozart wrote
for Giovanni succeeds in seducing the audience too, making him a
genuinely attractive character, just as he had with Cherubino's
naive but potentially tiresome teenager. And then the notion of
retribution, so suavely achieved in *Figaro*, is developed here in *Don
Giovanni* to literally cataclysmic proportions, partly through the
development too of the dramatic devices of disguise and darkness,
exacerbated now by the sheer quantity of grievances levelled at the
offender. And where in *Figaro* the very revolutionary nature of the
subject-matter yielded some rich insights into class-consciousness,
and into the human injustices of social hierarchies, these are continued in *Don Giovanni*: Leporello and Masetto both retain the
anger of Figaro, and Zerlina the essential servility of Susanna.
Again in the final outcome, the greatest optimism for the future
resides in the representatives of the lower orders, in *Figaro* in the

marriage between Susanna and Figaro, and their fundamental decency and happiness; and in *Don Giovanni*, amidst the scattered wreckage of so many lives, in the union between Zerlina and Masetto, and perhaps too in Leporello's dogged abilities to survive. As before, Da Ponte's libretto is bejewelled with lines of a quite remarkable richness, and Mozart never failed to honour them with music of matching understanding.

Mozart and Constanze arrived back in Prague at the beginning of October 1787, with most of the opera written: Wolfgang did after all know all but one of the voices for whom he was writing. Da Ponte followed them a week later. Given that the royal performance of this new work was scheduled for 14 October, it is not in the least surprising that it was nowhere near ready within such a short time: quite apart from the singers having to learn and absorb all this new music, and rehearse a complex and lengthy production, they were at the same time performing in other operas, and so their availability for rehearsal was even more restricted. Emergency measures were taken. The premiere of *Don Giovanni* was postponed for ten days, and the Imperial couple were entertained instead with a hastily remounted performance of *Figaro*. It was hardly an appropriate choice of subject for the newly-weds, who not surprisingly walked out of the theatre before the end of the opera. The following day they left Prague altogether, thus missing completely the work that had been devised for their delight. More serious perhaps, from Mozart's point of view, was that Da Ponte had to leave too: Salieri (and their *Tarare*, now renamed *Axur*) required his immediate presence in Vienna. When one of the *Don Giovanni* cast became ill, the premiere had to be postponed yet again; and it was not until 29 October that the work was at last presented, sadly without half of its creative team, mercifully perhaps without its intended dedicatees (if *Figaro* was an unsuitable wedding present, *Don Giovanni* was even more preposterous), but, thrillingly, in the presence of none other than Casanova, who had travelled to Prague expressly to see it.

Despite all the crises and changes of plan, Mozart was obviously in good spirits. He and Constanze spent time with their great friends the Duscheks in their Villa Bertramka, just outside Prague; and Josefa Duschek persuaded Wolfgang to write her a new concert aria, locking him in his room until he had finished it. He responded by insisting that she then sightread it, and made sure that he wrote some fiendishly difficult and unconventional intervals in 'Bella mia fiamma', K528.

As always with Mozart's 'tailor-made' operas, the music that he wrote in *Don Giovanni* is greatly indicative of the quality of his cast. He already knew the raw, erotic energy of 'fiery' Luigi Bassi, who had played the Count, and he drew extensively on it for his Don Giovanni, as he did on Bassi's great gifts as an actor and a mimic. Bassi did however complain to Mozart that, of his two arias, one ('Fin ch'han dal vino') was almost manically driven, and the other ('Metà de voi') was more concerned with plot than with singing, and that therefore he would like an opportunity to show off his ability to spin a lyrical line. So Mozart wrote him the sublime serenade, 'Deh, vieni alla finistra', and Bassi was satisfied. Felice Panziani had sung Figaro, and was especially known for his comedy and for his great ability with text; so he now became Leporello, a richly rewarding role, blessed with one of the most famous of all arias, the 'Catalogue' of Giovanni's lovers that he mercilessly enumerates for poor Elvira. The bass Giuseppe Lolli doubled the roles of the Commendatore and Masetto, as he probably had those of Bartolo and Antonio in *Figaro*. Only the tenor Antonio Baglioni was new to Mozart, as he was to Bondini's company, and most of his music, including his (at that point) one aria, was written after the Mozarts had arrived in Prague. But, as that aria ('Il mio tesoro') shows, he was a singer of grace, stamina and good coloratura; and he would reappear importantly later in Mozart's life.

The three women, headed by the boss's wife Caterina Bondini as Zerlina, were all remarkable singers. Donna Elvira was sung by Caterina Micelli (who had most probably played Cherubino); and Donna Anna was Teresa Saporiti, who had joined Bondini's company at the age of nineteen, and sung for him in Dresden and Leipzig as well as Prague (where almost certainly she would have sung the Countess). She had a reputation for good looks, a highly-strung temperament and a radiant voice, and Mozart was to deploy all these avidly. (She must also have enjoyed remarkably good health, for she apparently lived to the age of 106.)

Clearly, Mozart was energized by the qualities of his singers, as he was by his continuing collaboration with Da Ponte, by his great popularity in Prague, and by the richness of the subject-matter. Perhaps, too, the rawness of his emotions after the death of his father, in May 1787, in some profound way contributed to yet another level of originality in *Don Giovanni*. There was major audacity and musical innovation, the most breathtaking being the use of three on-stage bands, in addition to the orchestra in the pit, playing different music in different time-signatures at the same time, in the finale to Act I. At the wedding party he throws for Zerlina and Masetto, Giovanni lays on all manner of activities, including three different dances, in order to draw attention from his designs on the bride herself. The very complexity of this had been set up in Giovanni's 'Champagne' aria:

> *Fin ch'han dal vino*
> *Calda la testa,*
> *Una gran festa*
> *Fà preparar.*

> Now that the wine
> has set their heads on fire,
> go and prepare
> a great party.

He had continued:

> *Senza alcun ordine*
> *La danza sia;*
> *Ch'il minuetto,*
> *Chi la follia,*

Chi l'alemana
Farai ballar.

Let the dancing
be completely wild:
They can do a minuet
or a gavotte
or a waltz.

And this is exactly what Mozart wrote in the party scene. But while, to all intents and purposes, the music seems to be 'senza alcun ordine', with three different stage bands tuning up and playing across one another, it is in fact of extremely sophisticated organization, the different layers fitting neatly together. (Like so many passages in Mozart's letters, this appears to be nonsense but in fact makes perfect sense.) He had once said that hearing much different music at the same time gave him 'plenty of ideas', and here is his quite phenomenal and seemingly effortless ability to reproduce them all at once. In the final scene of the opera, when Giovanni is calmly eating his supper before the arrival of Elvira and then the statue of the Commendatore, Mozart could not resist using a stage band again, as, clearly following custom, Giovanni's meal was accompanied by tunes from popular shows. With a gleeful touch, Mozart quoted from Martin y Soler's *Una cosa rara*, Sarti's *I due litiganti*, and, hilariously, from his own *Figaro*. (These quotations would have been even funnier at later performances in Vienna, but would have made their mark too with the well-versed Prague audiences.) And at Don Giovanni's final damnation, Mozart used again a device he had first deployed to enormous effect during the storm scene in *Idomeneo*, and wrote for an off-stage chorus. The addition here of unseen and unworldly voices, together with trombones (instruments traditionally associated with church music, and suggestive therefore of divine retribution), adds immeasurably to the impact of the moment, and to its enduring terror.

But, as always, it is in the musical characterization that Mozart overwhelmingly excels, and in *Don Giovanni* nowhere more than in his portrayal of the three women. Zerlina, as sung by Caterina Bondini, would probably have been considered the 'prima' donna, and seems to represent pure sexuality, the most irresistible bait for Giovanni himself. From her first appearance, with Masetto and her fellow country folk on her wedding day ('Giovinetti, che fate a l'amore'), her music is appropriately peasant-like, with uneven, 7-bar phrases in a rustic 6/8 metre. (This contrasts sharply with the aristocratic dignity – however unstable – of the music for Anna and Elvira.) But when Zerlina is seduced by Giovanni, he makes something lyrical and elegant of her. Even in the simple recitative preceding their famous duet, Mozart gave Giovanni hypnotically repetitive vocal patterns as he enumerated Zerlina's attractions – her eyes, her lips, her fingers ('quegli occhi briconcelli, quei labretti si belli, quelle dituccie candide e odorose'). The duet itself, 'Là ci darem la mano', is in A major, like that for the Count and Susanna (which of course Bassi and Bondini had sung together), and at first she tries to resist him ('Vorrei e non vorrei' – I want it, and yet I don't want it). But her resolve melts completely, in a chromatically descending collapse ('non son più forte' – I haven't the strength) as Giovanni strokes her into submission. At just the right moment, he leads her into a gentle 6/8 (her own metre) for 'Andiam, andiam, mio bene' (Let's go, darling), and she joins him, willingly and finally ecstatically. The duet has become one of the most alluring in the entire operatic repertoire, and says as much about the theatrical chemistry between Bondini and Bassi as it does about Mozart's own understanding of gentle conquest.

At her next appearance, Zerlina (who has been dragged away from Giovanni by Elvira) has to make it up to Masetto: quite understandably he is furious at having been abandoned by his bride on his wedding day. She tells him he should punish her, but then let them make peace. The text of her aria, 'Batti, batti, o bel Masetto / La tua povera Zerlina' (Hit your wretched Zerlina, Masetto), could have been set in an altogether angular, even violent way. But Mozart understands that this is Zerlina's own form of seduction, and one that is quite as successful as that of Giovanni himself. It is an aria of infinitely alluring simplicity, enhanced by an obbligato solo cello; and at the end of it, Masetto too is lulled into playful submission. Then, during the party at Giovanni's house, Zerlina is all but seduced again, but screams for help (legend has it that Mozart taught Caterina Bondini to do this by pinching her bottom). After that she sings constantly with Masetto, as if she is literally clinging to him. But she has to use all her effusive sweetness again in the second act, after Giovanni has beaten up poor Masetto. Da Ponte's text for this scene between them is seductive, beautiful and naughty. As Masetto shows Zerlina the bruises and wounds all over his body, she observes lightly, 'Non è gran mal, se il resto è sano' (If the rest of you is fit, there's no problem). Again Mozart set Da Ponte's gloriously erotic text in an utterly beguiling manner, and the aria 'Vedrai carino' literally arrests the apparently unstoppable, even accelerating, flow of the main story (the fall of Don Giovanni), as the dramatic focus hovers over two ultimately less important roles. Caterina Bondini, Prague's favourite singer, certainly had her moment of complete glory, and generations of Zerlinas have been grateful to her ever since.

In the final outcome, Zerlina and Masetto scamper off together, grateful to have survived the dramatic events they have witnessed. Anna and Elvira cannot share their relief, however: there has been gratification at the final justice of Giovanni's end, but absolutely no satisfaction. Anna's journey through the opera is perhaps the greater of the two, for, unlike Elvira, she starts it (before we see her) in a state of innocence. Both Da Ponte and Mozart are teasingly tight-lipped about the extent to which Anna (if at all) actually welcomed an unidentified, attractive charmer into her room at night. But whether she did and then had second thoughts, or whether she was genuinely startled by his presence, her first appearance is absolutely compelling: as Giovanni tries to run away from his failed seduction, she clutches at him, screaming, 'I will never let you get away with this.' She calls for help, and, when her father arrives, flees back into the house. By the time she returns with Ottavio and others, Giovanni has long gone, and she is confronted with the corpse of her murdered father. This utterly appalling moment motivates her for the rest of the opera, and it is brilliantly handled by both Da Ponte and Mozart. In inarticulate bursts of shocked accompanied recitative, Anna is almost ghoulishly fascinated by the reality of her father's death, by the blood, and by his wound ('Quella sangue – quella piaga'). She begins to lose her grip, and eventually collapses altogether: 'Padre mio . . . caro padre . . . padre amato . . . io manco . . . io moro'. (And this music is even more searing in the knowledge that Mozart wrote it while coming to terms with the death of his own father.) When she recovers from her faint, railing even at poor Ottavio in her confusion, she becomes consumed with determination to avenge her father's blood. In more accompanied recitative she makes Ottavio swear to help her, and together they sing of the crisis in which find themselves. Both Anna and Ottavio are entirely human and credible in this scene; and Anna's gathering obsession now to make Giovanni pay is surely coloured for her by the thought that, somehow, it is all her fault.

After Giovanni's next thwarted seduction (that of Zerlina, interrupted by Elvira), Anna and Ottavio come upon him and – for they know him well – ask for his friendship and help on this terrible day. Relieved not to be recognized, Giovanni smoothly complies. But Elvira interrupts the proceedings again, and firmly tells Anna not to trust him ('Non ti fidar, o misera / Di quell ribaldo cor'). Anna and Ottavio are greatly sympathetic to Elvira ('Cieli! Che aspetto nobile! Che dolce maestà!' – What noble bearing, what imposing sweetness!), and although Giovanni tries to tell them that Elvira is crazy ('La povera ragazza / E pazza, amici miei'), they remain convinced that she is not ('Non hà l'aria di pazzia'). In hesitant, disjunct and falling phrases, they begin to have grave and unwelcome misgivings. And as Elvira leaves, cleverly followed by Giovanni who feigns concern for all of them, Anna at last recognizes Giovanni's voice, and therefore the awful truth: he was her attempted seducer, and her father's murderer. In another brilliant scene, alternating between near-hysteria and icy resolve, she tells Ottavio exactly what happened that night, making the remarkable suggestion that she thought the man who came into her room was Ottavio himself. Mozart sets this line over a completely static string chord; and, especially in the midst of such turmoil, the doubtful veracity of this statement is quietly underlined. Anna retrieves her momentum, and launches into an enormous aria about honour and vengeance ('Or sai che l'onore'), with wild leaps, high tessitura and aggressive word-painting as she sees again the horrific image of her father's fatal wound. Teresa Saporiti's dramatic and vocal skills were well exploited in this scene, which ends with a real surprise, a gentle cadence. The ambiguity of this ingenious touch of Mozart's has challenged generations of interpreters.

At Giovanni's party, Anna, Elvira and Ottavio, masked now as if at a Venetian Carnival celebration, work together as a team to track down Giovanni and bring him to justice. He escapes, of course; and by the second act it is clear that Anna's composure is beginning to crack. Ottavio is perhaps being over-solicitous, inviting her to dry her tears and lean on him, but she understandably insists that she needs to grieve. When Leporello, disguised as Giovanni, is discovered with Elvira, and (in the sextet) then unmasked to reveal his true identity, to the total mystification of everyone else, Anna cannot cope at all, and rushes from the scene. Ottavio, never completely sensitive to Anna's mood, believes that her best course would be to marry him straight away, and in their next scene together he suggests as much. She is appalled: 'O Dei, che dite? In si tristi momenti?' she cries (How can you ask this now?). He tells her she is cruel to him, and this really shocks her: 'Crudele? Ah no, mio bene!' And at last she becomes tender with him. In her aria, 'Non mi dir', she tries to tell him that she really does love him ('Tu ben sai quant'io t'amo'), but that the timing is quite wrong for them to marry. Expressed in long, cantabile lines, this is Anna's most lyrical moment. But she becomes agitated again, in an allegro moderato section, when she suggests that, perhaps one day ('Forse un giorno') heaven will smile upon their marriage; but as Anna's music becomes more acrobatic, the audience is told (by Mozart) that she herself has grave doubts that such a day will ever come. Sure enough, in the epilogue after Giovanni's dreadful end, when Ottavio tries yet again to persuade her to marry him, she begs to be given one more year in which to mourn ('Lascia, o caro, un anno ancora'). She really does need to sort herself out.

Donna Anna began the opera therefore as the innocent daughter of the Commendatore, safely betrothed to the reliable, respectable Don Ottavio; and she ends it in a state of real fragility, traumatized, grief-stricken and lost. For Donna Elvira the journey is not so vast, but it is equally troubled, and, at its end, equally unresolved. At her own first appearance – brilliantly signalled by Giovanni himself, who interrupts his own thoughts by literally smelling the approach of a woman ('Zitto! mi pare sentire odor di femina!') – Mozart tells the audience that Elvira is already disturbed and damaged. 'Ah, chi mi dice mai / Qual barbaro dov'è?' (Who can tell me where the wretch is?), she sings, in rhythms identical to those of the first aria of Elettra in *Idomeneo* ('Tutto nel cor mi sento'). And, sure enough, Elvira's music is distracted, miserable and furious. She has short fragments of phrase, wild contrasts of dynamic, and swirling accompaniment in the strings. And she too is bent on results: 'Gli vò cavare il cor' (I want to tear his heart out). Giovanni, observing all this at a distance, fails at first to recognize her; but when he steps out of the shadows to offer her his assistance, she of course identifies him. And as she accuses him of having treated her so shamefully, she tells the audience exactly what happened to her: as was clearly his common practice, Giovanni had apparently slipped furtively into her house, given her three days of the greatest pleasure, and promised to marry her. (Casanova, sitting in the audience, may perhaps have raised his eyebrows at this point.) So now Elvira wants to get her own back, although she is not exactly clear what she means by this. Giovanni cleverly slips away, instructing Leporello to 'tell her everything'. And he does, in his 'Catalogue' aria, counting out, country by country, the exact number of con-quests (over 2,000, evidently) that Giovanni has made. Elvira's resolve for vengeance is thoroughly refuelled.

At her next appearance, Elvira interrupts Giovanni's seduction of Zerlina: she pulls the couple apart, and tells Zerlina to run away from such a traitor: 'Ah, fuggi il traditor!' Her brief aria (just 45 bars long) is extremely effective, set in jagged lines and dotted rhythms, completely dispelling the erotic serenity of 'Là ci darem la mano'; and Zerlina does indeed flee. But when, in the quartet, Elvira approaches Anna and Ottavio, warning them for their part not to trust Giovanni, her tone is calm, sorrowful and dignified, and they believe her, joining forces with her to track down their prey. If Elvira's aim was at the very least to get in Giovanni's way, thus far she has been extremely successful.

But early in the second act there is one of the cruellest episodes in the opera. Elvira is at her window, confessing to herself that she still loves Giovanni ('Ah taci, ingiusto core'). Giovanni and Leporello overhear this. Giovanni anyway has designs now on Elvira's maid, and tells Leporello to pretend to be him, and lure Elvira away. As Leporello acts out the role of ventriloquist's dummy, Giovanni sings for him what is evidently one of his little serenades of seduction (for 'Discendi, o gioia bella' will become 'Deh vieni alla finestra' when he sings it to the maid). And poor Elvira falls for it. This is at once one of the most glorious and the most disturbing moments in the entire opera. Dramatically it is heartless: Elvira is being horribly and humiliatingly tricked, Giovanni is ruthlessly exploiting her vulnerability, Leporello is sniggering in the background; and the music is of heartstopping beauty. Mozart seems to be delivering the scene from Elvira's point of view, as her private melancholia gives way to tentative excitement when she hears Giovanni's honeyed tones. And yet the presence of the two men, the layers therefore of dramatic complexity, and the whole thrust of narrative and pace give the scene tremendous depth and clarity. As an encapsulation of the combined brilliance of Mozart and Da Ponte, there is no finer nor more succinct example.

The cruelty of Leporello's disguise as Giovanni continues in the recitative, as Leporello now begins to enjoy himself; and he

succeeds in getting Elvira away. We meet them next in a dark courtyard, at the beginning of the sextet. Elvira is frightened of the dark,
and fearful too of being left alone there, and her heart palpitations
are heard in her music. When Leporello is cornered by Anna,
Ottavio, Zerlina and Masetto, she leaps to his defence – 'E mio
marito, pietà' (Have mercy on my husband). But as Leporello
removes his disguise and begs forgiveness, she, like the others, is
stunned almost into speechlessness: 'Deh! Leporello?' they gasp,
'Che inganno è questo?' (What on earth is going on?), and they all
join together for a truly turbulent fugue of swirling, angry, brilliant
counterpoint, 'Mille turbidi pensieri'. After Leporello's flight,
Elvira remains silent (in that first Prague version), leaving Ottavio
to try to take charge of the situation. She appears again briefly in
the supper scene, begging Giovanni now to change his ways; but
her pleas meet only with derision. She can do no more, and rushes
from the room, passing as she goes the terrifying spectacle of the
statue of the Commendatore, whose supernatural presence will
shortly achieve what the combined efforts of the earthly avengers
could not. And when it is all over, and the exhausted survivors draw
breath and survey their futures, Elvira announces her intention to
enter a convent. Her life in the outside world has been ruined.

News of the success of *Don Giovanni* spread fast, and in Vienna
Joseph II immediately requested a production there. (By the time it
happened, in May 1788, the Emperor was on the battlefield fighting
the Turks, and missed the whole event.) Vienna could certainly produce a cast as gifted as that in Prague. There were only two
newcomers to Mozart: Don Giovanni would be sung by Francesco
Albertarelli, a young baritone who would make his Viennese debut
in the Salieri–Da Ponte *Axur*, one month before *Don Giovanni*; and
Don Ottavio by Francesco Morella, whose own debut was as
Almaviva in the Paisiello *Il barbiere di Siviglia* in the same season.
But the rest of the cast were old friends. The two Francescos were
back: Benucci as Leporello, and Bussani as the Commendatore and
Masetto. And the three women were Mozart's Countess, Luisa
Laschi, as Zerlina; and, as Donna Elvira and Donna Anna, Caterina

Cavalieri and Aloysia Lange, together again for the first time since *Der Schauspieldirektor*. It was a truly stellar cast.

Given these different singers – and a different audience too – Mozart and Da Ponte did make some changes to the opera. They omitted the Epilogue altogether, preferring to give their Viennese public the spectacular conflagration of Don Giovanni's end as a final image, rather than pull the focus back on to the more rational (albeit generally unhappy) remaining characters. (This shortened version was to be preferred throughout the nineteenth century.) Other changes involved specific singers. Clearly Francesco Morella did not have the vocal flexibility of Antonio Baglioni, and could not cope with the demands of 'Il mio tesoro', so Mozart wrote him the slow, lyrical and sweet 'Dalla sua pace'. But this did not substitute for 'Il mio tesoro': Mozart and Da Ponte put it in the first act, and rewrote completely what happened after the sextet in Act II. In the Vienna version, Leporello did not make his escape, but was seized by Zerlina, tied to a chair and threatened with a razor. It is a not unsuccessful scene, deriving perhaps from that for Blonde and Osmin in *Die Entführung*, and both Mozart and Da Ponte gave it richness yet levity. The Viennese audiences therefore had a lacuna of rough hilarity amidst the darkness of the second act, and Benucci and Laschi too were given a presumably welcome opportunity to display their own combined comedic skills.

But the biggest change for Vienna was what immediately followed the Zerlina–Leporello scene: Caterina Cavalieri, as Elvira, got a new soliloquy. (Perhaps she was aware of just how much extremely exposed music there was for Aloysia Lange as Anna, and their old rivalry still obtained.) And, as in the soliloquy for the Countess in the second half of *Figaro*, Elvira has a recitative and aria of real, private soul-baring, and it shows her in an altogether new light. Having just been utterly humiliated, discovered with Don Giovanni's servant while believing him to be the man himself, she seems to be in total despair, agonizing about 'excesses' and 'horrible enormities'. But the shock of this recitative is that she is not expressing self-pity, but concern for Giovanni. It is for the safety of his soul that she fears. And in her aria ('Mi tradì quell'alma ingrata' – The wretched man betrayed me) she spells out the truth: although she has been appallingly treated by Giovanni, she only has to look upon his face ('ma se guardo il suo cimento') and she is utterly aroused: she still loves him. The real turbulence of this realization is expressed in jagged virtuosity (that Cavalieri speciality), word fragmentations and phenomenally unexpected harmonic and melodic progressions. As ever, Mozart has seized on Cavalieri's remarkable musicianship and technical expertise, and deployed them in such a way as to give real insight into Elvira's character and situation. But the big difference between her soliloquy and that for the Countess in *Figaro* is that, where the Countess had a healing change of heart and ended her scene in radiant optimism, poor Elvira's self-revelation only confines her all the more to her bleak hopelessness.

~

WHEN THIS VIENNESE *Don Giovanni* was mounted in May 1788, Aloysia, as Donna Anna, was five months pregnant with her sixth child. But she was not the only cast member in that state: Luisa Laschi (Zerlina) was in her seventh month, and in due course she had to leave the production. (Her first child, born the previous year, had died almost immediately, and she was probably anxious for her second – sadly, this one also died.) Laschi was replaced by a new arrival in Vienna, the slightly older Adriana Gabrielli.

Originally from Ferrara (and therefore often labelled 'La Ferrarese'), Gabrielli had studied as a young girl at the Conservatorio dei Mendicanti in Venice, where Burney had heard her in 1770 and been greatly impressed by her 'very extraordinary compass of voice, as she was able to reach the highest E of our harpsichords, upon which she could dwell a considerable time, in a fair, natural voice'. She ran away from the Conservatory, and was briefly married to one Luigi del Bene, the son of a papal ambassador in Venice, with the result that throughout her career her name appeared in a confusing number of manifestations, severally

Adriana Gabrielli, Adriana del Bene, Adriana Ferrarese del Bene, and so on. In the 1780s she appeared in London, at the King's Theatre, and then later in Milan and Trieste. She arrived in Vienna early in 1788, was cast as Diana in Martin y Soler's *L'arbore di Diana* (to a Da Ponte libretto), and became an overnight sensation. She also became Da Ponte's mistress, and, especially after her substitution as Zerlina, an important member of the Mozart–Da Ponte circle.

The end of 1788 was not a good time either for the Mozarts or for Vienna. Wolfgang and Constanze were recovering from the death of their daughter Theresia, and, without regular income, also had real money concerns. Vienna too was in a perilous financial state, for the Emperor's campaigns against the Turks were draining the coffers; early in 1789, Joseph even announced his intention to suspend the Italian opera company altogether. Da Ponte moved quickly to raise a petition, and persuaded the Emperor to change his mind; but the livelihoods of everyone involved in operatic activity in Vienna now seemed more than precarious. Nevertheless, in the summer of 1789, *Figaro* was remounted, with Caterina Cavalieri as the Countess, Adriana Gabrielli as Susanna, and Francesco Albertarelli (recently Vienna's Don Giovanni) as the Count. As the hottest property in operatic Vienna, Gabrielli could ask for her 'own' new music, and so Mozart wrote her 'Un moto di gioia', K579, to replace 'Venite inginocchiatevi' in Act II, and 'Al desio di chi t'adora', K577, to replace (astonishingly) 'Deh vieni e non tardar' in Act IV. Joseph II was so pleased with this revival that, in September 1789, he asked Mozart and Da Ponte for a new opera; and between them they devised, not a reworking of an old libretto, nor the retelling of an old story, but a completely new subject on a contemporary theme: *Così fan tutte*.

The genesis of this new opera is not entirely clear. According to Constanze, the libretto was first offered to Salieri, who rejected it – possibly because he considered its subject-matter wholly inappropriate for opera, that province of ancient heroes and noble ideals. And indeed, on the surface, the story is frankly absurd. Ferrando

and Guglielmo, the two young fiancés of the sisters Fiordiligi and
Dorabella, are challenged by an older friend, Don Alfonso, to try to
capture each other's sweethearts. They should appear to leave town,
return in disguise so as not to be recognized by the girls, and then
court the opposite partner. They would be assisted by the girls'
maid Despina, who would enter fully into the spirit of the game and
herself adopt disguises (first as a doctor, and then as a lawyer); and
the women would indeed fall for the charms of the wrong man.
Originally entitled *La scuola degli amanti* (The School for Lovers),
there was a distinct suggestion of lessons being taught to a fickle
society. But there would be much opportunity too for high comedy,
largely at the expense of the two women.

There had been couple-swapping plots before this proposal.
Salieri himself had set Casti's *La grotta di Trofonio*, in 1788, with
great success; and even Shakespeare's *A Midsummer Night's Dream*
would have been familiar to Viennese audiences. But the exchange
of partners in both these stories, and many others like them, was
achieved through the device of magic and the supernatural, and
here in the new story there was no such forgiving licence. Any
change of heart would be seen as the entire responsibility of the
people concerned. It is hardly surprising that the respectable Salieri
refused to have anything to do with such a libretto.

But when Da Ponte brought the idea to Mozart, the two composers realized that incomparable riches were to be gained by
opening up this Pandora's box of emotion. For the story was much
more than a lighthearted comedy put before a society eager for
superficial gossip and anecdote. In a way, it was an encapsulation of
an Enlightenment subject, concerning the traditional challenges to
love, honour and duty. But the emotional chaos that such mischief
engendered was potentially vast, and this was real grist to the combined mill of Mozart and Da Ponte. As Fiordiligi and Dorabella try
to adhere to the mores and conventions of their society, to their
whole upbringing and contemporary manners, they gradually discover them to be without foundation, and absolutely no defence
against any onslaught on their emotions. Stripped therefore of any

moral or spiritual guidance, they become isolated and vulnerable. And so, as told by Mozart and Da Ponte, the story ends with another heap of emotional ruin: human behaviour has effectively been mocked, and most devastatingly penetrated too. The new title, *Così fan tutte* (All Women Are like That), would have come to Mozart and Da Ponte as they considered the whole ironic thrust of the story; and one of them would have quoted Basilio's line from the Act I trio in *Figaro*, 'Così fan tutte le belle'. Almost as a private joke, they built on this, making 'Così fan tutte' a seminal line for the men at both the beginning and the end of the opera. And Mozart even set it up in the overture, distributing the very notes of Basilio's line among the woodwinds, deceptively feather-light, beguilingly sweet.

Mozart and Da Ponte cast their opera entirely from people they knew. The two sisters Fiordiligi and Dorabella would be played by Adriana Gabrielli and another soprano, recently arrived in Vienna, Luise Villeneuve. She too came from Italy, where she had had great success at the Teatro San Moisè in Venice, in Martin y Soler's *Una cosa rara* and *L'arbore di Diana*; and indeed it was as Amor, again in *L'arbore di Diana*, that she made her Viennese debut in June 1789. (It is tempting to speculate that Adriana Gabrielli might have repeated her great interpretation of Diana, even though she was about to appear as Susanna in the *Figaro* revival, and that the two sopranos had therefore already been seen together on stage.) Mozart wrote two insertion arias for Villeneuve in *L'arbore*: 'Chi sà, chi sà qual sia', K582, and 'Vado, ma dove', K583; and when she went into Cimarosa's *I due baroni* he similarly gave her 'Alma grande e nobil core', K578. All these arias show that her tessitura was lower than that of Aloysia Lange or Caterina Cavalieri, or indeed Adriana Gabrielli; but she was enormously expressive, and agile too in her coloratura. There are even suggestions that she might have been Gabrielli's sister, in which case Mozart and Da Ponte would have been thrilled to find such perfect casting for Fiordiligi and Dorabella.

Ferrando would be sung by the tenor Vincenzo Calvesi.

Although he had yet to perform in a Mozart opera in Vienna, he had been a leading lyric tenor there since 1785, when he had appeared in Paisiello's *Il re Teodoro in Venezia*. Subsequently he had been seen in Salieri's (couple-swapping) *La grotta di Trofonio* and Bianchi's *La villanella rapita*, also in 1783, Martin y Soler's *Una cosa rara* in 1786, and *L'arbore di Diana*, with Laschi and Mandini, in 1787. For *La villanella rapita* Mozart had written a new trio and quartet, and so Calvesi's voice and capabilities too were well known to him before he began writing *Così fan tutte*.

And the rest of the cast were all old friends. Francesco Benucci, back from his trip to London to see Nancy Storace, and incidentally to perform extracts from *Figaro* with her on the stage of the King's Theatre in the Haymarket, would play Guglielmo. Alfonso would be Francesco Bussani, now elevated to the post of Vice-Director of Spectacle, but still singing too; and his wife Dorotea, who had created Cherubino in 1786, would play Despina. The Bussanis did not have the most cordial relationship with Da Ponte, who was to accuse Francesco of being 'a jack-of-all-trades, save that of an honest man',[56] an intriguer, and even an 'enemy'; but he would certainly make use of all these supposed attributes in the character of Alfonso. And if he mistrusted Dorotea Bussani too, she nevertheless served him well. She must have been a remarkably versatile performer: from the adolescent page, Cherubino, in 1786, to the worldly, vivacious maid Despina, capable of all manner of disguises, in 1790, was already quite a leap. But in 1792, still only twenty-nine, she would play an elderly aunt, Fidalba, in Cimarosa's runaway success *Il matrimonio segreto*. Again, her versatility and depth as a singing actress would be well exploited by both Mozart and Da Ponte.

All six characters in *Così fan tutte* are drawn with incomparable richness by Mozart and Da Ponte, and, yet again, it is the women who benefit most from their penetrating understanding. Ferrando and Guglielmo do, of course, make a painful transition from confident young playboys, ready to gamble unthinkingly with the affections of their girlfriends, at the start of the opera, to confused lovers at the end of it. The chemistry between them, controlled and manipulated as it is by the cynical, even cruel Don Alfonso, is never less than fascinating. Their easy, blokish camaraderie is gradually punctured by competition, envy and resentment, and in the penultimate scene of the opera they all but come to blows. Yet the destruction of the women's security is even greater, for Fiordiligi and Dorabella are innocent participants in the game that goes so badly wrong. Their passage from carefree society girls to distraught neurotics is all the more merciless because they have had no active part in the collapse of their world. Unlike the Countess, or Donna Elvira, who are seen to be in distress from their first appearances, these women begin in a state of thoughtless bliss, and end, like their maid Despina perhaps, in one of wretched disillusionment.

And Mozart, so familiar anyway with the reality of sisters who sang, charted the fall of Fiordiligi and Dorabella even in their music. From the very beginning, they seem to be virtually inseparable, singing identical lines with identical coloratura, then locked together in thirds as they share their easy contentment. In their young, privileged, affluent lives, nothing much has so far troubled them, the most serious blot on the horizon seeming merely to be the late arrival of their fiancés. (And here Da Ponte recognizes the natural, unguarded colloquialism of siblings, as Dorabella – rather shockingly after such a sublime opening duet – asks of her sister, 'Ma che diavol vuol dir che i nostri sposi ritardono a venir?' – But where the devil are they?) The arrival first of Alfonso and then of Ferrando and Guglielmo with their unwelcome news (the story is that they have been called away to the battlefield, as indeed any young man could be in the winter of 1789) changes the temperature of the scene. In the first, glorious quintet, the girls continue to react identically, with emotion and a little fear, as the boys act out their pretended dismay, and Alfonso gamely supports them. After the announcement that Ferrando and Guglielmo must leave forthwith, there is a tearful parting in the second quintet ('Di scrivermi ogni giorno' – Promise to write to me every day). Here individual syllables are separated as if by sobs for all four lovers (as Alfonso stifles his inclination to laugh) before the flood of emotion brings abundant lyricism, bound by an exquisite viola line, and punctuated by wide dynamic contrasts. Mozart was especially proud of this quintet, as Constanze was later to recount; and there was resonance in it for him too, who, after he had dragged himself away from Mannheim and Aloysia in December 1778, had written to his father:

> For me, to whom nothing has ever been more painful than leaving Mannheim, this journey was only partly agreeable, and would not have been at all pleasant, but indeed very boring, if from my youth up I had not been so much accustomed to leave people, countries and cities, and with no great hope of soon, or ever again, seeing the kind friends whom I left behind.[57]

After the departure of the boys, Fiordiligi and Dorabella sing their sublime prayer 'Soave sia il vento' (May the breezes be gentle). Still in thirds, they are joined together now in bereft dejection, and even Alfonso affects to console them.

It is in their next scene that the two sisters begin to show their individuality. As they return to their sitting room, where Despina has prepared their breakfast, Dorabella suddenly loses control, and in a melodramatic aria, 'Smanie implacabili', she unleashes veritably adolescent hysterics. She demands solitude and a darkened room, she hyperventilates, and, Elettra-like, she calls upon the Furies, to whom she will present a wretched example of tragic love. Mozart has great fun with this exaggerated display of self-pity, and supplies turbulent undercurrents in her accompaniment too: restless strings, and wailing cries from the supporting winds. When eventually Despina prises out of the girls what exactly is their problem, her tough line of practicality sends them both running from the room; and they only reappear when Ferrando and Guglielmo return in their ludicrous disguise as 'Albanians'. Still unsettled by Despina's attitude, Fiordiligi and Dorabella call her crude names ('Ragazzaccia tracotante' – Arrogant slut) for having allowed men into their house on such a day, and, musically clinging together in their thirds once more, toe the conventional line. They explode with forte outrage to the intruders, and breathe piano apologies to their absent lovers. Ferrando and Guglielmo are delighted.

But when Alfonso emerges from his observation post and feigns astonished pleasure at meeting two of his dearest friends, it is time for Fiordiligi to take control of the situation. 'E in casa mia che fanno?' (But what are they doing in my house?), she demands; and the boys' reply takes them completely off guard. 'Amor . . . qui ci conduce' (Love brought us here), they croon over a seductive cushion of string sound, whereupon they concoct, line by line, turn and turn about, their first gallant thrust in the game of flirtation. Dorabella is dumbfounded, but Fiordiligi roars into action: 'Temerari!' (How dare you!). In a tough, forthright and extremely angular accompanied recitative she declares that the sisters' hearts are not available, as they are entrusted elsewhere, and that they will remain faithful to their fiancés. 'Come scoglio' (Like a rock), she continues in her aria, now thoroughly in her stride; she will stand to resist any onslaught. And Mozart raids every corner of Gabrielli's formidable technique, describing her impregnable 'scoglio' in a musical line of immense compass and power, with vast leaps of range, dazzling (Cavalieri-like) coloratura, and marvellous fortitude. And when Guglielmo vainly tries to enumerate their good points and physical credentials, Fiordiligi and Dorabella flee exasperated from the room, leaving the boys helpless with the most successful operatic laughter ever written.

At the beginning of the finale to the first act (and the first half of the opera) the girls are back together again in close harmony and gentle imitative counterpoint, but now of dismay, as opposed to the playful happiness of their opening scene. When the 'Albanians' rush in, claiming to have taken poison, Fiordiligi and Dorabella yell for Despina, who tells them to stay with the men while she goes to fetch a doctor (herself in the first of her disguises). But a subtle change now occurs, and it is Dorabella who leads, showing more than a passing interest in the two young men ('Che figure interresanti!' – What interesting faces!). Increasingly the girls find themselves curiously attracted to the strangers, and privately confess to Zerlina-like weakenings ('Più resister non poss'io' – I can't resist much longer). They end the act in a state of continued outer resolve, but inner emotional confusion.

By the beginning of the second act Fiordiligi and Dorabella have recovered a little of their equilibrium, and cling sanctimoniously to the 'correct' position. But they are rattled, and again speak roughly ('Cospettaccio!', 'Che diavolo!') and even cruelly to Despina, especially when she proposes that, to counter any rumours of impropriety, they could tell the inquisitive outside world that the new admirers were hers. Dorabella flatly dismisses the suggestion: 'Chi vuol che il creda?' (Who would believe that?). But, still on the side of the young men, Despina tries to teach Fiordiligi and Dorabella how to ensnare a new lover, and after she has left the room, the girls do now reveal cracks in their armour. Again it is Dorabella who takes the initiative, playfully leading her sister into a giggling charade of choosing one of the two Albanians; and as their little enacted scene develops, with extended ornamental melismas on 'Che spassetto io proverò!' (What fun I'll have!), the accompanying instruments giggle and sigh too. Already Fiordiligi and Dorabella are a step removed from the massive resolve of the Act I finale. And when, in the following scene, they encounter their suitors again, there is no longer any aggressive resistance, no hint of rocks, but a soft, polite unease. Ferrando and Guglielmo lay on a wind band and a small choir to serenade them; Despina and Alfonso give all four young people a quick lesson in social engagement, and leave them alone. At first the scene is charming, full of adolescent embarrassment as, truly unable to take control of the situation, they all resort desperately to idiotic smalltalk about the weather and the foliage. But again it is Dorabella who is the first to succumb, easily submitting to Guglielmo's clumsy flirtartion. Alone together, they sing a duet ('Il core vi dono' – I give you this heart), full of double meanings, significant pauses and silences, as the real gravity of what is happening strikes them. Their vocal lines answer each other at first, but then come together on their heartbeats. Soon Dorabella is singing in close harmony with Guglielmo, and they leave entwined in each other's arms.

Fiordiligi meanwhile is desperately resisting the attractions of Ferrando, and when at last he leaves her alone she is in a true state of panic. And here, in exactly the same position in the opera as the soliloquies for the Countess, or for Cavalieri's Viennese Donna Elvira, is a pivotal, crucial, accompanied recitative and aria for Fiordiligi. She longs for Ferrando to return, and cries after him, but checks herself. And so she confesses that she is totally aroused by him: 'Io ardo, e l'ardor mio non è più effetto d'un amor virtuoso' (I am on fire, and my passion is no longer that of a virtuous love). With shaking stabs of string accompaniment, as if to smite herself with the reality of her shameful feelings, she lists them: 'E smania, affanno, pentimento, leggerezza, perfidia e tradimento' (This is madness, anguish, remorse, fickleness, deceit and betrayal). And then, Countess-like, Fiordiligi embarks on a glorious, slow, simple line, as she begs forgiveness from her absent Guglielmo: 'Per pietà, ben mio, perdona'. Da Ponte's text here overflows with guilt and remorse, and a frail attempt to hope that her constancy might drive away her hateful desires. But whereas in *Figaro* the Countess's references to constancy turned her around, giving her hope and optimism, here Fiordiligi's attempt at resolve only leads her back into her 'vergogna e orror' (shame and horror). She sings more wide, desperate, vocal leaps, and doleful ornamentation; and throughout all this, most significantly, she is shadowed by a prominent solo horn, traditionally the instrument of the cuckold. The fast section to Fiordiligi's aria is agitated, repetitive and angular, as she continues on her path of overwhelming guilt and self-chastisement, and apologizes to Guglielmo, whose trust deserved better reward ('Si dovea miglior mercede, caro bene, al tuo candor'). Both Da Ponte and Mozart have recognized and exploited the unbearable poignancy of Fiordiligi's solitary confrontation with a seemingly

cruel world, devoid of moral or spiritual guidance. The Enlightenment, it seems, has failed her.

When Fiordiligi joins the other women, she finds that, to
Despina's great delight, Dorabella has already changed allegiance.
Miserably, Fiordiligi confesses to them that she too is affected by
her new admirer: 'Io amo! E l'amor mio non è sol per Guglielmo'.
So now Dorabella works on her sister, with the playful aria 'E
amore un ladroncello' (Love is a little thief). Written in 6/8, like so
much of Despina's music, she offers the same sort of cheerful
advice that their maid had offered them at the beginning of the first
act: love is a serpent who can bring you sweetness and content, but
who can also make you miserable if you try to deny him. Alone
again, Fiordiligi has a brilliant idea: she and Dorabella must dress
up in Ferrando and Guglielmo's uniforms, and follow them into
battle. And, as the hidden men observe her, she tries to build her
enthusiasm for the path she must take. She wraps herself in
Guglielmo's jacket and imagines herself in his arms: she is in the
key of A major, and she begins to retrieve her joy. But Ferrando
emerges from his hiding place and tells her that if she leaves he will
die of grief; and suddenly her aria of determination becomes a duet
of seduction. In desperation she tears them away from A major to
C major ('Son tradita! Deh, partite . . .' – I am betrayed – leave
me!). But Ferrando persists, using her new key to plead passionately with her to kill him if she cannot love him; and Fiordiligi
begins to falter. Her energy, like her resistance, gradually dissolves:
she sends up a helpless prayer, 'Dei, consiglio!' (Heaven help me).
And Ferrando, now calm and controlled and infinitely sweet (and
back in A major), appeals to her with simple, unadorned ardour:
'Volgi a me pietoso il ciglio' (Look on me with mercy). He offers
himself as a lover and a husband, and she can only gasp 'Giusto ciel'
as she weakens. With the significant help of an oboe, which completes the phrases she cannot, she finally capitulates: 'Hai vinto; fà
di me quel che ti par' (You have won: do with me what you want).
And at last they embrace joyfully. Now it is they who sing together
in close harmony, with ecstatic little flourishes of purely sexual

energy. The conquest of Fiordiligi, an altogether different matter from that of Dorabella, has been achieved in the course of a musical number that began as an aria of steadfast resolution, and moved through surprise, passionate protestation and the most tender supplication, to utter jubilation. Mozart and Da Ponte have excelled even themselves: there is no finer, or more human, musical depiction of such a transformation.

After the duet, there is a truly distressing scene between the men, and Ferrando and Guglielmo practically beat each other up. But Alfonso, triumphant and detached, calmly tells them to marry their new loves: women are all the same, after all. And, turning his knife in their raw wounds, he makes his pupils in his 'School for Lovers' repeat with him his miserable mantra: all women are the same. They do: 'Così fan tutte'.

The finale to Act II, the denouement to the opera, opens in a mood of the greatest jollity, with enormous energy generated in the orchestra, and servants and musicians scurrying around, preparing for the wedding. The four young people seem a contented unit now, literally in harmony with themselves, and it is the newly serene Fiordiligi who proposes a gentle toast: 'E nel tuo, nel mio bicchiero / Si sommerga ogni pensiero' (May every care be drowned in your glass and in mine). First Ferrando and then Dorabella join her in what becomes a sublime canon; only Guglielmo, who so recently witnessed the loss of his Fiordiligi, cannot bring himself to take part. Despina's appearance disguised as a lawyer to marry them is interrupted by Alfonso's cruel masterstroke – the 'news' that the girls' former lovers are returning. Fiordiligi and Dorabella are musically thrown back to each other, singing again in their thirds, gasping with fear of what might happen next. Ferrando and Guglielmo, as confused now as are the women, return as themselves and eventually reveal their Albanian disguises to Fiordiligi and Dorabella, who plead with them for forgiveness. But while they accept their apologies, the men utter the devastating lines, 'Te lo credo, gioia bella / Ma la prova far non vò' (I believe you, my beauty, but I can no longer trust you). Despite all Alfonso's advice to join hands and embrace each other, the four lovers are thoroughly bewildered and mortified. They obediently join with Alfonso for the opera's coda, repeating the beliefs of the Age of Reason:

> *Fortunato l'uom che prende*
> *Ogni cosa pel buon verso*
> *E trà i casi e le vicende*
> *Da ragion guidar si fà.*

> Happy is he who takes
> the right side of everything
> and through all tribulations
> lets Reason guide him.

But there is no doubt at all, from Mozart's brittle, almost manic setting of these words (allegro molto) that he too has lost all faith in this Enlightenment philosophy.

Both Fiordiligi and Dorabella have travelled long roads in *Così fan tutte*. Not unlike Elinor and Marianne Dashwood in Jane Austen's *Sense and Sensibility* (written just eight years after *Così fan tutte*), one of them attempts rigidly to impose self-control while the other is more immediately demonstrative of her emotions; one is upright and determined, the other more melodramatic and demanding. But they both end up, like the men as 'instructed' by Don Alfonso, wiser, more troubled and, in truth, more adult. The same cannot be said for Despina, for she actually begins the opera in a state of cheerful, worldly cynicism (an altogether more benign cynicism than that of Alfonso). But she too is dismayed and ashamed by the consequences of a game into which she entered willingly, but whose outcome she could not foresee.

Da Ponte's Despina, in fact, could have been a completely different woman in the hands of someone other than Mozart. From her very first recitative, in which, Leporello-like, she complains of the hardship of being a lady's maid, through her mystified reaction to the girls' distress, to her own first aria about men ('In uomini'), the text is tough, jaded and bitter. Exasperated by the naivety of Fiordiligi and Dorabella, she effectively tells them to snap out of it and grow up (which of course, in due time, they do), and advises them that all men are false and deceitful, and therefore untrustworthy. And yet, as interpreted by Mozart, this toughness is softened. Despina has clearly had great experience of the opposite sex, but she is never less than charming, vivacious, witty and full of common sense. 'Do you expect to find fidelity in men, in soldiers?' she asks at the start of her aria. But the question is delivered with delicacy and even mirth, and as she gets into the main section of the aria ('Di pasta simile son tutti quanti' – They are all made of the same ingredients), Mozart gives her a rustic 6/8, and circular phrases with contrasts of dynamic to emphasize the repetitive false-ness in men. Her advice to her charges is to love men as it is convenient for themselves: 'Amiam per comodo'; and only here, in the final section of the aria, does Despina's light touch seem a little forced ('La la ra, lara la,' she bravely trills), and there is a sense of real pain beneath her carapace. Da Ponte's text was already fascin-ating. But Mozart's realization of it has, yet again, endowed it with a depth and richness undetectable on the printed page of the libretto.

In her scenes with Alfonso, when she enters (for financial con-sideration) into the whole 'Albanian' charade, Despina is once more vivacious, canny, amusing and amused. Again, her philosophy of life and love, as stated before the Act I finale, seems hardbitten. Answering her own question as to what love is ('Amor cos'è?'), she gives her definition: 'Piacer, comodo, gusto, gioia, divertimento, passatempo, allegria' (Pleasure, convenience, taste, enjoyment, amusement, pastime and fun); but it is no longer any of those if it brings pain and torment. Then when she is disguised as a doctor to minister to the men, Despina loves taking charge of the situation, and beginning to pull the strings of her puppet-like mistresses. And it is she who is the vehicle for Mozart's in-joke about his old friend Dr Mesmer, whose magnet can so miraculously cure her patients of any effects of poisonous substances.

By the beginning of the second act, Despina can see that her young ladies are beginning to weaken, and she redoubles the didactic line, telling Fiordiligi and Dorabella to keep an eye to the main chance, and if necessary to take more than one lover at a time ('Mangiar il fico e non gittare il pomo' – Eat the fig and keep the apple too). When the girls insult her by pouring scorn on her suggestion that they tell the world their new suitors are coming to see her, she takes a Susanna-like line: 'Non hà forse merto una cameriera d'aver due cicisbei?' (Doesn't a chambermaid deserve a couple of admirers?). But Mozart gives her aria 'Una donna a quindici anni' another rustic, 6/8 lilt and swagger, as she enumerates again what any fifteen-year-old girl should know about ensnaring lovers; and she allows herself a little self-congratulation as she leaves them, knowing that she has made more than a little headway.

In the garden scene, after Ferrando and Guglielmo have had the girls serenaded, Despina and Alfonso now demonstrate to their charges how they should proceed. But Despina (and Mozart) startle everyone by interrupting this little lesson of social comportment with a sudden flash of exasperation. The music becomes accompanied recitative, as Despina effectively tells the girls to face realities. 'Quello ch'è stato è stato', she declares (What's done is done), and, with almost Fiordiligi-like firmness (forthright rhythms and arpeggios) she becomes truly severe, in a statement of double meaning:

> *Rompasi omai quell laccio*
> *Segno di servitù.*
>
> Break this knot,
> this sign of servitude.

But, almost as if she knows she has overstepped herself, she then softens again into her 6/8 deportment lesson; and she and Alfonso slip away, chuckling delightedly at the situation they have created.

After the inevitable capitulation of Fiordiligi and Dorabella,

Despina enjoys her second disguise at their wedding, posing now as the lawyer who will marry them. Here Mozart is merciless in his caricature of the legal profession (as he had been with the twitteringly incompetent Don Curzio in *Figaro*), for Despina's utterances are monotonous, longwinded and incomprehensible. After Ferrando and Guglielmo have returned as themselves, Despina is quick to try to lighten what is potentially a very difficult situation: they pull her, still disguised, out of hiding, and she reveals her true self: 'E Despina mascherata' (It's only me in disguise). But when she too realizes that the 'Albanians' have been Ferrando and Guglielmo all along, she is truly appalled, abandoning any sense of fun, or allegiance to Alfonso, and joining with the girls in their horrified disgrace. Her final utterance, before the brittle Enlightenment epilogue in which she too must take part, is one of confusion and shame. Her carapace has finally cracked completely.

Così fan tutte does not have the sensational and gruesome ending of *Don Giovanni*, nor even the shocking public humiliation of the aristocracy of *Figaro*. Its relatively intimate, domestic scope made it somewhat mystifying to its first audiences in 1790; and thirty years later even Constanze confessed that she did not much admire its plot.[58] But this final collaboration between Mozart and Da Ponte can be seen as a summation of their combined gifts, for in it they address that most fundamental of issues, the attraction between men and women, and in so doing they expose all manner of truths about human nature and behaviour. All six characters, and especially the women, are drawn with multifaceted exuberance, and are completely recognizable as members of a contemporary society. Da Ponte perhaps betrayed his own private allegiances and prejudices: for his (then) beloved Adriana Gabrielli he created the absolutely magnificent role of Fiordiligi; for his supposed adversaries, the Bussanis, he devised an ending where both their characters would have to assume shameful responsibility for the chaos that had unfolded. But there is nothing ordinary about this libretto: even more, perhaps, than Da Ponte's two earlier works for Mozart, *Così fan tutte* is brilliantly constructed, and rich in quite fascinating detail. And as Da Ponte raised his standard, Mozart accordingly followed. He rejoiced in the vocal talents especially of Gabrielli, Villeneuve and Calvesi, and in the dramatic and comedic skills of all his performers; and he produced a score as consistently glorious and elevating as any ever written.

~

THE PLEASING SUCCESS of *Così fan tutte*'s performances was abruptly interrupted by the death, on 20 February 1790, of the Emperor Joseph II. Although this once-adored monarch had in his later years become deeply unpopular (on hearing of his death, his almost octogenarian Chancellor Kaunitz remarked, 'How very good of him'), Vienna dutifully went into official mourning, and therefore closed all its theatres. *Così fan tutte* would only resume its performances in June. The death of the Emperor also marked the beginning of one of Mozart's most difficult periods. He was constantly ignored at every grand celebration (the accession of Leopold II in March, and, in the autumn, his Frankfurt coronation, and the huge Habsburg double wedding in Vienna); Constanze was ill; and even his own creative spirit seemed curiously fallow. Then in the spring of 1791 there was another blow. Da Ponte, together with Adriana Gabrielli, was banished from Vienna, as a result (according to him) of outrageous cabals against them at Court; and so Mozart lost for ever his most thrilling collaborator. (Soon after they left, Da Ponte and Gabrielli themselves separated, with some acrimony.) But it was not all bleak. *Così fan tutte* was taken up by the city of Prague, which had always been such a supporter of Mozart. Pasquale Bondini had sadly died in the summer of 1789, on a journey to Italy; but he had in any case recently handed over the reins of his company to his colleague Domenico Guardasoni, who had long wanted to entice Mozart back to Prague for a new opera. And in Vienna, meanwhile, Mozart had renewed his friendship with the man who would succeed Da Ponte as his most exciting and energizing partner, Emanuel Schikaneder.

Now in his late thirties, just four years older than Mozart,

Schikaneder too was enjoying a hugely colourful life. He was edu-
cated by the Jesuits in Regensburg, and then became an actor. By
his mid-twenties he had already played Hamlet, Macbeth and even
King Lear, and his early familiarity with the craft as well as the
poetry of Shakespeare would remain a crucial part of his theatrical
make-up. He was also something of a composer, and in Innsbruck
in the 1775–6 season had put on the comic opera *Die Lyranten*, for
which he had written both the text and the music. In 1777 he
married an actress, Eleanora Arth, and they both joined Franz
Joseph Moser's company in Nuremberg. The following year
Schikaneder took over the management of the company and toured
it extensively for many years. Their residence in Salzburg in the
winter of 1780–81 had brought him into the Mozart family's
acquaintance, and genuine friendship had been established. When
Mozart left Salzburg for Munich and *Idomeneo* (and indeed for
good), Schikaneder had come to the Tanzmeisterhaus to see him
off. Buried though he was in composing his new opera, Wolfgang
had found time to write an aria for Schikaneder, 'Zittre, töricht
Herz, und leide', K365a, and send it back to Salzburg for one of
his comedies. In 1784 Schikaneder was in Vienna, appearing at
the Kärntnerthor-Theater for three months. The friendship with
Mozart was renewed, and Schikaneder put on a revival of *Die
Entführung* in November. In the following season he also appeared
at Vienna's Burgtheater. But at this point his wife left him for a rival
impresario, Johann Friedel, and with him formed a company which
eventually settled at the Freihaus-Theater in Vienna. Schikaneder's
own company spent the next seasons touring again, to Salzburg,
Augsburg and Regensburg (where Schikaneder became a Freemason). But when Friedel died in March 1789, Eleanora contacted
Schikaneder, and the couple were reunited. Schikaneder brought
his company back to Vienna, amalgamated it with Friedel's, and,
with the help of some impressive financial backers (including
Joseph von Bauernfeld, who would later translate Shakespeare into
German for Schubert) reopened the Freihaus-Theater in July 1789
with his own comic opera, *Der Dumme Gärtner aus dem Gebirge*. For

both Schikaneder and the Freihaus-Theater it was the beginning of a hugely successful period, which would last into the next century.

The new company at the Freihaus-Theater was an extremely impressive gathering. Like Schikaneder himself, many of his colleagues were multitalented all-rounders, and they burned with theatrical fire. Benedikt Schack from Prague had been with Schikaneder since 1786. He was a fine tenor, a talented flute-player, and also a composer. He wrote much of the music for Schikaneder's singspiels, often in collaboration with his colleague, the superb bass singer Franz Xavier Gerl (who was almost certainly a former pupil of Leopold Mozart, for he had sung as a boy chorister in Salzburg). From Friedel's company Schikaneder inherited Johann Joseph Nonseul, an older actor who also sang small roles, and had had much experience too in theatre management; and Mozart's sister-in-law Josefa Hofer, a soprano of astonishingly high range and spectacular coloratura, like her sister Aloysia. New members of the amalgamated company in 1789 were Mozart's original Barbarina, young Anna Gottlieb, now aged fifteen, and another tenor–composer, Jakob Haibl, who would later become Sophie Weber's husband. These artists not only worked at the Freihaus-Theater but were also housed there, for Schikaneder had established his new company on what was effectively a self-contained campus. Mozart felt instantly at home with Schikaneder and his colleagues: he began to frequent their little community, forming great friendships especially with Schack and Gerl (it was for Gerl, and the company's principal double bass-player Herr Pichelberger, that he wrote his concert aria 'Per questa bella mano', K612, in 1791), and entering into great theatrical discussions with Schikaneder himself. In the course of these, in the spring of 1791, they conceived their joint project, *Die Zauberflöte*.

However much Schikaneder's natural inclination was to present the serious classical repertoire in his theatre, he had long since found it necessary to balance this with magic rescue operas and comic singspiels. He had created the character of 'Dummer Anton', a development of the Punch-like Hanswurst of popular Viennese theatre, and initiated a series of seven singspiels around him, beginning indeed with *Der Dumme Gärtner*. As an impresario, he insisted on presenting true visual grandeur, and his productions were famously elaborate, with opulent scenery, live animals, spectacular lighting and many magic effects. All these aspects of Schikaneder's work would find their way into his new collaboration with Mozart. But its most crucial and defining ingredient was the fact that both he and Mozart were Freemasons. At the time, Masonry was rather in need of a helpful boost, since its activities were deeply mistrusted by the new Emperor. The multidimensional production that Schikaneder and Mozart devised together would therefore not only combine elements of 'Dummer Anton'-type pantomime (a sympathetic comic character, and archetypal good and evil characters) with those of a rescue opera in the tradition of *Die Entführung* (a young prince would rescue an abducted girl), and include some alluring magic tricks (a queen would appear out of a mountain, an old woman would change into a young one, bread and wine would be turned into stones and water). It would also, in effect, present an allegorical justification and clarification of the whole movement of Freemasonry, depicted in all its recognizable symbols as a force for good, overcoming those of evil.

The details of the plot and its whole structure would undergo many shifts and changes as Schikaneder and Mozart created their new singspiel. But eventually they settled on a narrative wherein a young prince, Tamino, is sent by the Queen of the Night to rescue her daughter, Pamina, from the clutches of a High Priest, Sarastro. He is given the birdcatcher Papageno as a reluctant companion, a magic flute to help him, and three young boys as occasional guides. But Tamino becomes convinced that Sarastro in fact is benevolent and wise, and, together with Pamina, he himself undergoes various trials in order to become accepted into Sarastro's order. Meanwhile Papageno has been seeking his own companion (a Papagena), and he too is rewarded. The Queen of the Night and her entourage are overcome by the power of the sun, and the work ends with a hymn of praise for the gods Isis and Osiris.

So at last Mozart was again in his element, collaborating with a brilliant and theatrically vital colleague on subject-matter that was of the utmost importance to both of them, and writing too for a highly gifted group of performers whom he knew well and loved deeply. Schikaneder erected a little wooden summerhouse in the courtyard of the Freihaus-Theater premises, and in June and July of 1791 Mozart was most often to be found there, working on *Die Zauberflöte*.

But it was while he was submerged in this major labour, and contemplating too his bizarre commission for Count Walsegg's Requiem Mass, that Mozart was visited again by Domenico Guardasoni from Prague. The new Emperor, Leopold II, was determined to appear concerned with all parts of his Empire, and, in contrast to his brother Joseph II before him, to respect therefore his ties with Hungary and Bohemia. For this reason he had followed his coronation in Frankfurt, in September 1790, with another in Hungary two months later. Now, after almost a year, he proposed to have yet a third coronation, in Prague at the end of August 1791. As late as July that year, Guardasoni was instructed by the Bavarian Estates to provide a new coronation opera; and, although he had only recently returned to Prague after taking his company to Warsaw, he hurried at once to Vienna to ask the Emperor's Court composer, Salieri, to provide it. When Salieri declined the invitation, Guardasoni naturally turned to Mozart, who accepted with alacrity. He was of course already heavily laden with work, but he was anxious at last to write something for the new Emperor, especially having been so humiliatingly ignored in all the celebrations of the previous year. And he was always keen to work in the National Theatre in Prague. But he would have little say in either the subject-matter or even the casting of this coronation opera: he was told that the libretto should be a reworking of an old opera seria text by Metastasio, *La clemenza di Tito*, originally written for Caldara over fifty years previously, in 1734. Furthermore, two principal singers from Italy, a soprano and a castrato, had already been cast in the major roles. Mozart knew nothing about either of them.

If Mozart had no time at all to worry about these departures from his by now accustomed creative practice, he did probably have some input into the actual shaping of the antiquated libretto. Since Da Ponte's ignominious departure from Vienna, his position as Court Poet had been temporarily held by another Venetian, Caterino Mazzolà, and it was he who modernized Metastasio's text, restructuring it from three acts into two, eliminating several sections, and turning many solo numbers into ensembles. In the few weeks that Mozart had between receiving his commission from Prague and actually going there, he would have divided his time between meetings with Mazzolà at Court, and with Schikaneder in their little summerhouse. When he left for Prague at the end of August, together with Constanze, his pupil Süssmayr and the clarinettist Anton Stadler, he had by no means completed his opera. And yet, nine days after they arrived, it received its first performance. The theatrical world is accustomed to apparently miraculous occurrences, whereby what seems to be lamentably unready for an opening night somehow undergoes an astonishing transformation in its final hours of preparation. The premiere of *La clemenza di Tito* was unquestionably one of these.

Mozart's second Prague opera is, however, decidedly different from his three great collaborations with Da Ponte, and from the growing masterpiece that he left behind in Vienna. It is relatively short; and within it the individual arias and ensembles too are short, with no major accumulative sweep of musico-dramatic energy such as he had developed so thrillingly with Da Ponte. After the manner of opera seria, every number is driven by a single affect, and even the few ensembles leave little room for the development of plot. But the most severe difference between *La clemenza di Tito* and its predecessors is that Mozart did not have time to write the recitatives. It was the faithful Süssmayr who composed these; and he diligently added serviceable music to Mazzolà's text. Without a doubt, this competent work was a major factor in getting the opera on stage at all. But its total lack of that touch of genius, which makes all Mozart's own recitatives as riveting as the orchestral

numbers that they so seamlessly link, gives the score a real uneven-
ness. For this reason it is likely that, in his heart of hearts, Mozart
considered *La clemenza di Tito* to be among his failures. Like his
never-finished C minor Mass for Constanze, and indeed the
Requiem that also awaited him back in Vienna, *La clemenza di Tito*
is greatly uplifting, and thought-provoking, and affords intense
musical satisfaction. But it is only a glorious torso, lacking limbs.

All but one of the singers for Leopold II's coronation opera
were new to Mozart. He would have been delighted that the title
role of the Emperor Tito, who shows saintly clemency as he forgives his potential assassins, was to be sung by Antonio Baglioni,
the creator of Don Ottavio in 1787. Tito's great friend but would-
be murderer, Sesto, was to be sung, in the tradition of Idamante, by
the Italian castrato Domenico Bedini, who had enjoyed a steady
career in Italian opera houses since 1770. He cannot have been
altogether in his prime, and it is possible that Mozart was dismayed
by him, for, in an article by Niemetschek in 1794, Bedini was
described as having been 'wretched'. (After the great Rauzzini,
Mozart seems never to have had much luck with his castrato
singers.) Sesto's music is often very demanding, and was quite
possibly beyond Bedini. But Mozart did have the good idea of
transferring some of his virtuosity to the orchestra, and specifically
to his great friend Stadler's clarinet. Sesto's most magnificent aria,
'Parto, parto', towards the end of the first act, has a superb part for
obbligato clarinet; and though in the final section of the aria it is
necessary for the voice and clarinet to share dazzling twists and
turns, the deployment of one brilliant performer could perhaps
mask the presence of a mediocre one. Stadler was already involved
as an obbligato soloist in an aria, 'Non più di fiori', which Mozart
had probably written long before he got his commission for *La
clemenza di Tito* (it appears in the manuscript score on different
paper), but which could serendipitously be used for the character of
Vitellia towards the end of the opera. And, like all excellent wind-
players, Stadler would have been keen to have as many prominent
and challenging solos as possible.

Also in the cast for *La clemenza di Tito* were three sopranos and a bass. Little is now known of two of the sopranos, Carolina Perini, who in the travesty tradition of Cherubino played the role of Annio, and a Signora Antonini who sang Servilia, Sesto's sister, and Annio's lover. The Roman prefect Publio was sung by Gaetano Campi, whose greater claim to fame resided in his marriage that year to the eighteen-year-old Polish soprano Antonia Miklasiewicz. Despite the fact that the couple went on to have no fewer than seventeen children (including four sets of twins and one of triplets), Antonia Campi had a good career, especially as an interpreter of Mozart roles (the Countess, the Queen of the Night, Constanze, Donna Anna, Vitellia). And when, on one of Constanze's visits to Prague in November 1797, a special concert was arranged, both Campi and his wife took part. There were arias and ensembles, and the Campis sang together with Constanze herself.

But the most pivotal role in *La clemenza di Tito* is that of Vitellia. It is she who, like Lady Macbeth, repeatedly urges Sesto (who worships her) to assassinate Tito, partly in revenge for her father Vitellius having been dethroned by Tito's father Vespasian, and partly because she had designs on herself becoming Tito's queen, but he has preferred first, Berenice, daughter of the King of Judaea, and, later, Servilia. Towards the end of the opera Vitellia undergoes a change of heart, as Sesto's loyalty and Tito's clemency affect her too. She publicly confesses her involvement in the assassination plot, and in turn receives her own Imperial pardon. Vitellia is a complex and great role, requiring wide dramatic and vocal skills, for there are elements in her of Elettra, of Donna Elvira, even perhaps of Mozart's imminent Queen of the Night. She would be sung by Maria Marchetti-Fantozzi, the other singer engaged by Guardasoni before Mozart even agreed to write the opera. And here, it seems, Mozart was relieved and satisfied. She was a tremendous success in the opera's premiere (Count Zinzendorf reported that Leopold II himself had found her performance 'enchanting'), and from there went on to have a great career throughout Italy and Germany.

Despite the lack of preparation time, the shortcomings of at least one of the cast, and the somewhat retrospective constraints of Mozart's return to opera seria, there is much glorious music to be enjoyed in *La clemenza di Tito*. Its first scene, between Vitellia and Sesto, is crucial to the setting up of the two principal characters. Vitellia's lines are wildly angular, energetic, and slightly disjunct; Sesto's, by contrast, are more lyrical and resigned. When, in their duet, they share an allegro, each of them confesses to 'mille affetti' (a thousand emotions), and only then is their music identical. When they learn that Tito has in fact sent Berenice away, Vitellia realizes she can still hope for his hand, and reverses her instructions to Sesto. He is understandably confused, and she pours scorn on him in her aria 'Deh, se piacer mi vuoi' (If you wish to please me). On the surface this seems to be a sweet, flute-enhanced minuet of wheedling persuasion. But, in true *Figaro*-fashion, it has sinister undertones, which emerge at the allegro section. There are disturbing five-bar phrases, and at the words 'Chi sempre inganni aspetta / Aletta ad ingannar' (He who expects to be betrayed will always invite betrayal) a combination of freedom and virtuosity that is at once alluring and cruel.

After this intriguing introduction, Vitellia's character is intensified at her next appearance. She has just learned that Tito has now chosen Servilia, not herself, as his Queen, and once more she urges Sesto to join the conspirators plotting to murder him. Potentially this exchange has the power of a similar conversation between the Macbeths; but again Süssmayr's recitative does little justice to its content. It does however set up Sesto's big aria, 'Parto, parto' (with Stadler's clarinet), tenderly pleading to Vitellia as he prepares to do her bidding. But when, in the next volte-face, Vitellia learns that Tito will make her his Queen after all, she is in turmoil, and tries desperately to call Sesto back from his murderous path. She leads an agitated trio ('Vengo . . . aspettate' – I am coming . . . wait), where her lines of panic are supported by perplexed comment from Annio and Publio. Vitellia's music is wayward and frenzied, with Elettra-like high tessitura, real harmonic surprise, and (was this a gamble?) a final flourish including a top D. Mozart did then write a superb accompanied recitative for Sesto, a disturbed soliloquy of more Macbeth-like doubt, dramatically interrupted by the spectacle of fire breaking out on the Capitol. (Clearly, stage conflagrations were Prague's speciality.) And at this point Mozart and Mazzolà restructured what in Metastasio were five separate scenes (for Sesto, Annio, Servilia, Publio and Vitellia), and turned them into a quintet, a riveting ending to Act I. Vitellia's contribution to this is total horror at what she has instigated, and fear for Sesto's safety too; but Mozart enfolds her into a mighty ensemble, supported by his hallmark offstage chorus, of political, physical and emotional fear. And, ever the architect of surprise, he ends this finale quietly, as horror subsides into grief.

In the second act Sesto confesses to Annio that he was part of the (failed) assassination plot, and Annio advises him to throw himself on the mercy of Tito. But Vitellia urges Sesto to flee, believing he will reveal that she too was involved. Publio arrests Sesto, and as he is taken away (in the trio 'Se al volto mai ti senti'), Sesto is sorrowfully lyrical, while Vitellia is torn between contrition and fear; and again Mozart can control all these emotions in a single musical unit. As the plot straightens itself out, Tito himself has the 'Countess' slot of heart-searching, conscience-battling soliloquy; and again the ensuing scenes of recitative between Sesto, Tito and Publio are all telescoped into a brilliant trio, where, contrary to the norm, the plot is carried in slow music, and dramatic asides are uttered in fast music. After Sesto's remorse aria, 'Deh, per questo', Tito's crucial recitative, in which he first signs and then tears up Sesto's death warrant, is again cause for major regret that Mozart did not write this music. But mercifully he did set Vitellia's big moment of transformation, when she decides to tell Tito the truth. Without knowing Maria Marchetti-Fantozzi, Mozart's accompanied recitative is perhaps a little brief and formulaic; but his formulae are never ordinary, and the music is still fresh and original. And it leads into one of the most celebrated numbers of the opera, Vitellia's 'Non più di fiori', with its other important obbligato part for Stadler, here playing the basset horn (a lower version of his clarinet). Even though Mozart had already composed this concert scena, its inclusion here is wholly appropriate, and brings to a superb conclusion the whole role of Vitellia, before she too is par-doned by the exemplary Tito and the opera reaches its pointedly and respect-fully Imperial conclusion.

When this coronation opera was premiered, on 6 September 1791, it was rather stiffly received by its lofty audience. But after the Imperial and Royal party had left Prague, the opera was shown repeatedly to the city's public, who were delighted with it. Mozart was no longer there to witness their adulation, as he had imme-diately to return to Vienna and Schikaneder's rehearsals. But he heard of *La clemenza di Tito*'s resounding success, largely from Stadler who of course remained in Prague to play his solos. And despite the circumstances of its whole creation and preparation, *La clemenza di Tito* did become one of Mozart's most popular operas over the next thirty years. In subsequent productions the important role of Sesto was generally seized by women, and most promin-ently (if surprisingly, for its range was so much lower than her own) by Aloysia. Almost certainly the opera really found its place when all the roles were evenly cast, as had been Mozart's experience in all his Viennese operas, and was about to be again.

～

BACK AT LAST in the Freihaus-Theater complex in Vienna, Mozart felt enormous relief and excitement as he rejoined his cast for *Die Zauberflöte*. His three great friends were to play the main male roles: Schikaneder himself the 'Dummer Anton'-based Papageno, Schack the flute-playing prince Tamino, and Gerl the priest Sarastro. Other members of their families would be involved too: Schack's wife Elisabeth was the third of the Three Ladies (hench-women to the Queen of the Night), Gerl's twenty-one-year-old wife Barbara was Papagena; Schikaneder's brother Urban was a priest, and Urban's daughter Anna one of the Three Boys (the other two being played by real boys). The experienced character-actor and singer Nonseul would take the part of Monostatos, one of the forces of evil. And the casting of the women was equally distinguished. Young Anna Gottlieb, still only seventeen, would play that embodiment of innocence and beauty, Pamina; and the evil Queen of the Night was to be Mozart's brilliant sister-in-law Josefa. After the somewhat arbitrary collection of imported singers that had been thrown together in Prague for *La clemenza di Tito*, this close-knit group was especially suitable to give unity to an opera of so many different aspects.

Much has been made of the Masonic symbolism in *Die Zauberflöte*, and especially of the mystic significance of the number 3 that has such importance in Freemasonry. Certainly there are three ladies, three boys, three temples; Tamino is advised to practise the three virtues of steadfastness, tolerance and discretion ('Sei standhaft, duldsam und verschwiegen!'); Sarastro reassures his priests that Tamino is virtuous, discreet and beneficent, the three qualifications for initiation into their order; there is the celebrated threefold chord from the beginning of the overture, which itself appears three times in the opera; and at the heart of it all there are three flats in the key signature of E flat major (or its relative C minor), in which so much of the opera resides, including its beginning and end. It could also be said that there are three plots. The first is a straightforward rescue plot, of Pamina by Tamino, and their passage together through life-changing challenges. The second is Papageno's quasi-comic plot, of his own series of baffling experiences, including even a suicide attempt, before he reaches his happy outcome of finding the woman of his dreams. And the third is an allegorical Masonic plot, in which Sarastro's benevolent order is assailed by potent forces of evil (the Queen of the Night, with her Three Ladies and Monostatos), and triumphantly overcomes them. With all these completely disparate elements flung into the creative pot, the result could so easily have been at best a kind of variety show, in which one turn succeeded another with little coordination between them, and at worst a disastrous mish-mash of chaotic confusion and a total absence of clear narrative. But with the combined creative artistry of Mozart and Schikaneder, *Die Zauberflöte* is an unquestionable masterpiece of clarity and passion, and it is utterly unique. With Da Ponte, Mozart had already broken any number of rules and moulds, and produced works of theatrical genius. Now, with Schikaneder, he was doing it all over again.

And, as always with Mozart, all these characters, whether of the cloister, or the world of magic, or popular theatrical tradition, are manifestly human, with recognizable emotions eloquently expressed. Sarastro may head a stern order bound by strict rite and regulation, but he is calm, warm and gentle in his dignified authority, even when he displays flashes of irritation with his adversary. Papageno is by no means merely a lovable fool, for he too shows vulnerability and integrity. And Tamino's upright decency is irradiated by the ardour of his commitment both to Pamina and to his search for truth. And, yet again, the women in *Die Zauberflöte* are drawn with profound human understanding. The Queen of the Night emerges from a mountain and sings in extra-terrestrial registers, but her grief at the abduction of her daughter, and then her obsessive fury and hatred of Sarastro, are understandable feelings. Her Three Ladies are not merely her officers, handy for supernatural plot-twisting and a certain amount of comedy too, but women who respond entirely naturally to the presence of a handsome young man, or to an irritating teller of lies. And Pamina is so much more than a beautiful story-book princess, for she is imbued with gentle sympathy, a forthright courage, and, in her own potential suicide scene, desolate vulnerability. That Mozart has yet again so staunchly taken the side of women is somehow all the more remarkable in this essential depiction of Freemasonry. For all that Sarastro's society is seen as benevolent, tolerant and just, there was decided anti-feminism in Masonic practice. Mozart and Schikaneder have not sidestepped this, for it is apparent in the exchanges between Sarastro and his priests. Rather they have met it head on;

and even so they have given the most profound utterances (if not to the Three Boys) to Pamina.

In the opening moments of the opera, Tamino is rescued from the clutches of a great serpent by the dramatic arrival of the Three Ladies. Mozart's writing for them, both as a group and in their separate lines, is predictably idiomatic. (It is extremely tempting to imagine that he might have been remembering his three Salzburg ladies – Lipp, Brauenhofer and Fesemayr – with their solid techniques and vibrant personalities, who had launched his operatic career a quarter of a century earlier.) Having with little ado dispatched the serpent and allowed themselves a moment of congratulation, they then become three romantic women admiring an attractive man. Their excitement is expressed in breathlessly fragmented words and sudden, unexpected forte chords, and although they end their scene in perfect harmony, departing together to inform their Queen of Tamino's arrival, they have established themselves as three individuals. There have been echoes not only of the competing divas, Mesdames Herz and Silberklang in *Der Schauspieldirektor* (when they propose that one of them should stay and take care of Tamino), but also of the playful sides of Fiordiligi and Dorabella contemplating the respective merits of their sweethearts.

It is during the ensuing (dialogue) conversation between Tamino and Papageno that the very mystique of the Queen of the Night is introduced. She is terrifyingly described by Papageno as a 'sternflammende Königin' (starbright queen), whom nobody has even seen. And after the Three Ladies have returned to punish Papageno for claiming to have killed Tamino's serpent, they set up the mystique of Pamina too, for they present him with her portrait which stirs new emotion in him ('mein Herz mit neuer Regung füllt'). By these simple theatrical devices, the audience is made to feel eager to encounter both these women long before they actually appear; and when they do there is no disappointment. The Queen has a marvellously dramatic entrance. As the Ladies shout 'Sie kommt! Sie kommt!' (She's coming!), the mountains part to reveal her. And Mozart reflects this in rumbling but animated syncopations in the strings (recalling the openings of his D minor piano concerto, K466, and of his 'Prague' symphony, K504 — both indications of creative buoyancy and exuberance), clambering arpeggios in the bass line, and a mighty crescendo. And here at last is Josefa Hofer, with all the technical traits of her sister Aloysia — magisterial accompanied recitative, a gloriously pathetic cantabile line in her andante section ('Zum Leiden bin ich auserkoren' — I am condemned to grief), and sensational coloratura, repeatedly hitting top Fs, in her allegro section ('Du wurst sie zu befreien gehen' — You must go and set her free). The famous difficulty of this aria has led to its virtually being adopted as the definition of demanding coloratura. But for a Weber girl, this was simply par for the course.

In the following quintet with Tamino and Papageno, the Three Ladies operate again as a team to effect the plot's business: they release Papageno from the padlock they clamped on his mouth (as a punishment for having told lies), hand a magic flute to Tamino and magic bells to Papageno, and tell the men that three young, gentle and wise boys will guide and advise them on their journey ahead. Here Mozart changes the whole pace and colour of the music, presenting (like the boys they describe) supremely simple, innocent progressions, perfectly controlled. And the Three Ladies vanish into the night, like their Queen before them.

Pamina's first appearance is almost as dramatic as that of the Queen. She is at the mercy of the wicked Monostatos, who is threatening to kill her. Although she pluckily maintains that she is not frightened of death, she faints in her fear of him. The arrival of Papageno brings pantomimic light relief, for his terror at the sight of Monostatos is mirrored by that of Monostatos himself, who darts away. After Papageno and Pamina have established each other's identity, they have one of the most tender scenes in the opera. They discuss the importance of love, and of the necessity for a man to find a woman, and vice versa: 'nichts Edler's sei als Weib und Mann' (nothing is nobler than a wife and husband). This is effectively a love duet, but it is sung by two strangers; and it is as brilliantly contrary as the first duet between Susanna and Figaro, in which a genuine bride and groom take no notice of each other. The duet for Pamina and Papageno, in the opera's home key of E flat, is one of the emotional centres of the whole piece. It is in two parts, the first of utterly enchanting simplicity, and the second of delicate ornamentation, and, throughout, it is rich in emotional integrity. However ardently Mozart was promoting the brotherhood of Freemasonry in *Die Zauberflöte*, presenting its virtues in the best possible light, he did not neglect this opportunity to provide a hymn to the beauty of human relationships. In just 49 exquisite bars of music, he has utterly dispelled all the cynicism of *Così fan tutte*.

Pamina and Papageno reappear together in the finale to Act I, excited at being on the point of finding Tamino. Papageno's magic bells save them from capture by Monostatos and his slaves, but, when Sarastro's imminent arrival is heralded, they both become extremely nervous at being discovered in a place where they ought not to be. Again it is Pamina who is strong. When Papageno asks her what they should tell Sarastro, she answers with pellucid simplicity, 'Die Wahrheit! Wär' sie auch Verbrechen!' (The truth – even if it is a crime). Schikaneder wrote more text for Pamina here, but Mozart chose not to use it; her single line, in his most pure of settings, said all that was required. And Pamina's subsequent confession and apology to Sarastro are in the same vein of honest integrity. Sarastro is gentle with her, and extremely understanding. But when they begin to talk of her mother, he does become stern, and his instructive philosophy is in stark contrast to that of the 'Mann und Weib' duet:

> *Ein Mann muß teure Herzen leiten*
> *denn ohne ihn pflegt jedes Weib*
> *aus ihrem Wirkungskreis zu schreiten.*

> A man must guide your heart,
> for without that, every woman
> oversteps her natural sphere.

And this bald dictum is set by Mozart as straightforward
accompanied recitative, literally as a matter of fact, lacking any
emotional warmth or ornament. But the chilly tension of this
moment is completely broken by the arrival of Tamino; and as he
and Pamina at last set eyes on each other, Mozart brings the
audience effortlessly back into the world of passion. 'Er ist's!' – 'Sie
ist's!' (It is he! It is she!) they ecstatically exclaim, for this is love at
first sight. The first act ends with Sarastro issuing orders that
Tamino and Papageno be blindfolded and taken into their temple of
trial, while he himself takes Pamina away separately.

At the beginning of the second act Sarastro and his priests agree
to admit Tamino to their brotherhood, and a trial of silence begins
for him and Papageno. Apart from Papageno's natural tendency to
chatter, the real test of their ability to remain silent comes in the
form of the Three Ladies. Operating now completely as a team,
singing therefore in close harmony, they taunt the men: 'Wie? Wie?
Wie? Ihr an diesem Schreckensort?' (Why are you in this dreadful
place?) they ask. Tamino refuses to engage in conversation with the
Ladies, though Papageno comments freely on everything they say,
becoming increasingly alarmed when they tell him that the Queen
of the Night is close at hand. When these busy warnings fail to
penetrate Tamino's silence, the Ladies try another tactic. 'Warum
bist du mit uns so spröde?' (Why are you so sharp with us?) they
sing, now in their most wheedling mood, with caressing strings and
calm winds. But that too is met with stern resistance, and, realizing
they have lost this particular battle, the Ladies decide to retreat.
When voices from within announce that the sacred threshold has
been defiled by the presence of women, they disappear in crashes of
thunder and lightning, and veritably comic shrieks of 'O weh!'.
Their power is decidedly on the wane.

Pamina, meanwhile, has really been having her own 'trials'. She
has first been all but molested by Monostatos, and then come face to
face with the enraged Queen of the Night. She urges her mother
to help her escape, but the Queen produces a knife and tells her
that she must kill Sarastro; suddenly, out of nowhere, there is an

agitated rumble in the strings, and the Queen bursts into her enormous aria: 'Die Hölle Rache kocht in meinem Herzen' (Hell's vengeance burns in my breast). There is none of her earlier lyricism here; she is wild and terrifying with fury, and Mozart emphasizes this by adding trumpets and timpani into all the stabbing forte chords: he meant to frighten everyone, including himself. And here again Josefa's brilliant technique was used to electrifying effect, for the music is of the utmost difficulty. There are repeated high notes, arpeggios again regularly hitting top Fs, and swirling triplet passages. When well sung, as it surely was when performed by Josefa (for otherwise Mozart would not have written such music), this aria invariably brings the house down.

As if all this were not enough of a trial for Pamina, Monostatos then reappears, and this time it is Sarastro who saves her from his odious intentions. Although she loyally tries to defend her mother to Sarastro, he is calmly firm with her, telling her in his sublime aria 'In diesen heil'gen Hallen' that revenge has no place in his sacred halls, but that love will lead a man back to his duty: he is in effect giving her licence to be associated with her prince. But when, later, she comes joyfully to Tamino, and he, still under his vow of silence, refuses to speak to her, she is stunned and uncomprehending. Her aria, 'Ach, ich fühl's', is a simple expression of utter desolation (I feel that the joy of love has gone for ever). The emotional power beneath this simplicity is vast, with an undertow of reflected pain in discordant woodwinds (the flute, oboe and bassoon of Susanna's 'Deh, vieni'), and seemingly spontaneous coloratura drawn from the anguish of the moment. Five years earlier, when Anna Gottlieb was only twelve, Mozart had given her Barbarina a similar aria of ingenuous wretchedness and staggering beauty. Now seventeen, the prodigiously talented singer had been rewarded with another jewel, and this time her more mature technique enabled him to intensify the emotional gesture and content; the result is 41 bars of musical perfection.

After the priests' chorus ('O Isis und Osiris') there is a scene (added later) which actually fractures the plot, making nonsense of

Pamina's next appearance. But in it Sarastro tells Pamina to bid Tamino a final farewell, and although he also promises them a happy reunion, the young couple take their tense leave of each other. Mozart is clear in his musical interpretation of it, for at first Pamina is heard on her own while the two men sing together, but eventually she and Tamino cling together in their music, even sharing a cadenza at the end of the trio, while Sarastro tries to tear them apart.

The Act II finale begins with the Three Boys, who herald the sunrise with some monumental Enlightenment statements. But Pamina is in distress, contemplating suicide; and from the sublime and positive trio for the Boys, the music suddenly becomes broken, almost like accompanied recitative. The Boys reassure her that Tamino does still love her (they still cannot tell her why he refuses to speak to her – 'Dieses müssen wir verschweigen'); and, convinced and moved by them, she joins them to sing their (and Mozart's) wonderful little moral:

> *Zwei Herzen, die von Liebe brennen*
> *Kann Menschen ohnmacht niemals trennen;*
> *Vedoren ist der Feinde Müh',*
> *Die Götter selbsten schützen sie.*

> Two hearts united by love
> can never be parted by weakness.
> Their enemies strive in vain
> for the gods protect them.

And so the scene changes into the most spectacular, both scenically and musically, of the opera, with two armed men standing guard over a rural place with a waterfall at one side and a burning fire at the other. Anticipating Tamino's final trials, these two men declare that, if he overcomes his fear of death by travelling through fire and water, he will be purified, and his soul will soar heavenward. Mozart set these most grave, veritably mystic words to a Lutheran chorale tune, 'Ach Gott, vom Himmel sieh darein' (as used in Bach's

cantata BWV 2), lending a truly solemn, cathedral tone to the proceedings. Like all chorale preludes, the music is both awesome and
somehow intimate, and a world away from that of serpents, lustful
ladies and birdcatchers, where the opera started. As the brave
Tamino is about to embark on these trials, Pamina's voice is heard:
'Tamino, halt! Ich muß dich seh'n!' (I must see you!) She is brought
in, and her exquisite line, 'Tamino mein! O welch ein glück!' is set
by Mozart with utter radiance, and can only come from one who
truly knows the pain of separation and the joy of reunion. And it is
Pamina who leads Tamino through the fire and water while he plays
his magic flute. Their shared triumph is roundly celebrated by the
offstage chorus.

After the Boys have rescued Papageno too from possible suicide,
and he has been reunited with his beautiful Papagena, they contemplate the joys of a long marriage and many children. And now it
remains only for the Queen of the Night and her cohorts to be
dispatched by the power of sunlight, and for her evil therefore to
be conquered by Sarastro's forces for good. The Queen's promises
to Monostatos are now meaningless, her powers are empty: she, her
Three Ladies and Monostatos are consumed in another monumental effect of thunder, lightning and blazing light (and
trumpets). And the final moral, sung by the chorus, draws on the
three central words of Masonic ritual – strength, beauty and
wisdom – as the opera reaches its magnificent conclusion.

But if this spectacular ending seems to put the seal on the
allegorical aspect of *Die Zauberflöte*, it is still the intimate presentation of human interaction which lingers long in the mind. And it is
Pamina herself, as first portrayed by the seventeen-year-old Anna
Gottlieb, who seems most to have moved Mozart, and has therefore
become the central focus of the whole multisided story. Here again,
perhaps, is Mozart's ideal woman. While she lacks the fiery side to
the character of Susanna (certainly it is hard to imagine her hitting
anyone), Pamina does inherit her sweetness, courage and strength.
She is steadfastly loyal, to Tamino and even to her mother, respectful to Sarastro, compassionate and sympathetic to Papageno, and

utterly honest in her every action. It is she whose authority reassures Papageno of the inevitability of perfect human love, and of the sanctity therefore of the union between 'Mann und Weib'; and it is she who leads her own 'Mann' through the trials which bring him his wisdom, his maturity and therefore his security. This seems to have struck a real chord in Mozart. He was, to be sure, entirely at home in Sarastro's (Masonic) world, which he respected, honoured and defended. But for him the presence too of a woman as companion and guide was absolutely essential.

After Mozart

~

MOZART'S OWN companion and guide, Constanze, was only twenty-nine years old when she was left a widow with a seven-year-old boy and a four-month-old baby. Wolfgang had died intestate. With no guaranteed income or any pension (this was Wolfgang's ultimate penalty for having left Salzburg employment), she was again facing real financial hardship.

Baron van Swieten, who had so capably dealt with the immediate funerary procedures, then addressed Constanze's longer-term financial position. Nothing could be done with Wolfgang's estate until his creditors had been paid off, and provision made for the welfare of his children. So an inventory was made of all his possessions, and everything on it was valued. Exempt from this inventory were manuscripts, for royal statutes had no taxable requirement of them – and in due course this loophole would provide Constanze with the means to secure a future for her children and herself. But it is unlikely that in those early and bewildered stages of bereavement she paid much attention yet to the potential gold-dust lying around the apartment. She and van Swieten would have been more preoccupied with paying bills and medical expenses, and, if any, creditors. But in fact, with Wolfgang's recent change in fortune, and no doubt with Constanze's organizational encouragement, he had paid off the loan she had arranged with

Lackenbacher. And his other two chief creditors, Lichnowsky and of course Puchberg, both showed great magnanimity and never claimed a penny. So, for the moment, Constanze was just about solvent.

On 10 December there was a memorial service for Wolfgang in St Michael's Church, organized, and indeed paid for, by his distraught friend Emanuel Schikaneder. The following day Constanze presented a petition to the Emperor.[1] In a dignified and carefully worded document (almost certainly drafted by van Swieten), she acknowledged that she had no right to a pension, since her late husband had not been in Imperial service for the statutory ten years. But she was trusting in the favour and generosity of the Court to hear her appeal, especially in view of Wolfgang's loyalty to it, and the cruelty of fate which 'took him from the world at that very moment when his prospects for the future were beginning to grow brighter on all sides'. She mentioned in passing that she was unable to apply for help from the Tönkunstler-Societät, which after all existed to support widows and orphans of its musician-members, because Wolfgang had never in fact 'thought to ensure provision for his dependants by enrolling'. (This was not strictly true: Wolfgang had applied for membership, but had been rejected on the technicality that he could not produce his baptism certificate. And indeed that same, wretchedly elusive document had almost prevented their wedding from taking place, and its requirement had had to be waived.) Constanze did in fact apply to the Tönkunstler-Societät for help; but, sticking doggedly to their rule-book, they replied tersely that Wolfgang's 'bereaved widow is neither at present drawing a pension from the funds of the afore-mentioned Society, nor has she any expectation of one in the future'.[2] The Court, however, in its own time, did look sympathetically on Constanze's application. Having made her supply various documents supporting her request, they eventually agreed to award her one third of Wolfgang's 800-florin salary, backdated to 1 January 1792. So Constanze would at least receive just over 265 florins per annum – though there was an emphatic clause to the effect that this was 'granted as a special favour and does not establish a precedent'.[3]

There would have been donations too from appalled and sympathetic well-wishers, as a number of newspaper articles had appeared in Vienna and beyond, outlining Constanze's situation, and some of these elicited gifts. But if Constanze had read her newspapers carefully, some stories would have upset her. She would have been outraged to learn of a rumour that Leopold Kozeluch was to be appointed to succeed Wolfgang as Kammermusikus, with a salary restored to 2,000 florins;[4] indeed, if it was true, it does seem incomprehensible that the emoluments of these two incumbents fluctuated wildly, and bore no reflection at all of their respective talents. And for her, of course, one third of 2,000 (as opposed to 800) florins would have been very welcome. Then another story, at once sensational and gruesome, would also have distressed Constanze. It concerned the Mozarts' friends Franz and Magdalena Hofdemel: Franz was one of the fellow Freemasons who had lent Wolfgang money for his journey to Berlin in 1789; his wife Magdalena had been one of Wolfgang's pupils. On 6 December, the day of Wolfgang's funeral, Franz Hofdemel had violently attacked his pregnant wife with a razor, slashing her face and hands; he had then cut his own throat. She survived this bloodied frenzy, but he did not. Rumours immediately spread, first, that Hofdemel had brutally disfigured his wife out of jealousy, believing her to have had an affair with her teacher, Mozart; and second, therefore, that Hofdemel had actually poisoned Mozart as part of the same grim scenario. Good newspaper copy though this was, it is unlikely that any of it was true, although what it was that drove poor Hofdemel to such crazed action has never been established. There were further petitions at Court, now on behalf of Magdalena Hofdemel; and, most interestingly, it was the women there, headed by the Empress Marie Louise herself, who became passionately concerned, and sent financial assistance to both Magdalena and Constanze. But these dramatic events and consequent rumours can have done little to ease Constanze's path towards emotional equanimity.

She was not however having to deal with this on her own: there was an enormous amount of support for her. In the same way that Herr Thorwart had become legal guardian to Constanze herself and her sisters when their own father had died in 1779, the Magistracy now appointed Dr Nicklas Ramor, an advocate, for her sons; and in her dealings with the Magistracy, Constanze nominated their still-devoted friend Michael Puchberg as her own representative. Several of Wolfgang's other old patrons and supporters rallied around her, including, as well as Baron van Swieten, the Countess Thun, and members of his Lodge ('New Crowned Hope'), who in June of 1792 opened a collection fund for Constanze and her children. Schikaneder's company had taken part in the memorial service, and various individuals among them made their own contributions. (In a gesture touchingly anticipating that of Colline in *La Bohème*, Benedikt Schack pawned his watch and gave the proceeds to Constanze.) Like all close-knit theatrical communities, they would have been deeply affected by the loss of someone who had effectively been one of them, and had certainly been largely responsible for their current buoyancy. With the immediate connection of Josefa and Franz Hofer, the welfare of Constanze and her sons would have been uppermost in their concerns. And above all, the carer of the Weber family, Sophie, who had been charged by Wolfgang on his deathbed to look after Constanze, would have applied herself to this responsibility with fervent dedication. The very passion of her memoir to Nissen, written so long after the events, testifies to the depth of her emotional involvement, and probably therefore to the success with which she carried out her obligation.

Beyond Vienna, too, other appalled friends rushed to try to help. In Prague, where they had come to look upon Wolfgang as one of the jewels in their own crown, they first held a church service in his memory. According to reports in the Viennese press, the ceremony had been arranged by the orchestra of Prague's National Theatre, and 120 of the city's musicians took part. One of the soloists was the Mozarts' great friend, Josefa Duschek (for whom Wolfgang had written the scena 'Ah, lo previdi' in 1777, and 'Bella mia fiamma' in 1787, and who had become and would remain close to Constanze). And, as the newspaper report carried it, 'solemn silence lay all about, and 1,000 tears flowed in poignant memory of the artist who through [his] harmonies so often turned all hearts to the liveliest of feelings.'[5] By the end of the year, those same musicians were planning a benefit concert for Constanze and the children.

Even further afield, in London, the tragic news reached Haydn. (He had indeed accepted the invitation of Johann Peter Salomon, and was now enjoying great success there.) He was, as he wrote to Puchberg, 'beside myself for some considerable time because of [Mozart's] death, and could not believe that Providence should so soon summon an irreplaceable man to the other world'. Longing to be able to do something, he asked for a list of all Wolfgang's works to be sent to him in London, so that he could make them known there 'for the benefit of the widow'. He also wrote to Constanze herself, promising personally to take charge of her son Carl's musical education, 'so as to some extent to take the place of his father'.[6] And he kept to his word: in due course Carl would go, at Haydn's suggestion, to study composition in Milan with Bonifazio Asioli. But before that, with the collaborative concern of many of Constanze's other sources of help, the boy was to go to school in Prague.

As Wolfgang's last letter to Constanze had indicated, the Mozarts were uneasy about the level of schooling that Carl had been receiving in Perchtoldsdorf. He was extremely healthy, 'because the children do nothing but eat, drink, sleep and go for walks'; and from that point of view 'he could not be in a better place, but everything else there is wretched, alas! All they can do is turn out a good peasant into the world.'[7] So they were thinking of moving him to a Christian Brothers' seminary. The death of Wolfgang was the obvious moment to take decisive steps about Carl's schooling, so Baron van Swieten paid for him to go to Prague where, under the watchful eye of Josefa Duschek and her husband Franz, he stayed with Franz Xavier Niemetschek, and was also schooled by him. This must have been a more satisfactory arrangement, for in later years Constanze would also send her younger son to the Niemetscheks. And since Niemetschek was in any case engaged in trying to write a biography of Mozart, it was presumably beneficial to both parties to have such close contact with the widow.

~

MEANWHILE CONSTANZE, WITH the help of van Swieten and others, had to attend to some issues relating to Wolfgang's music. The most pressing of these was the problem of what to do with the Requiem. It lay unfinished; but if it could somehow be completed, Constanze would receive the rest of the commission money. She did not, in the first instance, ask Süssmayr to continue the work he had begun with Wolfgang and complete it in the way in which Wolfgang had been trying to demonstrate as he died. (Years later, Constanze seemed to think she had been 'annoyed' with Süssmayr, although she could not remember why.) Instead she contacted another young composer, the twenty-six-year-old Joseph Eybler, who had very possibly assisted Wolfgang in rehearsals for *Così fan tutte* in 1790, and had a good reputation in Vienna as a composer and a singer – better, no doubt, than Süssmayr's. Within weeks of Wolfgang's death, Eybler signed a statement in which he undertook to complete the work by the middle of Lent. But he was soon daunted by his labour. Early in 1792 he returned the unfinished score to Constanze, who, having now apparently got over her irritation, handed it back to Süssmayr, just as Wolfgang had intended. Süssmayr strained earnestly to adhere to Wolfgang's desperate guidelines, and at last produced a score which, however unequal it may have been in its patchwork, was at least complete. Keeping a copy for herself, Constanze sent the Requiem Mass to its patient commissioner, Count Walsegg, and received her money.

But this was not the end of the story, either for Constanze or for the Requiem itself. Hardly surprisingly for a venture founded on deceit, the ensuing web did indeed become truly tangled. Misled perhaps by Constanze and her negotiators, Walsegg believed that Wolfgang had composed everything in the Requiem except the last movement (the *Agnus Dei*), and that once that had been completed, the score that he paid for and received was now his, and he could do whatever he wanted with it. So in his usual fashion he copied it out, 'note by note in his own hand', according to Anton Herzog, and then passed it on to his musicians to make individual orchestral parts. But those musicians were of course familiar with the Count's customary plagiarism, and in any case knew from Anton Leitgeb (the 'grey messenger') of the dealings with Mozart. As each movement came their way, they 'followed the progress of this exceptional work with mounting interest'[8] – and indeed their gradual assembly of the Mozart Requiem is greatly to be envied. The date originally planned for the first performance of Walsegg's supposed Requiem was 14 February 1792, the anniversary of his young wife's death. But because of all the delays (Constanze's bereaved confusion, Eybler's failure to deliver, and eventually Süssmayr's clumsy completion), that date was long past. Walsegg was probably surprised too by the very scale of Mozart's conception of his Requiem, for he realized he could in no way muster the required forces in his castle in Stuppach, and began to plan instead for a performance in nearby Wiener-Neustadt. This did not happen until 12 December 1793, when Walsegg himself was the conductor. (Herzog had prepared the choir.) He then repeated the performance closer to home, in the church of Maria-Schulz in Semmering, on 14 February 1794, the third anniversary of his wife's death. But although he had originally intended this to be an annual event, he never performed 'his' Requiem again. Almost certainly, he must by then have realized that he had been rumbled.

And indeed, given the single degree of separation between Count Walsegg and Constanze (their mutual friend Michael Puchberg), it is astonishing that he even imagined he could get away with his vastly scaled plagiarism. Constanze and her supportive circle, headed by Baron van Swieten, must have got wind of the Count's deceptive preparations. True, Walsegg had paid for the score, and, if he had proposed to perform it under the name of Mozart, that would have been perfectly reasonable. But the very injustice of Walsegg's attempting to pass Wolfgang's composition off as his own may well have prompted some retaliatory action. Using material that they had retained between them, Constanze, Süssmayr and Eybler organized their own performance, almost a year before Walsegg's, on 2 January 1792. It was given at the establishment of Ignaz Jahn in Vienna, and attended by many Viennese dignitaries, including Salieri. According to press reports, a sum of more than 300 ducats was raised for Constanze and her children. Count Walsegg must have read of this event, and could do nothing about it, although the preparations for his own performance were now beyond the point of no return. He did try pathetically to save face with his own musicians. According to Herzog,

> The Count tried to say to us that he was a pupil of Mozart's and he had often sent [his Requiem] to him piece by piece to be looked through. Shortly before Mozart's death he had sent him the completed Benedictus for this purpose. After Mozart's death the score, from the beginning up to the Agnus Dei, had been found, and people believed it was a composition of Mozart's, so deceptively similar were their handwritings.[9]

But perhaps even he finally saw the futility of such an outrageous falsehood. All he could do now was delay his own plans for a few months, so that no direct comparison could be made between the two supposedly different Requiem Masses.

It is significant that there had never apparently been any contractual document either between Walsegg and Wolfgang, or between Walsegg and Constanze. And Constanze was clever. She never named the 'unknown commissioner' of the Requiem, in any statement to any biographer, nor even in any correspondence. When Breitkopf and Härtel came into the story, and eventually published Mozart's Requiem, she still withheld Walsegg's name.

According to Herzog, the Count was furious to see the score in print, and 'at first intended to take serious measures with the widow Mozart'. But in the end he merely asked for 50 ducats (the equivalent, presumably, of what he had paid in the first place), and some copies of the printed version, and disappeared. The whole truth of this gothic tale was eventually revealed only in the mid-twentieth century, when a full account by Anton Herzog — written in 1839 after the death of almost all the original protagonists except Constanze and himself, but suppressed at the time by the Imperial Library in Vienna — finally came to light. By then, of course, the rumours, the claims and counter-claims, the accusations and counter-accusations, and certainly the myths, had become ever more knotted and surreal, and much acrimony had settled on Constanze. But Herzog's disclosures proved once and for all that every deception stemmed from Count Walsegg's curious condition of musical kleptomania, and that Constanze's actions were motivated not only by the need for money, but also by a desire to identify and protect the property — that precious final creation — of her late husband.

AFTER WOLFGANG'S DEATH, brief obituary notices had appeared in several newspapers across Europe, generally stating the basic facts (Wolfgang's age, date and place of his death, his position as I & R Kammermusikus, and his heirs), and occasionally embellished by some editorial statement along the lines of 'exceptional natural gifts'. But soon there were plans afoot for much longer obituaries, and even biographies. Constanze herself cooperated fully with Niemetschek in Prague, supplying documentation as well as many verbal anecdotes and opinions. And meanwhile, a young German scholar based in Gotha, Friedrich von Schlichtegroll, was exploring other routes in order to amass material for his own publication. Between 1790 and 1806, Schlichtegroll published 34 volumes of obituaries, at six-monthly intervals. Mozart was an obvious candidate of his *Nekrolog auf der Jahr 1791*. These two publications were therefore being prepared in parallel. And while Niemetschek's biography was a rather leisurely exercise, based on the input from Constanze and recent family friends, and would not appear until 1798, Schlichtegroll's article used material from Salzburg sources, and was published in 1793. If the relations between the Salzburg and Vienna sides of Wolfgang's life (or, more specifically, between Nannerl and Constanze) had never been exactly relaxed, they were now to become seriously strained.

For it is here that Nannerl comes back into the picture. She and Wolfgang had effectively lost contact after the death of Leopold. She had had no letter from him since 1788, and had not actually seen him since 1783. She probably remembered the happy period of *Idomeneo* in Munich, for the Carnival of 1781, as the last proper family time she had spent with her father and brother together. It was after that visit that they had literally gone their separate ways – she and Leopold back to Salzburg, and Wolfgang to Vienna where his life had changed immeasurably. Since then she had been in Wolfgang's company for just three months, and even then she had had to share him, for the occasion was the visit of Wolfgang and Constanze to Salzburg in 1783. The last letter she had received from her brother had apparently been extremely cheerful, as he had sent her his latest keyboard works, told her about his appointment at Court, and alluded modestly to the success of *Don Giovanni*. The siblings had not even communicated to each other the births (and deaths) of their children. In those years of silence between them, Wolfgang's daughter Anna Maria had been born and died within the hour, in November 1789, but his healthy son Franz Xavier had been born in July 1791. Nannerl meanwhile had had two daughters: Johanna (always known as Jeanette), born on 22 March 1789, and Maria Babette, who was born on 17 November 1790 but had died six months later.

It is not even known how Nannerl was informed of Wolfgang's death, let alone the extent of her desolate resignation as she accepted the loss of the last member of her immediate family. But when she was approached on behalf of Schlichtegroll, and asked to contribute to an obituary of her brother, she responded with whole-hearted generosity and diligence. It was not Schlichtegroll himself who contacted her. He had initially written to Albert von Mölk, a canon and consistorial councillor at the Cathedral in Salzburg, and asked him a series of questions about Wolfgang's early life. Mölk had known the Mozart family since childhood, and so forwarded his questionnaire to Nannerl in St Gilgen. When she had completed her responses, in a long draft of a letter to which she would subsequently refer as her 'article',[10] she sent it back to Mölk, assuming he would make a copy of it for Schlichtegroll and return the original to her. But Mölk took it as it was, added a few sentences of his own, and forwarded it directly to Schlichtegroll.

Overjoyed (or, as he put it rather more blandly, 'pleasantly surprised') by the wealth of material from such an important source so close to Mozart, Schlichtegroll immediately wrote back, again through Mölk, with a list of supplementary questions for Nannerl. And, when she received these, Nannerl realized to her horror that her 'article' had already been absorbed into the system. ('I should fairly scold you,' she wrote to Mölk, 'that, without writing to me beforehand, you [sent Schlichtegroll] my written article.') She was now being asked for more specific and personal details of her brother's childhood: Wolfgang's favourite playtime activities, the subjects he most liked to learn, and, most startlingly, his 'faults'. She instinctively shied away from these, claiming loyally that she could 'only charge him with a single one . . . that he had too soft a heart, and did not know how to handle money'. She then enlisted the assistance of Andreas Schachtner, he whose trumpet had so traumatized Wolfgang as a child (and who indeed made this revelation in his own responses to Schlichtegroll's questions), and withdrew from the arena. In her communications to Mölk, and therefore to Schlichtegroll and posterity, her comments were thoughtful, generous, honest, fair and extremely touching. And perhaps the compilation of these affectionate memories was for Nannerl at last some kind of cathartic process, whereby she released any family tension from the last few years. The prevailing tone of them is one of loving pride, just as it had been of her childhood years.

It was the few sentences that Mölk himself added to Nannerl's first 'article' that caused the problems. First, he clarified the identity of his star witness, Nannerl, and praised her own musical abilities, especially as a teacher ('even to the present, one can single out the students of Nannette Mozart from all the others by the care, precision and correct fingering in their playing'). Next, he described all the Mozart family as good-looking: Leopold and Maria Anna were 'the handsomest couple in Salzburg', and Nannerl herself 'a regular beauty', though young Wolfgang had been 'small, frail, pale in complexion, and completely lacking in all pretensions of face and form'. And then came the damage.

> Apart from his music he was and remained almost always a child; and this is a major trait on the dark side of his character; he would always have need of a father, a mother, or some other supervisor; he was unable to handle money, married a girl not suited for him against the will of his father, and that's why there was such domestic disorder when he died and afterwards.

Mercifully, Schlichtegroll, in his largely free interpretation of Mölk's opinions, did not include the lines about Constanze and her unsuitability as a wife. (She was after all still very much alive, and Schlichtegroll did respect her sensibilities.) But he did paraphrase the rest of Mölk's statement, with the result that the following paragraph appeared in his *Nekrolog* article:

> Just as this rare individual early became a man in his art, so on the other hand he remained in virtually all other respects — this must in all impartiality be said of him — eternally a child. He never learned to discipline himself, and he had no feeling for domestic order, for the proper use of money, for moderation and the judicious choice of pleasures. He was constantly in need of a father figure, a guardian, who would look after the mundane matters attendant to his well-being, for his own spirit was constantly preoccupied with a host of completely different ideas and thus lost all

sensibility for other serious considerations. His father was very much aware of this weakness, this lack of self-discipline, in him and, for this reason, provided the son with his mother as travelling companion to Paris when his own duties chained him to Salzburg.[11]

Mölk, and therefore Schlichtegroll, were almost certainly reflecting general Salzburg prejudice (the Gospel according to Leopold?). So, in 1792, there was still residual animosity toward the troublesome black sheep of Colloredo's court, who had abandoned his father and sister and chosen to live his life altogether elsewhere. When Schlichtegroll's obituary was published in 1793, Constanze would have read these hurtful and derogatory words, appearing as they did in tandem with material that can only have come from Nannerl, and she would have drawn her own defensive conclusions. In the following year, 1794, Schlichtegroll's *Nekrolog* was reprinted in Graz, and Constanze exercised a monumental gesture of disdain, of which Wolfgang himself would surely have been proud. She bought up all 600 copies of the work, and destroyed them.

~

ON 22 AUGUST 1793, Cäcilia Weber died at the age of sixty-six. Like Maria Anna Mozart, her life been fraught with difficulty, but greatly enriched by the talents of her children. She had endured the early loss of her two sons, and then a long widowhood, during which she had presumably been supported by the activities of her lively and gifted daughters. But she had certainly earned her keep: throughout the 1780s, when Aloysia and Constanze were continually producing children, she was always on hand as a practical, nursing grandmother (a pleasure, sadly, that Maria Anna Mozart never enjoyed); and she was involved in every illness or crisis (Constanze's bereavement especially) of all her family. She must however have gained enormous pleasure from their successes, above all those of the dazzling Aloysia, whose profile in Vienna and beyond in the 1780s and 1790s was as high as any; and she was close to all three of her gifted sons-in-law.

For Cäcilia Weber's daughters, her passing was truly the end of an era, and most especially for Sophie, who had taken care of their mother after all her sisters had married and left home. And in the following years there were more life-changing events for the Weber sisters. Aloysia separated from Joseph Lange in 1795; Josefa's husband, Franz Hofer, died in June 1796. For a period, all four sisters were effectively single again. Josefa remained a member of Schikaneder's company until well into the new century, and in addition to her numerous performances as the Queen of the Night, she trespassed into Aloysia's territory, singing the roles of Donna Anna (or Donna Laura, as she appeared in *Don Juan*, the German-language version of *Don Giovanni*), Fiordiligi (or Leonora, in *So machen sie's alle*), Constanze in *Die Entführung*, and Madame Herz in *Der Schauspieldirektor*. She was often partnered by a young singer-actor, Friedrich Sebastian Mayer. He sang Sarastro to her Queen of the Night, and was also the Pasha Selim to her Constanze in *Die Entführung*; and at the end of 1797 she married him. (He was fourteen years younger than she.) Their careers continued in parallel for the rest of their singing lives, though inevitably his lasted longer – and was somewhat enriched in 1805 when he created the role of Pizarro in Beethoven's *Fidelio*.

Constanze meanwhile continued her relationship with the city of Prague, with its supportive musicians, and of course with the Duscheks and Niemetschek, who between them were taking care of Carl and his education. In February 1794 she and Carl both attended a memorial concert for Wolfgang in Prague. Josefa Duschek sang at the concert, and also spoke warmly and passionately about all the Mozarts. The Prague *Neue Zeitung*, as ever sympathetic to Constanze and her situation, reported that 'Mozart's widow and son both wept tears of grief at their loss, and of gratitude towards a noble nation.'[12] There had been some putative scheme for the ten-year-old Carl to appear in the Salieri–Da Ponte opera *Axur*, as a young boy offered up for sacrifice. But Constanze vetoed this, anxious to keep her son out of a limelight intensified by his famous name. This change of plan, too, was reported with understanding by the Prague *Neue Zeitung*, which reiterated its support for Constanze ('who is full of respect and gratitude towards the Prague public'), claiming to have leapt to her defence lest she be accused of 'a capriciousness of which she is entirely innocent.'[13]

But however anxious Constanze was at this stage to keep her children out of the performing arena, she herself began to contemplate her own return to it. And it is likely that her sisters encouraged her. As Aloysia became increasingly estranged from Joseph Lange in the mid-1790s, she devoted more time to Constanze and her cause. In December 1794 Constanze organized a special concert performance of *La clemenza di Tito* in Vienna, and Aloysia sang the role of Sesto. All the musicians and singers performed without fee, and the takings went to Constanze and her children. The success of this event encouraged Constanze to mount a repeat performance in the following March, with a somewhat expanded programme, for Wolfgang's dramatic D minor piano concerto (K466) was played, with one Ludwig van Beethoven as the soloist. Fortified by the warmth and the rewards of all these ventures, in both Prague and Vienna, Constanze planned a concert tour of Germany in the autumn of 1795, for herself and Aloysia, and a pianist, Anton Eberl. The package was extremely attractive to audiences. Nostalgic enthusiasm for Mozart's music was growing fast in Berlin, Leipzig, Hamburg, Linz and Graz. (Salzburg was never on the itinerary.) That it was to be performed by his widow and her sister, who happened to be one of the greatest singers of her day, was irresistible. The concerts were well received, and brought in good sums of money.

In her time on the road, Constanze's organizational and entrepreneurial skills developed considerably. She parted company for a while from Aloysia, and peeled off to visit King Friedrich Wilhelm II of Prussia. He was anxious to help Mozart's widow as much as possible: he had already bought a number of scores, and was now to take possession of a special copy of the Requiem. Constanze delivered it herself, and also managed to get permission from His Majesty to mount a performance of *La clemenza di Tito* in Berlin. It is tempting to imagine that, had he lived, even that entrepreneur par excellence, Leopold Mozart, might have applauded her industry.

On their return from the concert tour, both sisters experienced some domestic upheaval. Constanze finally moved out of the apartment in Rauhensteingasse, where Wolfgang had died, and settled briefly in Krugerstrasse. In fact in the next four years, quite apart from her new travelling activities, she moved house twice more, in a state of domestic restlessness reminiscent of the early days of her marriage. Aloysia had an even greater uprooting. Perhaps anxious not to be in the same environment as her now estranged husband, she accepted a contract at the Schröder'schen Theater in Hamburg, where she had performed with Constanze on their tour. Two years later, in 1798, she moved on to Amsterdam, and joined the German Opera company there; and in the early years of the nineteenth century she had contracts also in Paris, Frankfurt and Zurich, where she was to settle for six years. So for a time she and Constanze went their separate ways. But Aloysia had unquestionably played her part at a crucial time for Constanze. In donating her time and her gifts to her sister, she had helped first to stabilize and then to boost Constanze's finances, and therefore her morale. By the time Aloysia went to Hamburg, Constanze had the confidence to continue on her own. She returned periodically to Prague, and during her visit in 1797 she was actually in such a strong financial position that she could lend Josefa Duschek 3,500 florins, an enormous sum of money, for the mortgage on the Duscheks' country villa. She was also becoming increasingly aware of the precocious talents of her younger son Franz Xavier, now six years old and being schooled in Prague along with his older brother. Contrary to her former determination to keep her children away from the public gaze, she let him take part in one of her concerts, singing Papageno's ingenuous 'Der Vogelfänger bin ich, ja' from *Die Zauberflöte*, to piano accompaniment.

But it was not just the concert tours that were beginning to bring in money for Constanze and her sons. In the mid-1790s she had also begun to realize the assets of the truly priceless legacy that her poor, intestate husband had left her, his music. In 1795, for instance, the piano score of *Idomeneo* was published, and several newspapers carried announcements inviting customers to subscribe to it, either through Constanze herself in Vienna, or, in another indication of supportive solidarity, through Josefa Duschek in Prague. With an enticing little marketing flourish, the advertisements made a special offer of eleven scores for the price of ten: Constanze was clearly beginning to feel confident in her commercial manoeuvres.[14] While in Leipzig with Aloysia, she had entered into dealings with the large publishing firm of Breitkopf and Härtel, possibly to publish the complete Mozart oeuvre. In the next few years, negotiations with them would become lengthy and tortuous, and she was going to need a cool head. But here again, Constanze had found extremely good support. Two men in particular helped to guide her hand, one an old friend, the other a new one.

The Abbé Maximilian Stadler (no relation of the Mozarts' clarinettist friend Anton) was a Benedictine priest and keen music-lover, who had known Wolfgang and Constanze from the early days of their courtship in Vienna, and had been at the periphery of their chamber music circle in the mid-1780s. In 1784 he had moved out of the capital, holding posts successively in the brand-new, spectacular monastery at Melk, and then in Lilienfeld, Krems-munster and Linz. In 1796, at the age of forty-eight, he returned to live in Vienna, and renewed his friendship with Constanze. She asked him to help her organize Wolfgang's autograph fragments and sketches, and as the Abbé immersed himself in these precious manuscripts, he attempted to put everything in order and prepare a catalogue. In due course Stadler was joined by a Danish diplomat, who lodged in the building in Judengasse where Constanze now lived. This was Georg Nikolaus Nissen.

Nissen was a year older than Constanze: she was by now thirty-five, he thirty-six. Born in Haderslev in South Jutland in 1761, he had worked as postmaster in Copenhagen before joining the Danish envoy to Regensburg. From there he was posted to Vienna as First Secretary at the Danish delegation, where his diplomatic skills as a calm, stable negotiator were invaluable in turbulent Napoleonic times. (Unlike Austria, Denmark sided with France.) If it was pure chance that brought Nissen to reside in the same building as Constanze, it cannot have been a continuing accident that they shared both of their next two addresses too. Like Wolfgang, Georg Nissen began as Constanze's lodger, became a good and close friend, and ended up as her husband. But, unlike Wolfgang, Nissen's progress to the altar was altogether very cautious.

It really was now a matter of some urgency for Constanze to get a complete edition of Wolfgang's music published. Interest in him was again on the rise, as the long-awaited biography by Franz Xavier Niemetschek at last appeared in 1798. In the six years since Wolfgang's death, Neimetschek had collected opinions, anecdotes and indeed documents from many sources, including Constanze. He had also read Schlichtegroll's article in the 1791 *Nekrolog*, and plundered its information on Wolfgang's early life in Salzburg. His *Leben des k.k. Kappelmeisters Wolfgang Gottlieb Mozart* was a generous portrait of his subject. It glossed vaguely over Wolfgang's faults (his poor handling of money and his tendency to trust people too easily), suggesting rather that his more difficult circumstances were simply due to bad luck. Constanze was paraded as a model wife, supportive and loving, who made her husband very happy, and who paid off his small debts after his death by mounting concerts in his memory. It was in this biography that many personal details first appeared before the wider public, including most dramatically the story of the commissioning of the Requiem, complete with its becloaked messenger.

Constanze was delighted with Niemetschek's book, not only for its glowing portrait of her marriage, but for the fascination with Wolfgang's music that such a sympathetic biography now generated. And, sure enough, some of this music was beginning to appear in print. In the pre-copyright era, any person who obtained any score, by any composer, from any source, could publish it; and pirated copies of music by Mozart were now appearing, as Constanze herself complained to Niemetschek. Even more damaging were the cases of other people's works being published under Mozart's name (for this would surely guarantee decent sales), and Constanze found herself accused of having appropriated these other pieces in order to make financial gains from them. Even her former colleague Anton Eberl (the pianist who had accompanied her and Aloysia on their tour in 1795) claimed in newspapers in Hamburg and Leipzig that three of his compositions had appeared as works by Mozart; and the editor of the Leipzig paper then begged the question by commenting that 'Mozart's widow has so little respect for the ashes of her husband that she willingly participates in illegal activities.'[15] All this was of course preposterous: Constanze would never even have contemplated gathering up material by inferior musicians when she had so much superlative music in her possession. It was certainly time to deal with the pirates.

Relations between the Mozart family and Breitkopf and Härtel actually went back a quarter of a century, for in 1772, and again in 1775 and 1781, Leopold Mozart had unsuccessfully tried to persuade the publishers to take some of Wolfgang's music. After Constanze's advances to them in 1795, they did begin to show some interest. But it was only after the Niemetshek biography appeared, and then another, much smaller, publisher, Johann Peter Spehr, printed six instalments of what was declared to be a collected edition, that Breitkopf and Härtel sprang into action. Without even consulting Constanze, they published their own announcement of a 'correct and complete' edition; and only then did Gottfried Christoph Härtel, the tough, thirty-two-year-old head of the firm, write a careful letter to the 'honoured lady and friend'.[16] He apologized for having made his announcement without first contacting her, but explained that he had been forced to do so because of Spehr's action. Constanze replied firmly, beginning, 'It did indeed seem strange to me that I would have to read in a public announcement about an undertaking which, without my participation, would be daring and difficult to execute.' She continued:

> Does anyone know how many manuscripts I still own – manu-
> scripts which have never been copied? Is there anyone who would
> disagree with me, Mozart's widow, if I were to announce publicly
> that no complete edition of Mozart's works is possible unless
> issued by me or with my assistance? Could a person turn to any-
> one but me for the publication of all his hitherto unpublished
> works, since I am the person who owns the autographs?

But she was of course keen to secure a contract (and Breitkopf and
Härtel were the most reputable firm), and so, she declared, she was
open to offers.

It was at this point that the Requiem reappeared, and became
something of a problem. Breitkopf and Härtel had acquired two
copies of it (for, again, any copyist could make scores of anything,
and circulate them), and now asked for the score in Constanze's
possession. Still deliberately withholding the name of Count
Walsegg, Constanze declared that she had held back from publishing it 'out of respect for the gentleman who had commissioned it on
condition that it never be published'. But she reckoned she could
'work things out with the gentleman in question', and get his permission to publish. She was adamant that Breitkopf and Härtel
should do nothing with their copies of the Requiem until she had
reached some agreement with Walsegg, for, technically, he had paid
for it and therefore owned it. She (or, more likely, the clever and
diplomatic Nissen) drafted an appeal to 'the anonymous patron',
and prepared to publish it in Viennese newspapers:

> More than seven years have gone by since the noble anonymous
> commissioned the late Mozart to write a Requiem, just a few
> months before the composer's death. Since during all this time the
> patron has not had the work published, Mozart's widow grate-
> fully takes this as proof that he is agreeable to her deriving some
> gain from such publication. But she wishes to make sure of this,
> for she has only noble feelings of respect and devotion towards
> that person. She therefore considers it her duty to insert notices
> in newspapers in Vienna, Hamburg and Frankfurt, inviting the
> gentleman to indicate his intentions within three months, after

which interval she will make so bold as to have the Requiem appear in an edition of the late composer's complete works.[17]

But Constanze never had to go into print with this announcement. Anxious to avoid a humiliating revelation of his own deceptions, Count Walsegg reappeared quietly, had his money refunded, received the promise of some published scores, and scuttled back into obscurity. So Constanze handed over her own copy of the Requiem, and washed her hands of it.

It was most likely Nissen who brokered the deal with Walsegg, and steered Constanze through the complexities of the Requiem's passage to publication. And he must also have been behind Constanze as she now worked to secure a proper contract with Breitkopf and Härtel for their complete edition of Mozart's music. On 9 November 1799 she wrote to ask them to pay her 1,000 ducats (4,050 florins) for all his scores, either payable in two instalments at six-monthly intervals, or (again showing her negotiating skills) in one lump sum of 900 ducats. She concluded her letter:

> I would be happy if you and I could come to an agreement over this, for you were the first one to have the idea (very agreeable to me) of issuing a proper edition of my late husband's works, as a fitting memorial to him. For this I would gladly offer you favourable terms.[18]

But Breitkopf and Härtel did not respond to this offer, probably thinking that she was asking too high a price, and that if they called her bluff she might drop it. Later that month, on the 27th, Constanze wrote again, threatening to 'sell all the music in my possession to another interested party, at a good price, in order to put an end to all this uncertainty'.[19] She gave them another two weeks to respond, and then, still hearing nothing, she issued an ultimatum:

> Since no answer has been forthcoming, it is evident that you are rejecting my terms. I therefore must tell you for the last time (though this should hardly be necessary) that, though I would

have liked to maintain our business relationship, I shall without fail sell all my husband's complete musical estate by the end of the year.[20]

And so she did. She had not been bluffing. In Offenbach, one Johann Anton André, aged only twenty-four, had just taken over his father's publishing house, and had indeed approached Constanze. Early in 1800 she sold the rest of her music to André for 2,550 florins (just over one half of what she had asked of Breitkopf and Härtel). So now two rival publishers were preparing printed scores of Mozart's music, and the battles between them became ugly and argumentative. Constanze's affiliation with André did not in the event turn out to be particularly happy, for he was slow with his payments and the quality of his publications was flawed. Härtel was naturally furious at having missed out on a complete oeuvre, and even brought Nannerl into the fray, trying to play her off with Constanze, and no doubt instilling more mistrust into an already strained relationship between the two sisters-in-law. But, sweetly willing though Nannerl was to cooperate, just as she had been with biographers, she could produce no additional scores for Breitkopf and Härtel, and apologetically referred them back to Constanze.

All the while these transactions were being negotiated, Breitkopf and Härtel were advertising their new edition; and, in an attempt to boost advance sales, they were also publishing biographical anecdotes about Mozart in their house journal, the *Allgemeiner musikalische Zeitung*. The editor of this was Friedrich Rochlitz. He asked Constanze and others to submit material for its columns, and Constanze cooperated fully. She handed over not only her own anecdotal testimony, but also precious letters, including, astonishingly, those that Wolfgang had written to his cousin, the 'Bäsle'. As she told Rochlitz, she felt that the inclusion of these, as well as letters to herself, her sister Aloysia and Michael Puchberg, would give a truly rounded picture of Wolfgang. But, mystifyingly, Rochlitz chose to ignore the content of the letters, preferring instead to present the more attractive copy that he was getting from

Constanze and Nannerl, and from the Niemetschek biography, now in print. He wrote many of the columns himself, and the whitewash picture that he presented was one of Mozart the victim, poorly treated by society. The cynical interpretation of these Rochlitz articles – some forty of them, appearing between 1798 and 1801 – is that they must have been good for sales.

By the turn of the century, though, Constanze's situation was at last stable. For all the tension in her negotiations with the publishers, she had now entered into agreements with two of them, and financially she was more secure than she had ever been. The Abbé Stadler and Georg Nissen had certainly played their part in these recent events, Stadler as organizer of the material, and Nissen as diplomatic negotiator. And indeed it was with the calm, civilized presence of Georg Nissen that Constanze felt, literally, at home. They now lived in the Michaelerplatz, under the same roof if not in the same apartment, in quiet domesticity.

~

CONSTANZE'S SONS, WHO had both spent some years in Prague receiving their musical and general education, were growing up. The elder, Carl, had left the Gymnasium in 1799 at the age of fifteen, and Constanze was now trying to steer him towards a career in business. In January 1800 she wrote to André, describing her son as 'well-mannered and with a good heart',[21] who spoke a little French and was beginning also to learn English and Italian. 'If he agrees,' she confided, 'I intend him to be in business.' Eventually she got her way, for Carl travelled to Livorno and entered an English business firm there as an apprentice. Like his father, he was enchanted by Italy, and in due course would decide to make his home there. But he was still reluctant to abandon completely the idea of a career in music. He moved to Milan where, with Haydn's long-promised recommendation, he took his composition lessons from Bonifazio Asioli. But he lacked confidence as a musician, and perhaps application too; and Constanze firmly believed that to continue on this path would actually be folly. On 5 March 1806 she wrote her son an extremely careful letter. 'I always, now and in the future, want what you want,' she began, but continued then by asking him to think appropriately for a man of his age. (He was twenty-one.) She acknowledged that he was 'not indifferent to music', and supposed that he worked hard at it ('You will know more about this than I do'). But she begged him to remember what she had often told him in the past, that 'no son of Mozart should ever be mediocre, for this would only bring shame rather than honour'. As if this tough little rejoinder were not enough, she also pointed out that Carl's younger brother (now fifteen) showed great talent (implying, correctly, that it was greater than his own) and told him she would hate 'to see one brother praised above the other'. But she concluded by putting the whole decision in his own hands, cleverly adding that if they both did well, 'my joy would accordingly be greater'.[22]

The comparison of Carl with his brother would have made its mark. From their earliest childhood Constanze had evidently realized that Franz Xavier had the greater talent, as she had shown by forbidding Carl's stage appearances but encouraging his brother's. To an extent Carl always resented this ('My mother had made the firm decision that not I but my brother . . . was to become a musician'[23]) and retained a thread of hope that he might yet be a composer or a performer. But in his mid-twenties he at last recognized the truth of his mother's realistic assessment, and returned to the business world. Eventually he became an official in the service of the Viceroy of Naples in Milan; his music-making remained a private pleasure.

Meanwhile, Constanze did indeed continue to rally her younger son. At some point it was decided to change Franz Xavier's names to Wolfgang Amadeus, as if even in name he was now to assume the identity of the father he had never known. Expectations of the young Wolfgang were high, and the pressure on him was great. He too had returned from Prague to Vienna, where his father's old colleagues were eager to help him. He was taught by no lesser men than Haydn, Salieri, Hummel (his parents' former lodger) and

Albrechtsberger. And in 1805, when young Wolfgang was fourteen, he gave a piano recital at Schikaneder's theatre. The public roared their appreciation, and a huge sum of money (1,700 florins) was taken; it must have been a great night for Constanze too. Other concerts followed, in cities where not only his father but also his mother had performed. But if young Wolfgang's early appearances were received with an enthusiasm born of earnest nostalgia, his own talents were reviewed with decidedly faint praise, and he began either to resent or to feel daunted by the limelight. At the age of seventeen, in 1808, he took a teaching post far from Vienna, in Galicia, at the extreme edge of the Austrian realm. So now both Constanze's sons had left home. But although family reunions were few after this point, they all kept in touch with one another by letter, and genuine if distant affection and mutual concern remained between them.

~

THE FIRST YEARS of the nineteenth century were uncomfortable for foreign diplomats in Vienna. Francis II, who had succeeded his father, Leopold II, was a deeply conservative Emperor, who swept aside the social reforms that had initially though not lastingly made his eldest brother, Joseph II, so beloved by his people. In Joseph's time, Enlightenment thought, heralding the idea of man as a free individual, had led to strong Viennese support for the revolutionaries in France; but under Francis II a new anti-revolutionary stance was adopted, with the disastrous result that France declared war on Austria. As the great Napoleon Bonaparte emerged, he was seen by the younger (Wordsworthian, Beethovenian) generation as the champion of the poor, embodying the principles of freedom and equality, as opposed to the repression of the ruling Habsburgs. But when in 1804 Napoleon declared himself Emperor (famously causing Beethoven to rename his third symphony, originally dedicated to Napoleon, the 'Eroica'), the Austrian people saw it as a betrayal of principle. Napoleon's two Austrian campaigns, in 1805 and 1809, were terrible times for the Viennese. Napoleon set up his own quarters in Schönbrunn, and his troops occupied the city. Austria's victory over France at Aspern in April 1809 was but a false dawn, for the French, preoccupied with fighting the British in Portugal, had rather taken their eye off the ball. Napoleon retaliated immediately, with a victory at Wagram in July; there were huge casualties on both sides. Between these two campaigns, many foreign diplomats fled from Vienna across the Danube to Pressburg (now Bratislava). Georg Nissen was among them, and he took Constanze with him. On 26 June 1809, while Napoleon was rallying and reforming his armies, Georg Nissen and Constanze Mozart were married in Pressburg Cathedral.

Life with her second husband was for Constanze an altogether different matter to life with her first. Georg Nissen was calm, solid and comfortable. While he cannot have begun to resemble the high-octane, hyperactive genius of Wolfgang, in his own way he adored Constanze as deeply and passionately as Wolfgang had. She had experienced extreme emotional turbulence, both in her twenties as Wolfgang's wife, and then in her thirties as his widow. Now, in her late forties, she was more than ready to devote herself to a man whose loving companionship brought her tranquillity and the greatest contentment. And her two sons, each in his remote outpost of Habsburg territory, approved greatly of their mother's new husband. They referred to him ever afterwards as their 'father', even between themselves, and always spoke of him with affection, respect and gratitude.

After their marriage, Georg and Constanze Nissen moved briefly back to Vienna, but they were not anxious to stay there. (Since Napoleon's victory at Wagram, the French were occupying the capital once more.) Nissen wanted to take Constanze back home to Copenhagen, and, at forty-nine, he was more than ready to leave diplomatic service. According to young Wolfgang, he had been planning this for some time. Wolfgang wrote to Carl: 'Our father . . . is so happy at the prospect of being reunited with his countrymen that he seems ten years younger. As you probably know it has been his wish for some years to leave Vienna for

Copenhagen.'[24] And so they did, in 1810. Before they left, they made various financial arrangements for Constanze's sons, and it was Nissen who wrote to them, outlining their affairs.[25] He informed them that the money that Constanze had so carefully accrued, through her travels and concerts and the selling of scores, was now a sum that would increase rather than diminish, and that in due course (Nissen naturally meant at the time of Constanze's death – 'and you and I both hope that this will be a long way off') it would be divided between the two of them. With the gentlest, most diplomatic and loving practicality, Nissen was reassuring his stepsons that he would not be touching any of their mother's money. At the same time Constanze sent Carl and Wolfgang each one of Mozart's precious keyboard instruments.

The Nissens then made their journey back to the Danish capital, and eventually bought a new property on Lavendelstraede, near the Town Hall, in 1812. Nissen was appointed as state press censor, a post which gave him security, a small but regular salary, and, most important of all, plenty of free time to pursue his own cultural interests. And Constanze took to her new home willingly. Copenhagen had had its troubles, and was still recovering, both physically and economically, from the British naval bombardment of 1807. But Constanze liked the city's culture and people; she also liked her new home and especially her garden. She spoke warmly of her new life in her letters to her sons.

Constanze's old life was by no means forgotten or ignored, however. Mozart's music was becoming increasingly popular now in Denmark, and the arrival of his widow would not have gone unnoticed in Copenhagen. She had visiting cards printed, proudly naming both her husbands: 'CONSTANZA Etats Raethin von NISSEN, gevesene Witwe Mozart'. And, in the best Mozart tradition, the Nissens regularly enjoyed evenings of chamber music in their own home. After several years, young Wolfgang visited his mother and stepfather in 1819, and rejoiced in 'the happy life they have led for twenty years'.[26] He was relieved to find his mother in such good form, confessing to his brother that he had not been sure what to expect after eleven years, but was thrilled that she seemed completely unchanged. Constanze revitalized her old skills, and organized a concert for him at the Royal Theatre (with tickets obtainable through her at the Lavendelstraede house). The programme involved singers too, from the Royal Danish Opera, and consisted entirely of Mozart's music. Constanze must again have been flooded with a kaleidoscope of emotions as she sat beside her second husband in his city that was now her home, listening to her son perform music by her adored and brilliant first husband – music to which in any case she could never listen with equanimity. As she approached her sixtieth year, her life circle must have seemed almost complete. But there was one more, extremely courageous, chapter to come.

~

IN A CURIOUS way, it was the spirit of Mozart that had bound Georg Nissen and Constanze together. After whatever serendipitous accident had brought them to live under the same roof, he had become ever closer to her through the work that he and the Abbé Stadler did for her. In marrying Mozart's widow, and partly taking responsibility for the upbringing of his sons, Nissen had taken his place at the very forefront of the Mozart family. At some stage in their marriage, husband and wife hatched the idea of Nissen writing a full-scale biography of Wolfgang. He had plenty of free time in Copenhagen. As a passionate music-lover, he deeply appreciated Mozart's music, especially since he had, literally, lived with so much of it. And of course he had unique access to the person who had shared Wolfgang's entire adult life. What he and Constanze both lacked was any detailed knowledge of Mozart's earlier years. As the Nissens approached the age of retirement in Copenhagen, they took an immensely bold decision: they would move to Salzburg, and research and write the biography there.

Quite apart from the whole physical upheaval of uprooting themselves from their comfortable Copenhagen home, and crossing many hundreds of miles to start again in a new environment, the psychological bravery of this move was considerable for Constanze. Memories of her single visit to Salzburg, with Wolfgang in 1783, cannot have been happy; and she had been deeply upset by the Schlichtegroll article in his *Nekrolog auf der Jahr 1791*, composed largely of contributions from Salzburg inhabitants. Above all, her relationship with her sister-in-law Nannerl, who would have to be a crucial, and willing, participant in this new biographical venture, had never been exactly easy, and there had been no direct communication between them for at least thirty years. However much Constanze looked forward to returning to her homeland, she must have been steeling herself to face residual animosity and disapproval in Salzburg. But, even as she battled with her instinctive reluctance, no fewer than three people were on hand to ease her path. The first was of course Nissen, the professional diplomat whose intelligence, charm and decency could dispel tension in any situation. The second was her son Wolfgang, who was also drawn to his father's birthplace. The third, and the most surprising, was Nannerl herself.

After Nannerl's uncomfortable contribution to the Schlichtegroll obituary in 1793, she had retreated again from public gaze. Her husband, Johann Baptist, had been raised to the nobility in 1792, and from then on all his family, including Nannerl, could title themselves 'von Berchtold zu Sonnenburg'. Nevertheless, St Gilgen was still essentially a 'wilderness', and there she quietly brought up her children Leopold and Jeanette, and continued to care too for her stepchildren, whose affection and respect she had gradually won. Breitkopf and Härtel tried to reel her into their dealings with Constanze over the publication of Wolfgang's music, and in her sweet naivety Nannerl might indeed have been thoroughly exploited by the tough businessmen from Leipzig. But in fact she could not help them. As she politely told Breitkopf and Härtel, she had forwarded all Wolfgang's music to her brother after the death of their father in 1787, and she 'no longer had contact with that world'.[27] (This did not stop Breitkopf and Härtel trying to use Nannerl to prise music out of other Salzburg composers, such as

Michael Haydn; but nothing ever came of this notion, and they soon lost interest in her.)

In February 1801 Nannerl's husband, Johann Baptist Franz von Berchtold zu Sonnenberg, died at the age of sixty-five. Within a few months, Nannerl packed up her possessions and left for ever her house by the lake in St Gilgen. As she returned at last to Salzburg, a widow with two children, her journey and situation were an almost exact replica of those of her maternal grandmother, three-quarters of a century earlier. But her children were older than Eva Rosina's little girls had been (Leopold was sixteen and Jeanette twelve); and Nannerl herself had quite considerable resources, for Berchtold had left her comfortably off. She also had her own musical gifts. After having taken lodgings in an apartment owned by her old friends the Barisanis, in what is now the Sigmund-Haffnerstrasse, literally around the corner from her childhood home in Getreidegasse, she began to give piano lessons again, and to an extent to pick up the threads of the Salzburg musical life that she had left seventeen years earlier. But she had yet more tragedy to endure, for Jeanette died in 1805, aged only sixteen. Nannerl buried her daughter in the Mozart family grave in the St Sebastian cemetery, beside her grandmother Eva Rosina and her father Leopold. (Berchtold's remains lay in his family's vault in St Gilgen.)

In her late middle age Nannerl's life continued to be a struggle. After Jeanette's death, she lost two of her stepchildren; and her own son Leopold joined the army to fight the French. In 1809 he was captured and imprisoned. (He did survive, though, and left the army to become a customs official, eventually settling in Innsbruck. He lived into his fifty-fifth year.) And then Nannerl's own health began to fail. Although she had certainly proved to be more robust than her frail brother, the serious illnesses that they had both endured in childhood had taken their toll on her constitution too, and she was now paying the price. Worst of all, she began to lose her eyesight, and this was the most spiritually debilitating infirmity for a woman whose greatest joy was still to sit at a keyboard and play it. But as Salzburg at last began to acknowledge the inestimable quality of her late brother, her own role as his surviving sister in the town of their birth was one she quietly enjoyed. She received visitors, displayed her family portraits and musical instruments, and was held in esteem by all who knew her.

In 1821 Nannerl received a most special visitor. Her brother's son Wolfgang, whom she had never met, contacted her and told her he wanted to make her acquaintance. Young Wolfgang was now thirty years old. His teaching job in the service of Count Baworowsky in Galicia, which he had taken in 1808 in order to escape the pressures of Vienna, had initially stimulated him (he felt instinctively happier as a large fish in a small pond), but ultimately bored and therefore depressed him. He left it in 1810, and tried his luck with another patron, Count Janizzewski, but this too failed to satisfy him. After only eighteen months there he moved to Lemberg (now L'vov), and resolved to make a living as a musician without any regular income or patronage. The parallel with his father is striking. In Lemberg he became the piano teacher to young Julia Baroni-Cavalcabo, who would one day become a celebrated pianist herself. Her father was a government councillor, and her mother, Josephine, was twenty-three years younger than her husband and only three years older than young Wolfgang. In due course Josephine became Wolfgang's mistress, and this forbidden, impossible relationship was to dominate the rest of his life. Josephine stayed with her elderly husband, but Wolfgang moved in with them, and his devoted infatuation for her never left him. Wolfgang's brother Carl was supportive of this unconventional arrangement (he in fact had one of his own), and would subsequently refer to Josephine as a 'saint'. When Wolfgang had visited his mother in Copenhagen, he had told her of his love for the ultimately unattainable Josephine, and Constanze had touched him by showing great pleasure at this news. (Wolfgang wrote delightedly to Josephine that Constanze and Georg Nissen 'love me so much that they cannot help loving anyone who loves me and whom I love'.[28]) But Constanze was in fact privately troubled by her son's infatuation, as she would confide years later to sympathetic visitors.

In 1819, at the age of twenty-eight, Wolfgang had embarked on an enormously ambitious venture, a concert tour of Europe. He would be away from Lemberg and Josephine for nearly four years. He had certainly inherited his father's wanderlust, but perhaps also his chaotic inability to reap proper benefits from a tour on such a scale. (Would that he had rather taken after his mother in this regard, or certainly after his paternal grandfather.) His wanderings across European cities in those years yielded little reward, and often depressed him. Like his father, he desperately missed the woman of his heart, feeling incomplete without Josephine. But he did have some joyful encounters and reunions, not least with his mother in Copenhagen, with his brother Carl in Milan, with his old teacher Salieri, with Beethoven too, in Vienna, and with his mother's brilliant cousin, Carl Maria von Weber, in Dresden. And finally, in Salzburg in May 1821, he met his aunt Nannerl.

For both aunt and nephew, this initial encounter was of extreme importance. These two essential loners found a wealth of common ground in their family connection. Wolfgang was thrilled to learn, first-hand, of his father's childhood, of his life with Nannerl and their parents. And Nannerl could release all her harboured love and affection for her lost brother on to the son who so resembled him. She showed him the house of their birth in Getreidegasse, and the Tanzmeisterhaus. She introduced him to many elderly people who had been his father's childhood friends, and who were moved to tears to meet him. She listened to him playing her piano, and maybe even played for him herself. What she then wrote so passionately in his album is barely recognizable as coming from the undemonstrative chronicler that she had always been:

> In my seventieth year I had the great joy of meeting for the first time the son of my dearly beloved brother. What delightful memories were evoked by hearing him play just as his father had played. These memories are treasured by his aunt Maria Anna, Freyfrau von Berchtold zu Sonnenburg, née Mozart.[29]

The bond was formed between Nannerl and young Wolfgang.

Whenever in the coming years he visited Salzburg, he was extremely attentive to his aunt, and without doubt he became for her the real joy of her declining years. In 1826, when the publisher André was preparing a new edition of the Requiem, and proposing that all its profits went to Nannerl, she declined this generous offer, not wishing to 'attract public attention'. She therefore passed all those profits to her two nephews, Carl (whom she had never met) and her new friend, Wolfgang.

It was shortly after Wolfgang's first visit to Salzburg that Constanze and Nissen arrived, and settled in a beautiful house in Marktplatz (now Altermarkt). From everybody's point of view, the timing could not have been better. Nannerl's delight at having discovered her nephew can only have warmed her attitude to his mother, whom she had not seen for nearly forty years. The calm and kindly presence of Nissen, the palpable success of his devoted marriage to Constanze, and above all the sincerity of their combined project – to produce a proper biography of Nannerl's brother – dispelled any residual suspicion (generated by Leopold, all those years ago) towards her sister-in-law. Nannerl became intrinsically involved in the biography, willingly handing over to Nissen all her letters and memorabilia, and no doubt being the key witness in Nissen's research into his subject's early life. Constanze would have breathed a huge sigh of relief. And, as Nannerl's health and eyesight continued to decline in the 1820s, it is clear that Constanze's natural Weber instinct to care for those around her now embraced her sister-in-law. At last, and for the remaining years of their lives, Constanze and Nannerl were united, not divided, by the man they had both loved.

～

Since Nannerl's return to Salzburg at the turn of the century, the city had changed considerably. As a result of Napoleon's Austrian campaigns, the semi-feudal Prince-Archbishopric had been swept away. In 1800 Mozart's old adversary, Archbishop Colloredo, had fled the city as the French troops advanced, and the Court was eventually abolished in 1806. Most of Salzburg's musicians migrated to Vienna; those who remained dealt only with church services, where, inevitably, standards declined. After a brief period of Bavarian rule, the Congress of Vienna in 1816 restored political stability, and Salzburg, to Austria. But the brilliance of this former episcopal seat had faded: in effect it was now no more than a stagnant provincial town. Nannerl would have mourned the emptying of Salzburg's musical resources – how different its cultural life now was to the bustling hub of activity that she had enjoyed in her childhood and early adulthood. And when Constanze arrived in 1820, she too would have been struck by the change in the musical environment, as compared with her previous experience back in 1783. But both she and Nannerl would have appreciated the peace and stability of nineteenth-century Salzburg. And they both lived long enough to witness the beginnings of its eventual artistic revival, centred entirely on the recognition, at last, of its debt to their Wolfgang.

Soon after the Nissens' arrival in Salzburg, they evidently travelled to Milan to visit Carl. The chronology of events is not entirely clear at this stage of Constanze's life, but it seems that they were in Italy for possibly as long as two years, for in 1823 she wrote to a composer friend, Christophe Weyse in Copenhagen, to apologize for having neglected her promise to him to try to spread awareness of his music there. For two years, she acknowledged, she had had many opportunities to do so, as Carl had organized weekly evenings of music-making for her.[30] At any rate, whenever exactly it was, this visit to Milan was a significant reunion for mother and son. Although Carl would remain the more remote of her two sons, both emotionally and geographically, the very length of the visit, and that tiny indication of Carl's efforts to please his mother, suggest that loving contact was restored. Wolfgang's visits to Copenhagen, Milan and Salzburg would also have drawn together the disparate elements of Constanze's family. Both her sons were genuinely fond of their stepfather; and now that she and Nissen had returned to Austria, the distances between them all, metaphorically as well as physically, seemed to have shrunk.

~

SALZBURG SUMMERS CAN be unbearably hot. In the eighteenth and nineteenth centuries, as in so many other cities, some residents chose to move out of the centre of town and into its cooler rural suburbs. Surrounded as it is by beguiling wooded hills (the Kapuzinerberg, Mönchsberg and Rainberg), Salzburg can offer much peripheral opportunity for airier tranquillity. And at some stage after their arrival in their new home, the Nissens too acquired a house in which to spend their summer months. Situated in Nonnberggasse, an energetic and steep climb out of town towards the Hohensalzburg fortress, the house had wonderful views, and a flourishing garden which, as ever, Constanze enjoyed enormously. The house was also just round the corner from the Nonnberg Priory, whose choirmaster Anton Jahndl was a passionate devotee and practitioner of Mozart's church music, and who became closely involved with Georg Nissen as he worked on the biography.

With Jahndl and another Salzburg colleague, Maximilian Keller, to help, Nissen collected articles about Mozart from every journal, newspaper and periodical that he could find. He either interviewed personally or wrote letters to anyone he knew had had contact with him, inviting memories, opinions and judgements. Especially important at this time were Mozart's closest family members. And it was here that Nissen's gentle diplomacy brought him the close cooperation of Nannerl, and, with her, the incomparable hoard of over 400 letters that she had partly accumulated herself and partly inherited from Leopold. Her very conversations with Nissen, especially about her father and her childhood, would greatly influence his eventual conception of the biography. And Constanze considered her own sisters too, though only one of them did contribute. The eldest, Josefa, had died in 1819, at the age of sixty, while Constanze was in Copenhagen. (Constanze maintained contact with her daughter, also Josefa, and her husband Carl Hönig.)

Aloysia, now also in her sixties, had retired as a performer, and returned from Zurich to Vienna where she was in demand as a singing teacher. But there is no evidence of any direct contribution to Nissen's project from Aloysia, and Constanze may perhaps have been reluctant to ask for one, given Aloysia's own early emotional involvement with Wolfgang. Her younger sister Sophie, on the other hand, was greatly important.

Sophie's life had also changed considerably since the death of their mother. In 1807, at the age of forty-four, she had at last married. Her husband, Jakob Haibl, was, like Josefa's two husbands, a member of Schikaneder's company, where he had not only performed as a tenor but also been involved in administration. (Within a week of Mozart's death, it was he who, on behalf of Schikaneder, had sent a libretto of *Die Zauberflöte* to the opera company at Mannheim, adding a sad little postscript, 'Herr Mozart has died'.) Like many of Schikaneder's company members, he was also a composer, and his popular singspiel, *Der Tiroler Wastel*, was performed 118 times by the company between 1796 and 1801. In 1806 his first wife Katharina died, and he moved to Djakovar (now Dakovo) in Slavonia. Sophie went with him, and on 7 January 1807 she married him in the Cathedral, where he was choirmaster.

So now Sophie too was asked by Nissen for her memories of Mozart, and especially to relive the part she had played in Mozart's last days; and she duly sent him her passionate, poignant account. Finally, Constanze's own sons were urged by their mother to make their own contributions to the biography. Young Wolfgang of course had no direct memory of his father, though he knew many musicians who had. Carl in Milan had had his childhood reminiscences, and now, like his brother, was in contact with others who could recall their own Mozartian experiences. As the replies came in, Nissen attempted to organize his rapidly growing piles of material into some sort of coherent shape. Even Constanze was overwhelmed by the ardour and diligence with which he worked. She wrote to Carl:

Day and night he sits, buried under stacks of books and journals –
stacks so high I can hardly see him. We would be hard put to find
another Mozart advocate like him – there is no end to his efforts. I
worry about the number of letters he has to write; they and all the
other work might harm his health which up to now, God be
praised, has been good . . . Tears come into my eyes as I write
this.[31]

Having assembled such a huge amount of material, Nissen
began to write. He started a Preface, and immediately revealed
his diplomatic even-handedness and fairness of judgement. The
advantage that his biography would have, he states, over the earlier
studies by Schlichtegroll and Niemetschek, was the enrichment of
his newly acquired hoard of letters. He had organized them and
categorized them, and clearly spent several months absorbing their
content. He had even cracked the codes that the Mozart family had
sometimes deployed (probably with the help of Nannerl), and
laboriously set out their complicated systems – they were basically
a form of elongated acronym. Nissen evidently admired Leopold
enormously. He praised all his good qualities: his exemplary organization, his intellect, his morals, and his brilliant education of his
son. And although Nissen gives the impression of having learned
all this from reading the letters, it is clear from his descriptions of
Leopold's educational methods, and of their practical interpretation on the children's travels in the 1760s, that he must also have had
first-hand accounts from Nannerl. Nissen does include references to
Nannerl and her mother, but really only as witnesses to the main
drama (the education and moulding of a genius boy) rather than as
participants. And indeed Nissen goes on to state that the best of all
the letters are those written between father and son ('man to man').
Unquestionably Nissen revered Wolfgang, but he was extremely
uncomfortable about certain aspects of his nature. The childish
vulgarity, the obsession with bodily functions, and of course the
inability to make provision for Constanze after his death, at best
puzzled him and at worst appalled him. But in spite of his own
scruples about basing his book on the contents of letters never

intended for publication, Nissen was resolved to tell the whole truth: any concealment would be a form of lying ('Verschweigung is schon Unwahrheit').

Nissen barely began this monumental task, however. He did not even complete his Preface. Constanze was right to worry that the sheer volume of work was potentially harmful to his health, for on 24 March 1826 Georg Nissen died suddenly, of 'paralysis of the lungs', at the age of sixty-five. For the second time in her life, Constanze was widowed. And, in another curious parallel with her first husband, Nissen had left her in possession of an unfinished, major, project.

Posterity has never quite forgiven Constanze for her attitude to graves. She did not accompany Mozart's coffin to its final resting place in the St Marx cemetery outside Vienna, nor did she ever organize a proper headstone for it. By the time she actually visited the cemetery, as late as 1808, more than the statutory ten years had elapsed; and in accordance with contemporary custom, the grave had been raked over, and the plot reclaimed for later occupants. Perhaps with this in mind, Constanze was much more actively involved with the remains of her second husband. The Mozart family did have their own appointed grave in the churchyard of St Sebastian in Salzburg. Already interred there were Wolfgang's maternal grandmother, Eva Rosina, his father Leopold, Nannerl's daughter Jeanette, and, bizarrely, Constanze's aunt by marriage, Genoveva, the mother of Carl Maria von Weber. Genoveva (whom Constanze, two years her senior, had delighted in addressing as 'Tante') and her husband Franz Anton had visited Wolfgang and Constanze in Vienna in 1788: Constanze's Carl was four years old at the time, Genoveva's Carl was nearly two. She too was a singer, and had actually sung in *Die Entführung*, in Meiningen in 1790, and again in Weimar in 1794. In the mid-1790s she was with Franz Anton in Salzburg, where he briefly held the post of Kapellmeister; and it was there that she died, of tuberculosis, on 13 March 1798, aged only thirty-four. Her tangential connection with the Mozart family must have made their plot in the St Sebastian cemetery the obvious place for her to be buried; and so she had been. If Nannerl in St Gilgen had had any objections to her family's plot being thus invaded, she had not raised them. So now Constanze continued along this somewhat crooked path of logic, and decided that Nissen too should be buried in that very same grave.

This was probably not Constanze's most tactful decision. Nor was it exactly thoughtful to erect a headstone for this crowded grave, with only the name of Nissen on it, ignoring therefore Nannerl's grandmother, father and daughter. Effectively, the Weber family had hijacked the Mozart family's burying-place, and this time Nannerl did resent the invasion. She had made a will back in 1823, stating her wish to be buried beside her father in St Sebastian's churchyard. In 1827, one year after Nissen's burial there, she added a codicil asking to be buried instead in the churchyard of St Peter's. Sympathetic though she may have been to Constanze in her new bereavement, Nannerl's altering of her own arrangements was a strong statement. A little tension, it seems, had been rekindled between the two women, and ironically by the death of a man who had done so much to bring them closer together.

Young Wolfgang may well have been instrumental now in bridging any new gulf between Constanze and Nannerl. He came straight to his mother's side after Nissen's death, but, without fail, continued to pay loving attention, too, to his increasingly blind and frail aunt. Relationships between the two households remained courteous and caring. And meanwhile Constanze herself gained great comfort from the presence of her son. She organized a performance of Mozart's Requiem in memory of Nissen, and Wolfgang conducted it. Again, this must have been for Constanze an occasion of multilayered emotion. And her younger son was not her only support in her second widowhood. In another remarkable family coincidence, her sister Sophie had lost her own husband, Jakob Haibl, on the very same day that Nissen died. As the two sisters shared commiseration and condolence by letter, they came to a decision that would affect the rest of their lives. Sophie packed up her house in Djakovor, and moved to Salzburg to live with

Constanze. Now the two sisters would provide each other with companionship and, that Weber speciality, care.

~

AFTER ALL THE labour that had gone into Nissen's researches for his Mozart biography, not to mention their very move to Salzburg in order to undertake it, Constanze was now determined to get the book finished. It would, after all, be a fitting memorial to both her late husbands. She still had the willing cooperation of Nissen's two local assistants, Jahndl and Keller. But Constanze felt that a stronger, more literary figure was needed to bring cohesion to the huge piles of material that Nissen had accumulated. She was right in her realization of the need for the book, but wrong in her choice of person to deal with it. Johann Friedrich Feuerstein of Pirna, near Dresden, was a medical doctor, a Mozart enthusiast and an old friend of Nissen's. He offered his services, and Constanze accepted them. She asked him to take over the whole project, and also to deal with the publishers, her old adversaries Breitkopf and Härtel. Feuerstein did so, and in due course the *Biographie W.A. Mozarts* appeared. But it was a very far cry from the painstakingly thorough presentation of information that Nissen had planned. Feuerstein cobbled it all together in a disastrously haphazard manner: there is absolutely no shape to the material; rather, the text is full of contradictions, repetitions and unidentified anecdotes. Whether Constanze ever actually read it, let alone approved of its content and style, must remain in some doubt. Within a few years, the relationship between Constanze and Feuerstein would end in bitter acrimony, for he withheld sums of money that she claimed to be rightfully hers. By the time she actually tried to retrieve these through litigation, he was of unsound mind and unable to testify. Constanze lost the case, and Feuerstein ended his days in a lunatic asylum.

But at the time when Feuerstein was doing his frantic patchwork, Constanze busied herself with the actual selling of it. The list of subscribers that she managed to enrol for the biography was highly impressive. It was headed, naturally, by the royal families of Austria and Denmark, followed closely by those of Bavaria, Saxony, Italy and Prussia. (The English king, George IV, does not appear among the supporters, although Constanze had written to him too.) Princes, dukes and counts flocked to subscribe, and eventually Constanze's list numbered more than 600 well-heeled enthusiasts. When the book appeared she was delighted, and wrote in her diary on 1 April 1829, 'it looks beautiful'. She then entered with equal energy into its distribution, sending crates of copies to all corners of Europe. Initially, sales were excellent, and the takings most gratifying. But the momentum did not last. After the first rush, everything slowed to a halt, and the book did not go into a second printing for over twenty years. Disappointment with the actual product had its inevitable effect on the biography's ultimate fortune in the commercial, musical and literary worlds.

~

SHORTLY AFTER THE publication of the Nissen biography, two English visitors came to Salzburg. Vincent Novello, celebrated now for founding his music publishing house, but known in his time also as a practising musician, travelled with his wife Mary across Europe to Vienna, and back. The purpose of their journey was threefold: to collect material for a projected English biography of Mozart; to present Mozart's sister Nannerl, whom they believed to be destitute, with a sum of money raised on her behalf in London; and to arrange some singing lessons in Paris for their daughter Clara (one of their eleven children). Their first arrival in Salzburg, in July 1829, was of such excitement to them that they deviated from their original itinerary and stayed there longer, abandoning altogether a planned visit to Prague. They then continued on to Vienna; and when in due course they returned homewards, they lingered in Salzburg once more. Both Vincent and Mary Novello kept diaries[32] throughout this momentous journey; and these have survived, to present posterity with instant contemporary portraits of Constanze, Nannerl, Sophie and young Wolfgang (who happened to be there at the time, visiting his mother and aunts) in Salzburg, and of Aloysia in Vienna.

Upon their arrival in Salzburg that summer, Vincent Novello wrote (in French, since he understood little German, and spoke less) to both Nannerl and Constanze, asking if he and his wife might call on them, and, in Nannerl's case, present her with his 'petit cadeau'. Constanze in fact replied on behalf of them both, apologetically explaining that Nannerl was not well enough to see them that day, but inviting them to her own house, to which her servant would lead them. So Constanze was clearly now in close contact with Nannerl's household, in what indeed was to be her final illness. Whether or not she saw her every day, she was monitoring her condition, assessing her ability to receive visitors, and politely dealing on her behalf with the outside world.

Over the next three days a warm and genuine friendship developed between the Novellos and Constanze. Their first meeting with her, up at the Nonnberggasse summerhouse on the afternoon of 14 July, left both Vincent and Mary Novello 'in a complete trance'. On the 15th they were taken by young Wolfgang to see Nannerl, and, after they had invited him to join them for lunch, then spent the rest of the day with Constanze again. She offered to take them on a little outing to Aigen the following day, so they instantly changed their plans for departure and accepted her invitation. On the 17th, before reluctantly leaving in the afternoon, they spent one last morning with Constanze in her town house on Marktplatz. As they said their goodbyes to each other, both parties agreed that the visit had been a huge success. Vincent Novello wrote in his diary: 'We at last parted with mutual anticipation of meeting again soon, whether at Salzburg or in London and with mutual promises of becoming in the meantime frequent correspondents. Altogether the three days I have passed at Salzburg with the widow and son of Mozart have [been] some of the most interesting, satisfying and gratifying that I ever enjoyed.' And Constanze wrote in hers: '. . . very attractive man and altogether charming wife . . . these good people left today, July 17th.'[33]

Given that Novello was a passionate devotee of Mozart's music, and that the main objective of his whole pilgrimage to Austria was to collect first-hand opinions of him from people who had known him, it was inevitable that this impressionable enthusiast would be completely overwhelmed by his Salzburg experiences. Before leaving home, he had acquired a copy of the Nissen biography ('the very first copy which arrived in England', he proudly reported to Constanze), and with his very limited German he had struggled his way through it. He had also prepared in advance a list of (not very penetrating) questions to ask Constanze, most of which would elicit answers that confirmed anecdotes related in the biography. But his recording of these responses in his diary, together with his descriptions of the circumstances and surroundings in which he found Constanze, and especially with the added insights and intuitions of Mary Novello as she recorded the same events, do release the most vivid portrait of Constanze the woman.

On the steep climb up to the Nonnberggasse house, Novello was already digging into his superlatives: 'The road leading to the House is of the most uncommon and picturesque description, and the House itself is placed in one of the most exquisite spots I ever saw.' And, as Mary Novello recorded, the house itself was unassuming but elegant and comfortable: 'The apartments, like most foreign ones, are not encumbered with furniture and the room she received us in opened to a cabinet which contained her bed, but it was tastefully covered with a bright green counterpane forming a nice unison with some flowers round the room.' These flowers almost certainly came from Constanze's garden, which she loved, and which Mary Novello described after their next visit: 'She was in her garden, which is beautifully situated halfway up the mountain and full of flowers, with Vines trellised up the sides and several seats which command the most delightful view perhaps in the world – the fine town, Palace and church to the left, the mountains covered with snows before and the Salzach river flowing beneath in a beautiful Valley.' And on the third day, when the Novellos and Constanze met in the town, Constanze brought Mary 'a beautiful bouquet of flowers out of her garden'. Within the house, the walls of Constanze's rooms were hung with the Mozart family portraits, as Vincent Novello recorded:

> Over the sofa, the one containing Mozart and his sister playing a Duett with the father sitting down and the Mother's portrait in a picture frame, over that the Portrait of her second Husband Mr von Nissen. In the other Room, the portrait of Mozart as a Boy with an embroidered waist and sword, and the picture of his two Sons in a very affectionate and graceful attitude as if they were fondly attached to each other . . . By far the best likeness of him in [Madame] Nissen's opinion the painting in oils done by the Husband of Madame Lange (the eldest sister of Mrs Nissen) from which the portrait of Mozart contained in her Biography – is unfinished but admirably done . . . in a wooden case as if it had been travelling.

That hauntingly unfinished Lange portrait captivated Mary too: 'the forehead is high and ample in the extreme, full of genius, the mouth of sweetness and beauty, both this latter feature and the nose are exaggerated in the engraving, they are much more delicate in the painting . . . Mozart had very delicate hands.'

As for Constanze herself, Vincent Novello attempted to be dispassionate in his description of her, but again the high emotion of the occasion rather overtook him:

> In her youth her Eyes must have been very brilliant and are still fine. Her face does not resemble the portrait given of her in the Biography. It is thin and has the traces of great care and anxiety in it, but when her features relax into a smile, the expression is a remarkably pleasant one. She is of a rather small stature, slim figure, and looks much younger than what I expected to find her. Her voice is low and gentle, her manners well-bred and prepossessing, unconstrained like a person who has lived much in society and seen a good deal of the world, and the way in which she spoke of her illustrious Husband (though not quite so enthusiastic as I should have expected in one 'so near and dear' to him) was tender and affectionate, and I could perceive a little tremor in

her voice whilst she was looking with me at his portrait and on two or three occasions when she was alluding to some of the last years of his Life, which was not the less affecting or pathetic, from its being involuntary, unobtrusive and partly repressed. Nothing could be more kind, friendly and even cordial than her behaviour to me during the whole visit. Altogether this Lady is, to me, one of the most interesting Persons now in existence.

Mary Novello, too, was overwhelmed to meet Constanze:

> When I first entered I was so overcome with various emotions that I could do nothing but weep and embrace her. She seemed also quite affected and said repeatedly in French 'oh quel bonheur pour moi, de voir les enthousiastes pour mon Mozart'. She speaks French fluently though with a German accent, in Italian she thinks better but as I do not converse in that language she politely continued in French. She is completely a well bred Lady, and though no remains of beauty appear except in her eyes such as the engraving prefixed to her biography of Mozart would indicate, yet she keeps her figure and a certain air, well, for a woman of her age, which I suppose must be sixty-five. [She was in fact sixty-seven.]

In the course of their several conversations, the Novellos and Constanze covered much ground, familiar territory of course to Constanze, for it can by no means have been the first time that she had been subjected to this sort of questioning. But occasionally her own affectionate insights into the behaviour and personality of her first husband, and into their life together, brought delightful new shine to a well-worn surface. They were discussing Mozart's compositional procedure, for instance, as Mary reported:

> When some grand conception was working in his brain he was purely abstracted, walked about the apartment and knew not what was passing around, but when once arranged in his mind, he needed no Piano Forte but would take music paper and whilst he wrote would say to her, 'Now, my dear wife, have the goodness to repeat what has been talked of', and her conversation never

interrupted him, he wrote on, 'which is more', she added, 'than I can do with the commonest letter'.

The Novellos found Constanze to have extremely acute knowledge of Mozart's music: she knew the operas by heart, and had often sung parts of them with and for Mozart; and she could certainly pass judgement on some truly awful performances that she had heard ('so very unsatisfactory that she could hardly recognize it as the composition of Mozart'). But listening to his music could still upset her. She confided to Mary Novello that she 'could not bear to hear either the Requiem or "Idomeneo" performed, the last time she heard "Don Giovanni", she was not calm for a fortnight afterwards'. Constanze told the Novellos that she thought Mozart's real cause of death was, quite simply, overwork, especially as he often composed through the night. But this unhappy memory was turned, by Constanze and her son, into a sweet revelation of Constanze's own nocturnal habits, as Mary Novello recorded: 'He frequently sat up composing until 2 and rose at 4, an exertion which assisted to destroy him. At present she rises at the same hour, but goes to bed, her son says, with the chickens.'

The dynamic and charismatic nature of Constanze in these joyful encounters rather overshadowed the additional presence of young Wolfgang, and of Sophie. But they were noticed. Sophie emerges as a slightly shadowy, quiet figure. At one point on that first visit, Vincent Novello and Wolfgang moved to the piano, where Wolfgang played and Vincent listened. Sophie went with them, preferring to be with the music than to chatter with Constanze and Mary on the other side of the room. And Wolfgang too seems to have been a slightly introverted, even troubled soul, a fact which Mary Novello rather acutely attributed to his carrying the burden of a famous name:

> In the room was . . . her youngest son, who though somewhat resembling his father seems to have no genius, and this feeling perhaps may cast a shade over his countenance rendering it rather heavy, and damps the ardour of his musical works reducing them

to mediocrity; something of this despair of effecting anything worthy of his father's name seemed to hang over him, otherwise he appeared goodnatured, modest, easy of access and frank.

But the Novellos were increasingly impressed by Wolfgang ('he improves much on acquaintance'), and especially by his kindness to his other aunt. For it was he who took them to see the frail Nannerl, and Vincent was 'particularly charmed by the respectful and kind cordiality with which Mozart's son behaved to her, calling her repeatedly "meine liebe Tante" and exerting himself to the utmost to ascertain and fulfil all her wishes'.

Nannerl had finally lost her sight in 1826, though she had still been able to play the piano. But early in 1829, in her seventy-eighth year, her frailty had increased considerably, and she had become bedridden; and, as with all chains of rumour, the reports of these infirmities had become distorted and exaggerated. By the time Vincent Novello heard them in London, poor Nannerl was understood to be not only blind and incapacitated, but effectively destitute too. So the warm-hearted Novello had raised for her the sum of 60 guineas, from seventeen subscribers. This he undertook to deliver himself, on his travels. His list of donors included the organist of St Paul's Cathedral, Thomas Attwood, who had studied composition with Mozart in Vienna for eighteen months in his early twenties, the composer Ignaz Moscheles, the pianist Cipriani Potter, the publisher J. B. Cramer, and the harp-maker and great friend of Beethoven, J. A. Stumpff. (Stumpff corresponded from time to time with Constanze, and indeed when the Novellos returned to London, they carried a letter to him from her.) Novello also had it in mind to mount a concert in London for the benefit of 'Madame von Sonnenburg'.

It is no doubt fortunate that Constanze managed to intercept some of the Novellos' misconceptions before they themselves met Nannerl. On their first afternoon in Salzburg, Constanze gently explained that her 'belle-soeur' could not enjoy the pleasure of actually seeing them when they presented her with their gift. She also made it clear that although Nannerl was infirm, she did not require charity. The Novellos learned of Nannerl's refusing André's offer of the profits from the Requiem scores, because she 'would not be made the subject of public observation'. And, Vincent Novello added, 'Madame Nissen thinks she would *not* like a concert to be given for her.' So Constanze had mercifully cut that one off at the pass. She had also signed the receipt for the 60 guineas on Nannerl's behalf, in order to save her any embarrassment. It is even possible that Constanze had actually contrived to postpone the Novellos' calling on Nannerl, in order to prepare the scene for her visitors. Nannerl still had her pride, and Constanze was especially sensitive to it.

Poor Nannerl was indeed 'blind, languid, exhausted, feeble and nearly speechless' when young Wolfgang took the Novellos to see her the following day. But she knew they were coming, and was by now extremely anxious not to miss them. She had spent a restless night worrying, and apologized profusely that she had not been able to receive them when they had first called. The Novellos were most moved by Nannerl's state, described with compassion by Mary:

> She is quite blind but suffers no pain, hers is entirely a decay of nature. She remains in bed like a person ready for the death stroke and will probably expire in her sleep. Her countenance, though much changed, even rather ugly, has something resembling her portrait. She is very fair and has most delicate hands. Like most blind people she is always alive to touch and kept our hands locked in hers, asking which was *der Herr* and which Madame, grieved very much that we could not speak German, 'kann nichts Deutsch'. Her voice is scarcely intelligible it is so low.

But Nannerl thanked them graciously for her 'cadeau', and removed any potential embarrassment by 'conceiving it was sent for her approaching name's day the 26th – the feast of St Anne'. The Novellos also discovered that, far from being penniless, Nannerl was attended by a servant who lived in the apartment with her,

ministering to her every need. This was one Joseph Metzger, whose
duties included those of a secretary, for it was he who wrote on her
behalf to thank Novello and his fellow subscribers for their gift.
And, as in Constanze's houses, on the walls there were family portraits, which Nannerl was especially keen for her nephew to show
her visitors, and other paintings too, as Vincent Novello noted ('I
particularly noticed those of Vandyke and Rembrandt'). So any
lingering notion of Nannerl's destitution was thoroughly dispelled
as soon as the Novellos entered her apartment.

They did not stay long with Nannerl, but did inspect, and indeed
play, her 'instrument on which she had often played Duetts with her
Brother'. Nannerl told the Nissens that, having not touched it since
she took to her bed, she had just two days previously tried to play
again, only to discover that her left hand did not function at all. The
last pieces she had actually managed, six months earlier, were little
excerpts from *Die Zauberflöte* ('Das klinget so herrlich'), and
Don Giovanni (the minuet). The reverential Vincent Novello
commented, 'This to me was a most touching proof of her continued sisterly attachment to him to the last.' (It was also, of course,
a definition of who Nannerl was, an almost territorial claim of identity with the name and the music of her brother.) The Novellos
took their tender parting: 'I fear she cannot continue much longer
in her present exhausted state [continued Vincent] – but whenever
the hour arrives which no one living can ultimately avoid, I can
only hope that it will not be attended with the least suffering, and
that she will calmly cease to breathe as if she were merely sinking
into a tranquil sleep.'

Vincent and Mary Novello tore themselves away from Salzburg
and continued on to Vienna, where they spent several days in more
Mozartian research. They were considerably fortified by intro-
ductory letters given to them by the willing Wolfgang, and had
fascinating meetings with, among others, the Abbé Stadler and
Joseph Eybler. And Mary Novello also met Constanze's other
sister, the now sixty-nine-year-old Aloysia. This fascinating
encounter came about because Thomas Attwood in London had

given them a letter for her – a fact which had occasioned a small
flash of irritation in Constanze when they had told her of this, for
Attwood had sent no message to her. Sure enough, Aloysia turned
up on the Novellos' doorstep. Vincent must have been out at the
time, for only Mary recorded their meeting. She found her to be 'a
very pleasant woman but broken by misfortune – she is parted from
her husband who allows her so little that she is obliged to give
lessons which at her age she finds a great hardship'. Mary cannily
used the occasion to seek Aloysia's advice on singing teachers for
her daughter Clara in Paris, and elicited some quite forthright
opinions: 'she declares that most of the Italian singers cannot read
the music they sing – nature has done much for them in a voice but
that they are quite ignorant of the science'. (As a good pianist and
all-round musician herself, Aloysia would indeed have been
exasperated by such deficiencies.) Aloysia also professed great
fondness for young Wolfgang, whom she loved 'better even than
her own children'. And at last the two women entered the area that
Mary will have been most anxious to explore:

> She told me Mozart always loved her until the day of his death,
> which to speak candidly she fears had occasioned a slight jealousy
> on the part of her sister. I asked her why she refused him, she
> could not tell, the fathers were both agreed but she could not love
> him at the time, she was not capable of appreciating his talent and
> his amiable character, but afterwards she much regretted it. She
> spoke of him with great tenderness and regret, as of her sister
> whose understanding she thinks very superior.

So, for all her professional feistiness, poor Aloysia now emerges
as a rather sad woman with real bitterness in her memories. She had
chosen to blot out any recollection of the considerable parental
opposition to her liaison with Mozart, preferring instead to retain a
romantic picture of star-crossed lovers. And although she and her
sisters were still close, the 'slight jealousy' in Constanze to which
she referred could perhaps more truthfully have been applied to
herself. When she politely expressed her regret to Mary that she

had never been to London, she actually blamed Constanze: 'she was much pressed by the English when at Hamburg to come, but had no one to go with, as Mme Mozart left her to present the Requiem to the King of Prussia'. It was Constanze who after all had had not one but two loving marriages, whereas her own had failed. Constanze was now living in extreme comfort while she was struggling at the edge of poverty. And ultimately, of course, it was Constanze's name, not hers, that would for ever be joined with that of Mozart. Like so many of her generation and kind, Aloysia had once received tumultuous applause in the great opera houses and concert halls of Europe, and now faced only bleakness and hardship.

As the Novellos headed back to London, they again stopped in Salzburg. By delightful chance, the first person they met was young Wolfgang, at the offices of the Diligence coach company as he was about to set off on a journey to the Tyrol. He informed them that Nannerl was in 'the same state of languor', but that his mother was 'in excellent health as usual'. They did not disturb Nannerl when they found her to be sleeping peacefully, but later that day did climb the hill to the Nonnberggasse house to call on Constanze and Sophie. To their dismay, Constanze was out – in fact herself on a vigilant visit to Nannerl. But Sophie pressed them to stay and wait for her return, and while they did so she opened up with her own Mozartian reminiscences. (The Novellos had rather ignored her two weeks earlier.) What both Vincent and Mary Novello wrote down was an account of Mozart's last days virtually identical to that which Sophie had sent to Nissen for the biography, almost as if the very process of composing it for her brother-in-law had provided her with a script from which she could easily satisfy the questioning of other enquirers. This was probably not the first time that Sophie had divulged her crucial role in Mozart's final illness, and it certainly had its effect on her English visitors. 'She also told me *that Mozart had died in HER arms*,' gasped Mary. With touching and commendable loyalty to her own husband, Sophie then showed the Novellos a Mass by Jakob Haibl, and Vincent politely praised it. Constanze eventually arrived home, and was genuinely delighted to find the Novellos there. Another afternoon of Mozartian conversation and genuine friendship was passed. And later that evening Constanze and Sophie surprised the Novellos by turning up at their inn. 'Both she and her sister came to us like old friends; placed themselves by our side at table, and paid us the compliment of partaking of our little Meal, without the least formality, and just as if they wished to convince us that they felt as much at home with us as at their own house.'

After supper the gallant Vincent insisted on walking the women home for their final farewell, climbing back up the hill to the little street past the nunnery. He was ecstatic: the moon was full, the countryside that it now so mysteriously revealed was exquisite, and Mozart's widow was on his arm. And Constanze too enjoyed the gentle companionship of the civilized Englishman of whom she had so quickly become fond, and confided to him her deepest anxieties about her Wolfgang and his Polish 'mistress'. Vincent was so touched by this moonlit, post-prandial baring of Constanze's soul that he did not even share its revelations with his wife.

~

ON 10 OCTOBER 1829, just over two months after the Novellos' visit, Nannerl died. She was seventy-eight years old. Although she must at times have felt, rightly, that her achievements as a musician represented a mere fraction of her potential, the life of Nannerl Mozart remains to this day one of the most fascinating for a woman of her time. Her earliest years were of an excitement, glamour, drama, effort and achievement that very few children of any period can possibly know. Her father immediately recognized her considerable gifts, and taught her superb technique at the keyboard, together with sight-reading and memory skills. Her younger brother was soon to outshine her, but their childhood was one of happily shared experiences and games, most of them involving the process of making music together. Nannerl inevitably found it a little difficult when attention was increasingly focused on Wolfgang, but she never let her flashes of sibling jealousy destroy the joy

and pride that she felt in his brilliance, and soon she adapted to glid-
ing along in his slipstream: 'I am only my brother's pupil,' she
would modestly declare.

The door to this wonderland was slammed in her face in her
late teens. As her father and brother strode happily off to Italy,
repeatedly and for several months at a time, Nannerl was suddenly
excluded from the very activities that had been her lifeblood. Her
joy in her brother's development was shifted: where she had been a
participant in it, she was now to be an observer. And despite the
fact that other girls and women of her own age in Salzburg were
pursuing exciting musical paths, her dictatorial father never even
contemplated the notion that she too might have a performing
career. She would have grown close to her mother as they fended
for themselves in Salzburg. But the tragic loss of Maria Anna, on
yet another trip from which Nannerl was barred, was devastating
for her. For a while she assumed the role of her mother in the
Tanzmeisterhaus, taking domestic responsibility for Leopold and
Wolfgang; and her gifts as a chamber musician flourished within
those walls, affording great pleasure to her listeners, her colleagues
and herself. But after the final departure of Wolfgang from
Salzburg, her involvement in his continued blossoming took yet
another step back. Although she still played regularly and with
great pleasure, her life at the beck and call of her domineering
father became increasingly claustrophobic.

Nannerl's marriage in her mid-thirties, to a selfish widower
several years her senior, does have the stamp of desperation. She
entered into it in the full knowledge that conjugal gains would be
achieved only with musical sacrifices, but even so she was probably
startled to discover the bitter reality of her decision. Her years in St
Gilgen constituted another shock to her artistic system: she could
not play at all, and she was now utterly severed from the dazzling
world of her brother. But while she did experience a kind of
bereavement for the loss of her playing days, she duly became a
wife, mother and stepmother, and stuck to this role loyally and
doggedly; she continued her duties as a daughter too, until

Leopold's death. But her relationship with her own children was complicated. Leopold had effectively confiscated her firstborn son in the most important early part of his life, and in due course she tragically lost both her daughters. She must have known the true meaning of loneliness.

After the death of her husband, Nannerl quickly returned 'home', as it must have felt, to Salzburg, and there at last, in her quiet widowhood, she seems to have discovered a sense of peace. She was cooperative with biographers and publishers, and whole-heartedly supportive of the Nissens' huge project, for in adding her weight to it she relived, and therefore enjoyed all over again, the thrills of her childhood. She suffered cruelly from the debilities of age (whereas, in her childhood, she had been hailed as a 'prodigy of nature', in her final years she was described as a 'decay of nature'), but evidently she bore these with dignity and grace. The arrival of her nephew Wolfgang, in her late life, brought her a new conduit for love and a reconciliation with her past, and perhaps, too, a roundness to her life as she entered her final sleep.

~

As INSTRUCTED IN the codicil to her will, Nannerl was buried in the churchyard of St Peter's Abbey, around the corner from her apartment, rather than in the cemetery of St Sebastian on the other side of the river, with the rest of her family. Her son Leopold inherited all her possessions, with the exception of a few named bequests to her stepgrandchildren and her servants. But Nannerl did specify that any items that had come from the Mozart side of the family, as opposed to the Berchtolds', should be returned to the next genera-tion of Mozarts after Leopold's death. As it happened, Leopold passed all these items straight on to Constanze and her sons; and, while he was about it, ordered a copy of the Nissen biography from her, before he faded back into Mozartian obscurity. The younger generation was certainly behaving with perfect propriety.

In Constanze's own final years, the marketing of the biography became one of her main preoccupations. She kept a record of all her correspondence relating to its sales and distribution, her *Tagebuch meines Brief Wechsels in Betref der Mozartischen Biographie*. In it she noted every transaction between 1828, when advance notices of the biography's imminent publication first appeared, and 1837. Her chief collaborators in this business partnership were Breitkopf and Härtel in Leipzig, Feuerstein in Pirna, André in Offenbach, and, a little surprisingly, for he was a big rival of Constanze's recently deceased cousin Carl Maria von Weber, Gaspare Spontini in Berlin. She also recorded in her *Tagebuch* her dealings with lawyers in Copenhagen on matters relating both to Nissen's estate and to her own will, which she regularly revised; and with her bankers, Schuller & Co., in Vienna. Constanze had become a shrewd businesswoman, determined, tenacious and razor-sharp.

But her *Tagebuch* included details of the rest of her correspondence too. Her letters to various friends and acquaintances across Europe appear there, including Nissen's relations (her 'cousins') in Denmark, her niece Josefa Hönig (daughter of her late sister Josefa) and her husband Carl. (Both these young people would in fact predecease her, in the early 1830s.) And of course there were letters to and from her immediate family. Carl and Wolfgang were both in regular contact with Constanze, and like all mothers she loved to hear from them: on 4 September 1831 she noted with delight, 'Since 14 June I have had 11 letters from Wolfgang, the dear boy!'[34] But she continued to worry about her younger son. She periodically sent him small sums of money, and was much happier about him after 1838 when at last he left Lemberg (still with Josephine and her husband) and moved to Vienna. There, at least, his talents 'might be better known and appreciated', as she had confided to Vincent Novello. She was less worried about Carl, securely employed as he was in Milan, and comfortable with his life as an Italian. But she learned with genuine distress, in March 1833, of the death of 'his Constanza', from a malignant growth, and she wrote to him immediately to pour out her sympathies. For here was Carl's other life. He too had evidently had an illicit relationship, and produced an illegitimate daughter whom he had named after his mother. If the girl's death was something Carl could share with Constanze, then she must have known about her granddaughter, and may even have met her on her visit to Milan. Meanwhile, both Carl and Wolfgang continued to visit their mother, Wolfgang rather more often than his brother. And indeed, the two sons of Mozart were also acquiring an important status in Salzburg, as the town at last began to plan a permanent foundation and memorial in the name of their father. They had even begun to make their own friends there.

The other members of Constanze's family who received care and assistance from her were her two surviving sisters. Sophie of course lived with her, and they looked after each other. And Aloysia too, struggling as she was in Vienna, was increasingly supported by her. In August 1830 Aloysia came to Salzburg for a short visit, and from November that year there are several payments to her recorded in Constanze's *Tagebuch*. Some of these subsidies, generally of 12 florins each, went through Constanze's bank in Vienna, but most of them were simply enclosed in letters. In 1831 Aloysia wrote to tell her sisters that her former husband, Joseph Lange, had died. This would have affected Constanze, not only for the memory of happy times that she and Aloysia and their husbands had shared nearly fifty years earlier, but also because of Lange's unfinished but deeply treasured portrait of Mozart that Constanze still had in her possession. In spite of Constanze's regular contributions to Aloysia's living expenses, there was apparently some further crisis in July 1832, and Aloysia wrote her sister a long letter appealing for more help, which Constanze immediately supplied. By the middle of the decade, it was decided that Aloysia too should come and live permanently in Salzburg, in close proximity to her sisters. Around 1835, she moved into an apartment in what is now the Dreifaltigkeitsgasse, just round the corner from the Tanzmeisterhaus. It is likely that, here too, family connections were instrumental in finding her this home, for one of Nannerl's stepsons, Karl Joseph Franz Berchtold, lived in the same building.

So now all three surviving Weber sisters were gathered in the town of Mozart's birth, drawn there by their intimate connection with his life and his music, and with one another. Aloysia was the first to go: she died on 8 June 1839, at the age of seventy-nine, and so would probably have been unaware of the by now accelerating interest in establishing the foundation in Mozart's name. The year 1841 would be the fiftieth anniversary of his death, and Salzburg was to mark it, and finally make its peace with him, by founding a conservatory, to be known as the Dommusikverein and Mozarteum, and by erecting a monument to him in the very heart of the town. Constanze's own robust health was now declining: the old injury to her foot had returned to trouble her, and she was plagued by gout. So she and Sophie abandoned their beloved Nonnberggasse house, and settled together in Michaelsplatz. It was in the centre of this square that the statue of Mozart was to be erected, and Constanze would be able to see it from her new lodging. She became deeply involved in the setting up of the Mozarteum, and tried hard to get Wolfgang appointed as its director. He was not in fact given the job, though he was tactfully made an 'honorary Kapellmeister'; but Alois Taux, who did become head of the conservatory, was a close friend to Constanze and to both her sons for the rest of their lives. As the festivities were planned for the unveiling of the monument and the commemoration of the half-centenary, Taux kept all the family informed. Wolfgang in particular was to play an active part in the music-making surrounding the events.

As it happened, these festivities had to be delayed for a year, because the monument to Mozart, by Ludwig Schwannthaler in Munich, was not ready. The unveiling of the statue, that resides to this day in the renamed Mozartplatz, eventually took place in September 1842. Carl and Wolfgang both came to Salzburg for the celebrations, and Wolfgang was indeed a prominent participant, conducting an anthem that he himself had put together from sections of *La clemenza di Tito* (to his own text), and playing his father's D minor piano concerto. Two thousand people were in the audience, many of whom had come from all corners of the world. At a certain point, according to one visitor, the proceedings were dramatically interrupted by the appearance of a 'very tall, thin and eccentric-looking woman, who at once exclaimed, as though addressing an audience, "Ich bin die erste Pamina" [I am the first Pamina] . . . This lady had ostensibly come from Vienna to join in our homage.'[35]

How appropriate it was that at this final, official reconciliation of Mozart with his birthplace, there should be a representative from his legions of beloved and talented women performers. And how appropriate too, perhaps, that it should be Anna Gottlieb, who shared his middle name, and who had created both the youngest and then the last of his great stage women. Sophie, who was also present, would of course have remembered her. And it is to be hoped that these women rejoiced in their reunion, and shared memories and reminiscences as they sat in Sophie's apartment, overlooking the newly named Mozartplatz.

But Constanze was not there. She had died six months earlier, on 6 March 1842, at 3.45 in the morning. She was eighty years old. The woman who had brought the greatest human joy to Mozart had outlived him by more than half a century.

~

No part of Constanze's long life had ever been tinged with the ordinary. From her earliest years, she and her sisters had stood out from the crowd. Their childhood was not without its upheavals and dramas: before Constanze reached adulthood she experienced the harsh tragedy of bereavement three times, with the death of her two brothers, and then, when she was seventeen, of her father. But the close-knit family was loving and lively, and especially united by the musical gifts they all shared. Not unlike the Brontë sisters, Josefa, Aloysia, Constanze and Sophie were different from other children around them precisely because of their creative and artistic talents. Constanze would have been somewhat over-shadowed by her two elder sisters, and especially by the family's high achiever, Aloysia. Glamorous, successful, extraordinarily gifted as an all-round musician, and attractive to all men, Aloysia's every prodigious development dictated the movements of the entire Weber family. Her appointment to Vienna in 1779, and then her marriage to one of the most acclaimed and high-profile actors in the city, provided great excitement for her sisters. But the theatrical personality of Joseph Lange was nothing compared to that of Mozart, the veritable fireball of musical genius that stormed their habitat and swept Constanze away as his bride.

The marriage between Mozart and Constanze has been some-what maligned, ridiculed and slandered by the cruel tongues of posterity. Constanze in particular has been seen as woefully inad-equate as the partner to a genius, and decried as a wife whose influence was demeaning, distracting and ultimately destructive. But on its own terms — that is, on their terms — the marriage was a great success. Life with Constanze was never dull. She was essen-tially a fun-loving companion, totally compatible with Wolfgang's physical needs, supportive, intelligent, and encouraging of all his activities. While nobody could possibly have been equal to his unique musicianship, Constanze did possess a discerning and edu-cated understanding of their art: according to Aloysia's generous statement to Mary Novello, it was superior to her own and prob-ably therefore to that of the rest of the Weber family. When Constanze took control (rather late, admittedly) of the business side of their married life, she did turn it around; and that early apprenticeship in financial organization stood her in great stead for her later years. But most important of all, Mozart adored Constanze unreservedly. Theirs was a marriage of immense devotion and concord, and its early truncation was brutal.

In her immediate bereavement Constanze discovered a particu-larly driven kind of energy as she sought to provide for her sons and herself. Carl and young Wolfgang were then somewhat side-lined, as Constanze's obsession with maintaining the Mozart flame grew. As a mother to small boys, therefore, she was not especially close, and though she planned her sons' education with the greatest care, she did tend to leave them to their own devices. But they never seemed to hold this against her: rather in the manner of most children sent away to boarding school, they took it all in their stride. In marked contrast to the relationship between Leopold and Wolfgang, that between Constanze and her sons was never intricate. Carl and young Wolfgang were always part of her life, but not especially central to it.

Constanze was indeed fortunate to sail into the safe harbour that was Georg Nissen. This intelligent and decent man, completely different temperamentally from Mozart, was steady, dependable and safe. And, like Mozart, he adored Constanze. With him she was entirely willing to escape from the mainstream of European life, and to go and live in Copenhagen for a long decade. She acquired a wisdom and maturity through her second marriage, and a general deepening of her innate characteristics. Through Nissen, probably, she developed her considerable business skills, becoming tirelessly vigilant in her affairs, and therefore extremely successful. But she was always generous with the monies that she acquired late in life, and neglected no opportunity to provide care and assistance for one or other of her family.

It was this propensity for warmth and care that had always characterized all of the Weber sisters, Mozart's 'other' family. It kept them in close contact throughout their lives: they supported one another at times of crisis, but simply enjoyed too the very pleasure of one another's company. And in their final years they were brought together again to exercise their loving care on a permanent basis. They were indeed fortunate to have one another's support. And Constanze, who had in childhood been less prominent, unquestionably ended up as the overseer and provider, and effectively therefore as the head of the family.

∼

THE PUBLISHED ANNOUNCEMENT of Constanze's death had been in Sophie's name. Neither of her sons was present at her funeral. She was buried beside Georg Nissen in the Mozart family grave, in the churchyard of St Sebastian. Her considerable estate was divided between Carl and Wolfgang; but there was also generous provision

for Sophie – of furnishings, clothes and linen in addition to money
– and there were smaller gifts too for individuals. Fifty years after
the death of her first husband, it was he who was magnificently providing for the descendants of both their families.

But there were not to be any more of them. Wolfgang died just
two years after his mother, on 29 July 1844, at the age of fifty-three.
He bequeathed everything to his beloved Josephine, to whom he
had remained passionately devoted all his life, and she returned all
the Mozart items and memorabilia – sheet music, manuscripts and
letters, portraits, a piano – to the Mozarteum. Sophie died on 26
October 1846, aged eighty-three. And Carl resisted all pressure to
come and live permanently in Salzburg (Taux at the Mozarteum
tried repeatedly to lure him there), preferring instead to remain in
Italy. In his seventy-second year, he did travel once more to
Salzburg, to join in the Mozart Centenary celebrations in 1856. But
in general he shunned the limelight, as he always had: Constanze
had been right to shield him from it when he was a child. He
returned to Italy, dividing his life between a modest summer house
in the village of Caversaccio (his version of the Nonnberggasse
house) and his apartment in Milan, where he, and the Mozart line,
died on 2 November 1858.

~

IN THE CEMETERY of St Sebastian in Salzburg, no inscribed stone
marks the graves of Aloysia or Sophie. But Constanze's final
resting-place is shared with five others, whose names are all tastefully displayed on three separate stones. These six cohabitants were
assembled, like a chaotic game of Mozartian 'Consequences', over
four generations. United for ever in stone are Mozart's grandmother Eva Rosina, his father Leopold, his wife's aunt Genoveva,
his niece Jeanette, his wife's second husband Georg Nissen, and, in
pride of place above them all, his beloved wife Constanze. How
uneasy a social gathering that might have constituted, had they all
chanced to come together in the living world. But the headstones
are eloquent too of absentees. There is no Maria Anna, whose

remains in Paris have long since been raked over. There is no Nannerl, though she is safely and independently immortalized in her grave in St Peter's, on the other side of Salzburg. Most poignant of all, there is no Wolfgang Amadeus Mozart.

Postlude

MY GREAT-GRANDFATHER used to say to his wife, my great-grand-mother, who in turn told her daughter, my grandmother, who reported it to her daughter, my mother, who used to remind her daughter, my own sister, that to talk well and eloquently was a very great art, but that an equally great one was to know the right moment to stop. So I shall follow the advice of my sister, thanks to our mother, grandmother and great-grandmother, and put a stop not only to my moral digression, but to my whole letter.

Mozart to Gottfried von Jacquin, 4 November 1787

Notes and Sources

L numbers refer to the letters published in *The Letters of Mozart and his Family*, ed. Emily Anderson. 3rd edition (Macmillan, 1985). (Some have had minor adjustments to the translation.) Letters not included in Anderson's edition have been directly translated from the German collection: *Mozart, Briefe und Aufzeichnungen*, ed. W. A. Bauer et al. (Deutsch and Eibl, 1962–1975) (referred to as *Briefe*).

Deutsch = O. E. Deutsch, *Mozart, Die Dokumente seines Lebens* (A. & C. Black Ltd, 1965) (English translation by E. Blom, P. Branscombe and J. Noble: *Mozart, A Documentary Biography*, 1966).

WM = Wolfgang	N = Nannerl
LM = Leopold	C = Constanze
MA = Maria Anna	'B' = the 'Bäsle'

Mozart's Family

1. Full quotation in Solomon, p. 23.
2. This reference to their impoverished union appeared in a letter LM wrote on their twenty-fifth wedding anniversary: L162, LM to MA, 21 November 1772.
3. Quoted in Deutsch, p. 9.
4. N's memoir, spring 1792, quoted *ibid.*, pp. 454–62.
5. Schachtner's memoir, in a letter to N, 24 April 1792, quoted *ibid.*, pp. 451–4.
6. N's memoir, *ibid.*
7. L2, LM to Hagenauer, 16 October 1762.
8. Quoted in Deutsch, p. 17.
9. L12, LM to Hagenauer, 11 July 1763.
10. L16, LM to Hagenauer, 20 August 1763.
11. From N's travel diary, *Briefe* 77.

12. L466, WM to the Baroness von Waldstätten, 28 September 1782.

13. L28, LM to Hagenauer, 8 June 1764.

14. From N's travel diary, *Briefe* 85.

15. Published in *Allgemeine Musikalische Zeitung*, Leipzig, 22 January 1800; reproduced in Deutsch, p. 493.

16. L31, LM to Hagenauer, 13 September 1764.

17. L39, LM to Hagenauer, 5 November 1765.

18. N's memoir, Deutsch, p. 457.

19. From Grimm's *Correspondance Littéraire*, 15 July 1766; quoted in *ibid.*, p. 56.

20. *Ibid.*, p. 57.

21. Quoted in Gutman, p. 207.

22. Quoted in Deutsch, pp. 67–9.

23. N's memoir, *ibid.*, p. 458.

24. L55, LM to Hagenauer, 3 February 1768.

25. L54, LM to Hagenauer, 23 January 1768.

26. *Opera buffa*: term used to describe Italian comic operas with recitative as opposed to spoken dialogue.

27. N's memoir, Deutsch, p. 458.

28. L106a, WM to N, 4 August 1770.

29. N's memoir, Deutsch, pp. 458ff, from which all the following quotations have been taken.

30. L71b, WM to N, 14 December 1769.

31. L73, LM to MA, 17 December 1769.

32. L77, LM to MA, 26 January 1770.

33. L99, LM to MA, 27 June 1770.

34. L72, LM to MA, 15 December 1769.

35. L78, LM to MA, 3 February 1770.

36. L79, LM to MA, 10 February 1770.

37. L123, LM to MA, 1 December 1770.

38. L107, LM to MA, 11 August 1770.

39. L110, LM to MA, 1 September 1770.

40. L91, LM to MA, 2 May 1770.

41. L87, LM to MA, 14 April 1770.

42. L125, LM to MA, 15 December 1770.

43. L98a, WM to N, 16 June 1770.

44. For example, L102a, WM to N, 7 July 1770 (retranslated), *et passim*.

45. L92a, WM to N, 19 May 1770.

46. L95a, WM to N, 29 May 1770.

47. L89, WM to N, 25 April 1770.

48. L87a, WM to MA and N, 14 April 1770.
49. L84a, WM to N, 24 March 1770.
50. L92a, WM to N, 19 May 1770.
51. L106a, WM to N, 4 August 1770.
52. L133a, WM to N, 20 February 1771.
53. L136, LM to MA, 18 March 1771.
54. N's memoir, Deutsch, p. 460.
55. L140a, WM to N, 24 August 1771.
56. L141a, WM to N, 31 August 1771.
57. L148, LM to MA, 19 October 1771.
58. L146, LM to MA, 5 October 1771.
59. L149, LM to MA, 26 October 1771.
60. L144a, WM to N, 21 September 1771.
61. L146a, WM to N, 5 October 1771.
62. L140a, WM to N, 24 August 1771.
63. L139a, WM to N, 18 August 1771.
64. L138, LM to MA, 16 August 1771.
65. Quoted in Deutsch, p. 138.
66. L155, LM to MA, 8 December 1771.
67. L161, LM to MA, 14 November 1772.
68. L162, LM to MA, 21 November 1772.
69. L162a, WM to N, 21 November 1772.
70. L164a, WM to N, 5 December 1772.
71. L170a, WM to N, 16 January 1773.
72. L166a, WM to N, 18 December 1772.
73. L160, WM to MA, 7 November 1772.
74. L165, LM to MA, 12 December 1772.
75. N's memoir, Deutsch, p. 461.
76. L180, LM to MA, 21 August 1773.
77. L181, LM to MA, 25 August 1773.
78. L178, LM to MA, 12 August 1773.
79. L179a, WM to N, 14 August 1773.
80. L178a, WM to N, 12 August 1773.
81. L191a, WM to N, 16 December 1774.
82. L192, LM to MA, 21 December 1774.
83. L194, LM to MA, 30 December 1774.
84. L195, LM to MA, 5 January 1775.
85. L202a, LM to MA, end February 1775.
86. L197, WM to MA, 14 January 1775.
87. *Nannerl Mozarts Tagebuchblätter*, ed. W. Hummel (Salzburg, 1958).

88. L205, WM to Padre Martini, 4 September 1776.
89. L206, WM to Archbishop Hieronymus Colloredo, 1 August 1777.
90. Deutsch, p. 163.
91. Quoted by LM in L211, LM to MA and WM, 28 September 1777.
92. L208, LM to MA and WM, 25 September 1777.
93. L209a, MA to LM, 26 September 1777.
94. L209, WM to LM, 26 September 1777.
95. L207, WM to LM, 23 September 1777.
96. L209a, MA to LM, 26 September 1777.
97. L211a, N to MA and WM, 29 September 1777.
98. L216a, N to MA and WM, 5 [6] October 1777.
99. L216, LM to MA and WM, 6 October 1777.
100. L222, LM to WM, 15 October 1777.
101. L226, LM to WM, 18 October 1777.
102. L230a, LM to MA and WM, 27 October 1777.
103. L213, LM to WM, 30 September 1777.
104. *Ibid.*
105. L219, WM to LM, 11 October 1777.
106. L219a, MA to LM, 11 October 1777.
107. L219b, WM to LM, 11 October 1777.
108. L219c, MA to LM, 11 October 1777.
109. L224, WM to LM, 17 October 1777.
110. L221c, MA to LM, 14 October 1777.
111. L228a, MA to LM, 23 October 1777.
112. L230, N to MA and WM, 27 October 1777.
113. L224a, 'B' to LM, 16 October 1777.
114. L226b, LM to WM, 20 October 1777.
115. L227, LM to WM, 23 October 1777 .
116. L231, LM to WM, 29 October 1777.
117. *Ibid.*
118. L232a, WM to LM, 31 October 1777.
119. L240, LM to WM, 13 November 1777.
120. L235, WM to LM, 4 November 1777.
121. L265a, N to MA and WM, 22 December 1777.
122. L247a, MA to LM, 23 November 1777.
123. L256a, MA to LM, 7 December 1777.
124. L258a, MA to LM, 11 December 1777.
125. *Ibid.*
126. L238, MA to LM, 8 November 1777.
127. L269, MA to LM, 3 January 1778.

128. L242, WM to 'B', 13 November 1777.
129. L254, WM to 'B', 3 December 1777.
130. L242, WM to 'B', 13 November 1777.
131. *Ibid.*
132. L269, MA to LM, 3 January 1778.
133. L267a, MA to LM, 28 December 1777.
134. L268a, N to MA and WM, 29 December 1777.
135. L284a, N to MA and WM, 9 February 1778.
136. L257a, N to MA and WM, 8 December 1777.
137. L272, LM to MA and WM, 12 January 1778.
138. L271, MA to LM, 10 January 1778.
139. L277, LM to WM, 29 January 1778.
140. L282, LM to WM, 5 February 1778.
141. L273a, WM to LM, 17 January 1778.
142 L275, MA to LM, 24 January 1778.
143. *Briefe* 412; L278, WM to MA, 31 January 1778.
144. L281, WM to LM, 4 February 1778.
145. L282, LM to WM, 5 February 1778.
146. L285, LM to WM, 11 February 1778.
147. L288, WM to LM, 19 February 1778.
148. L288a, MA to LM, 19 February 1778.
149. L296a, WM to N, 7 March 1778.
150. L289a, MA to LM, 22 February 1778.
151. L292a, MA to LM, 28 February 1778.
152. L293, WM to 'B', 28 February 1778.
153. L299a, MA to LM, 24 March 1778.
154. L302, LM to MA and WM, 20 April 1778.
155. L301, LM to MA and WM, 6 April 1778.
156. *Ibid.*
157. L300, MA to LM, 5 April 1778.
158. *Ibid.*
159. L303a, MA to LM, 1 May 1778.
160. L305, MA to LM, 14 May 1778.
161. L307, MA to LM, 29 May 1778.
162. L308, LM to MA and WM, 11 June 1778.
163. L309, MA to LM, 12 June 1778.
164. L311, WM to LM, 3 July 1778.
165. L319, WM to LM, 31 July 1778.
166. L311, WM to LM, 3 July 1778.
167. L312, WM to the Abbé Bullinger, 3 July 1778.

168. L315a, WM to LM, 20 July 1778.
169. L315b, WM to N, 20 July 1778.
170. L319a, WM to N, 31 July 1778.
171. L319, WM to LM, 31 July 1778.
172. L333, LM to WM, 24 September 1778.
173. L337, LM to WM, 19 October 1778.
174. L345, WM to LM, 18 December 1778.
175. L348, WM to LM, 29 December 1778.
176. L322, WM to the Abbé Bullinger, 7 August 1778.
177. L354, WM to 'B', 10 May 1779.
178. *Nannerl Mozarts Tagebuchblätter*, p. 44.
179. *Ibid.*, p. 71.
180. L369, LM to WM, 4 December 1780.
181. L357, LM to WM, 11 November 1780.
182. L363, WM to LM, 24 November 1780.
183. L376, WM to LM, 16 December 1780.
184. L387, WM to LM, 1 December, 1780.
185. L366, N to WM, 30 November 1780.
186. L382a, N to WM, 30 December 1780.
187. L359, WM to LM, 15 November 1780.
188. L396, WM to LM, 4 April 1781.
189. L393, WM to LM, 17 March 1781.
190. L409, WM to LM, 9 June 1781.
191. L401, WM to LM, 9 May 1781.
192. L405, WM to LM, 19 May 1781.
193. L415, WM to N, 4 July 1781.
194. L491, WM to LM, 7 June 1783.
195. L415, WM to N, 4 July 1781.
196. L425, WM to N, 19 September 1781.

Mozart's Other Family

1. L281, WM to LM, 4 February 1778.
2. L273a, WM to LM, 17 January 1778.
3. L281, WM to LM, 4 February 1778.
4. L283a, WM to LM, 7 February 1778.
5. L292, WM to LM, 28 February 1778.
6. *Ibid.*
7. L299, WM to LM, 24 March 1778.
8. *Ibid.*

9. L336, WM to LM, 15 October 1778.

10. L318, WM to Aloysia Weber, 30 October 1778.

11. L329, LM to WM, 3 September 1778.

12. L331, WM to LM, 11 September 1778.

13. L333, LM to WM, 24 September 1778.

14. L342, LM to WM, 23 November 1778.

15. Nissen, *Biographie W. A. Mozarts*, pp. 144–5.

16. L348, WM to LM, 29 December 1778.

17. L401, WM to LM, 9 May 1781.

18. L404, WM to LM, 16 May 1781.

19. L405, WM to LM, 19 May 1781.

20. L417, WM to LM, 25 July 1781.

21. L421, WM to LM, 22 August 1781.

22. L405, WM to LM, 18 May 1781.

23. L415, WM to N, 4 July 1781.

24. L418, WM to LM, 1 August 1781.

25. L426, WM to LM, 26 September 1781 .

26. L436, WM to LM, 15 December 1781.

27. L438, WM to LM, 22 December 1781.

28. L447, WM to N, 20 April 1782.

29. L448, WM to C, 29 April 1782.

30. L455, WM to LM, 27 July 1782.

31. L453, WM to LM, 20 July 1782.

32. L455, WM to LM, 27 July 1782.

33. L456, WM to LM, 31 July 1782.

34. L457, WM to the Baroness von Waldstätten, late July/early August 1782.

35. L458, WM to LM, 7 August 1782.

36. *The Travel Diaries of Vincent and Mary Novello*, p. 116.

37. L458, WM to LM, 7 August 1782.

38. L471, WM to LM, 19 October 1782.

39. L473, WM to LM, 13 November 1782.

40. L474, WM to LM, 20 November 1782.

41. L484, WM to LM, 29 March 1783.

42. L489, WM to LM, 7 May 1783.

43. L478*, from Nissen, p. 687.

44. L478, WM to LM, 8 January 1783.

45. L486, WM to LM, 12 April 1783.

46. L488, WM to LM, 3 May 1783.

47. L492, WM to LM, 18 June 1783.

48. L493, WM to LM, 21 June 1783.

49. L495, WM to LM, 5 July 1783.
50. L494, WM to LM, 2 July 1783.
51. *Nannerl Moẓarts Tagebuchblätter*, p. 89.
52. *The Travel Diaries of Vincent and Mary Novello*, p. 113.
53. L477, WM to LM, 4 January 1783.
54. Nissen, p. 476.
55. *The Travel Diaries of Vincent and Mary Novello*, p. 96.
56. L499, WM to LM, 31 October 1783.
57. L501, WM to LM, 10 December 1783.
58. L513, WM to LM, 15 May 1784.
59. L515, WM to LM, 9 June 1784.
60. L256, WM to N, 21 July 1784.
61. *Briefe* 801; L517, WM to N, 18 August 1784.
62. Quoted back at LM by WM in L441, 16 January 1782.
63. L524, LM to N, 21 February 1785.
64. L523, LM to N, 10 February 1785.
65. *Ibid*.
66. *Ibid*.
67. L527, LM to N, 16 April 1785.
68. Quoted in Halliwell, p. 505.
69. L528, WM to Professor Anton Klein, 21 May 1785.
70. L531, LM to N, 3 November 1785.
71. L533, WM to Franz Anton Hoffmeister, 20 November 1785.
72. *Briefe* 881, LM to N, 22 September 1785.
73. *Reminiscences*, p. 128.
74. L471, WM to LM, 19 October 1782.
75. L542, LM to N, 17 November 1786.
76. L543, LM to N, 12 January 1787.
77. *Briefe* 1019; Deutsch, p. 283.
78. L544, WM to Baron Gottfried von Jacquin, 15 January 1787.
79. *Ibid*.
80. L546, WM to LM, 4 April 1787.
81. L547, WM to Baron Gottfried von Jacquin, end May 1787.
82. L548, WM to N, 16 June 1787.
83. As reported to Wilhelm Kuhe, and recorded by him in *My Musical Recollections* (London, 1896), pp. 8–9.
84. Deutsch, p. 304.
85. Lorenzo Da Ponte, *Memoirs*, p. 180.
86. Deutsch, p. 323.
87. *Ibid*., p. 325.

88. L554, WM to Puchberg, mid-June 1788.

89. L559, WM to C, 8 April 1789.

90. L561, WM to C, 13 April 1789.

91. L562, WM to C, 16 April 1789.

92. L565, WM to C, 23 May 1789.

93. Deutsch, p. 526.

94. *Ibid.*

95. L570, WM to C, early August 1789.

96. *Ibid.*

97. L577, WM to Puchberg, 23 April 1790.

98. Deutsch, p. 362.

99 L583, WM to Puchberg, 14 August 1790.

100. L584, WM to C, 28 September 1790.

101. *Ibid.*

102. Anton Herzog, *Wahre und ausführliche Geschichte des Requiem von W. A. Mozart.*

103. *Ibid.*

104. L598, WM to C, 7 June 1791.

105. L599, WM to C, 11 June 1791.

106. *Ibid.*

107. *Ibid.*

108. L610, WM to C, 6 July 1791.

109. Deutsch, p. 510.

110. L614, WM to C, 7–8 October 1791.

111. L616, WM to C, 14 October 1791.

112. Deutsch, pp. 524–6.

Mozart's Women

1. Nissen, p. 272.

2. 'Allgemeines einfaches Grab', as opposed to a communal grave ('gemeinschaftlich').

3. L546, WM to LM, 4 April 1787.

4. *Briefe* 1250, N to Breitkopf and Härtel, 4 August 1799.

5. *Verzeichnis aller meiner Werke*, English facsimile, 1990.

6. L440, WM to LM, 12 January 1782.

7. L428, WM to LM, 13 October 1781.

8. L309a, WM to LM, 12 June 1778.

9. *Ibid.*

10. L339, WM to LM, 12 November 1778.

11. L318, WM to Aloysia Weber, 30 July 1778.

12. L381, WM to LM, 27 December 1780.

13. L499, WM to LM, 31 October 1783.

14. L88a, WM to N, 21 April 1770.

15. L121, LM to MA, 17 November 1770.

16. L125, LM to MA, 15 December 1770.

17. L285, LM to WM, 11–12 February 1778 .

18. L95a, WM to N, 29 May 1770.

19. L285, LM to WM, 11–12 February 1778.

20. L164, LM to MA, 5 December 1772.

21. C. Burney, *The Present State of Music in Germany, the Netherlands and United Provinces* (London, 1775).

22. L163, LM to MA, 28 November 1772.

23. L165, LM to MA, 12 December 1772.

24. L167, LM to MA, 26 December 1772.

25. L168, LM to MA, 2 January 1773.

26. L164a, WM to N, 5 December 1772.

27. L193, LM to MA, 28 December 1774.

28. Burney, *op. cit.*

29. *Ibid.*

30. L313, WM to LM, 9 September 1778.

31. L367, WM to LM, 1 December 1780.

32. L356, WM to LM, 8 November 1780.

33. L383, WM to LM, 30 December 1780.

34. L245a, MA to LM, 20 November 1777.

35. L426, WM to LM, 26 September 1781.

36. L494, WM to LM, 2 July 1783.

37. L426, WM to LM, 26 September 1781.

38. *Ibid.*

39. L480, WM to LM, 5 February 1783.

40. L426, WM to LM, 26 September 1781.

41. *Reminiscences*, p. 99.

42. L489, WM to LM, 7 May 1783.

43. L528, WM to Professor Anton Klein, 21 May 1785.

44. L489, WM to LM, 7 May 1783.

45. *Memoirs*, p. 131.

46. L428, WM to LM, 13 October 1781.

47. In *An Extract from the Life of Lorenzo Da Ponte* (New York, 1819).

48. *Memoirs*, p. 136.

49. L412, WM to LM, 20 June 1781.

50. *Reminiscences*, p. 49.

51. *Ibid.*, p. 48.

52. *Ibid.*, p. 118.

53. *Ibid.*, p. 125.

54. *Ibid.*, pp. 135–6.

55. *Memoirs*, p. 175.

56. *Ibid.*, p. 159.

57. L345, WM to LM, 18 December 1778.

58. To Vincent and Mary Novello, *Travel Diaries*, p. 94.

After Mozart

1. Deutsch, pp. 421–2.

2. *Ibid.*, p. 439.

3. *Ibid.*, p. 446.

4. *Ibid.*, p. 426.

5. *Ibid.*, p. 427.

6. *Ibid.*, p. 434.

7. L616, WM to C, 14 October 1791.

8. Herzog, *op. cit.*

9. *Ibid.*

10. Deutsch, pp. 454–62.

11. Schlichtegroll, *Nekrolog auf das Jahr 1791* (Gotha, 1793; repr. Ed. J. H. Eibl, 1974).

12. Deutsch, p. 469.

13. *Ibid.*, p. 471.

14. *Ibid.*, p. 476.

15. *Ibid.*, p. 487.

16. The documentation for all this correspondence is to be found in Gärtner, *Mozarts Requiem und die Geschäfte der Constanze* (English translation by R. G. Pauly: *Constanze Mozart: After the Requiem*, 1986).

17. Deutsch, p. 488.

18. *Briefe* 1263.

19. *Ibid.* 1269.

20. *Ibid.* 1271.

21. *Ibid.* 1275.

22. *Ibid.* 1370.

23. Gärtner, pp. 69–70.

24. *Ibid.*, p. 139.

25. *Briefe* 1388.

26. Gärtner, p. 143.
27. *Briefe* 1250.
28. Gärtner, p. 143.
29. *Ibid.*, p. 148.
30. Quoted in Constanze Nissen-Mozart, *Tagebuch meines Brief Wechsels*, ed. R. Angermüller (1999), p. 24.
31. Gärtner, p. 174.
32. *The Travel Diaries of Vincent and Mary Novello*, from which all the following quotations are taken.
33. Constanze Nissen-Mozart, *Tagebuch*, p. 73.
34. *Ibid.*, p. 105.
35. W. Kuhe, *My Musical Recollections* (London, 1896), p. 12.

Select Bibliography

Original sources

Hummel, W. (ed.), *Nannerl Mozarts Tagebuchblätter*, Salzburg 1958

Mozart, Leopold, *Versuch einer gründlichen Violinschule*, Augsburg 1656; trans. E. Knocker, *A Treatise on the Fundamental Principles of Violin Playing*, London 1948

Mozart, W. A., *Verzeichnüss aller meine Werke*, facsimile reproduction, London 1990

Nissen, G., *Biographie W. A. Mozarts*, Leipzig, 1828; latest publication with foreword by R. Angermüller, Hildesheim, 1991

Nissen-Mozart, Constanze, *Tagebuch meines Brief Wechsels in Betref der Mozartischen Biographie (1827–1837)*, ed. R. Angermüller, Salzburg 1999

Letters and documents

Anderson, E. (ed.), *The Letters of Mozart and His Family*, London 1938; revised 3rd edition, S. Sadie and F. Smart, London 1985

Bauer, W. A., Deutsch, O. E., and Eibl, J. H. (eds), *Mozart: Briefe und Aufzeichnungen*, Kassel 1962–75

Deutsch, O. E. (ed.) *Mozart. Die Dokumente seines Lebens*, trans. E. Blom, P. Branscombe and J. Noble, *Mozart: A Documentary Biography*, London 1966

Eisen, C., *New Mozart Documents*, London 1991

General

Blom, E., *Mozart*, London 1935, revised 1962

Brauenbehrens, V., *Mozart in Vienna, 1781–1791*, trans. T. Bell, London 1989

Brophy, B., *Mozart the Dramatist*, London 1964, revised 1988

Clive, P., *Mozart and His Circle*, London 1993

Crankshaw, E., *Maria Theresa*, London 1969

Da Ponte, L., *An Extract from the Life of Lorenzo Da Ponte*, New York 1819

– *Memoirs of Lorenzo Da Ponte*, trans. E. Abbott, New York 1967

Gärtner, H., *Constanze Mozart, After the Requiem*, trans. R. Pauly, Munich 1986

Gutman, R., *Mozart: A Cultural Biography*, New York 1999

Halliwell, R., *The Mozart Family*, Oxford 1998

Hildesheimer, W., *Mozart*, Frankfurt 1977; trans. Marion Faber, London 1983

Hodges, S., *Lorenzo Da Ponte: The Life and Times of Mozart's Librettist*, London 1985

Kelly, M., *Reminiscences of Michael Kelly*, ed. R. Fiske, London 1975

Levey, M., *The Life and Death of Mozart*, London 1971

Mann, W., *The Operas of Mozart*, London 1977

Medici, N. and Hughes, R., *A Mozart Pilgrimage: The Travel Diaries of Vincent and Mary Novello in the Year 1829*, London 1955

Robbins Landon, H. C., *Mozart and the Masons*, London 1982

– *1791: Mozart's Last Year*, London 1988

– *Mozart: The Golden Years*, London 1989

– (ed.), *The Mozart Compendium*, London 1990

Sadie, S. and Eisen C., *The New Grove Mozart*, revised London 2001

Shaffer, P., *Amadeus*, London 1980

Solomon, M., *Mozart: A Life*, London 1995

Spaethling, R., *Mozart's Letters, Mozart's Life*, London 2000

Stafford, W., *Mozart's Death*, London 1991

– *The Mozart Myths*, Stanford 1991

Steptoe, A., *The Mozart–Da Ponte Operas*, Oxford 1988

Tyson, A., *Mozart: Studies of the Autograph Scores*, London 1987

Wheatcroft, A., *The Habsburgs*, London 1995

Acknowledgements

I believe that the seed for this book was germinated in my early childhood. Hearing any music of Mozart on recordings, I would become utterly absorbed, and I soon found myself wanting to know more about the boy composer, who would die when still a young man. When I discovered that he had had a musical sister, who had performed with him across Europe for many years, I was even more intrigued. (I fear that, ludicrously, I rather identified with her.)

By the time I reached adulthood my communion with Mozart's music was profound, thrilling and consoling. My employment at that supreme Mozart establishment, Glyndebourne, and then my appointment as Artistic Director of the London Mozart Players, cemented my professional commitment ot the composer. I made a six-part television series on him for the BBC, and in due course recorded all the mature symphonies, and many concertos and arias. The 1991 commemorations of the bicentenary of Mozart's death were an enormous focus on all aspects of his life and work, for all musicians across the world. Among countless Mozartian activities, I became increasinlgy interested in Constanze and her family; and, together with Elizabeth Jane Howard, spent happy hours planning a possible television play on the four Weber sisters. Most recently, at the approach of 2006 and the 250th anniversary of Mozart's birth, I widened my fascination yet again. And thus the present project, covering Mozart's family, Constanze's family, Mozart's interpreters and the roles they created, came into being.

Many significant individuals have accompanied me on this fascinating journey. For years I have discussed the idea with my great friend Simon Callow, himself a formidable writer as well as an actor and director (truly a Schikaneder personality): significantly he created the role of Mozart in

Peter Schaffer's brilliant play *Amadeus*, and he has been my frequent stage partner, as reader of Mozart letters in concerts of his music. Simon introduced me to his literary agent Margaret Hanbury, and then she led me to both Macmillan and HarperCollins. Georgina Morley at Macmillan, and Hugh van Dusen at HarperCollins, like Maggie, have been model guardians of this project, taking care of this very part-time author by offering equal measures of guidance, encouragement, freedom and (gentle) admonition.

The Mozart field has been enormously well mined, and for this book I have done no original research in dusty libraries, discovering documents hitherto unnoticed. But I have read copiously the fruits of others' diligence (some of which is listed here in a select bibliography) with admiration, respect and gratitude. Andrew Eggert has assisted me greatly in hunting down obscure publications, and then discussing their content with me. Other individuals who have made significant contributions to my researches, discoveries and perspective are Mike Ashman, Nonie Beck, Imogen Cooper, John Cox, Brian Dickie, Geraldine Frank, Ruth Halliwell, Julian Hope, Felicity Lott, Diane Paulus, Adam Pollock, Richard Stockes, and Erna Schwerin and her organization, the Friends of Mozart.

When the book was in typescript, two close friends read it. Both Ellen Rosand, my long-time musicological mentor (and fellow Venetian), and Nicholas Kenyon, whose first version of his own book on Mozart was neatly exchanged with mine (we read each other's), made observations and comments of inestimable value, and I am immensely grateful to them. And above all I offer profound thanks to all my other colleagues in the musical and theatrical worlds, with whom, over the last three decades, I have had the privilege of performing the music of Mozart. These include especially 'my' two orchestras, the London Mozart Players and Chicago's Music of the Baroque, and the opera companies Glyndebourne and English National Opera. In addition to these, my professional path has taken me to many organizations in Europe, America and Australasia, and every singer, instrumentalist, director and designer has contributed therefore to my ever-enriched vessel of Mozartian experience.

Index

Illustration Credits

a = above, b = below, l = left, r = right

AKG Images: p. 1 (Musée Condé, Chantilly), p. 3a & b (Internationale Stiftung Mozarteum/Erich Lessing), p. 4a, p. 5a (Internationale Stiftung Mozarteum), p. 5b (British Museum), p. 6a (Hunterian Art Gallery, Glasgow/Erich Lessing), p. 6b (Internationale Stiftung Mozarteum), p. 7br, p. 8 (Internationale Stiftung Mozarteum/Erich Lessing), p. 12, p. 13b (Deutsches Theatermuseum), p. 14al, p. 15a & b, p. 16al (International Stiftung Mozarteum)

Art Archive: p. 2a & b (Internationale Stiftung Mozarteum), p. 9b (Musée du Château de Versailles), p. 11br (Mozart Apartment, Vienna), p. 14b (Society of the Friends of Music, Vienna)

Bridgeman Art Library: p. 9a (Kunsthistorisches Museum, Vienna)

Internationale Stiftung Mozarteum (ISM): p. 7a & bl, p. 10a

Lebrecht Music and Arts Photo Library: p. 11al, ar, bl, p. 13a, p. 14ar, p. 16ar